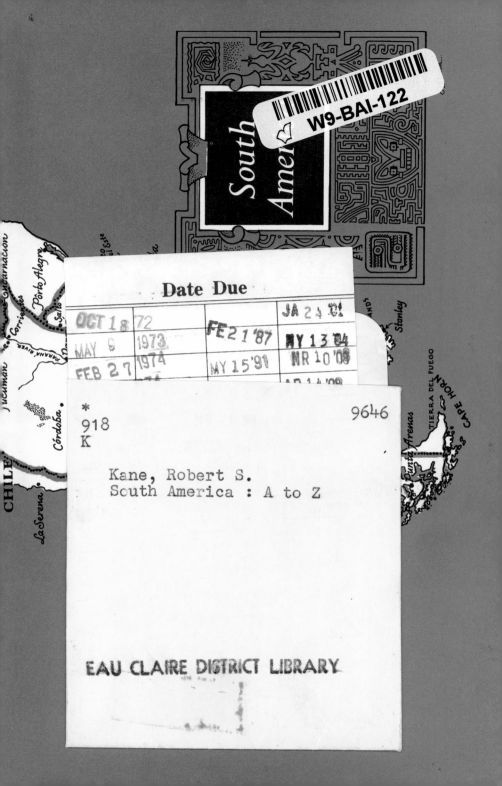

South
Ameri♥

W9-BAI-122

Date Due

OCT 18 72		JA 24 01
MAY 9 1973	FE 21 '87	MY 13 04
FEB 27 1974	MY 15 '91	MR 10 08

SOUTH AMERICA A TO Z

"The essential qualities of a true Pan Americanism must be the same as those which constitute a good neighbor, namely mutual understanding, and through such understanding, a sympathetic appreciation of the other's point of view. It is only in this manner that we can hope to build up a system of which friendship and good will are the cornerstones."
—FRANKLIN D. ROOSEVELT, 1933

"The inter-American system represents not merely the unity of governments but the unity of people, not only a common goal for a political alignment but a common vow to improve man's economic, social and political well-being . . . an Alliance for Progress. We will be in the Nineteen Sixties more than good neighbors."
—JOHN F. KENNEDY, 1961

BOOKS BY ROBERT S. KANE

Africa A *to* Z
South America A *to* Z

South America

A to Z

ROBERT S. KANE

Photographs by the author

Maps by Louise E. Jefferson

WITHDRAWN

Doubleday & Company, Inc., Garden City, New York

For Aunt Lottie, with love

Library of Congress Catalog Card Number 62–7651
Copyright © 1962 by Robert S. Kane
All Rights Reserved
Printed in the United States of America

CONTENTS

INTRODUCTION   vii

SOUTH AMERICA ALPHABETICALLY   xii

SOUTH AMERICA: THE BACKGROUND   1

The Sixth Grader's Favorite—Geography Revisited—
History in a Hurry: B.C. (Before Columbus), A.C.
(After the Conquistadors), The Colonies Become Sover-
eign, The OAS: A Regional UN, The United States and
South America, The Alliance for Progress, Common
Heritages?—"A Rose by Any Other Name . . ."

SOUTH AMERICA: TOURIST TERRITORY   19

A Belated Awakening—Boning Up on South America
(Governmental, Intergovernmental, Voluntary, Business,
and Educational Organizations, and Museums Which
Deal with South America)—Tourist Cards and Visas—
Obtaining a U. S. Passport—Inoculations and Health—
Climate—Packing Simplified—Photography—Customs—
Your South American Hosts—Shopping—Embassies
and Consulates—Currency—Tipping—Sight-seeing and
Guides—Private Clubs—Mail—Language—Where To
and How Much: Balancing and Juggling, Three Types of
Trips, Selecting a Travel Agent, The Absolute Basics of
a 'Round South America Air Itinerary, A Few Package
Tours, Daily Expenses, The World's Greatest Interna-
tional Travel Bargain, Other Air Fares, Two A–O.K. Air-
lines: Panagra and Varig, Other Airlines Serving the
United States and South America, Airlines Operating
within South America, European-South American Air
Services, By Sea to South America—Major Passenger
Lines Serving the Continent, Other Cruises, Shipboard
Life, Freighter Travel, Driving in and through South
America.

EASTERN SOUTH AMERICA   61

    ARGENTINA   65

    BRAZIL   101

    THE GUIANAS   144
       British Guiana   151
       French Guiana   154
       Surinam   156

    PARAGUAY   162

    URUGUAY   175

    VENEZUELA   193

WESTERN SOUTH AMERICA   211

    BOLIVIA   215

    CHILE   235

    COLOMBIA   261

    ECUADOR   286

    PANAMA   310

    PERU   325

INDEX   360

MAPS

    EASTERN SOUTH AMERICA   62
    WESTERN SOUTH AMERICA   212
    CONTINENT OF SOUTH AMERICA   Endpapers

INTRODUCTION

". . . El que lee mucho y anda mucho, vee mucho y sabe mucho."
—CERVANTES: *Don Quixote*

(*He who reads much and travels far, sees much and learns a great deal.*)

There can be no denying that we are a nation of stereotypers. But we are at last beginning to realize that Africa is not the continent our geography books and Tarzan movies suggested. We are coming to recognize, if belatedly, that Asia is considerably more than Yul Brynner-type monarchs and Kipling heroes. And now, we're taking a realistic look at our own front yard, and finding it full of surprises.

Where, indeed, is that South America populated by Carmen Mirandas and mustachioed gallants who while away their non-siesta hours in song, dance, and guitar playing? Can it be that the lands of the pampas are not exclusively populated by maté-drinking Gauchos. Is not Carnival a year-round occupation? Is it true that our Latin neighbors are not always a little tipsy from heady wine, perpetually a little exhausted from the rigors of flamenco, invariably in the midst of operetta-type revolution?

Has that South America of the romantic gone, like the antebellum U. S. South, with the wind? Not entirely, of course, but to an extent which still astounds far too many headline-reading, movie-going Americans, who until recently ventured to see very little of foreign shores for themselves, except perhaps the *boîtes* of Paris, the pubs of London, and the beaches of Bermuda.

Now, though, the well-traveled American is coming to the conclusion that "abroad" means more than the capitals of Western

Europe. He is branching out—to Tokyo and New Delhi, to
Moscow and Belgrade, to Accra and Nairobi, and—to La Paz
and Montevideo. He is concerning himself with the less developed
areas of the world, which it has not at all been the fashion to tour,
to talk of, or indeed, to be informed about.

Three factors seem to have engendered this change: the miracle
of the jet airliner, the tremendous reductions in air fares, and the
search for new travel frontiers by those who've already trodden
the beaten path.

Factor number two—those lowered transport tabs—has wrought
a change not only in the quantity of travelers to South America,
but in their age. It is what has made possible the increasingly big
exodus of students, young university graduates, and inquisitive
career girls to South America. Until more recently than I like to
recount, our Latin neighbors were quite thoroughly convinced that
the United States was a nation of the elderly—retired and near-
retired executives and farmers and physicians and professors, and
their vivacious, vitamin-packed wives.

Now, though, the ball has started rolling. Our appetites have
been whetted and we need not have six months of leisure, or an
immense bankroll in order to satisfy them. We have the wherewithal, the curiosity, and some of us have even more. "We hope
to open people's minds, show and tell them what Americans are
really like, and erase some of the false impressions" the spokesman
for a group of seven New Jersey college students told the press
on the eve of a recent 27,000-mile jaunt through South America
which they'd billed as a Good Will Tour.

For other travelers, an itinerary need not fall in the 27,000-
mile category, nor need it be specifically labeled "good will."
A vacation, after all, is a time for relaxation and pleasure, be it
taken in Mendoza or Miami. Still, the curious traveler to South
America today will, in the course of his pleasures, come across a
good deal more than what he's seen in the wide-screen travelogue,
if he'll but open his eyes. Of course, there will be the magnificent
Andes, the balsa boats of Lake Titicaca, the grand boulevards of
Buenos Aires, the brilliance of Rio's harbor, the ingenious cuisine

of Peru, the skyscrapers of Caracas, and the great Colonial art of Ecuador.

But tilling land in the shadow of the Andes, fishing in the waters of Titicaca, strolling the boulevards of Buenos Aires, eating the *ceviches* of Lima, pounding typewriters in the offices of Caracas, praying in the lovely churches of Quito are the South Americans themselves—no more stereotypes, in their eyes, than are you and I, in ours. Cultures, customs, cuisines, amusements, monuments, natural wonders of their own? Of course. And very worth knowing and seeing and tasting and experiencing and photographing they are.

But the people themselves want knowing and we deserve their acquaintance, too. Even though our government has repeatedly blundered in South America and our business community has too often been concerned with profits rather than people, we have a good deal to be proud of. We're not so bad after people get to know us. And vice versa. But that's half the battle. And be it in Spanish, Portuguese, Quechua, English, sign language, or a combination thereof, the effort—now more than ever before, particularly in South America—is worthwhile, for both guest and host.

This book may help, both as a general companion for the traveler, and as a primer for the stay-at-home. What's inside? It is safer for an author to say what his book is not, rather than what it is.

South America A to Z is not a laboriously-detailed Baedeker, with detailed instructions on how to get to the Avenida 9 de Julio in order to walk south three blocks to the intersection of Calle San Martín, where if one looks left, a statue of the Risen Christ can be observed tucked away between a rose arbor and a weathered wall (c. 1742), whose sculptor was a Jesuit monk born thirty-seven years earlier in Salamanca, Spain, of mixed Catalan-Andalusian parentage, and with a tick in the left eye, the result of a childhood trauma. But it does attempt to convey the flavor of the continent, its great and not-so-great cities, its principal bucolic landmarks, its peoples and their cultures, as well as capsules of geography and history, both past and present, with names occasionally named, opinions occasionally expressed (sometimes negative), and allusions to political situations, all too often avoided like the plague by writers of books on travel.

What else is this book *not?* Well, it's not an Airline and Steamship Timetable, but the transport picture to and within South America is dwelt upon in terms of the lay reader. It is not a complete Hotel and Restaurant Guide, but it does not neglect those important ingredients of a journey. And it is not a Directory of Shops, although once again the highlights are touched upon to the extent that the casual traveler will find them helpful.

To continue, this book is not an ostrich-type guide, hiding from unpleasantness, poverty, dirt, disease, and dictatorship. It attempts, on the other hand, to recognize the charm and the color and the distinctiveness of the cultures of South America, whose strength and resonance manifest themselves despite the aforementioned conditions and not—as is often the prevalent view—because of them. It does not attempt to ignore U.S. complicity in South America's travails, nor does it, alternatively, blame all of our Latin neighbors' woes on Uncle Sam, there being more truth than alliteration to the oft-repeated "It takes two to tango."

Finally, *South America A to Z* is written for the thinking traveler, the tourist who does not need to be told in a book to fasten his seat belt when boarding an aircraft, who knows that it is the travel agency or transport company or hotel desk which is the ideal source for the answers to those often dreary specifics of contemporary travel, and who looks upon a trip as something of an adventure instead of an antiseptic, anticlimactic line-by-line copy of what the man who wrote the book said to see, eat, drink, fly over, or avoid.

We have got, it seems to this traveler, to live a *little* dangerously when we go abroad. Why not have a drink at a seedy bar on the waterfront? Why not venture a walk through a red-light district at night—if you really want to? How about an unescorted stroll through a university campus, even without an official translator or prearranged appointment—or a ride at rush hour on the subway or trolley car or bus? Can not a meal be pleasant and stimulating in a restaurant where shopworkers or factory hands eat? Must we dwell constantly on the oft-described "lovely residential sections" which have a monotonous sameness in every city of the Americas. And—but it's time to stop with prefatory remarks and get on with the show. And a show it is, in the very best sense of the word—vibrant with change, color, conflict, and with a dramatis personae whom it behooves us to get to know, even if on occasion we get our hands dirty or our shoes dusty.

—ROBERT S. KANE

SOUTH AMERICA ALPHABETICALLY

Country	Government	Capital	Area (Sq. Miles)	Population
Argentina	Republic	Buenos Aires	1,084,359	20,956,000
Bolivia	Republic	La Paz-actual Sucre-legal	416,040	3,462,000
Brazil	Republic	Brasília	3,287,199	65,790,000
British Guiana	Self-governing colony	Georgetown	83,000	540,000
Canal Zone	U.S. territory	Balboa	553	55,000
Chile	Republic	Santiago	286,396	7,627,000
Colombia	Republic	Bogotá	439,553	14,132,000
Ecuador	Republic	Quito	105,743*	4,298,000
Falkland Islands¶	British Colony	Stanley	4,618	2,500
French Guiana	"Overseas Department" of France	Cayenne	65,000	31,000
Panama	Republic	Panama City	28,753	1,000,000
Paraguay	Republic	Asunción	157,047	1,768,000
Peru	Republic	Lima	506,189	10,857,000
Surinam	Domestically self-governing territory of the Kingdom of the Netherlands	Paramaribo	54,300	220,000
Uruguay	Republic	Montevideo	72,153	2,803,000
Venezuela	Republic	Caracas	352,150	6,709,000

*Including Galápagos Islands
¶ Claimed by Argentina and called Islas Malvinas by Argentina

South America

THE BACKGROUND

*"We are . . . neither Indian nor European, but a species midway
between the legitimate proprietors of this country and the . . .
usurpers."*
                                                    —SIMÓN BOLÍVAR

THE SIXTH GRADER'S FAVORITE

It's not at all difficult to perceive why South America is the
sixth grader's preferred continent: it's the easiest—on the surface,
anyway. It has the fewest countries, North America and Australia
excepted. (North America doesn't really count, because we live
here, and Australia is more a single country than a continent.)
It's the simplest to draw in outline from memory—more essentially
triangular than any of the others, with the smoothest coast lines,
lots of unencumbered ocean water surrounding it, and those easy-
to-place Andes Mountains which follow the Pacific coast line. It
has but two principal languages, if one omits the three little
Guianas, which are not all that little but which usually are
omitted, and even the sixth grader has no difficulty in remembering who speaks what: Brazil (which, as everyone knows who has
seen *Charley's Aunt,* is "where the nuts come from") has the
monopoly on Portuguese, and all the others speak Spanish—
neither being rated as chic a language as French.

The "principal products," to borrow the textbook phrase, are relatively few. The inhabitants appear to be either Gauchos in baggy pantaloons or Indians in gay ponchos. The animals are funny-face llamas of which the zoos are full. Pizarro (whose name begins with a P) conquered Peru (the first letter of which is P, so that's easy to remember), a man named Bolívar freed a lot of countries from Spain and since then most have had revolutions every few months which no one—least of all a sixth grader—could be expected to memorize. And Rio de Janeiro has one of the best natural harbors in the world. Next continent, teacher!

Well, the kids *do* size up some basics, and if it is true that they end up with more stereotypes than facts, it is probably also true that they are among the best-informed residents of the United States on matters Latin American, which is not saying a great deal, and which is as good a reason as any for the brush-up which follows.

GEOGRAPHY REVISITED

South America is near the bottom of the list when it comes to geographical superlatives. It's not the biggest of the continents (the area is 6,850,000 square miles), and it's one of the most sparsely populated (population about 140,000,000—considerably less than that of the United States). It is by no means tiny, however, extending some forty-six hundred miles from north to south and—at its widest—some three thousand miles from east to west. Brazil, its biggest country—which covers half the area and contains about half the population—is bigger than the continental United States. And the whole continent is about twice the size of China.

The great Andes, which extend the length of the continent, are magnificent to climb, look down from, and traverse. But they make communications difficult and tend to split the continent in two. They range from two hundred to four hundred miles in width,

average some thirteen thousand feet in height, and number among
their most impressive peaks the highest in the Western Hemisphere—Aconcagua—at 23,081 feet. (More than a dozen others
exceed sixteen thousand feet so that one can understand why
South Americans are not overly impressed with the Rockies.)

The continent is not all mountains, there being many plains,
forested, scrub, and otherwise; a good bit of healthy highland,
with the great river systems a major influence, geographical and
economic.

From the top of the map to the bottom, these include the
Magdalena, connecting the heart of Colombia to the Caribbean;
the Orinoco, flowing through the Venezuelan llanos, or plains,
and separating from land (along with the waters of the seas) the
forest-highlanded Guianas, which extend geographically, if not
politically, into Brazil and Venezuela; the amazing Amazon, some
four thousand miles long, extending from the Atlantic to the
Peruvian highlands, carrying more water than any other river in
the world, and draining (with its tributaries) a two-million-square-
mile basin; and the Río de la Plata, the estuary of the Paraná and
Uruguay rivers, which cuts into the Atlantic coast where Argentina
and Uruguay meet, and on whose waters move the produce of the
rich Argentine Pampa.

To the north is the scrubby Chaco, a plain extending into
Paraguay, the Mato Grosso tablelands, and the uplands of central
and southern Brazil. Way to the south is windy, rugged Patagonia,
separated by the Strait of Magellan from the Chilean-Argentine
island of Tierra del Fuego, and Cape Horn. The principal
desert area is the copper-rich, nitrate-laden Atacama Desert of
northern Chile and southern Peru. There are magnificent lakes
in the northern Patagonian playland of Argentina and Chile, but
the biggest on the continent is fabled Titicaca, in the Bolivian-
Peruvian Andes, and the wealthiest—fortunes in oil are extracted
from beneath its waters each day—is immense Maracaibo, in
Venezuela.

There is, too, the Isthmus of Panama, through which one of the

globe's great canals has been incised. Though until fairly recently
Panama was a province of a South American republic—Colombia
—it is now often (but not always) considered a part of Central
America. But in this book—primarily because the traveler to the
southern continent invariably visits it—it is being treated as a
part of South America.

South America runs the climatic gamut, and although the climate
will be dealt with more extensively in the pages which follow, it
is worth noting here that although the bulk of the continent is
in the torrid zone, important parts are not, there being considerable
areas with mild temperate climate; others, though in the tropics,
are naturally air-conditioned by reason of their high altitudes.

HISTORY IN A HURRY

B.C. (Before Columbus): South America's first visitors—and they
were to become permanent residents for many, many centuries—
were Neolithic Asians who are believed to have arrived by
means of the Bering Strait, and gradually spread themselves—
rather thinly—throughout the continent, evolving cultures which
varied according to physical environment. The first of their great
civilizations was the Mayan, in Central America, which had its
heyday at about the same time the ancient Romans had theirs,
and which distinguished itself by excellence in astronomy, the
construction of palaces and pyramids, even a written language. It
was on its last legs by the time the Europeans arrived to crush it.

Farther south, in South America proper, there were a number
of other Early American communities, ranging from the advanced,
imperialist-communist Incas of the Andean highlands, and the
highly-developed Chibchas of Colombia, to the backward inhabitants of southern Patagonia and the Amazon basin, and the brave,
independence-loving Araucanians of Chile—all of which (and
more) are dealt with in succeeding chapters of this book.

A.C. (After the Conquistadors): The first of the Europeans to
change all this—as we all know—was Christopher Columbus,

who first arrived more or less by accident, while on an India-hunting expedition. (So convinced was he that he'd found India that the name he gave to the indigenous people—Indians—has stuck, and continues to this day to create terminological confusion with the inhabitants of India.) It was not until his third voyage, in 1498, that Columbus actually visited the South American continent, when he reached the mouth of the Orinoco, in what is now Venezuela.

What he did, to understate, was start the ball rolling. The Iberian countries—Spain and Portugal—were both anxious to fill their coffers and develop empires. They had just emerged from centuries of Moorish rule and needed to re-establish themselves as viable states. Spain, even more than Portugal, wanted to swell the ranks of Christiandom and to implant its culture—which it considered the greatest in the world—wherever it could, by force or otherwise. Both countries, of course, wanted the wealth and power and prestige which the New World (new to Europe only, that is) could provide. And they were to have just what they sought, for some three centuries, thanks to their emissaries: dedicated Jesuits and other clerics, gold-hungry adventurers, aristocratic courtiers and planters, and poor but ambitious peasants.

What they accomplished is, even in retrospect, difficult to fathom. Against fantastic odds—mountainous altitudes which made breathing difficult, killing diseases which were strange to them and which they were unable to arm themselves against, tropical heat and humidity, vast territories which had never been charted, understandably hostile peoples—they made a continent their own, subduing the great majority of the Indians, enriching themselves and their sovereigns, reproducing their own civilizations, making of a long-inhabited but barely developed continent a glittering colonial empire.

Their method—their entire approach—was cruel, repressive, totalitarian, and with notable exceptions devoid of the faintest touch of humanity. Treachery, murder, pillage, enslavement, lust, greed—these typified the Iberians in South America.

But their system worked. The breaks were in their favor. Within a decade after Columbus' third expedition the Atlantic coast had been explored as far south as the Río de la Plata. The Pacific was discovered by Balboa. Magellan sailed through the strait which bears his name. Pizarro went south from Panama and conquered, with a relative handful of men, all of Inca-held Peru. The remarkable Chibchas, in the northern interior, were rendered powerless.

And from these key points the Spanish conquistadors and the Portuguese *bandeirantes* advanced even more into the interior, founding such cities as Asunción in Paraguay, Santiago in Chile, Córdoba in Argentina, breaking through the uncharted vastness of Brazil, mining silver in the rarified Bolivian mountains, erecting beautiful churches in high Quito and opulent palaces in strategic Lima, shipping their treasures back to Europe from Panama, Callao, the Brazilian ports, and later Buenos Aires; tilling the land, as well. At the same time they were fighting off other Europeans—the French, Dutch, and British—who wanted to get in on the act, and who raided their newly rich, brilliantly fortified ports.

Assimilation with the indigenous American? It could be called that, but enslavement is the better word. The Spaniards concentrated in areas where there were great concentrations of Indians, whom they ruthlessly impressed into plantation and mine labor. The Portuguese on their part of the continent (and the two roughly adhered to a dividing line decreed by the Vatican, with the eastern areas going to the Portuguese and the remainder to the Spaniards) found the local Indians unsatisfactory as laborers, and exploiting Brazil's nearness to Africa, brought over untold shiploads of Negro Africans, whom they enslaved on their plantations.

What evolved was a reproduction of the medieval caste system of the mother countries—neither of which (unlike England in North America) had the slightest heritage of representative, parliamentary government to export. At the top were the European-born administrators, landowners, and clergy. Next in the social strata were the creoles—American-born descendants of the Europeans. They were followed by the great mass of racially mixed people—

mestizos (Indian-European) and mulattoes (Negro-European). (Thanks to their centuries of Moorish-Moslem occupation, neither the Spaniards nor the Portuguese have the same racial inhibitions of the northern Europeans; they brought few of their women with them at first, and proceeded without compunction to cohabit with—and later marry—both Indian and Negro women.) Way at the bottom of the social heap were the purebred Negroes and Indians. Though long since freed as slaves, they continue, by and large, to live in poverty, on the lowest economic rung of the ladder.

The colonies become sovereign: Independence came to all of the South American colonies, save the Guianas, in the early decades of the nineteenth century, thanks to the military genius of Simón Bolívar, mainly in the north, and José de San Martín, mainly in the south, both of whom helped in the liberation of a cluster of lands, and were aided in their work not only by locals of each country, but also by the British. The events which led to independence, and the aftermaths, are briefly recounted in later chapters. But the impetus for freedom and the pattern of achieving it are uniform throughout. The independence fought for—and gained—was by and large independence for the creoles. They resented their position of inferiority alongside the European-born aristocrats who outranked them. And they disliked the heavy taxes they paid to the sovereigns in the mother countries. What they wanted—and what they achieved—were economic liberty and the opportunities to run their own lands without colonial overlords.

As for the great masses—well, things changed relatively little for them. The feudalistic organization of the colonies remained, under republican guise. Oligarchies—composed of landed gentry and military brass—took over where the viceregal representatives of the crowns left off (except in Brazil, which started off as a monarchy). The great heroes of independence—Bolívar and San Martín—were more military geniuses than egalitarian-minded liberators, although Bolívar was the first Pan-Americanist, and San Martín—the more selfless and social-minded of the two—might have effected greater influence had he not departed for Europe and self-imposed exile shortly after his great victories.

Lacking a broad popular base, almost all of the new republics found it difficult to function at a constitutional level; some, in recent years, have made tremendous strides in the realm of stability. Uruguay, in this century, changed from tyrant-dominated oligarchy to smooth-functioning, socially-advanced, representative democracy. Brazil has had a relatively bloodless political history, transforming itself from colony to monarchy to republic fairly peaceably, and remaining at peace with its neighbors for more than a century. The other republics have a less admirable record. Power has changed hands far too frequently and at gunpoint more often than not, with the support of the military generally the deciding factor on "ins" and "outs" in the presidential palaces.

The rich have remained rich—going along with whoever was president, paying virtually no taxes, and wanting only to be left alone to enjoy the luxurious way of life at which the Iberians and their descendants are excelled by no one. Middle classes are still virtually nonexistent in countries like Bolivia and Paraguay, and only just beginning to be of consequence in many of the other republics.

The OAS—a regional UN: What Simón Bolívar attempted at the Congress of Panama in 1826—an organized inter-American system—was finally formalized in 1890, when the First International Conference of American States took place in Washington. Its members joined together as a body called the International Union of American Republics—mainly to collect and distribute business intelligence of mutual value, by means of a Commercial Bureau in the American capital. Twenty years later the Commercial Bureau became the Pan American Union, and in 1948, at the Ninth International Conference of American States, in Bogotá, Colombia, a charter was agreed upon which reorganized the inter-American system and took the name, Organization of American States. The Pan American Union, long since housed in an opulent Spanish Colonial-type palace in Washington, was designated the secretariat of the organization. Consequently, both names are still used concurrently, and remain a source of confusion to the uninitiated.

OAS' principal function—and one at which it has had some

success—is the creation of workable machinery for settling inter-American disputes peaceably. There have been no international wars in the hemisphere since 1947, when the republics adopted a treaty of reciprocal assistance. José A. Mora is Secretary General.

Other OAS conferences: Besides the aforementioned Washington and Bogotá historic conferences, others of note included Santiago (1923), at which the Pan American Highway had its beginnings; Montevideo (1933), at which the members established the principle that "no state has the right to intervene in the internal or external affairs of another" (which was violated by the United States in connection with the abortive invasion of Cuba in 1961); Mexico City (1945), at which was signed the Act of Chapultepec, wherein the states agreed to consult on common measures of defense in case of actual or threatened aggression, and amplified the principle that "an act of foreign aggression against an American state would be considered an act of aggression against all" by broadening it to include aggression on the part of *any* nation, American or non-American; and Rio de Janeiro (1947), at which was adopted the Inter-American Treaty of Reciprocal Assistance, or Rio Treaty, establishing a system of collective hemispheric security.

OAS specialized agencies: Little publicized in the United States press, but hardly insignificant, are the frequently-called OAS technical conferences on such matters as housing, health, sanitation, tourism, and social welfare, which have accomplished a not inconsiderable amount. And important, too, are the all too obscure specialized agencies of the OAS: the Pan American Health Organization (PAHO), the Inter-American Children's Institute (IACI), the Inter-American Commission on Women (IACW), the Pan American Institute of Geography and History (PAIGH), the Inter-American Indian Institute, the Inter-American Institute of Agricultural Sciences, and the Inter-American Statistical Institute (IASI). All have made beginnings in the kind of program for which there is a crying hemispheric need, and which, it is hoped, will be tackled head-on, on a crash basis, by the Alliance for Progress.

OAS and its agencies work closely with the UN and its agencies;

it considers itself a "regional agency" within the United Nations framework, and there has been considerable co-operation between, for example, the OAS Pan American Health Organization and the UN's World Health Organization, and UNESCO and the Inter-American Cultural Council. The UN also functions in Latin America, through its Economic Commission for Latin America (ECLA). And it goes without saying that all the American republics are members of the UN.

The United States and South America: More often than not, since the colonies became republics, the United States has supported dictatorships with the same enthusiasm as representative governments, playing the imperialist game when expedient (i.e., the Panama Canal), providing arms so that the armies of each state were equipped to (a) put down popular revolts and (b) make war on each other. Until President Kennedy took office in 1961, the only truly bright spot in Latin American-U.S. relations was during the Franklin D. Roosevelt period. F.D.R. still is remembered affectionately in South America. There are a number of thoroughfares which bear his name; the most recently-designated is a street in Buenos Aires—named after him in 1961—sixteen years after his death. Roosevelt's Good Neighbor policy, largely implemented through Secretary of State Cordell Hull and Under Secretary Sumner Welles, was primarily a program of fair, unpatronizing treatment toward the Latin American republics which yielded big dividends. (Among them: World War II support, particularly from Brazil, the only South American republic which sent troops overseas.)

But the Good Neighbor policy passed into oblivion after World War II, when America concerned itself primarily with war-torn Europe, later with Asia and those countries in general which it considered the most vital in meeting the threat of the Soviet Union. The lands to the south seemed of little consequence. North of the Rio Grande it seemed unimportant that America gave the impression of being buddy-buddy with dictators like Pérez Jiménez of Venezuela, Rojas Pinilla of Colombia, Odría of Peru, Stroessner of Paraguay, Trujillo of the Dominican Republic, the Somoza family of Nicaragua, and Batista of Cuba. (The only post-World

War II dictator whom it was fashionable to dislike in the United States was Perón.)

But our policies did not go unnoticed in the southern continent. For despite the tremendous development which was going on in the great cities, and despite the advances made in industry, transportation, and other areas, the poor were remaining poor. Appreciable segments of American industry (although there were, and are, important exceptions to the rule) took great profits out of the continent, and put little into it. To many Latins, it appeared that U.S. policy was geared to the interests of American business in South America.

Toward the close of the Eisenhower administration, the handwriting on the wall became somewhat less blurred in Washington, and at the Inter-American Conference in Bogotá in late 1960, a five-hundred-million-dollar social-development fund for the Latins was promised by the United States. It was not a great deal of money (other areas of the world have received far more than Latin America since World War II), but it was indicative of U.S. awareness of reality. However, had not Fidel Castro dramatized the plight of the Latin masses, no one can be sure that a great deal more would have been done—until it was too late. But Castro's propaganda fired intellectuals, students, and many workers in the Latin countries.

The Alliance for Progress: Castro's battle cry made it crystal clear to the Latin governments and the American government that if a massive aid program was not forthcoming from the United States, it would come from the Communist world. And so, in 1961, shortly after President Kennedy took office—even before the fiasco of the U.S.-financed and directed Cuban invasion—Washington began to move rapidly. President Kennedy appointed a "task force" for Latin America—whose key men were Adolph A. Berle, lawyer, teacher, and longtime Latin specialist; Arthur A. Schlesinger, Jr., Harvard professor and author of *The Age of Roosevelt,* Richard N. Goodwin, young member of the White House staff, and later appointed Deputy Assistant Secretary of State for Latin American Affairs, and Lincoln Gordon, now ambassador to Brazil—to come up with a meaningful program. And they did: the administration dubbed it the Alliance for Progress.

President Kennedy gained Latin American support for his program after proposing it in an address, by means of a good-will tour undertaken by Adlai E. Stevenson, his ambassador to the United Nations, who had a substantial firsthand acquaintance with the continent and whom many of its citizens would no doubt have liked to see as president of the United States. Stevenson's eighteen thousand-mile tour was in great contrast to the infamous trip taken by then Vice-President Richard Nixon, during the Eisenhower period. Although in a few places small groups of militant pro-Castro students hissed and booed, the welcome for Stevenson was generally warm and gracious, as it had been previously when he toured the continent as a private citizen, and as it had been in every region of the world where he has traveled; with the exception of Mrs. Franklin D. Roosevelt, America has no better roving ambassador, official or otherwise.

Ambassador Stevenson returned to the United States convinced that social reform, including a drastic shakeup in land ownership, was urgently needed, as were other changes, many of which the Latins themselves would have to undertake. "The leaders of the Americas know today," he reported to Secretary of State Dean Rusk upon his return, "that they must identify themselves with essential changes that are demonstrably for the benefit of all the people."

"The underprivileged have been caught up in the winds of change," he wrote. "They are tired of promises. They want action, results—not for their grandchildren, but for themselves. They must be shown that their interest lies in making the Alliance for Progress work."

"Communism," he emphasized, "and its alter ego, Castroism, thrive on urban slum conditions and on rural insecurity. The poor . . . who are no longer passive politically, must see reasons for hope in life under free institutions. When they do, the statesmen of the Americas will be more free to plan for long-term development without being distracted by fears of rebellion and revolt. We cannot look for strong brothers-in-arms to the south of us against a common enemy as long as any of our fellow American nations are sapped by stagnation and social decay."

The only truly sour note in the Stevenson trip was the visit which his Washington superiors scheduled with the Paraguayan dictator, Stroessner. Just what was accomplished by this courtesy call on the continent's last remaining dictator, and a ruthless one at that, is difficult to fathom. It was obvious, though, from press reports, that Mr. Stevenson found his Paraguayan stopover personally distasteful; he made it short (a single day) and correct, but no more.

At any rate, as a result of the otherwise solid groundwork laid by Mr. Stevenson on his trip, the finance ministers of the American republics met in Uruguay in August 1961. Their meeting—the Inter-American Economic Conference—resulted in the Declaration of Punta del Este, in which they agreed to co-operate with the United States in effecting the reforms necessary for the gigantic Alliance for Progress crash program. Whether they follow through remains to be seen. An awful lot of toes will be stepped on if the governments take the action they should. Many rich men who pay little or no income tax—and never have—will resist. Great landlords will balk against their vast, peon-worked estates being broken up. Certain business interests, for whom the *status quo* means tremendous profits, will be unhappy. Certain civil servants —in many instances many more than would be necessary in a hundred years—will look with disfavor on their little empires being disintegrated. Corruption and graft, in part the result of ridiculously low salaries paid to even the highest officials, will have to be routed, and that will not be easy.

The Alliance program is ambitious. It involves a minimum of twenty billion dollars in foreign aid, pledged over a decade, with more than half from the United States, the rest from international agencies, Western Europe, and private capital. It embraces agreements which will help stabilize Latin countries' export incomes in such fields as coffee and tin. And in the area of social reform, it sets as its goals six years of free schooling for all children, literacy for fifty million now illiterate; eradication of malaria; major public-housing programs; potable water supplies for more than half the populations; agrarian changes under which large landholdings would be broken up; and drastic modification of taxation systems, whereby national incomes would be redistributed "to benefit those who are most in need."

President Kennedy, in a message to the Punta del Este delegates, termed the Alliance a "heroic effort." "Its success," he wrote, "demands the participation of all our people—of workers and farmers, businessmen and intellectuals, and above all, of the young people of the Americas. For to them and to their children belongs the new world we are resolved to create."

And Supreme Court Justice William O. Douglas, who sees the world on frequent travels from the vantage point of off-the-beaten-path itineraries, has emphasized what U.S. aid programs should *not* be. Too often, he declared in a 1961 address, "they have widened the gulf between the rich and poor," helping to create the vacuum into which the Communists easily move and which launched recipients "on military projects that gave them such an amount of armament that they crushed all dissident elements, with the result the liquidation of democratic influence and the entrenchment of feudal overlords."

The Alliance for Progress notwithstanding, it is imperative that intelligent appointments to the foreign service be made—from stenographers to ambassadors. Generally, the Kennedy appointments have been a vast improvement over many (but by no means all) of those of previous years. Still, the naming of deLesseps Morrison, former mayor of New Orleans—one of the most heavily segregated of American cities—to the post of Ambassador to the Organization of American States was hardly ingenious. Say what one will about aristocratic caste systems, there is no Latin American community with a formal color bar, and there never has been. Legal segregation such as that practiced in the southern United States is unheard of in South America, and many millions of South Americans are nonwhite or of mixed race.

The U.S. domestic racial situation is a cross to bear in Latin

America, as in every continent. And the insular U.S. communities in many South American cities—exclusive, well-scrubbed, socially and culturally detached from the stream of Latin life—make very few friends for Uncle Sam.

But in many other ways the United States seems at long last to be on the right path in South America. The appointment of Robert F. Woodward, a diplomat with long and excellent Latin American experience, as Assistant Secretary of State for Inter-American Affairs, was widely applauded on both sides of the Rio Grande, as was the appointment of Teodoro Moscoso—chosen by President Kennedy as the first Puerto Rican to serve as a U.S. ambassador (to Venezuela) and ex-head of Puerto Rico's successful Operation Bootstrap—as co-ordinator of the Alliance for Progress program, with the title, Latin American area administrator of the Agency for International Development. Welcome, too, was the naming of Chester Bowles—imaginative, courageous, humane —as special Presidential adviser for Latin American, African and Asian affairs. The State Department continues the practice of cultural exchanges begun during earlier administrations. The Peace Corps sent one of its first two groups to a South American country (Colombia) and another early mission to Chile. The Kennedy administration arranged for an enormous, multi-million-dollar advance of credits (from America and other countries) to help Brazil through a current economic crisis, and for a vitally-needed loan to Bolivia, where the revolutionary government is attempting to do, without the aid of Communists or of Castro, what no other government has done in Bolivia's history: raise the standard of living of all Bolivians. There has been commendable help—in the form of $100 million, plus technical aid—given to Chile for rehabilitation of its earthquake-torn areas. And the Operation Bootstrap program in Puerto Rico—which has made commendable strides forward in the last decade—is something to which the United States can and does point with pride.

The United States cannot approach its aid programs to Latin America as it did post-World War II aid to Europe, when spurts of cash helped the members of an already trained, educated,

professionally and occupationally competent society get back on
its feet. The Latin picture is of a different world. The need is not
only for funds, but for many more qualified individuals to put
them to work fruitfully—and of these there are but a relative
handful.

There is an awareness, too, of the importance of combating
the Communist propaganda offensive in Latin American countries, and the administration in Washington is complementing its
economic and social aid programs with a program which is expected to far exceed that of previous years, when approximately
$15 million was devoted to propaganda, in contrast to an estimated
$100 million expended by the Communist bloc. The Castro forces
are also at work in Latin America, and as previously mentioned,
their program is not without appeal to masses of poor workers,
many students, and many intellectuals, to the extent that most
South American governments favor a U.S. policy which would
ignore the Castro government, rather than alienate it, and would,
at the same time, concentrate instead on the kind of positive,
fruitful program which the Alliance for Progress typifies.

Although all South American governments are anti-Communist,
and against Soviet intervention in the Western Hemisphere, many—
including the major ones—do not see the Castro regime as a Russian satellite. A number have potentially revolutionary internal
forces to contend with, which they cannot afford to antagonize.
Moreover—and this is significant—many Latin Americans are
sympathetic to the goals of the Cuban revolution, if not all of its
methods and its affinity to the Soviets. By late 1961, only one key
South American government (Venezuela) had severed diplomatic
relations with Cuba. Of the other eight Latin American republics
which had taken similar action, only two (Uruguay and Paraguay—
both small countries) were South American. And there was reluctance, in deliberations of the O.A.S.—at the 1962 Foreign Ministers' Conference in Uruguay—to take further action against Cuba.

Luis Muñoz-Marin, who knows the Western Hemisphere both as
governor of the American commonwealth of Puerto Rico and as a
Spanish-speaking Latin, warned in a late 1961 address that Latin
American development should not be impeded by "any obsession

with Fidel Castro and Cuba." The United States, he said, "should not support a tyrannical government merely because it vigorously denounces Castro or cries with constant alarm that an alternative to its rule is Communist dictatorship." And he predicted that certain Latin governments would adapt socialistic measures "in an effort to reshape their economies or carry out necessary public services."

Common heritages? It is important, too, that we not take too seriously the frilly harkings-back to "common heritages" which are so often the content of public addresses on inter-American affairs. We are not, of course, without any similarities of background. But the ex-Venezuelan Foreign Minister, Dr. Ignacio Luis Arcaya, hit the nail on the head in a recent talk with some U.S. journalists: "When your United States came into being in an armed struggle with Great Britain, your own ancestors had a culture of throwing off feudalism. You had had the beginnings of democracy even in England itself long before you drew up your Declaration of Independence. You had the primer, the early education of at least the beginnings of freedom. We of Spanish heritage and culture [and he might have added Portuguese, too] had nothing but absolute monarchy or tyranny from which to spring. Democracy to us cannot come as full-blown as it did to a people of your background. It is impossible to use the same analytical and emotional motivations in the freeing of Latin American colonies which have endured through history under state control or rigid monarchy."

What must be done, Senator Mike Mansfield—the Majority Leader of the United States Senate and a former Latin American history professor—wrote in the New York *Times* Magazine, is to bring what he terms the developed "beachhead societies" of the coasts to the poverty-stricken masses in the underdeveloped interior. "Between the minority and the majority," he stated succinctly, "is a social lag that can be measured in centuries, even millennia." Or, as Secretary of State Dean Rusk has put it: "We believe that freedom and progress are historic partners and that the alleged choice between rapid progress and free institutions is false. But this we must prove."

"A ROSE BY ANY OTHER NAME . . ."

Before he departs for South America, and time after time during his visit, the American will be cautioned to refer to himself as a "North American," on the grounds that to call himself an "American" is to imply that citizens of the southern continent are not Americans, the point being that we are all Americans. I suggest that this is, to a great extent, terminological malarky. The name of our country is the United States of America, and our citizens are known as Americans by millions of Europeans, Africans, and Asians. To go along with the "North American" phraseology is to deny ourselves proper national identification. There are, after all, two other countries on the North American continent—Canada and Mexico. Should not—if one follows through with this line of logic—Canadians and Mexicans ignore their nationalities and also be known only as North Americans? Or should we, perhaps, call ourselves United Statesians? Should the Swiss stop calling themselves Swiss and be designated only as Europeans, or the Japanese be known only as Asians? Carry the matter to South America: no Argentine or Venezuelan or Bolivian or Uruguayan is asked to refrain from identifying himself with his country. Why we should be discriminated against in this matter, simply because four centuries ago unimaginative mapmakers named two continents after one man?

It is not terminology that will solve problems existing between the peoples of the two continents, or resolve their inequities. Can't we desist from assuaging our guilt by going along with this patronizing silliness? I consider myself an American—a citizen of the United States of America—whether I'm in Tokyo, Paris, Accra, Montreal, Mexico City, *or* Caracas. But you, of course, may want to go along with the "North American" terminology; doing so can preclude possible arguments along the way.

South America

TOURIST TERRITORY

*"Of journeying, the benefits are many, the freshness it brings to
the heart, the seeing and hearing of marvelous things, the delight
of beholding new ways, the making of lifelong friends. . . ."*
—SAADI: *Gulistān* (1184)

A BELATED AWAKENING

The breakthrough has been made. The two major stumbling
blocks in the South American tourist picture have been removed.
The first was time. It took twenty-two hours to fly from New York
to Buenos Aires, which few Americans realize is more distant
from New York than Moscow. But now jet planes zoom down
to the Argentine capital in twelve hours—and to nearer destinations in considerably less time. The second was money. It cost a
good bit more to encircle the continent of South America than
it did Europe. But now a round-trip air ticket costs less than an
air circuit of Western Europe.

Now, Americans who want to have a look at their own front
yard, and a visit with neighbors whom they should know much
better than they do, are taking advantage of the cheap fares and
fast service, to the extent that even the South American governments—notoriously lethargic about matters touristic—are beginning to perk up.

Until very recently, American transport companies bore the entire brunt of travel promotion to South America. Airlines like Panagra and shipping concerns like Grace Line printed the folders, lithographed the posters, took the full-page ads, whetted the curiosities of the traveler, provided the travel agent, and the press, with the ammunition that set Americans in a southerly travel direction. They are still doing more than their fair share.

But the South Americans themselves have come on the scene, and are being accorded a warm welcome. The crack Brazilian airline, Varig, was the first to jump on the band wagon in full force; others, including the governments themselves, have followed suit. Today, every South American country has a government department which concerns itself with tourism. Two (Surinam and Colombia) have opened branch offices in the United States which deal exclusively with tourist information, and a third (Brazil) handles tourist matters in a division of its Trade Bureau's American branch. Several others have equipped their embassies and consulates to handle travel inquiries intelligently, and two—Venezuela and Chile—are planning to open tourist information offices in the United States, like those of Surinam and Colombia.

The record cannot yet touch that of Europe's, nor that of many of the West Indian countries. Even distant Asia has been more aggressive and so have a surprising number of African states. But a start has been made, and it just may be that the new cheap fares and the new quick jets will spur even more action. One would hope that those countries which have not yet simplified entry procedures will emulate the leaders in this respect—Uruguay, Argentina, and Chile, for example—and dispense with bothersome tourist cards and/or visas. One hopes that before long *every* South American government will—in conjunction with its tourist industry—open up multilingual information centers in its capital city and in the United States.

Meanwhile, the prospective traveler may well wonder, what is the tourism picture like now? The answer, in a word, is: excellent—bashful, un-Madison Avenue governments notwithstanding.

There are fine hotels throughout the continent—and not just in the capital cities, either. Not a single important touristic attraction —urban, resort, or remote—is without first-class or de luxe accommodation.

And in many, many instances, one can go far off the beaten path and still be eminently comfortable. New hotels are going up all the time, and in every country. Local businessmen are often the owners, and in addition, four great United States organizations— Hilton Hotels International, Intercontinental Hotels Corporation, Hotel Corporation of America and Sheraton Corporation of America—are on the scene, operating hotels under contract from the local owners and with dominantly local staffs. In several countries —particularly Peru, Uruguay, and Venezuela—attractive government-operated inns dot the countryside. And in the great cities the range of accommodation runs the gamut of luxury, as do restaurants, cafés, and night spots.

Getting about is rarely difficult. The airlines now fly *everywhere* —and the word is used advisedly. Railroads have been ingeniously built through some of the most exhilaratingly beautiful mountain passes in the world. Boats and steamships ply the principal lakes and rivers. Every government is concerning itself, in varying degrees, with the construction of new roads, and progress continues to be made on the Pan American Highway, which is already in use in a number of areas. Travel agents have sprung up in full force; all offer bilingual service which is occasionally imaginative, invariably competent; many are members of ASTA, the American Society of Travel Agents. Self-drive cars are everywhere available. The credit-card plans—particularly American Express—have members all over the continent. Customs men, with rare exceptions, are courteous, unstuffy, and expeditious. Air terminals and harbor facilities are more often than not modern, and frequently luxurious.

Person-to-person hospitality? In my experience it is warmer, more generous, and more gracious on no other continent. In every South American country citizens are curious about Yankees, anxious to meet and talk with them, proud to show them about. There are exceptions, of course, as there are among the countries of any continent, and among the individuals of any country. But the welcome mat is out, from Tingo María to Tierra del Fuego.

BONING UP ON SOUTH AMERICA

Herewith, a capsulized roundup of some of the organizations which deal exclusively with Latin America, or include Latin America in their activities. The prospective visitor—indeed, anyone interested in the continent—does well to acquaint himself with their programs and publications.

Governmental and intergovernmental organizations: *The Organization of American States* (Pan American Union, Washington, D.C.) is described on pages 8–10. It answers inquiries from individuals and organizations on its functions through the Division of General Information. Its Sales and Promotion Division sells a variety of nominally-priced publications, all of which are listed in a free catalogue. *The United Nations* (United Nations, New York) deals in many ways with Latin America, makes many gratis reports available through its Office of Public Information and Documents Distribution Section, and distributes its publications through its Sales Section. The *UN Economic Commission for Latin America* (ECLA) is devoting current efforts toward such goals as the formation of a Latin American regional market. It has twenty Latin American states as members, plus several others, and co-operates with the Inter-American Economic and Social Council of the OAS, and other UN-related agencies. The *United Nation's Children's Fund* (UNICEF, Box 1618, Church Street Station, New York) has more than two hundred current child-care projects in Latin America. The *UN Special Fund* undertakes a wide range of technical-aid programs in a number of South American countries, ranging from power studies in Argentina to vocational training in Colombia. The *Food and Agricultural Organization* (FAO) has its experts in several Latin lands.

The *International Bank for Reconstruction and Development* (World Bank, 1818 H Street, N.W., Washington, D.C.) has concentrated its loans to Latin nations in the public-utilities field. *The International Labor Organization* (ILO, 917 Fifteenth Street, N.W., Washington, D.C.) has co-ordinated the work of five international organizations in a project known as the Andean Program, which has attempted improvement in the economic and social integration of the Indian populations of Peru, Ecuador, and Bolivia. The *United Nations Educational, Scientific, and Cultural Organization* (UNESCO, Paris, France, and 801 Third Avenue, New York) has a wide range of Latin American activity, including efforts at improving rural primary-school education. The *World Health Organization* (WHO, 1501 New Hampshire Avenue, Washington, D.C.) works closely with the Pan American Health Organization and its secretariat, the Pan American Sanitary Bureau —aligned with the Organization of American States.

The Inter-American Development Bank (801 Nineteenth Street, N.W., Washington, D.C.) works closely with the OAS and the UN Economic Commission for Latin America. It was founded in 1959 and is associated with the administration of the U.S. government's Latin American social-development program.

The United States Government has available many publications and documents concerning Latin America, emanating from the *State, Agriculture, and Commerce departments, the U. S. Information Agency,* the *Senate Foreign Relations Committee,* and the *House Foreign Affairs Committee.* Some are obtainable directly from the committee, department, or agency; others from the *U.S. Government Printing Office* (Superintendent of Documents), Washington, D.C.

Voluntary organizations: *American Foundation for Cultural Popular Action* (350 Fifth Avenue, New York) supports the manifold activities of Cultural Popular Action, a mass-literacy program; *American International Association for Economic and Social Development* (30 Rockefeller Plaza, New York), a Rockefeller-sponsored nonprofit corporation, deals in rural rehabilitation pro-

grams, in co-operation with the OAS and the governments of the
countries in which it operates; *American Organization for Rehabilitation through Training* (ORT, 222 Park Avenue South, New
York) runs vocational-training schools in several South American
countries; *Association for International Development* (347 Grand
Street, Patterson, New Jersey) sends Catholic professional and
technical specialists to participate in Latin American community-
development projects of a wide variety; *CARE* (660 First Avenue,
New York) provides such diverse materials as medical supplies,
vocational-training equipment, food parcels, and textbooks in
many Latin American countries; *Overseas Education Fund*
(1026 17th Street, N.W., Washington, D.C.) in co-operation
with the League of Women Voters, helps Latin American women's
groups further participation in their countries' affairs, exchanges women's groups for seminars; *Catholic Relief Services of
the National Catholic Welfare Conference* (350 Fifth Avenue, New
York), through local agencies in South America, provides medical
materials, helps establish welfare agencies; *Church World Service*
(475 Riverside Drive, New York) unites the relief and rehabilitation programs of the Protestant churches affiliated with the
National Council of Churches, provides material aid, works with
churches in community self-help, medical, agricultural projects; the
Ford (477 Madison Avenue, New York), *Rockefeller* (111 West
50th Street, New York) and *Kellogg* (Battle Creek, Michigan)
foundations have all interested themselves in Latin American projects; *Inter-American Association for Democracy and Freedom*
(45 West 45th Street, New York, monthly publication: *Hemispherica*) devotes itself to fighting against totalitarianism in all its
forms and fighting for civil and political liberties; *Inter-American
Press Association* (22 East 60th Street, New York, monthly
publication: *Press of the Americas*) has members representing major publications of the Americas, concerns itself with press freedom,
promotes cultural and technical exchanges, maintains a scholar-
ship program, awards annual citations to outstanding hemisphere
journalists, and reports on press conditions regularly through its

Freedom of the Press Committee; *Inter-American Regional Organization of Workers* (20 West 40th Street, New York) is affiliated with the International Confederation of Free Trade Unions, promotes, by a diverse program, the cause of trade-unionism in the Latin American countries; *Maryknoll Missioners* (Maryknoll, New York), a Roman Catholic order, operates schools, dispensaries, credit unions, agricultural programs, and community-leadership classes in a number of Latin countries; *Meals for Millions* (115 West 7th Street, Los Angeles, California) is a mass-food-distribution organization; *Pan American Society of the United States* (630 Fifth Avenue, New York) makes awards to citizens of the Americas, gives fellowships for graduate work by Latin students in U.S. universities, holds luncheons and dinners to honor visiting leaders; *YWCA* (600 Lexington Avenue, New York) conducts training programs for leaders from Latin countries, and exchange programs under which Latin American women spend six months in the United States observing community-service programs, while American women do likewise in the Latin countries.

Business organizations: *Chamber of Commerce of Latin America in the United States* (29 Broadway, New York) promotes increased trade between the Americas; *Binational Chambers of Commerce*—all in New York—include *Argentine-American* (11 Broadway), *Brazilian-American* (22 West 48th Street), *Chilean-American* (149 Broadway), *Colombian-American* (160 Broadway), *Ecuadorian-American* (535 Fifth Avenue), *Peruvian-American* (11 Broadway), and *Venezuelan-American* (441 Lexington Avenue). The *coffee growers* maintain promotion offices in the United States and offer free material on their product: *Pan American Coffee Bureau* (120 Wall Street, New York), *Brazilian Coffee Institute* (120 Wall Street, New York), and *National Federation of Coffee Growers of Colombia* (120 Wall Street, New York); *W. R. Grace and Company* (3 Hanover Square, New York) publishes—and makes available without charge—the quarterly *Grace Log*, on Latin American affairs (including tourism), and its diverse business interests (which include the Grace Line and, in part,

Panagra Airways); available from it, too, is a brief but thoughtful book, *It's Not Too Late in Latin America,* by J. Peter Grace, the firm's president, in which Mr. Grace advocates among other things, "a lend-lease program to provide Latin Americans with U.S. road-building, land-clearing, irrigation and transportation equipment to colonize and develop its millions of fertile acres of virgin land." *The First Bank of Boston* (Boston, Massachusetts, and Buenos Aires, Argentina) publishes a delightful sight-seers' booklet on Buenos Aires. *Chase Manhattan Bank* (Chase Manhattan Plaza, New York) publishes the free quarterly *Latin-American Business Highlights. Sears Roebuck* (925 South Homan Avenue, Chicago) has gratis material on its interesting Latin American operations. *Vision* (635 Madison Avenue, New York), a United-States-published newsweekly (editions in Portuguese and Spanish only) with a wide Latin American circulation, also publishes in English—for U.S. readers—the *Vision Latin American Letter,* a biweekly political-economic report ($18 annually).

Educational organizations: *The Association for Latin American Studies* (c/o Prof. H. L. Johnson, Indiana University, Bloomington, Indiana) functions "to promote Latin American studies in all fields of knowledge in co-operation with other scholarly agencies"; *Inter-American Schools Service* (1785 Massachusetts Avenue, N.W., Washington, D.C.) an agency of the American Council of Education, acts as a clearing house for financial assistance and educational advice for some three hundred Latin American schools established by private American citizens, corporations, and religious groups. *The Joint Committee on Latin American Studies* (230 Park Avenue, New York) is an agency of the American Council of Learned Societies and the Social Science Research Council, founded in 1959 to establish a program for the advancement of research on Latin America, on a grant of the Carnegie Corporation of New York. An outstanding leader among the university centers of Latin studies—of which there are far too few—is the *Institute of Hispanic-American and Luso-Brazilian Studies* at *Stanford University* (Stanford, California). Its excellent monthly journal, *Hispanic American Report,* edited by the institute's director, Ronald Hilton, deserves a far wider readership. Among the others: The *University of Florida's School of Inter-American Studies* (Gainesville) which offers advanced degrees and publishes the quarterly *Journal of Inter-American Studies,* and the new *Latin American Institute* founded in 1961 at *Columbia University.* Of importance, too: the *Junior Year in Brazil* program of *New York University* (New York City 3), conducted annually at the University of São Paulo.

Museums: Many United States museums contain collections relating to South America. However, the country's most comprehensive exhibits of Latin American Indian art—both pre-Columbian and contemporary—are those of the *Museum of the American Indian,* Broadway at 155th Street, New York, whose curator, Dr. Frederick Dockstader, is an outstanding expert in this field. Other museums with especially good pre-Colombian collections include the *United States National Museum,* a division of the Smithsonian Institution, Washington, D.C.; the *American Museum of Natural History,* New York; the *Brooklyn Museum,* Brooklyn; the *University of Pennsylvania Museum,* Philadelphia; the *Peabody Museum* of Harvard University, Cambridge, Mass.; the *Chicago Museum of Natural History,* Chicago; the *Art Institute of Chicago,* Chicago; the *Anthropological Museum of the University of California,* Berkeley, Calif.; and the *Museum of the University of California at Los Angeles.* A rich collection of the traditional arts of Spain—unique in the United States—is that of the *Museum of the Hispanic Society of America,* Broadway and 155th Street, New York; some of its displays are of Colonial South American origin.

NOTE: *The Foreign Policy Association-World Affairs Center* (First Avenue at 47th Street, New York) is a nationally-unique and extremely valuable clearing house of information on international affairs, with a stimulating, many-faceted program serving business, community, educational, professional, religious, and labor groups, as well as individuals. Facilities include a bookshop specializing in foreign-affairs publications, an audio-visual service, meeting rooms, displays of program materials. The FPA-WAC publishes *Intercom* magazine and in many ways does a superb job of helping keep America intelligently informed about the very small world in which we live—inter-American and otherwise.

TOURIST CARDS AND VISAS

It is sad but a fact that about half of the South American countries still require tourist cards or visas. (It is likewise sad but a fact that the United States does too, although the new U. S. Travel Service is trying to make things a little easier for visitors to our shores.) But to get to the point: seven South American countries require only proof of identification (i.e., a birth certificate) or a valid passport of American tourists, not one of which has yet attempted to overthrow the government. (The honor roll: Argentina, Bolivia, British Guiana, Chile, French Guiana, Surinam, and Uruguay.) For the others, tourist cards or visas—obtainable through the travel agent booking one's trip, the carrier on which one departs, or directly from consulates—remain a requisite. Before applying, one needs a valid *passport* or proof of identification, a *health certificate* indicating a valid vaccination for smallpox, a *transportation ticket* to show the authorities that there will be no difficulty in leaving their country (travel agents issue letters, certifying that the ticket is being prepared, in cases where it is not ready at the time of making application for tourist card or visa), and, very often, passport-size *photographs* (the quantity varies with the country—have a good dozen ready, if the trip is to cover the continent). Paraguay asks for additional nonsensical documents and when you ask its officials why, they ask if you know how difficult it is for foreigners to enter the United States; *that* shuts you up.) *The specific requirements of each country are included in the chapters on each country, which follow*. Note, though, that they are for U.S. citizens traveling as *tourists,* not planning to remain in a single country more than thirty days. For others—persons on business missions or planning stays longer than a month—regular visas are usually required, the details of which can be furnished by travel agents, each country's consulates, or the consular sections of the embassies in Washington. (Exceptions: British consulates for British Guiana, French consulates for French Guiana, Dutch consulates for Surinam.) It seems worth mentioning here that unless one is making a brief trip to a single country which does not require a passport, but only "proof of identification," that one should have a passport and carry it along; it is the best document an American (or a citizen of any country) can have when abroad—of far more value, in the long run, than a birth certificate or other means of identification, no matter how valid. Travel agents who specialize in South American travel are familiar with tourist-card and visa procedures, and with whatever changes are made in them from time to time; they know, too, the locations of the consulates. If one is going to a number of countries, it is essential that enough time be allotted for this predeparture malarky. Start the ball rolling several weeks ahead. With the aid of a travel agent it's all quite painless; done on one's own it provides an introduction to the people and the red-tape peculiarities of the countries to be visited; each nation, including the United States, has its own.

OBTAINING A U. S. PASSPORT

The passport-application procedure has become so quick and simple that old-timers are now mumbling that it's *too* easy to go abroad. To obtain a first passport, one needs a birth certificate (or a notarized affidavit of birth vouched for by a relative or long-time friend), ten dollars, two passport-size photos (front view, three inches by three inches, on a white background, in color if you like—and yes, Passport Director Frances G. Knight says you *can* smile). The passport is valid for three years and can be renewed for two additional years for five dollars. Applications must be made in person at the Department of State Passport Offices in New York, Miami, San Francisco, Washington, Boston, Seattle,

Los Angeles, Chicago, and New Orleans, or, in other cities, at the office of the clerk of a federal court. Allow ten days to two weeks but don't be surprised if the passport comes in the mail even sooner; extra-quick service may be requested.

INOCULATIONS AND HEALTH

For re-entry into the United States—and for entry into *every* South American country—a valid *smallpox vaccination* is necessary; it must be not less than eight days or more than three years old, and should be validated by the local board of health. Generally, no other inoculations are required of visitors, but it is usually advisable to play it safe and have also such "regulars" as *typhoid* and *paratyphoid,* and if one wishes, *typhus, tetanus, polio,* and, as a precaution for one or two areas, *yellow fever,* plus *diphtheria* for youngsters under ten who have had positive Schick tests. Generally, vacationing visitors find that besides the required smallpox, typhoid and paratyphoid suffice. But one is advised to check with one's own physician. Additional helpful information on keeping fit abroad is contained in *A Traveler's Guide to Good Health,* by Colter Rule, M.D. (Dolphin), and in Dr. Rule's regular column in *Travel* magazine (50 West 57th Street, New York).

To drink or not to drink? The tap water, that is. In major cities, particularly Buenos Aires and Montevideo, it is perfectly potable. In smaller places it is always advisable to drink it boiled or to order bottled water (both at the table and for one's room), of which there are good brands everywhere. The important thing is not to panic if you've gulped a mouthful, without thinking, in even the most doubtful of places; chances are it won't hurt you.

B.A.-Belly, Chileitis, the Rio Runs and assorted similar afflications can come as the result of overeating and overdrinking in a new place—*any* new place in *any* country. Moderation and a good night's sleep every night constitute Doc Kane's prescription for a pleasant trip.

CLIMATE

Americans—perhaps because so many of them live in some of the world's most disagreeable climates—are often overly climate-conscious when it comes to foreign travel. Rarely do they realize that the conditions so often experienced at home—the summer humidity of the great cities, North and South; the raw, biting winters of the North and Midwest—innure them to just about *anything* when they go abroad, and that includes much of South America, at any time of year. Manaus, in the heart of the Amazon, is no more uncomfortable than many August days in Manhattan, Saint Louis, or Washington—let alone New Orleans or Atlanta. Winter in Buenos Aires, on the other hand, is snowless and mild— Americans normally regard it more as spring. Rio is hot at Christmastime, but hardly objectionable with its superb beaches— which surely Omaha cannot boast of on the Fourth of July.

Worth noting, too, are the effects of the great mountains and highlands on climate. Many equatorial South American points are cool all year round, thanks to their elevation—Quito, La Paz, and Cuzco, for example. The hottest parts of the continent are not on the equator but on the fringe of the Caribbean—and there again, ocean breezes and beaches offset high temperatures.

Climatic conditions, country by country, are duly noted in succeeding chapters. But if a generalization can be made, it is that South America can be visited at any time of the year. The American spring, summer, and early autumn months are the coolest in the temperate and subtropical zones; the remainder of the year—from November to March—is by and large the pleasantest period for the tropics. Rainy seasons—when, it must be emphasized, rains are usually intermittent—need rarely be a deterrent, there being sufficient "bright periods"—to quote the British weather reporters—to permit of considerable sight-seeing.

PACKING SIMPLIFIED

The what-to-pack bugaboo need not be that at all. Air travelers, by now accustomed to forty-four-pound (economy and tourist classes) and sixty-six-pound (first class) limitations have learned that the best rule is: easy does it. Wash-and-wear garments, with percentages of such fibers as dacron which preclude frequent pressing, are, of course, the easiest to care for. Laundry is never a problem; every hotel will do it quickly and well. Extra-speedy service—for which there is, of course, a surcharge—is generally available; if the laundry is turned in before breakfast it is back in one's room at dinnertime.

The "travel-light" policy hinges on acceptance of the fact that it is not necessary to appear in a smashing new costume every day of the week. When moving about, one sees people for periods often so brief that they're not able to note the variety of one's dress, even if they're so inclined. Quantities of each item of clothing depend, of course, on individual stubbornness, as well as baggage allowances for air travelers; those going all the way via first-class on passenger ships are of course unrestricted in this regard, and they will want to include dress clothes for evening wear (including dinner jackets for men) and beach-type regalia for daytime pool and deck activity. No arrests will be made for violations, but in general it is worth noting that South American men, in the cities, wear jackets and ties, as a rule, and South American city-women are not slacks-and-shorts types. Men should not need to be reminded that visits to government and business officials—regardless of climate—call for a jacket and tie; I mention this only because I have never yet got over the embarrassment of being among a group of U.S. journalists received by the president of the Republic of Panama, a number of whom were in sports shirts and khakis; the president was gentleman enough not to mention this marked disrespect for his office, but it was duly noted. Resort wear resembles that of comparable places on the other continents, and for rural expeditions, comfort and practicality are the keynotes in dress.

A basic **woman's wardrobe**—and I am here indebted to a number of distaff travelers for counsel—should include two lightweight travel suits; several blouses that can be worn with suit skirts; at least one extra-full skirt for active sight-seeing; a pair of late-afternoon or cocktail ensembles, in either linen, cotton, or uncrushable silk; a serviceable wool dress for the highlands and other cool places; several changes of lingerie and stockings; housecoat and slippers, both as light in weight as possible; two pairs of low-heeled walking shoes, preferably with closed toes; two pairs of dressier shoes; a topcoat (preferably waterproof) which can double as a raincoat; a crushable hat, a swimsuit, and cosmetic and toilet requisites—replenishable in all the major cities. The aforementioned cocktail dresses are invariably adequate for big-city parties and theater nights. The woman who expects to be involved in a heavy social life should know that her counterparts in most parts of South America dress in good—and often high-style—taste.

A **man's wardrobe,** based upon my experience, should include a dark (gray or navy blue), medium- or summer-weight dacron-and-wool suit which is appropriate for both day and evening wear in the cities; a cotton-dacron cord sport jacket; a pair of gray dacron-and-wool medium- or summer-weight slacks, for wear with the cord sport jacket and with several short-sleeved sport shirts, as well as at least one long-sleeved sport shirt; a pair of khaki or chino slacks, convenient for resorts and rural exploration; a supply of regular long-sleeved shirts (wash-and-wear fabrics are handy) which may double as sport shirts; a good choice of ties—there being no better or lighter-in-weight variety-adders for the suit and sport-jacket combinations; a pair of wash-and-wear pajamas (the kind that dry in a few hours); a raincoat with detachable wool liner which will serve also as topcoat and bathrobe; socks, underwear, and handkerchiefs; a hat, if you wear one; two pairs of comfortable shoes (one may be loafers and thereby double as bedroom slippers); a swimsuit; two sweaters—one

long-sleeved and one sleeveless; and, of course, a toilet kit—the
contents of which can easily be replenished in any city. If the
itinerary will include the cool highlands or temperate zones during the South American winter, add a winter-weight worsted suit
(it need not be overly heavy) and, if you like, a muffler and un-
lined gloves.

Both men and women will want to take sunglasses, an extra
pair of eyeglasses, and a copy of the prescription (for wearers
of glasses); some Band-Aids, a roll of Scotch Tape (it has innumerable uses on a trip), an envelope of rubber bands and paper
clips—also valuable at the most unexpected times; a few packs
of Chiclets and/or Life Savers—for the occasional small aircraft
whose crews do not serve them, on take-off or landing; a half-
dozen of the cheapest ball-point pens—they are occasionally lost
when filling in landing cards, customs forms, etc.; several plastic
bags—of inestimable convenience all along the way; a pocket-size
flashlight; small Spanish-English and/or Portuguese-English dic-
tionaries for travelers whose Spanish and Portuguese is not all it
might be; printed or engraved personal or business cards; a plastic
bottle of aspirin; an antidiarrhea preparation (just in case); names
and addresses of friends of friends to contact; and, it goes without saying, this book! It's not at all necessary to carry soap; a
single cake is more than enough, for virtually every South American hotel provides it; it can be easily filched, in case of dire need,
from aircraft washrooms, or, for that matter, purchased everywhere. It might be worth noting, too, that the toilet paper in
hotel bathrooms is often of facial-tissue quality; South America is
not Europe.

PHOTOGRAPHY

The professional or semiprofessional photographer needs no
briefing in this regard, except perhaps a reassurance that South
America is eminently photogenic. The novice or nonprofessional

might want to consider these pointers: (1) Keep a tiny bag or two of Silicagel (or a similar preparation, easily obtained from photo-supply shops) in your camera case or gadget bag to fight the moisture, in those areas where it's prevalent. (2) Airmail exposed color film home only if you feel you are to be away longer than is absolutely safe; the mails in South America (of which more later) are not always reliable. Kodak film is packed with cloth mailing bags, each with address label attached. It goes directly to a U.S. processing laboratory, from which it is mailed to any address you note on the label. Black-and-white film—not nearly so sensitive as color—can be kept with you for a long period, preferably in a plastic bag or airtight container. And though experts might doubt me, I would say exposed color film would be safe in one's baggage for as much as three months. (Air-conditioned hotel rooms are good repositories for exposed color film; if your room is air-conditioned, leave the machine on while you're out during the day, and when the maid turns it off, turn it back on! (3) Ask your photo dealer—if you're not already an expert —to recommend an all-purpose filter for bright sunlight, and, perhaps, a sunshade. (4) Carry with you as much film as you've space for; don't worry, you'll use it all! Customs officials in most countries ordinarily believe you when you indicate that the film is for your own use—at least if you've an honest face. If not, partially open the packages, and write your name and address on them, thereby indicating that the film is for your own use. (5) Black-and-white film is stocked almost everywhere in South America; color film is sometimes scarcer and invariably more expensive than in the United States. *Film availability in each country is noted in the succeeding chapters of this book.* (6) In my experience Kodak Plus-X is the ideal black-and-white film, and Kodachrome is excellent for color. (7) In certain areas of South America— especially the Andean areas—women do not like their photograph taken, particularly without advance permission (I can't blame them). Often military installations cannot be photographed. Where there is any doubt, ask before snapping, and if accompanied by a guide, let him break the ice, where necessary. Often, people like to be remunerated when posing as models—as well they might. In such instances it is wise to set the price in advance, hand over the money, and then snap away.

CUSTOMS

In South America: Every country has lists a mile long of what can and can not be imported by foreign travelers, but this book is not about to go into the sordid details. Generally, customs officials are polite and sensible, particularly with tourists. It is always wise to level with them as regards cameras (which in some cases must be registered), film, cigarettes, and tape-recorders. Portable typewriters are never a problem, and actually, neither are the above-mentioned articles, so long as the customs official is assured that they are for one's personal use, and the quantities are reasonable. Everywhere, representatives of airlines and steamship companies are on hand to assist their passengers. Customs inspectors like to be regarded as officials of their governments—which, of course, they are. The best rule in South America, as on every continent: speak politely when spoken to; let *them* initiate the conversation,

Returning to the U.S.: In the apparent belief that it would help to close the dollar gap between our exports and imports, Congress (at President Kennedy's request) enacted legislation, effective September 9, 1961, which limited the amount of duty-free exemption on purchases made by Americans abroad. The current limit is $100, instead of the $500 which had been allowed for travelers once every six months. The $100 exemption is allowable once every thirty days. (The U. S. Virgin Islands alone remain in a privileged $200 category; congratulations, Virgin Islands lobbyists!) Even though the majority of U.S. travelers abroad will not feel pinched by the new legislation—the Customs Bureau estimates that well over half spend less than $100—the Treasury Department believes that foreign tourist purchases by Americans will be cut by as much as $150 million, which is but a fraction of the $2 billion spent annually by U.S. citizens abroad, on travel expenses and purchases.

American travel specialists had urged Congress not to tamper with the $500 limit, but rather to spur foreign travel to the United States to close the dollar export gap. The new United States Travel Service is attempting to do just that but Congress stubbornly went ahead and lowered the duty-free allowance anyway. Had there been more battlers opposing the curtailment of the $500 limit—Paul J. C. Friedlander, travel editor of the New York *Times*, fought valiantly but without nearly enough organized support—the outcome might have been otherwise. It remains to be seen just how many business enterprises abroad—on every continent—close down as a result, how many friends the United States has lost as a result of such a short-sighted move—and how many Americans travel only to shop.

At any rate, it is worth noting that *the value of goods brought in duty-free is figured on wholesale, not retail prices.* One is well advised to have merchants abroad so indicate on sales slips, which can be requested by customs officers at U.S. ports of entry.

Also worthy of note: you may still ship, *duty-free,* without having to declare them, and *not* counting as part of your $100 allowance, gifts or parcels not exceeding a total value of $10. Send *as many as you like* from wherever you like, but not more than one parcel per day *to the same recipient.* Mark each such package "GIFT—TOURIST PURCHASE—VALUE UNDER $10." Remember, too, that *antiques,* duly certified to have been made before 1830, are admitted duty-free, and do not count as part of the $100 quota; neither do *paintings* of any date, if certified as original. Also exempt from duty, but as a part of the $100 quota: one gallon (which generally means five "fifths") of liquor, and one hundred cigars (or a carton of cigarettes). Members of a family traveling together may pool their exemptions to cover large purchases. And—this is important—there is no restriction on how much one may bring in above the $100 limit so long as the duty is paid; on many items the duty is surprisingly moderate.

YOUR SOUTH AMERICAN HOSTS

"Es preciso bailar al son que se toca."
—OLD SPANISH PROVERB

(*It is necessary to dance to the tune that is being played.*)

Americans invariably find their welcomes warm and gracious
in South American countries, especially when they refrain from
incessant verbal comparisons which—when made by citizens of
a rich country like the United States—can be odious, as can
obsequiousness and a patronizing attitude. The tendency toward
singling out those citizens of a country who are either poor or of
a darker skin color as "natives" is not one which promotes good
will. The Negro in Salvador is just as much a Brazilian as the
resident of an Oscar Niemeyer house in São Paulo, and the Indian
living on the shores of Lake Titicaca is a Bolivian, just as is the
official in the foreign ministry for whom you may have a letter
of introduction.

Knowing about everyday matters like food can help a great
deal. *Cuisine specialties of each country are indicated in later
chapters,* but for a thorough, and delightful, gastronomic introduction to the continent, read *The Art of South American Cookery,*
by Myra Waldo (Doubleday, 1961). And, if at all possible, have
a meal at the Fonda del Sol (Avenue of the Americas at 50th
Street, New York) in advance of departure. This is the outstanding Latin American restaurant in the United States, with truly
authentic cuisine and a strikingly handsome décor, the highlights
of which are ingeniously designed displays, by Alexander Girard,
of Latin American folk art. The Avenue of the Americas, on
which the restaurant is appropriately situated, is not without an
inter-American flavor, even though stubborn New Yorkers still
refer to it as Sixth Avenue, its earlier name. It is lined with street-
lamp plaques bearing the crests of all the American republics.
And where the avenue meets Central Park, there are imposing

equestrian statues of two great South Americans. One is of José de San Martín, a gift to the city of New York from the city of Buenos Aires; the other is of Simón Bolívar, and was presented by the Republic of Venezuela.

It is always wise, especially on a relatively whirlwind round-the-continent tour to have straight in one's mind the countries one is visiting, and the cities within those countries. The traveler who, in Quito, enthuses over the "Ecuadorian" meal he has just had in La Paz, or the tourist newly arrived from Rio who in Buenos Aires comments to an Argentine about "you South Americans," as if they were all the same, cannot expect a particularly enthusiastic reception. The overecstatic gusher, who finds even the most sordid slums possessed of a quaint, exotic charm, is also suspect; one need never rave to one's hosts over anything one finds distasteful. Frankness is always to be preferred over hypocrisy.

SHOPPING

When one considers that the Spanish and Portuguese civilizations have heavy overtones of the long occupation of the Moors with their inventive culture, and that added to this in South America are the cultures of the African, the indigenous Indian, and assorted other infusions, it is easy to perceive how rich a treasure-trove are the shops and markets. *Interesting purchases are discussed in later chapters, country by country, with specific sources frequently suggested.* Purchases can be shipped home to avoid overweight when flying, but this is more difficult in some countries than in others, and one is advised to inquire of procedures in advance of buying anything heavy or bulky. Lima, Peru, is probably the most convenient shipping point on the continent.

Bargaining is often the rule in the public markets and smaller shops. One simply offers a good bit less than the first price asked by the merchant; a compromise fee is agreed upon if the seller is willing to deviate from his original price; if not, he so indicates.

Department stores and bigger shops in the great cities—Buenos Aires and Rio de Janeiro, for example—sell at fixed prices. But when, even in these places, merchandise is not price-labeled, one can feel free to bargain, or to ask for a discount if the order is a substantial one.

Always inexpensive—and invariably welcomed by friends at home —are the cigarettes of the South American countries, and the often-handsome boxes of matches sold at tobacco counters. (*Note for smokers:* Smoke the local brands while traveling; filtered and mild blends generally are available—considerably cheaper than U.S. makes in every country but Panama.)

EMBASSIES AND CONSULATES

American embassies are found in every South American capital, save those in the three Guianas, where the chiefs of the U.S. missions are consuls-general, ambassadors being accredited only to sovereign nations. There are, outside of the capitals, U.S. consuls-general and consuls in many important cities, commercial and maritime. In addition, there are offices of the United States Information Service in every capital and many other cities, whose function is to disseminate information on America to residents; to operate, in some places, American libraries (invariably popular with local people and very worth visiting), and to assist American journalists, writers, researchers, and technical specialists in making contacts and gathering material. It is among the functions of the embassies and consulates to assist visiting Americans with any unusual difficulties—booking hotel rooms and arranging for sight-seeing *not* being among these. One should have no hesitancy at all in seeking special assistance, and one should not countenance run-arounds—sometimes the case in the larger, more impersonal embassies in the great capitals. The quality of personnel varies, as might be expected. At times it is surprisingly high; at others, mediocre and unimaginative. Still, in no foreign post is the life as depicted in Hollywood; foreign-service life has more than its share of frustration as well the manifold problems—educational, domestic, health, child-rearing—which come of residence in a strange land.

CURRENCY

American Express travelers' checks are recommended; they are safe and recognized everywhere. Take a good many in ten-dollar denominations. Carry along, too, about thirty one-dollar bills. These are negotiable for purchases of drinks and cigarettes on many international flights, and also come in handy for last-minute use just before leaving a country when it would be inconvenient to cash a traveler's check. There is no need to stock up on South American currencies in advance of departure; a few dollars' worth, for use upon arrival, might be helpful, but none are available at bargain rates in the United States, as is the case with some European currencies. Handy for on-the-spot conversions from dollars into local currencies is Richard Joseph's *World Wide Money Converter and Tipping Guide* (Doubleday, $1)—*really* pocket-size, and at the same, convenient and easy to use; I never travel without it.

Thievery is not commonplace, at least in my experience (I've never had anything stolen anywhere in South America). But one does well, nonetheless, to obtain a theft-insurance policy from either a travel agent or an insurance company. The American Express Credit Card Plan is by far the most popular of any of the American plans in South American hotels, shops, restaurants, and night spots, and having a membership in it can be most convenient.

TIPPING

Tipping on land: The only tip-happy country is Panama, where tourists of one sort or another have been commonplace for centuries. But even Panama is restrained in contrast to such lands as Italy and Egypt. Elsewhere in South America one tips as one would at home, except in places where a service charge is added to the bill, at which times additional small tips are appreciated but never, never requested. *Tips on tipping, country by country, are contained in later chapters.* Everywhere it is wise, if possible, to have a good supply of change on hand when checking into and out of hotels.

Tipping at sea: There are no hidebound regulations covering shipboard tipping, but here is a suggested guide to minimum tips: For *shorter one-class cruises* (less than a fortnight): $12 each for the room and dining-room stewards, depending on services rendered. For *medium-length one-class cruises* (sixteen–eighteen days): $20 each for the room and dining-room stewards, $10 for the deck steward. For *longer cruises:* $25 each for room and dining-room stewards in first class, $10–$15 in cabin class; $5–$10 for bath steward (if used) in first class, $4–$5 cabin and tourist classes; deck steward $10 first class, $4–$5 cabin and tourist classes; chief dining-room steward $5–$10 first class, $3–$5 cabin and tourist classes, if special services have been rendered; pool and gym attendants—again depending on services rendered—$5–$10 first class, $4 cabin and tourist classes. Bar stewards, barbers, beauticians, and bellhops are tipped for individual services, as ashore. Ship's officers—and these include the purser and assistant pursers—are not, of course, tipped. On long trips— three weeks and upwards—tip twice: midway and at the end of the voyage; otherwise, tip at journey's end.

Tipping aloft: No such animal; the airlines forbid it. Porters at air terminals who carry luggage from customs to car or bus *do* expect tips; fifteen cents a cart-pulled bag is a good average.

SIGHT-SEEING AND GUIDES

Every capital, major city, resort, and rural point of interest has travel agencies which offer either guided group tours or individual escort. Often, however, sight-seeing is included on tours arranged by one's home travel agent, prior to departure from the United States—in which case there is no problem whatsoever. Taxi drivers often serve as good guides, provided they speak your language. Self-drive and chauffeur-driven cars may be hired everywhere. Hotel porters and concierges are always good local-information sources, as is the local press. In many cities, English-language papers are published; they always contain currently up-to-date information on local attractions. Everywhere, regardless of how extensive one's guided tours, additional shoe-leather expeditions are recommended—as long, leisurely, and frequent as possible.

The guided tours, particularly in the great cities, hit only the highlights—and not even the major ones, in many cases. Stay long enough, if possible, to poke around on your own. Wander through a department store, peep inside an "unfamous" church, watch a class in session through a school window or courtyard, take in a movie, relax for a bit on a park bench or at a café table, stroll through a university campus, engaging in conversation, if it's feasible, with a student or professor. And look up the friends of friends you've been told about—particularly if they're citizens of the country you're visiting; Americans, while often eminently worth meeting and knowing, are found in great quantities at home.

PRIVATE CLUBS

The names of leading private clubs—city, country, sporting, and "service"—are indicated in the chapters on each country. It should go without saying that they cannot be visited without cards or letters of introduction. These often can be obtained from clubs of a similar nature to which one belongs at home. And in countries served by Panagra, representatives of that airline are often able to arrange temporary memberships. Many cities have branches of such clubs as Rotary and Kiwanis, which hold regular luncheon meetings at leading hotels; they, of course, welcome with open arms members from foreign countries. Private-club memberships, it might be noted, are invariably representative of the small wealthy class of each country or of its insular foreign (mainly English-speaking) communities—worth knowing, of course, but hardly typical.

MAIL

If your itinerary is planned in advance, have letters addressed to you in care of your hotels along the way. American embassies and consulates (where they exist) will also hold mail for you, but unlike hotels, which are open day and night, they are closed evenings, Saturday afternoons, and Sundays and holidays, so that you can't always claim your mail just after arrival. Correspondents should allow a good week for delivery via airmail in every country except Brazil and Paraguay, where service is unbelievably and infuriatingly slow and unreliable. An airmail letter sent from New York will be in Rio or São Paulo within a few jet hours, but what happens to it after it arrives is one of the great mysteries of the international postal world. It *may* be delivered, in the aforementioned cities, within a week. But it may not be delivered for three weeks. For other Brazilian points, three weeks must be considered a *bare minimum*. In Paraguay one does well not to count on letters *ever* being delivered—although they are, on occasion. Elsewhere on the continent, mail delivery is generally efficient and reliable. The regular airmail letter rate was raised in 1961 from ten to fifteen cents per one-half ounce. International air letters, obtainable at all U.S. post offices, are ten cents—a nickel cheaper.

LANGUAGE

English is spoken more than one might imagine. More and more schools teach it, and many young citizens of the various South American republics are anxious to practice it—and a good many older educated people speak it well. There is rarely a hotel, transport terminal, travel agency, or major shop without English-speaking personnel. Spanish is, of course, the official language of every South American republic except Brazil, where Portuguese takes its place. Dutch is the official language of Surinam, French of French Guiana, and English of British Guiana—the only such countries on the continent. However, there are millions of Bolivians, Ecuadorians, and Peruvians who speak only Indian languages, and the same obtains with the Indian minorities of other countries. *The language situation in each country is dealt with in succeeding chapters.* Nowhere in this book will the reader find phrase lists in Spanish and Portuguese, for the simple reason that the author has never known anyone to use them. The best bet, if one doesn't speak the language, is a pocket dictionary, where individual words can be found at a glance. Recommended for use in advance of departure: "Hear How to Converse in Spanish," a two-side LP record which is an excellent primer in fundamentals for the traveler, recorded with great clarity by Lou Garcia, the bilingual public-relations director of Panagra Airways, and skillfully edited by Professor Susana Redondo de Feldman of Columbia University's Spanish Department. The disc is ⚹CHH/21 in Carlton Records' "Hear How" series, and sells for less than two dollars in record and department stores; included with it is Panagra's handy little Spanish-English dictionary.

WHERE TO AND HOW MUCH?

"The wise traveler, the self-indulgent and the happy one, is he who never looks at his timetable and hides his watch."
—JOHN MASON BROWN

Balancing and juggling: How much money is budgeted for the trip. How much time is available? Would you like to sample bits and pieces of South America, or concentrate on portions of it? Are you after the restful, relaxing kind of journey which is best taken by ship? Would you rather spend more time on dry land,

and less time traveling, in which case air is the solution? Or might a combination of the two—easily arranged—be preferable? These are the basic questions of the preplanning stage.

Three types of trips: What must be decided next is the degree of effort you yourself want to put into the details of the trip. There are three major types of journeys: (1) *independent* travel, in which you purchase your own transportation tickets, book your own hotels, arrange for your own sight-seeing—either in advance, or as you go along; (2) group travel, on a *package tour* purchased in advance from a travel agency; (3) individual travel, but by means of a travel agent's *prearranged individual itinerary,* with some or all arrangements—transportation, hotels, sight-seeing—made for you prior to departure. There are advantages to all three. The solitary traveler might enjoy the companionship afforded by group tours. The student on a tight budget, or the veteran traveler who knows the ropes, might enjoy "free-lancing" his trip as he goes along. Most travelers prefer the third-mentioned procedure whereby a travel agent tailors the basic arrangements— transportation and hotels, for example—to the traveler's order, and the traveler himself proceeds unescorted but with the assurance that his major requirements are taken care of, and with the advantage that he's going just where he wants, for as long as he wants. (If desired, and at slight extra cost, he can be met upon arrival at each point by his travel agent's local representatives.)

Selecting a travel agent: It is important to secure the services of a travel agent who is reputable and efficient (members of ASTA— the American Society of Travel Agents—are invariably good bets) and who knows South America, makes a specialty of South American business, and keeps abreast of developments in South American tourism. American Express, with offices throughout the United States and many in South America, is one such; another is Martin Tours, with headquarters in New York's Empire State Building. Both are expert at planning individually-tailored itineraries and offer a wide variety of package tours as well. Also worth knowing about are the package tours—exclusively for unattached men and women, divided by age group—offered by Bachelor Party Tours.

There are, of course, many good agents all over the country.

The absolute basics of a 'Round South America air itinerary should include—at least in my opinion—Rio de Janeiro, São Paulo, Salvador, and Brasília, Brazil; Iguassú Falls, on the Brazilian-Argentine-Paraguayan border; Asunción, Paraguay, because it must be seen to be believed; Montevideo, Uruguay, with an excursion, particularly if it's summer, to Punta del Este; Buenos Aires, Argentina; the Argentine Lake Country in and around Bariloche, all too often omitted from itineraries or offered as an optional "extra" when it should be a requisite; Santiago, Chile, with excursions to Valparaíso and, if summer, Viña del Mar; the Chilean Lake Country, ideally combined with the aforementioned Argentine lakes, and again frequently suggested as an expendable "extra" when it should be a basic; La Paz, Bolivia—left out of routings more often than not when it's the center of one of the greatest tourism regions of the continent (the altitude need be avoided only by persons with heart disease); Lima, Peru; Cuzco and Machu Picchu, Peru—these, too, are tacked on as occasional extras, when a trip to Peru which skips them is as absurd as a visit to Argentina which omits Buenos Aires; Quito, Ecuador, and an excursion to at least one major Indian fair, such as Otavalo— far more meaningful than the granite monument marking the equator; Cartagena, Colombia—for a taste of Caribbean South America; Panama City, Panama, and the Canal. These are, I repeat, the *basics,* and the basics only. I offer them with the full realization that there will not be time for all on many itineraries— and time for many more on others. They are listed, too, with the knowledge that every traveler has tastes and interests of his own; what I find interesting may be a bore to you—and vice versa!

A few package tours: *Package tours* being offered run a wide gamut; a few examples: a two-week tour of Chile, Colombia, and Ecuador for about $700, inclusive, to and from Miami; another two-weeker to Peru, Chile, Argentina, Uruguay, and Brazil for about $900 from Los Angeles; a three-week tour of five countries including Argentina, for about $1000 from and to Miami; a twenty-three-day around-the-continent tour, covering seven coun-

tries including Brazil and Uruguay for a little over $1200 from
New York; an eighteen-day Ski Tour from Miami to Portillo,
Chile, and return, for about $700. There is an iterminable variety;
travel agents and airlines are acquainted with the lot.

Daily expenses: How about day-to-day expenses (exclusive of
transportation) if one is traveling independently or on a prearranged individual itinerary? They vary according to one's living
style. For as little as $10 a day, one can eat three meals, sleep in a
modest but decent hotel, and sight-see on public transport—and
via shoe leather (there's no better way, actually). For about $20–
$30 a day, one can get along very comfortably in South America—
stay in top hotels, eat fashionably, and have enough left over for
guided sight-seeing and some shopping. And for de luxe travel—
really shooting the works—the budget would run $40 per day and
up.

Any suggestions on a really inexpensive way of getting about the
whole continent? I should say I have; read on.

The world's greatest international travel bargain: There is no
doubt about it: the biggest value in travel abroad today is the
'Round South America air ticket: $599 jet-economy, and even
less—$538—via piston aircraft. This figure, based on a New
York–Buenos Aires routing, takes the passenger some twelve
thousand miles, is valid for a *full year,* and allows for stopovers
in *every* South American country, plus *every* Central American
republic, Mexico, a number of West Indian points, and several
cities within the United States, en route. I'll list the stopovers
later on, but first let me make a few comparisons to prove what a
fantastic deal this round-the-continent ticket is.

Take Moscow: it's 4650 miles from New York, in contrast to
Buenos Aires, which is 5297 miles from New York. Still, the
New York–Moscow round-trip jet-economy fare is $799—$200
more than the Buenos Aires rate. Take Athens, considerably closer
to New York than Buenos Aires: round-trip jet-economy New
York–Athens, $756. Take Rome, even nearer to the States than
Athens: round-trip jet-economy fare New York–Rome, $620.30.
In other words, *one can fly to every major country in the Western*

*Hemisphere save Canada—and many minor ones, too—for less
than the cost of a swing around Western Europe.*

What is included? Here's the breakdown: New York, Washington, Miami; San Juan, Puerto Rico (*or* Montego Bay and Kingston
in Jamaica; plus Port-au-Prince, Haiti, and Ciudad Trujillo,
Dominican Republic—all four); Caracas, Venezuela; Port of
Spain, Trinidad; Georgetown, British Guiana; Paramaribo,
Surinam; Cayenne, French Guiana; Belém, Brasília, Rio de
Janeiro, São Paulo, Pôrto Alegre—all in Brazil (*or,* in place of
Pôrto Alegre, Iguassú Falls and Asunción, Paraguay); Montevideo,
Uruguay; Buenos Aires, Argentina; Santiago and Antofagasta,
Chile; La Paz, Bolivia; Lima, Peru; Guayaquil and Quito, Ecuador;
Cali, Bogotá, Medellín, and Barranquilla, Colombia; Panama City,
Panama; San José, Costa Rica; Managua, Nicaragua; Tegucigalpa,
Honduras; San Salvador, El Salvador; Guatemala City, Guatemala;
Mexico City, Mexico; Houston, Texas; New Orleans, Louisiana;
Birmingham, Alabama; Atlanta, Georgia; New York. *Wow!*

Now, it would require a hardy soul to take in all of these places
on a single trip—even allowing himself the full year for which the
ticket is valid. And I am not recommending that one do so. But
this ticket is so unusual in air travel, and so relatively little-known,
that its full potential seems well worth enumerating.

Other air fares: For the traveler on a business mission to a single
South American destination, or the holidaymaker who would like
to concentrate his trip on a specific region of the continent, regular
fares might be more applicable. One, for example, is New York–
Lima, with stopovers allowed in Ecuador and Panama as well as
in Central America and Mexico, jet-economy, $460. Another, of
interest to skiers, would be from Miami to Santiago, Chile (near
the Portillo ski resort), and return, $475 jet-economy. On the east
coast, where Rio de Janeiro, Brasília, São Paulo, and other Brazilian cities might be one's major goals, the round-the-continent
ticket remains the best buy, although travelers who want to visit
only Caribbean points, in Colombia, Trinidad, and Venezuela, for
example, would do better with a ticket routing them only to that
area.

First-class air fares are, naturally, considerably more costly than
the bargain-rate economy tickets, but there is, of course, more leg
room, more thickly upholstered seats, more elaborate meals
(served with wine and liqueurs), and complimentary cocktails. The
first-class fare, 'Round South America, is $1143 jet, with a one-
year validity to the ticket; $950 jet for a ticket valid only forty-five
days, and $904 for piston (nonjet) service.

Two A-O.K. airlines: Panagra and Varig: A pair of airlines, both
pioneers in Latin American aviation, are eminently worth knowing
about when making plans for a trip to the southern continent. Both
are operated with the creative imagination, technical skill, and concern for the passenger which set them apart in the South American
aviation picture, and both deal *exclusively* in inter-American transportation; knowing this hemisphere well is their business. One line
is United States founded and operated, and typifies far-sighted
American aviation at its very best; the other is Brazilian, and manifests the exciting futuristic spirit of that immense country.

Panagra's relatively young life deserves recounting. In 1928 its
fleet consisted of a minuscule single-engine Fairchild monoplane
(passenger capacity: four). Today it makes more jet flights than
any other airline operating in South America.

The 8878-mile Panagra network of today is a far cry from the
line's first flight thirty-four years ago, from Lima to Talara, Peru,
which marked the beginning of scheduled commercial air transportation along the west coast of South America. Panagra lost
no time in expanding; it went south from Lima to the seaport of
Mollendo, north to Guayaquil in Ecuador (linking Peru and
Ecuador with a scheduled air service for the first time); then to
other cities, as far south as Chile and as far north as Panama. The
cargo in those days was mostly mail, transported Pony Express
style; tiny landplanes were used for the overland routes, and
amphibians for the overwater hops.

Panagra's next historic feat involved less than eight hundred
miles of flying. But the points connected were Santiago and Buenos
Aires, separated by some of the most rugged terrain on the globe,
the high peaks of the Andes. There was nothing, before Panagra

changed things, but a railroad perched on the sides of the jagged mountains; crossing them was a two-day operation—and possible only in good weather.

Panagra's trimotor plane departed from Buenos Aires, and crossed the Cordillera through the Upsallata Pass at the then un-heard-of altitude of eighteen thousand feet, and landed in Santiago eight and a half hours later; the first commercial flight across the Andes was history. The trip by air from New York to Buenos Aires could then be completed in eleven days—less than half the time it took by ship. It was down to a week by 1930, by which time another historic flight had been made, in two parts by two pilots, one of them Lloyd R. "Dinty" Moore, who flew what was then considered an impossible dawn-to-dusk hop between Peru and Panama in order to deliver mail cargo on schedule to the other pilot, Charles A. Lindbergh, who took it north from Panama to the States. Their joint effort proved that scheduled air service between the Americas was an accomplished fact, and Panagra went on weekly scheduled service.

By 1946 the elapsed time between Panama and Buenos Aires was down to less than twenty-four hours, and by May 1960 Panagra had introduced DC-8 jets to cut travel time between New York and the Argentine capital to less than twelve hours. The line's handsome green-and-yellow Douglas DC-8s are the only jets serving the continent with berths. They accommodate forty first-class and seventy tourist-class passengers in attractive cabins which include a Fiesta Lounge and a snack bar. Jet routes serve cities in Panama, Colombia, Ecuador, Peru, Bolivia, Chile, and Argentina. Still other aircraft—four-engine DC-7s and DC-6Bs—call at such cities as Cali, Quito, Talara, La Paz, and Antofagasta.

Panagra's record—technical, safety, and otherwise—is one of of the most enviable in international aviation. And it's my con-viction that the service provided by its multinational, bilingual staff of green-uniformed stewardesses—from all of the countries on its routes—is one of the secrets of its success. Together, that is, with the excellent meals it offers, and the extras it provides—Tourist Corners in its offices in every city on its route, where free information is provided to travelers on all manner of topics touristic; public-relations representatives in the leading cities on its route, to assist journalists and others with special missions in South America; a South American Tourist Information Center at its New York headquarters in the Chrysler Building; and a Ski Desk (at the same address) which provides up-to-the-minute reports on snow conditions at the Chilean ski resorts during the American summer months. Slogans can often be corny and meaningless, but Panagra's—"The World's Friendliest Airline"—is no exaggeration. It extends even to U.S.-Latin American relations, through a travel-fellowship program, by means of which well over three hundred South American university students have been awarded Panagra grants for study in the United States, in co-operation with the Institute of International Education.

Varig had its beginnings—humble ones too—two years before Panagra's. It was born in 1927, with its fleet a solitary Dornier Wal flying boat which operated over 175 miles of small coastal towns in southern Brazil. Since then it has grown to become the fifth largest airline in the world, in terms of route miles, operating a 102,000-mile route, with its headquarters in Pôrto Alegre, the bustling capital of the state of Rio Grande do Sul, and with a staff of more than eleven thousand.

In 1959 Varig was the first Brazilian company to go jet, when it inaugurated Caravelle service between New York and São Paulo. The following year it pioneered again, with the first Brazilian jet service (Boeing 707 Intercontinentals) between New York and Brasília, the new capital.

Varig's operation has been progressive in other respects. It is unique among the world's airlines in that 85 per cent of its stock is employee-owned. Even its president, Ruben M. Berta, is a kind of Horatio Alger; as a young man he was one of the founders and in Alger fashion came right along to the top, guiding the airline's growth, which closely followed that of Brazil's in the economic field.

The early flying boats were gradually exchanged for land planes; new cities were added to the routes as airports were constructed.

Varig was the first Brazilian carrier of airmail; it not only delivered the first such mail, but was commissioned by the Brazilian government to print and sell the country's first airmail stamps.

The line became an international operation in 1942 with a route to Montevideo, Uruguay, then expanded its domestic service, so that it now flies to some sixty points in northern, central, and southern Brazil, including the interior states of Paraná and Santa Catarina. By 1955 it was flying from New York to Rio, via Santo Domingo and Belém. In 1961 it acquired Real, another Brazilian line, and incorporated the extensive Real routes and services within its own. Its jet service now extends all the way from New York, Los Angeles, and Miami to Buenos Aires, which it reaches on one-stop jet flights. It flies as well, with piston craft, to Rio via Santo Domingo, Trinidad, and Belém, in northern Brazil, it connects Brazil with the Orient by means of a Rio–Tokyo service, and it has a jet route, too, between Los Angeles and Rio via Mexico City, Bogotá and Lima.

Even before Varig entered the international field, its flights were known for the excellence of their on-board service. On the new intercontinental jets this reputation is even more enhanced, by such first-class features as a rolling wine cart with a wide selection of vintage wines and champagne; sumptuous full-course dinners followed by liqueurs, extra-large uniformed cabin crews, under the supervision of a nonuniformed Varig-created Executive Hostess, who take extra-special care of passenger requests and see to it that the famous Varig meals—served on gold-trimmed white china—are flawlessly presented. Elegance in recent years has become the most overused word in the English language. But it describes a Varig flight perfectly. There is no more pleasurable means of transporting oneself to—and through—South America, all the way to Buenos Aires. And it is worth knowing, too, that Varig offices everywhere on its route serve also as information depots for visitors; included among these is, of course, the U.S. headquarters of the line, at 634 Fifth Avenue, in Rockefeller Center.

Other airlines serving the United States and South America include APA (Panamanian), Miami–west coast; Argentine Airlines

(Aerolineas Argentinas), New York–east coast; Avensa (Venezuelan), Miami–Caracas; Avianca (Colombia), New York–Jamaica–west coast; BOAC (British), New York–west coast; Braniff (U.S.), New York, Dallas, and Houston to east- and west-coast points; CEA (Ecuadorian), Miami–west coast; LAN–Chile, Miami–west coast; Viasa (Venezuelan), U.S.–Venezuela, Colombia, Peru; Pan American (U.S.), east coast. *From Canada:* Canadian Pacific, Montreal and Vancouver–west coast.

Airlines operating within South America include Argentine Airlines (Aerolineas Argentinas), with excellent, highly recommended domestic services; Avensa (Venezuelan); Avianca (Colombian); Causa, a Uruguayan line which operates quick, hour-long flying-boat "shuttles" between the downtown harbors of Montevideo and Buenos Aires; CEA (Ecuadorian); Cruzeiro do Sul (Brazilian); Faucett, a Peruvian line which operates highly recommended services throughout Peru; LAB—flights throughout Bolivia; LAN–Chile; LAV (Venezuelan); Panair do Brasil—often unpleasant food and service; Pluna (Uruguayan); RAS (Colombian); Varig—no better domestic services in Brazil; VASP—Brazilian, and good.

European-South American air services are operated by a number of noted international lines, which fly between many European cities—often via Dakar, the Senegalese capital, located at that part of Africa which is the closest to the Americas, or Monrovia, Liberia—and Rio de Janeiro, Recife, Montevideo, Buenos Aires, and Santiago. The lines include Air France, Alitalia, Argentine Airlines, BOAC, KLM Royal Dutch Airlines, Scandinavian Airlines System, and Swissair. It is possible, utilizing these services, to include Europe on a triangular South American trip, flying from the United States to South America, from that continent to Europe, and from Europe back to the United States.

By sea to South America: There is no more luxurious cruise service in the world than that linking U.S. ports with those in South America. Four major passenger lines ply between the two continents, three linking the States with east-coast ports of the southern continent, a fourth concentrating on the South American west coast. Arrangements may be made with all to utilize their services for part of a journey, and those of an airline for the remainder, allowing more time ashore, and convenient transportation to points within the interior. Here's the line-up:

Grace Line, a division of W. R. Grace and Company, an American firm which over the years has developed extensive commercial interests of a varied nature in South America, and which knows the continent intimately, operates a variety of passenger services to the Caribbean, Panama, and the west coast of South America, as far south as Chile. Its most popular offerings are weekly *thirteen-day luxury cruises,* on the new all-first-class fully air-conditioned luxury liners *Santa Paula* and *Santa Rosa,* on which all rooms have private bath, and facilities include large outdoor swimming pools, night clubs, handsome public rooms, open-deck recreation areas, and excellent food. Sailing from New York, ports of call include Curaçao, N.W.I.; La Guaira, the port of Caracas, Venezuela; Aruba, N.W.I., Kingston, Jamaica; Port-au-Prince, Haiti; Fort Lauderdale, Florida. From $395. Grace's *Casual Cruises* last seventeen to nineteen days, depart weekly from New York on air-conditioned cargo-passenger *Santas.* There are accommodations for fifty-two passengers, all staterooms are outside and with bath, and there are swimming pools. Shipboard life is considerably more informal and less dressy than on the luxury sailings. Ports of call include Puerto Cabello and La Guaira (Venezuela), Barranquilla and Cartagena (Colombia). From $445. *West Coast Cruises* depart weekly from New York, pass through the Panama Canal to ports in Colombia, Ecuador, Peru, and, fortnightly, sail as far south as Chile. Available in connection with these trips are inclusive *Jewel Box Casual Cruise-Tours,* with twenty-six- to thirty-one-day itineraries covering coastal cities and interior points—reached by plane as well. Ships are fifty-two-passenger, air-conditioned *Santas,* similar to those used in the Casual Cruises. From $785. Unusual, too, are *'Round South America Cruises,* with Grace ships covering the west coast, connections made by Panagra to the east coast, and passage on ships of other lines completing the journey. The rate is a real bargain:

about the same as the round-trip rate to but one coast. Additionally, Grace offers *freighter trips* in twelve-passenger *Santas* departing from New York weekly for the Panama Canal and the west coast of South America, and also from Western U.S. ports to South and Central American points.

Argentine State Line (Flota Mercante del Estado República Argentina) operates its fleet of three *Río* liners—the *Río de la Plata, Río Jachal,* and *Río Tunuyan*—between New York and Buenos Aires, with calls at Rio de Janeiro, Santos, and Montevideo on the southbound journeys, and at Santos, Rio, Trinidad, and La Guaira, Venezuela, northbound. The ships are all handsomely decorated, fully air-conditioned, with a limit of 116 passengers— all first class. Cabins are outside, and with either private or semi-private bath, and the public rooms—lounges, bars, libraries, dining rooms, children's playrooms—are spacious and pleasant. There are, of course, swimming pools and sports decks. The cuisine combines the very best of Argentina, Europe, and the United States, and the *ambiance* aboard is delightfully Latin. Minimum all-year-round fares are $550 one way to Rio, $990 round trip to Rio; $600 one way to Buenos Aires or Montevideo, $1080 round trip Buenos Aires or Montevideo. Sailing time, New York–Buenos Aires (and vice versa), is seventeen days.

Delta Line has as its passenger fleet the sleek, modern luxury-liners *Del Norte, Del Sud,* and *Del Mar,* sailing from New Orleans and Houston, and calling at Saint Thomas, V.I., Rio de Janeiro, Santos, and Buenos Aires southbound, and Santos, Rio, Curaçao, N.W.I., and New Orleans northbound. The time aboard, from New Orleans (with two days in port at Houston) to Buenos Aires, is twenty-two days. All three *Dels* are fully air-conditioned, courteously-staffed post-World War II ships, with a limit of 120 passengers each—all first class. They all feature opulenty-decorated cabins and public rooms, spacious swimming pools and sports decks, and the excellent food one would expect from vessels originating in New Orleans. Minimum fares: New Orleans–Rio, $500; New Orleans–Buenos Aires, $600; round trip New Orleans–

Buenos Aires–New Orleans, $1080; 10 per cent discount on all fares during months of April and May.

Moore-McCormack Line's two handsome ships, the *Argentina* and the *Brasil,* are the newest passenger liners in the American merchant marine—each fully air-conditioned, with two swimming pools, sports decks, theater, a myriad of public rooms (including a separate section for youngsters). All staterooms are outside, with private bath.

On regular sailings the ships are at sea fifteen days, between New York and Buenos Aires, with ports of call including Barbados, Rio de Janeiro, and Santos, southbound, and Santos, Rio, Salvador, and Trinidad, northbound. Minimum fares to Rio, one way $575; round trip thrift season (March 1 to December 31) $1035; round trip high season, $1050; Buenos Aires—one way $675; round trip thrift season $1215; high season $1350. Moore-McCormack also operates special cruises on the *Brasil* and *Argentina,* some of which follow the routes of the regular sailings, others concentrating on Caribbean and Brazilian ports. Rates begin at $890 (twenty-four days), $1110 (thirty-one days), and one-way passages are also available. In addition the line operates Cargo Liner cruises on its freighters, sailing from U.S. East and West Coast ports.

Other cruises are conducted—usually during late autumn, winter and early spring—by lines which concentrate on other areas of the world during summer. Among these are: American Export, Canadian Pacific, Cunard, Greek, Holland-America, Home, Norwegian-America, and Swedish American. For a complete listing, consult American Express' *Guide to All Cruises,* published every autumn and obtainable free from American Express, 65 Broadway, New York. See also the cruise roundups published periodically in *Travel* magazine and the travel sections of such newspapers as the New York *Herald Tribune,* New York *Times,* and *Christian Science Monitor.*

Shipboard life—at least for the passengers—is the laziest form of existence known to man, and thoroughly delightful. Stewards and stewardesses are at one's beck and call, the purser or his assistants are great question-answerers and workers of miracles; deck chairs (to be reserved with the deck steward and usually free on South America sailings) are fine for morning naps and afternoon snoozes; the bars, swimming pools, sports decks, public rooms, and restaurants are invariably appealing, and clothes are rarely the problem that first-time passengers often consider them to be. During the day they are casual. For dinner, first-class and one-class passengers dress, except on the first and last nights out and on Sundays. Most times there are organized shore organizations at ports of call; these are charged for additionally, but are completely optional; many passengers prefer to team up on their own, hiring a car or taxi, or simply meandering about on foot. The choice is one's own. If you're not planning to return home on board ship, ship your excess baggage home from the port at which you land, or pack within the forty-four- or sixty-six-pound air limit, so that there is no excess baggage when you switch to an airplane. For additional packing information, see pages 32–34; for tips on shipboard tipping, see pages 41–42.

Freighter travel is something else again: completely informal— no dressing for dinner, considerably less luxurious quarters, meals in the wardroom with the ship's officers, and often, very flexible schedules: sailing dates may be delayed, ports of call canceled and others substituted. There are usually small passenger lists, a dozen or less, and bookings are generally made months in advance. Among the many lines which operate passenger-carrying freight services to South America (in addition to those already mentioned) are the *Booth Steamship Company,* whose ships sail from New York to Belém, at the mouth of the Amazon, in Brazil, thence up the Amazon to the interior ports of Manaus, Brazil, and Iquitos, Peru, and vice versa, and the *Alcoa Line,* which operates special cruises from Trinidad into the interior of Surinam, as well as other services from U.S. ports, many quite luxurious. (See page 159.) The list of freighter lines is a long one. Travel agents in possession of up-to-date editions of two directories—the *Official Steamship Guide* (U.S.-published) and the *ABC Shipping Guide* (published in England)—are well equipped to answer inquiries in this regard.

Driving in and through South America: Someday—and there is no one in a position to hazard an exact date—the Pan American Highway system will extend from Alaska to southern South America. Meanwhile, the traveler who attempts to drive from one continent to the other is a rarity. The highway is still far from completed, and many sections of it are not yet paved. Still, there have been hardy souls who have made the trip, occasionally using trains and ships in addition to roads. The best highway stretches are in Venezuela, Chile, Argentina, Uruguay, Peru, Ecuador, and Colombia. But without a Land Rover or Jeep, a strong constitution, and unlimited time, other means of transport are recommended. Until the governments of the Americas—who are the builders of the highway, in conjunction with the Organization of American States—finish their task, motorists with a yen to motor are generally better off renting cars in South America, for excursions from the major centers. To drive on the southern continent one should have an *Inter-American Driving Permit,* which is honored in every country save Uruguay, which accepts the *International Driver's License;* both are obtainable (at two dollars each) through automobile clubs in the United States. *Further information:* AAA International Travel Department, 250 Park Avenue, New York.

E A S T E R N
South America

ARGENTINA

BRAZIL

THE GUIANAS
British Guiana
French Guiana
Surinam

PARAGUAY

URUGUAY

VENEZUELA

Caracas
VENEZUELA
Georgetown
Paramaribo
BR. GUIANA
SURINAM
FR. GUIANA
Cayenne
Atlantic Ocean

BRAZIL
Brasilia

PARAGUAY
Asunción

ARGENTINA

URUGUAY
Buenos Aires
Montevideo

EASTERN SOUTH AMERICA

*"El Dorado beckoned not only to the Spaniards and the Portu-
guese, but also to the British, the French, the Dutch, and more recently to the people of Germany, Italy and the United States.
All . . . have been at work, each one guided by its own peculiar
objectives, attitudes and technical abilities."*
—PRESTON E. JAMES: *Latin America*

What distinguishes eastern South America from the western
region of the continent is not so much language (there are Spanish-speaking countries as well as Portuguese-speaking Brazil, and
both tongues are of the Romance family) or nearness to Europe
(for Europeans appeared on both coasts within decades of each
other). Terrain is the big differentiating factor. The east's elevated portions pale in contrast to the towering peaks and high
plateaus of the western Andes. And it is the culture that has
resulted from the lofty environment of the Andes that, to a
great extent, accounts for the differences between the two areas.

That is why, perhaps, the first-time traveler to South America
tends to negate what he is about to experience in the east. What he
has heard of in this region are the great cities which have evolved,
unhampered by the physical elements which have helped impede
progress in the west. Are they not, he wonders, quite similar to our
own? Are they worth a look? The questions are loaded, and therefore difficult to answer. But to begin with: they *are* different. And
to continue: they are but a tiny part of eastern South America.
Caracas, Rio, Buenos Aires, Montevideo, São Paulo, Brasília—
fascinating, all of them; great, a few of them; easy to spend entire
holidays in, some of them. But to know eastern South America,
one must go beyond.

There are, for example, the three, still offbeat Guianas, the vastness of Amazon Brazil, the great bulk of Venezuela, rarely visited
except for its capital, chief port, and oil center, where the vestiges

of the Colonial era have all but disappeared, unlike the lesser cities where they still remain. There is coastal Brazil north of Rio and Santos; Recife, at once new and old, rich and poverty-stricken; Salvador, an inexplicably brilliant mélange of Portugal and Africa; and the surprisingly progressive towns of the Brazilian south and interior—Pôrto Alegre, Belo Horizonte, Curitiba, to mention but three.

There is that freak of nature hugging the borders of Brazil, Paraguay, and Argentina—the falls of Iguassú. There are the interior cities of Argentina, wonderfully like what they were when the Spanish colonists came down from the mountains of Peru to establish them as Little Spains—Córdoba and Salta among them. There is Argentine Patagonia, whose palatial lake resorts are unsurpassed on any continent. And there are the two "guay" countries, as unlike as the day and the night: poor, police-state Paraguay, and enlightened, welfare-state Uruguay.

The visitor in eastern South America need never worry about either boredom or a dearth of variety. The great cities are each in themselves distinctive. And beyond—in the Pampa of Argentina, the *sertões* of Brazil, the Chaco of Paraguay, the jungles of the the Guianas, the mountains of Venezuela, the plains of Uruguay—there are worlds he very possibly did not know existed.

ARGENTINA

(*República Argentina*)

Entry requirements: *Easy as pie—just a valid passport; no visa or tourist card.* **Best times for a visit:** *The purpose of one's trip is the determining factor. Skiers and winter-sports enthusiasts might prefer the Argentine winter, which is the U.S. summer. Sun-worshipers' tastes might make the warm-weather months—the U.S. winter—preferable. In Buenos Aires, winters are mild—no snow and virtually no frost—but summers can be as hot as those of the United States. Buenos Aires averages: winter 54°, summer 77°, autumn and spring, 63°. The far northern tropics are hot and humid, the deep, deep south is dry and windy.* **Currency:** *The peso (designated by the $ sign), of which there are about eighty-three to the dollar, subject, of course, to fluctuation.* **Film availability:** *Both color and black-and-white film can be hard to find; one is wise to have an adequate supply upon entering the country.* **Language:** *Spanish, but this being the third largest Spanish-speaking country of the world, the Argentines have evolved an accent of their own, modifying the language as Americans have English, and Brazilians,*

*Portuguese. There is a good deal of English spoken in the
major cities and resorts; quite a bit of Italian, some French
and German.* **Domestic transport:** *The most comprehensive
rail system on the continent; a fine government airline (Aerolineas Argentinas) with excellent domestic services throughout the country, some private airlines, as well; steamer
services on rivers leading to Uruguay and Paraguay, and a
fair road network.* **Tipping:** *Hotels and restaurants add a
rather frightening service charge—24 per cent—to bills;
additional tips from millionaires are always welcome. For
other services: 10 per cent.* **Business hours:** *Major Buenos
Aires stores are open from 9* A.M. *to 7* P.M.; *smaller ones
take two- or three-hour lunch breaks.* **Further information:**
*Panagra, Chrysler Building, New York, and Buenos Aires,
Argentina. Varig Airlines, 634 Fifth Avenue, New York,
and Buenos Aires, Argentina. Dirección Nacional de Turismo, Buenos Aires, Argentina. Argentine Tourism Agency,
Empire State Building, New York; Argentine Embassy, Washington, D.C.*

INTRODUCING ARGENTINA

Ask Mr. John Doe of Main Street what comes to mind in connection with Argentina, and he'll no doubt answer, "Buenos Aires"
(which will undoubtedly be pronounced incorrectly) and "Perón."
If he has remembered a little geography and is allowed to ponder
a minute, he might add "Patagonia," possibly "beef," and con-
ceivably "Gaucho." Fine, as far as it goes. But that will be about
it, and pitifully little it is, when one considers that this is the
second largest country of the continent, the fourth largest of the
Americas, and the eighth largest of the universe, with a length
about as extensive as the width of the United States, a capital
which is one of the half-dozen truly great cities of the world, a
people with verve and vitality to whom the stereotype of *mañana*

is as foreign as it would be in, say, the Netherlands, and a history where the pattern of development has in some ways paralleled that of the United States.

Argentina, for circumstantially valid—if deplorable—reasons, has had precious few truly democratic periods in its history, and despite its name—which derives from the Latin (*argentum*) for silver—it is not a land of rich natural resources. It is these lacks which have created great difficulties, existing to this day. But there have been plus factors on which the Argentines have managed to build a remarkable country, with a relatively high standard of living (including a very high literacy rate), along with which has evolved a rich and distinctive culture, largely of European origin to be sure, but peculiarly Argentine, as that of the United States is American.

The irony is that Argentina almost wasn't. It didn't grow like Topsy after the first conquistador plunged the flag of Spain into the earth, with an official muralist on the spot, recording the scene for posterity—as seems so often to have been the case in the New World. Argentina's establishment required several attempts. The last, which proved successful, was the work of colonists already resident in the then leading city of southern South America—Asunción—now, paradoxically, the ramshackle capital of Paraguay, one of the most decrepit, backward countries on the face of the globe.

A backward glance: The *turista* for whom the Americas are named—Amerigo Vespucci—was probably the first European to see Argentina, in 1502. More sailor than settler, he moved right along and the Indians saw no more white men until 1516 when Juan Diaz de Solís sailed up the Río de la Plata, probably by accident, while looking for a southwest passage to the Orient. He, too, whipped on, as did Ferdinand Magellan, on his 1520 voyage, which included a quick excursion up the Plata estuary. Sebastian Cabot and Diego García both journeyed up the Paraná and Paraguay rivers in 1527. They attempted the first Argentine settlement, but the Indians could see no reason to welcome them and proceeded, rather promptly and with great efficiency, to destroy their little village. The founders escaped and sailed back to Spain, and it is possible that it was Cabot who named Argentina, so impressed was he reputed to have been with the silver ornaments of his unhospitable Indian hosts.

"Never say die" had become the password, and Pedro de Mendoza tried again in 1536, with the site of his village the present Buenos Aires. His fate was not unlike Cabot's, and a colonizing lull ensued, lasting four and a half decades.

It was not until 1580 that another attempt was made, with Juan de Garay the expedition director. He and his followers came from Asunción, which had been thriving since its establishment in 1537 as the first permanent settlement in southern South America. De Garay's colony had rough going but it stayed in business—just barely. Not until 1592, though, when an exceptionally able conquistador administrator, Hernando Arias de Saavedra, took over, did it get on its feet.

Spaniards, coming from the Andean regions of Peru and Bolivia, made settlements during this period in what is now western Argentina, and because of their situation they prospered, supplying the mountain mining towns of the region. But Buenos Aires stagnated—or nearly stagnated—for almost three centuries. The Argentine territory had been put under the control of the viceroyalty of Lima by the Spanish, with the wealth of Peru shipped to the motherland via Panama, rather than Buenos Aires, whose residents busied themselves competing against, and then fighting, the Portuguese, who a good bit of the time managed to keep control of the Banda Oriental, the extreme eastern region of the country which is now Uruguay.

In 1776 (and the date was *not* July 4) the Spanish broke down and gave Buenos Aires some recognition: it was finally designated a free port and the capital of a viceroyalty which extended as far north as southern Bolivia. Who knows but that this might have been enough to satisfy the locals on the scene, had not the ubiquitous British attacked? That they did in 1806, chasing the Spanish viceroy home in the process, but at the same time precipitating Argentine independence.

The creoles, or Argentine-born colonists, came to realize their collective strength when they united to evict the British in 1807, and on May 25, 1810 (May 25 is the Argentine National Day), an antiroyalist junta took over. Formal independence of the "United Provinces of La Plata" was proclaimed at Tucumán (where the decisive battle with the Spanish had been won) six years later, and among the leading figures of the new state was José de San Martín, of whom much more was to be heard in ensuing years.

The young republic: But the new United Provinces had birth pangs which were to continue even beyond the toddlers' stage. Civil war followed civil war, *caudillo* followed *caudillo,* unrest followed unrest, and the pattern which emerged was one of centralists—those favoring a strong unitary government in Buenos Aires—*vs.* federalists, who made Dixie's states-righters pale in contrast, and whose strength lay in the forces of Gauchos and their aristocratic employers. The Gauchos' idol, Juan Manuel de Rosas, became dictator in 1829, and a reign of terror—one of the most horrible in South American history—continued for the next seventeen years. By the time Rosas was routed, in 1852, federalism had triumphed, to the extent that the unitarists of Buenos Aires had that city actually secede from the republic, after the capital was moved to Paraná. Its troops, not long after, fought the federalists, and won.

Buenos Aires again became the seat of the government, and Bartolomé Mitre (one of the noted writers who did his best work in exile during the Rosas regime) was elected the first president, under a newly promulgated constitution. Mitre's administration saw Argentina, Brazil, and Uruguay team up in the Triple Alliance War to defeat the Paraguayan tyrant, López. Argentina gained little as a result of being a co-victor in this war, but it did begin, under Mitre, to institute governmental reforms, build schools, and expand public works.

In 1880 Buenos Aires suffered a rebuff: it was no longer to be the capital of its province; this honor went to nearby, smaller La Plata, but the larger city remained the seat of the federal government, and its economy—and commercial importance—began to grow by leaps and bounds, thanks to the development of the great Pampa, or plain, which it bordered. The Argentines had found their place in the world; by planting the Pampa with alfalfa and importing fine strains of cattle from Europe, they became one of the great meat-producing countries of the world.

Another boon to their growth was the opening up of the south, where settlement had been sparse as long as hostile Indians were extant.

Good-by, Indians, hello immigrants: These were killed off quite as ruthlessly as were their brothers in the United States, and concurrent with their demise the last decades of the nineteenth century saw many industrious immigrants from Europe—particularly Italy, Spain, and other countries including Britain—swell Argentina's population and help it along to modernity. By 1900 some six million had crossed the South Atlantic to a new homeland.

The British were probably the most extraordinary. They imported the first shorthorn cattle, sailed the first steamship to dock in Buenos Aires, imported polo (now a leading Argentine game) and a host of other sports including soccer and golf, were responsible for the beginnings of the meat-packing industry, made the initial, and often major, investments in early banks, insurance companies, factories, telephone and radio systems, and capitalized and constructed the excellent railroad system. Most British-founded enterprises are now Argentine owned and controlled (the railroads are nationalized), but the Anglo-Argentine community remains a significant—and peculiar—segment of the country's life, with the Buenos Aires suburbs its hub. Anglo-Argentines have retained an incredible identity with Britain over the years—unlike any other immigrant group in the Americas, except for a similar but much smaller community in Chile.

Anglo-Argentines born today will be completely bilingual in English and Spanish, will no doubt worship at an Anglican church, be members of exclusively Anglo-Argentine clubs and cricket teams, marry Anglo-Argentine spouses, read the English-language daily published by Anglo-Argentines in Buenos Aires, and be as knowledgeable about things British—including the day-by-day comings and goings of the royal family—as the resident of London or Leeds. They are at the same time as Argentine in their loyalties as the most Spanish of their compatriots.

Still, Argentina, even with its hard-working new citizens, was not without problems. There were attempts to decrease the power of the great feudal landholders whose vast *estancias* would probably impress even Texans. But these did not meet with great success, nor did efforts to minimize the political role of the army, which inclined itself toward alliances—first with conservatives, later with labor—which often ended in *coups d'état*. One wishes that the British, with their strong parliamentary background, had concerned themselves more with politics than they did. But in Argentina, as in South Africa, they concentrated on business and the making of money, leaving politics to their compatriots. The result in South Africa was the domination of the government by the fanatic, nationalistic Afrikaners of Dutch descent. The result in Argentina was a preponderance of reactionary, oligarchical regimes, and only occasional liberal administrations which introduced voting reforms and social legislation.

Twentieth-century Argentina: Argentina remained neutral during World War I. Its last external war was over a border dispute with Chile in 1902, after which the Christ of the Andes statue was erected as a monument dedicated to future peace between the bordering countries. The Argentines entered World War II on the side of the Allies just before the war was over—in time to qualify them for charter United Nations membership.

It was during the World War II period, while the rest of the globe was otherwise preoccupied, that Argentina's internal affairs became chaotic. One man followed another into the President's Palace. In 1944 a military junta took over the government; one of its members was Colonel Juan D. Perón. He got himself elected president in 1946, and instead of returning Argentina to constitutional government—which so many Argentines had been led to expect—he set himself up as a fantastically corrupt and vulgar dictator, with the aid of the laboring masses, whom he hoodwinked into believing he was helping, and of his beauteous, ex-showgirl wife, Eva, who became a kind of co-dictator.

Argentina turned into a concentration-camp state, run by the vain, glory-seeking Peróns, with the connivance of the army and assorted hangers-on from such diverse fields as the clergy, the intelligentsia, and the politicians of the extreme right. (There had been a substantial pro-Nazi element in Buenos Aires prior to and during World War II, toward which Perón was sympathetic.)

The Perón madness continued until 1955, by which time the dictator had virtually ruined the economy of Argentina. When his wife died of cancer in 1952, Perón took up with a teen-age schoolgirl, and almost concurrently found a new enemy: the Catholic church. At this point the Argentine people began to resist. Even the military no longer remained loyal to their leader. The navy revolted first, abortively, but it had started the fireworks: tension mounted and riots broke out in the capital. They were followed by a combined army-navy-air-force uprising, and on September 19, 1955, Perón was forced to resign and flee on a Paraguayan gunboat to Asunción, and the temporary hospitality of dictator Alfredo Stroessner. He has, since then, lived in Venezuela (with the then dictator Pérez Jiménez), the Dominican Republic (with the late dictator Trujillo), and Spain (with the still thriving dictator Franco), and he has never given up plans to return, retaining a large following among workers and other cohorts who to this day long for his return, and who labor to support his cause.

The post-Perón period: Following Perón's exile, an army junta took over, under a serious-minded, honorable officer, General Pedro Eugenio Aramburu. He promised that he would hold elections as soon as practicable, and he kept his word. In 1958 Arturo Frondizi, a competent, level-headed conservative, was freely elected to the presidency. His administration has faced both economic and political crises, but it continues to weather the storm. Argentina has been making a gradual return to normalcy. Its press (which includes such excellent papers as *La Nación* and *La Prensa* and is among the best in the world) is again free. The economy—thanks to an austerity program particularly stringent on imports—

has progressed, and the standard of living has improved. Foreign investment has been resumed.

Still, the Peronistas—who supported Frondizi's election, but who have never been supported by Frondizi—make trouble.

The armed forces, too, are a knotty problem. They absorb a staggeringly heavy proportion of the budget, and more often than not consider themselves the sole judges of policy in matters economic, political, and international. The major opposition party—Radicals of the People—is considerably to the left of the president and frequently attacks his conservative economic policy as U.S.-dictated and "imperialist." But official government policy—not to mention individual Argentine-American relationships—is warmly pro-United States, and not without reason: in mid-1961 the United States (with the World Bank) granted Argentina nearly $205 million in loans for industrial development and agreed to send a trade mission to Argentina to help her expand her exports to the United States. Since 1946 Argentina has received $452 million in loans and nearly $2 million in grants from the United States and the Export-Import Bank. The United States has assisted in many other ways, as well, in recent years. If the Frondizi government, which has survived thirty *coups d'état* since it took office in 1958, does not remain in control, it will not be because the United States has neglected it.

YOUR VISIT TO ARGENTINA

Argentina on the map, especially compared with its giant neighbor, Brazil, appears deceptively compact. But it is hardly the suburban extension of its capital which all too many visitors take it for. The area is more than a million square miles, which is a third that of the continental United States, and five times that of France. Argentina's southern tip, at the Strait of Magellan, is a little over 2100 miles from its northern frontier with Bolivia. (Other neighbors: Chile, Paraguay, Uruguay.) At its widest bulges it extends east-west for almost a thousand miles. Its coast line totals 1600 miles.

Topographically, few countries top it: towering above the Andean chain which constitutes its long frontier with Chile is 23,081-foot Mount Aconcagua, the highest peak in the Americas. In the far north are the sun-baked forests of the Chaco, in the center are the quarter-million miles of the great plain known as the Pampa, which is the heart of the Argentine economy and population. And to the south, below the Colorado River, is Patagonia, parts of which are gloriously green, mountainous, and wooded (this is the famed Lake District), in contrast to the remainder which is eternally wind-swept, generally arid, and sparsely inhabited, containing a quarter of the country's area, but less than half a million people out of a total population exceeding twenty millions.

The undisputed core of the country—economically, culturally, and politically—is the capital. The cities of the Andean foothills were the earliest to thrive, but Buenos Aires overcame them as the Pampa became rich. With the Río de la Plata as its front door and the Pampa as its back yard, the town of "good airs," which languished as a neglected backwater settlement for much of its first three centuries, has become in less than a hundred years one of the glories of the globe. In no other South American country does the chief city play a more important role. Every facet of the republic's life revolves around it. The traveler to Argentina must know Buenos Aires, and ideally, will start his Argentine visit there.

But synthesis of the country though it is, Buenos Aires should not be one's sole Argentine destination. It is a difficult city to break away from, but the exit should be made—to great *estancias* and still-Colonial towns on the Pampa, to the lovely southern lakes, the proud and venerable Andean cities, the great falls of Iguassú on the Brazilian-Paraguayan-Argentine frontier, the delightful resorts of the Atlantic coast, and perhaps, to the tiny towns amid the immense sheep ranches of southern Patagonia, and the half-Argentine island of Tierra del Fuego.

Argentina is more diverse than many of its inspectors ever come to realize. It has, besides the contrasts which every country can justifiably claim, a distinctive bracing quality—an atmosphere which is simultaneously Iberian in its dignity, New World in its energy, peculiarly Argentine in its intriguing complexity. It takes a longer visit than most have time for to know Argentina well. But even a brief courtship is invariably satisfying. One *likes* Argentina at first glance, and this admiration more often than not turns to affection the longer one's involvement. There is no denying the ugly side of the Argentine personality; those remaining manifestations of its lopsided semifeudal social structure, which have made possible the reigns of a string of dictators, attracted foreign Nazis, nourished native-born Fascists, and made difficult the attainment of a genuinely democratic state, cannot be condoned. But, at the same time, the other side of the coin encourages one to believe that his affection is not displaced. Argentina produced José de San Martín, the most selfless of the South American independence leaders. Argentina, geographically remote from the great centers of world influence, built itself into a great state the hard way— by developing through agriculture and cattle, rather than quick-and-easy gold or silver.

Argentina knows the value of the printed word and the limitless potential of the human mind. It is a literate nation, where the school and university are commonplace rather than the exception to the rule, where the artist is respected, and where the press has distinguished itself way out of proportion to the quantity of the readership.

And Argentina has as a part of its collective personality those rare, seldom-found attributes, style and taste. It was indeed the Peróns' lack of these—their blatant, gaudy vulgarity—which probably contributed as much to their downfall as did the tyranny and madness of their dictatorship. While this is hardly the preferred criterion in such matters, it is, particularly in Argentina, of some importance.

It is easy today for the visitor to get about Argentina. Aerolineas Argentinas' planes make it possible to reach every region of the country effortlessly, comfortably, and economically. The trains are good, too, as are roads in some areas. Standards in hotels are high; one eats well—often superbly well—everywhere. And the Argentine is the ideal host—courteous, helpful, gracious, more often than not charming, and with a sense of humor. I hope you get to know him, and his exciting country.

Buenos Aires: Buenos Aires is a "walking city," and only some of the great ones are walking cities. Rio de Janeiro, for example, is geographically difficult in this respect; its principal regions are too diffused to be of a piece and other means of transport than the feet are needed for a full appreciation. Tokyo, until the visitor gets to know it intimately, is too confusing a city to walk about in comfortably. In Cairo one is too easily spotted as a foreign visitor by ambulatory salesmen to make walks pleasant. Cape Town, while physically beautiful, has the immoral stigma of apartheid all about. New York, though, is wonderful for walks—easy to get about, varied in its façade, so used to visitors that they easily blend in with the terrain. London is undeniably a walker's paradise, with no rhyme or reason to its layout; Paris, of course, fills the bill, too; Calcutta, Quito, Copenhagen, Rome, Boston, and São Paulo all qualify.

But no city is in any way more admirable for the stroller than Buenos Aires. It appears to have been designed by promenaders for promenaders. All the accoutrements are there, and in quantity: eye-filling bench-filled plazas, conveniently-placed sidewalk cafés —here called *confiterías*—where one may linger over a cup or glass long after its been drained; gloriously verdant parks, enticing displays in shop windows, wide boulevards, elegant and formal; smaller, animated streets on a lesser but nonetheless pleasing scale; the cool, quiet sanctuaries of exquisite old churches for respite, the sumptuous façades of *fin-de-siècle* mansions and palaces which contrast with the towers of newer, more functional skyscrapers, for aesthetic interest; the lobbies—and indeed the public facilities—of fine hotels for rendezvous and rest stops, the *Porteños* themselves—tastefully urbane, with an "I-know-where-I'm-going" gait in their step; and the general tone of the town—

brisk but never frenzied, stylish but never faddish, smiling but never foolishly grinning.

There are more beautifully situated cities—Rio and San Francisco, La Paz and Stockholm come to mind. There are cities with more oomph—New York and Hong Kong are examples. And there are cities where the efficiencies of the twentieth-century entrepreneur—The Businessman—are more evident, Chicago and Hamburg perhaps typifying these. But Buenos Aires still stands out in the crowd. All it requires is a little time, a part of which is best spent in aimless meandering.

This is not to say that there should not be a sense of order and planning in one's explorations. The travel agencies, City Service being a good example, offer a variety of urban and suburban tours which give one the feel not only of the central portion of the city but of its outlying districts and the countryside—urban, suburban, and rural. It might be as well not to dwell on Buenos Aires' size, at least if one is easily terrified of great cities, for B.A.—and there is no objection to calling it B.A.—though spacious, does not exude the impersonal, unfriendly air some metropolises do. Still, there are some 3,750,000 *Porteños* within the city itself, and the population of Greater Buenos Aires is close to six million. However one looks at it, this is the biggest city of the continent, and if one takes the Greater B.A. population figure, the second city of the Americas.

Much of Buenos Aires is modern, great portions having been built or rebuilt since the turn of the century, by which time the old city, dating back to 1580, had got too big for its britches. The general plan of the central area is a simple rectangular one, with masses of square blocks and the streets which border them supplementing the two principal thoroughfares. One is the Avenida de Mayo (pronounced *my-o*) with the venerable Plaza de Mayo at one of its extremities and the broad Plaza del Congreso at the other. The other is Avenida 9 de Julio (*nuavay-day-hulio,* phonetically, in case you've occasion to pronounce it). Reputedly the world's widest Main Street, it also serves as a rooftop for a vast underground garage. The main shopping areas are north of the Plaza de Mayo. Streets whose names are worth knowing include Calle Florida—narrow, and closed to vehicular traffic most of the day, for the convenience of shoppers and window shoppers; Calle Santa Fe, and Calle Corrientes—ablaze after dark with the blinking signs of cinemas, theaters, and night spots.

The Boca is a wharfside district with a piquant Italian flavor— dotted with restaurants and cafés, small shops, an open-air theater, gay streets whose houses are uninhibitedly painted in the primary shades of the color wheel, and a street population heavily maritime. The Avenida Costanera spans the river front beyond the wharves. It has been bedecked with gardens, open-air swimming pools, and a succession of glorified refreshment stands which dispense the spicy and delicious Argentine sausage and beefsteak specialties lumped under the all-embracing term *parrilladas*.

But that should be only a starter. What follows is a selective breakdown of Buenos Aires' principal attractions. In planning excursions it is well to remember that public transport is good: there are subways (a system of five lines, with the fare one peso); streetcars, with graduated fares beginning at fifty Argentine cents; buses, whose fares start at a peso, and increase, depending upon the distance traveled; micro-buses, with smaller seating capacities, faster service, and a slightly higher rate; trolley buses, beginning at one and a half pesos; taxis—which are almost impossible to find at rush hour or lunchtime, but which are cheap when obtainable; and "private limousines," which the doormen of hotels produce in lieu of taxis, and which are three times the price.

Sight-seeing requisites include Casa Rosada, the headquarters of the president—of pink-hued stone, with a richly furnished interior, and a lovely setting in the Plaza de Mayo; the Old Congress, on the Plaza de Mayo, built in 1863, now a national monument, and the base of a bank superimposed above it; the Cabildo, also on the Plaza de Mayo, originally built in 1710, is the birthplace of Argentine independence, and today a national museum with furniture, documents, and paintings which tell the story of the revolution; the cathedral, which completes the Plaza de Mayo complex, dates from 1618 and contains the tomb of San Martín, an ever-burning lamp in his memory, and a perpetual guard, in the blue-and-red uniform of his Grenadiers.

The Teatro Colón is one of the outstanding opera houses of the world—and one of the most magnificent, with its own symphony orchestra, opera company, and ballet, an opulent gold-and-scarlet interior which includes lounges, lobbies, restaurants, and an unbelievably enormous stage; the Congress Building—domed in the manner of the Capitol in Washington—dominating the pigeon-filled green Plaza del Congreso, and containing the Senate and Chamber of Deputies; the Banco de la Nación, possibly the greatest banking edifice in the world, occupying an entire block.

Leading museums: The Museum of Fine Arts, with both modern and older paintings and sculpture of Argentines, other South Americans, North Americans, and Europeans, plus unusual colonial wood carvings from the provinces; the National Museum of Decorative Arts, with superb displays and collections dating back to the Colonial era; the National Historical Museum, a graphic presentation of Argentina's history, with a great many San Martín mementos, including furniture from the French house where he died in voluntary exile; the Mitre Museum and Library, with manuscripts and documents of the nineteenth-century writer-statesman Bartolomé Mitre; the Isaac Fernandez Blanco Museum of Hispanic-American Art—a great colonial collection.

Principal churches: San Ignacio de Loyala, built in 1710 and the oldest intact building in the city, unhappily now devoid of most of its original furnishings and treasures; La Merced (1732), with a superb organ, and an altar carved by Indians under Jesuit tutelage; El Pilar, with a lovely yellow plaster façade, is two centuries old and now the parish of the city's wealthiest people; the American Church, the first of its kind in South America, built in 1863; St. John's Pro-Cathedral (Anglican), dating back to 1831, when half of its cost was defrayed by the British government, for the Anglo-Argentine community.

Other requisites: Plaza San Martín, with a statue of the Liberator; the adjoining Plaza Británica, with a clock tower presented by the British community to the city; the University of Buenos

Aires, one of the Americas' largest, with an enrollment of some
twenty thousand students; Palermo Park—one of the most beautiful in the New World, with an exquisite Andalusian tiled patio, a
gift from Spain, as well as rose gardens, ponds white with chattering ducks, miles of winding paths and bridge-covered water-
ways, and the adjacent Botanical Gardens, zoo, and race track,
which seats 45,000 avid spectators at weekend races throughout
the year, interchanging its schedule with that at suburban San
Isidro; the various livestock markets (cattle, sheep, and horses;
cows and pigs, wool and hides), which are the sites of lively
auctions easily viewed by visitors; the great houses and mansions,
particularly those in the neighborhood of the Plaza San Martín,
some of which are now government ministries, private clubs, and
foreign embassies, and would include the Palacio San Martín (now
the Foreign Ministry), the Army Officers' Club (with a small
museum of its own), the handsome French Embassy and, though
not quite in the mansion category, the Plaza Hotel—one of the
city's landmarks.

Suburbs and environs of Buenos Aires: An *estancia* visit, easily
arranged by a travel agency, provides a picture of that facet of
Argentine rural life which is the mainstay of the economy. On a
day's excursion one is introduced to the routine of a great ranch,
with its comfortable owner's house, barns and shops, simple
Gaucho quarters, and to the business of the *estancia*—cattle, and
often sheep and horses, as well. Some trips include lunch at the
estancia, in the form of an outdoor barbecue, or *asado,* with fresh-
killed beef grilled on spits over the open fire, to the accompaniment of Gaucho folk music.

Interesting suburban communities include *Belgrano,* where the
British and American communities hole themselves up from the
non-English-speaking *Porteños,* with their own schools, clubs, and
churches; *Hurlingham,* with the elaborate, English-style Hurlingham sports club and a largely Anglo-Argentine population; *Olivos,*
on the Río de la Plata, at once a suburb and a center for swimming,
yachting, fishing, and golf, with the summer home of the president
and the year-round homes of a great many Americans and Anglo-

Argentines; *San Isidro,* still a bit Colonial but largely a summer resort for *Porteños,* prettily situated on the banks of the Plata; *Luján,* forty-five miles from Buenos Aires, and the country's leading Roman Catholic place of pilgrimage, with a seventeenth-century statue of the Virgin occupying the place of honor in an elaborate basilica, each arch of which is named for an Argentine province. The old town hall, or Cabildo, is the site of an excellent museum: the Colonial and Historical Museum of the Province of Buenos Aires.

La Plata, thirty-five miles from Buenos Aires, is the capital of Buenos Aires province, and a substantial city of some 350,000. It is also a thriving port, the site of a number of universities and other schools, a Museum of Natural History which has an enviable international reputation with people who are experts on museums of natural history, a delightful zoo in the same park which contains the museum, as well as an observatory; a race track which vies with the two in Buenos Aires, the impressive government and public buildings, a petroleum distillery of the government oil monopoly (YPF), and, on the nearby Islas de Río Santiago, the Argentine Naval Academy and a yacht club. Founded in 1882 when it was decided that Buenos Aires City would no longer be capital of its province, La Plata is a completely modern town, designed to function as the provincial capital and education center. It is, though, despite its relative newness, a town with a likable, perky bustle.

Mar del Plata and other beach resorts: *Porteños* are likely to advise against summer visits to Buenos Aires. "Everyone," they are prone to say, "will be away—at Mar del Plata." They exaggerate. Life goes on in Buenos Aires, summer heat or no, but it is true that literally hundreds of thousands of city dwellers, from the capital and elsewhere, make a beeline to Mar del Plata between November and April, during which time the population swells considerably from its year-round 160,000. Like La Plata, Mar del Plata is also a commercial port. But it is as a resort that it shines —hugging the marvelously craggy cliffs of the Atlantic, with five miles of beaches; dozens upon dozens of hotels running the gamut

of luxury; a pair of casinos; the opulent villas of wealthy vacationers, and the simple cottages of the less affluent; all manner
of private clubs—beach, yacht, and otherwise; and central streets
which after dark each evening are a carnival of merriment and
movement, with holidaymakers of all ages darting from café to
restaurant to casino to hotel to boardwalk to club to cinema. I
know of no resort where the night life has quite the spontaneous,
unrehearsed, and appealing frenzy of Mar del Plata. It calls for
sleep-late mornings, lazy forenoons and lunches on the beaches,
late-afternoon showers and naps, leisurely drinks followed by way-
after-dark dinner, and then the diversions of café and casino. The
sun is brilliant, the water blue and—one must be honest—*cold,*
the surf strong, and the life wonderfully relaxing.

Bristol is the main beach with masses of canvas *cabinas* and
behind them the principal hotel and casino. Grande is a more
exclusive beach with private clubs and estates adjacent to it;
Perla is more middle-income; there are numerous others. One can
easily make a choice after a morning's walk along the *corniche* on
the cliff which towers over them. There are swimming pools for
those who prefer them, deep-sea fishing, golf, boating.

Nearby are *Mar Chiquita,* a lagoon whose specialty is calm,
surfless bathing; *Balcarce,* a hill resort in the interior; *Miramar,*
a smaller, less expensive, somewhat more subdued version of Mar
del Plata, with a casino of its own, a number of good hotels, and
an exceptionally handsome setting, and *Necochea,* another rival
to Mar del Plata, with superb beaches preferred by some to those
of Mar del Plata, and again a casino.

Bahía Blanca is herein mentioned principally because it is the
major city of southern Argentina, below Buenos Aires; an important port situated, as its name implies, on a bay (which is not,
however, white), and a departure point for trips to the nearby
hills of the Sierra de la Ventana.

Bariloche and the lakes (see also pages 247–52, which deal with
the adjoining Chilean Lake District): Four hours from Buenos
Aires via Aerolineas Argentinas (and forty-five hours by train)
is Bariloche, the neo-Swiss town which is the unofficial capital

of a district of lakes, mountains, and glaciers unsurpassed by any other Alpine region on any other continent.

To visit southern South America and to miss the lakes—which ignore national frontiers and extend themselves from Argentina over the Andes into Chile—is to commit a touristic blunder of the first order. For the traveler in Argentina en route to Chile who does not want to miss the experience of the exciting Andean flight from Buenos Aires to Santiago—and this is one of the greatest air journeys of international travel—the lakes can be treated as an excursion from the Argentine capital. Alternatively, they may be inspected while one is en route from Argentina to Chile, with additional stopovers in their Chilean counterparts as part of the journey to Santiago. The reverse routing—Santiago to the Chilean and Argentine lakes to Buenos Aires—is popular with travelers bound for Argentina from Chile. The point is to include the region, by one means or another. Time to be allotted can be as little as four or five days, although great numbers of Argentines, Chileans, and other South Americans—joined each year by an increasing quantity of Americans and not a few Europeans—spend entire vacations in the area. And well they might: it is fantastically beautiful—cool and green in summer, white and crisp in winter, with fine accommodations and tiptop winter skiing and summer fishing.

The town of Bariloche straddles the southern shore of the inland sea known as *Lake Nahuel Huapí*—the chief body of water in the district, which is now a national park bearing the lake's Indian name. A community of some twenty thousand, Bariloche is dotted with chalet-type hotels, public buildings (including an interesting museum of northern Patagonian history), and private homes, with the Cerro Otto—a hill which is of mountainous proportions—at its back door, and the even taller Cerro Colorado a little south.

An advance request made with one's room reservation will assure transportation from airport to hotel. The top two hostelries are a good way from both town and airport, and the route—along the shores of the lake, with snowy-peaked mountains making up

the shore line and reflecting themselves in the blue waters—is
such that one drives along in stunned silence, preferably to either
the small, beautifully situated Tunquelen Hotel or the large and
quite splendid Llao-Llao. Both are government-owned and flawlessly run. The Llao-Llao (pronounced *Jao-jao,* with *j* soft in each
case) is named for the neighborhood in which both are situated,
with the larger ingeniously placed on a peninsula between Lake
Nahuel Huapí and the smaller Lake Moreno.

Within the area are trails and roads for leisurely hikes. The
waters themselves are great for fishing or simply for camera
safaris via motorboat. Excursions can be made to any number
of points—*Victoria Island,* amid Lake Nahuel Huapí, with its
unusual forest-research station; the *Limay River,* for trout fishing; *Lake Traful,* reached by a drive through the *Encantado
Valley* with its grotesque rock formations; the trio of *lakes* immediately south of Nahuel Huapí: *Guillelmo, Mascardi, Gutiérrez,* the last-named with its Grotto of the Virgin of the Snows; *El
Bolsón,* a mountain village to the south, and *Esquel,* amid excellent hunting country and near still more lakes, these being *Puelo*
and *Epuyén.* To the north is *San Martín de los Andes,* on the
shores of *Lake Lacar* and near the *Lanín National Park,* named
for the snow-coated volcano that dominates it.

Regardless of how one's itinerary within the lakes works out,
the scenery is never dull: venerable trees dominate the verdant
forests, millions of flowers—foxglove, fuchsia, primrose, daisies,
lilies—blanket the fields; glaciers protrude onto the very shores
of the azure lakes; waterfalls, brisk and foamy-white, appear at
unexpected intervals, and people—who seem midget-sized, so
grandiose is the setting—are relatively few and far between, even
during the tourist season, but so relaxed that one would rarely
know that many are desk-bound, apartment-dwelling clock watch-
ers for most of the year.

From the hotels at Llao-Llao, one can tour the enormous Lake
Nahuel Huapí (it is forty miles long and at times six miles wide)
via small motor-powered craft or on the larger *Modesta Victoria,*
a yacht-sized steamer which doubles as excursion boat and as the

first means of transport *for those visitors going on to Chile*. The first stop, if one is Chile-bound, is at *Puerto Blest,* on *Brazo Blest*—one of the many fiord-like "arms" of the big lake. From there one continues by bus to *Puerto Alegre* on *Lake Frias,* where by means of another boat one arrives less than half an hour later at *Puerto Frias,* Argentine customs, and a waiting bus for a roller-coaster-type journey through the *Pérez Rosales Pass* to *Casa Pangue,* and *Peulla,* in Chile. From Peulla one can proceed north to *Santiago,* via the Chilean lakes and the port city of *Puerto Montt.*

Southern Patagonia: The only part of Patagonia which most visitors to Argentina traverse is the aforementioned, and very distinct, Lake District. South of the lakes, Patagonia is something else again—an immense plateau with a population density of a fraction of a person to a square mile, with near-constant winds, considerable dust blown about by those winds, not nearly enough rain, and surprisingly moderate temperatures—about 50° in summer and 35° in winter.

Great stretches of southern Patagonia are bleak desert. That condition, together with the paucity of natural ports and the geographical isolation, have tended to limit the development of the region. The chief industry is the raising, clipping, and slaughtering of sheep (18 million of them!) on great *estancias* in those regions where there is enough moisture to provide grass for grazing.

Though first visited by Magellan in 1520, it was the Anglo-Saxons who became the most important settlers in Patagonia— there are colonies of English and Scots, and, for nearly a hundred years, the Welsh have been on the scene, at *Puerto Madryn* and more recently, at nearby *Trelew.* The former, on a sheltered coastal bay, was settled by a hardy band of 150 Welsh determined to found a New Wales in the New World. They almost perished, at one point, thanks to a disastrous flood, but sent for compatriots from Wales to replenish their thinning ranks, and even accepted a handful of United States immigrants. Through schools, churches, and a press of their own, they have attempted to keep the Welsh language and culture. Spanish is gradually taking over, but the mellifluous language of the town's ancestors is still spoken, and sung. Trelew, the other Welsh settlement, is newer, larger (about twelve thousand), and more prosperous, but without the dramatic history of its poorer neighbor.

Comodoro Rivadavia is Patagonia's largest city, with a population of about twenty-five thousand, a military base, and an eleven-hundred-mile pipeline through which the petroleum of the area is transported to Buenos Aires. Other Patagonian mainland towns include *Río Gallegos,* where residents make their livings at tallow-making, and trade in sheepskins and wool; *Santa Cruz,* on a river by that name, on which boats ply to *Lake Argentino* in the Andean foothills, and *Puerto Deseado,* the point of departure for visits to the awesome 580-square-mile *Lake Buenos Aires.*

Tierra del Fuego, the island separated from the mainland by the Strait of Magellan, is part Argentine, part Chilean, and the site of the world's southernmost town, *Ushuaia*—on the Argentine side. There are only seventy-five hundred souls resident in the Argentine portion of the island, which is flat in the north, Andean in the south, and fairly moist all about. Ushuaia claims twenty-five hundred of the population, and, fortunately for the visitor, is in the gloriously mountain southern section, amid white peaks, black rivers, turgid cataracts, and green forests. Cut in from the sea are a maze of splendid fiords, the likes of which are found only in Norway. Near the town is a wondrous glacier, easily viewed on excursions which the local Club Andino is happy to arrange for those rare visitors to this lonely part of the world.

Iguassú Falls and the northeast: Northeast Argentina embraces the vast scrubby, hot plains of the Chaco (which extend into Paraguay and Bolivia) and the region of Mesopotamia, which embraces a trio of provinces, including Misiones, where there remain the ruins of the fantastic communities built by the early Jesuits and their Indian converts. Also in the northeast is one of the great natural wonders of the world—*Iguassú Falls.* On the Igaussú River, at a point where Argentina, Brazil, and Paraguay converge, the great falls can be visited from any of the republics, and are treated in the chapters on each of these countries. The visitor on a 'Round South America air journey beginning his trip in the east, is advised to make his stop on the Brazilian side of the falls, en route south to Paraguay and Argentina. But the visitor in Argentina who would like to include the falls on his itinerary need only fly north from Buenos Aires, in a few hours, or, with six days at his disposal, proceed by boat from the capital to *Puerto Iguazú*. One can also make the trip on a combination train-boat or train-bus journey, going by train as far as Posadas, and taking either boat or bus from there to the falls. The means of transport pales in contrast to the spectacle which greets one upon arrival.

The falls lie a dozen miles up the Iguassú River from Puerto Iguazú, in a virtually uninhabited forest setting. The only towns are the aforementioned Puerto Iguazú on the Argentine side, and *Foz do Iguassú,* across the river in Brazil. Each country offers hotel accommodations, but it must be admitted even here in this chapter on Argentina that the Brazilian hotel is directly at the falls and within view of them, while the Argentine hotel is some distance away. At any rate, the falls are something to behold: above them, the river is some 4300 yards wide, there are cataracts for two miles above the 200-foot-high precipice over which the water flows, at a width of 2700 yards. Niagara's height is less by 30-odd feet, and, of course, its setting is practically urban. The best months, weather-wise, for a visit are May–November, when it is cooler. But even during the remainder of the year, the heat and humidity are worth countenancing. And at all times the falls are unbelievably beautiful. One can not see them all at once, except from the air. Footpaths lead to the various sections: Bosetti, more often than not with a rainbow emerging from its spray; San Martín, possibly the most dramatic; the smaller but still lovely Two Sisters, and still others—Three Musketeers, Devil's Throat, Mitre—which can be approached by canoe for close inspection, provided one has a raincoat along. Stay at least a full day and a night; longer for return visits to favorite vistas. And don't be without adequate film on each falls excursion. From every angle, this masterpiece of nature cries to be photographed.

Posadas: South of Puerto Iguazú, on the "arm" of Argentina which extends east into Brazil and Paraguay, is Posadas, capital of Misiones province, and just across the Alto Paraná River from Encarnación, Paraguay. There is nothing distinctive about the town itself. It is noteworthy because not far from it are ruins of the some thirty *misiones* or settlements, founded by the Jesuits and built by their Guarani Indian converts, in the early seventeenth century. They gave their names to the modern province in which they are situated, and at least one—*San Ignacio Miní*—is worth detouring for. Converging from its central plaza are the remains of a score and a half of uniformly proportioned streets, each containing exactly ten one- or two-story stone houses, now mostly roofless. These were the homes of the Indian converts, whom the Jesuits not only Christianized, but Westernized as well. When they moved to the *misiones,* the Guaranis changed into European-style clothing, worked as European-style craftsman or farmers, and, particularly on the settlements over the border in Paraguay, intermarried with Europeans. Besides the dwellings of this old town, there are other evidences of its past: a large church, an old cemetery, a school, a priests' cloister, a dining hall, workshops, warehouses—most all of which are embellished in finely-designed bas-relief sculpture. By 1614 San Ignacio Miní had some two thousand residents. The entire town—like the other *misiones*—was built by them under Jesuit tutelage, their handiwork including superb sculpture and painting.

Despite raids by bandits from Brazil and mass flights to safer regions, the *misiones* flourished, and by the middle of the eighteenth century, some thirty had a combined population of 100,000. There is no reason to believe they would not have continued flourishing, and possibly changed the course of history in this region of Argentina and bordering Paraguay, where they also existed (see chapter on Paraguay), had not Charles II of Spain expelled their Jesuit administrators in 1767. The Dominicans took over, but the Indians did not do well under them, and by the time the Paraguayan dictator, Francia, came to power in 1814, the *misiones* were so poor and weak that he ordered them evacuated.

San Ignacio was burned and lost in the thickness of the forest until it was rediscovered in the late 1890s. It is now under the protection of the Argentine government, and some of its treasures have been moved to the Isaac Fernandez Blanco and Colonial Art museums in Buenos Aires.

Corrientes, capital of the province which bears its name, not far south of Posadas, dates back to 1588, and numbers among its Colonial treasures a still-handsome Government Palace, a Renaissance cathedral, an early nineteenth-century church—La Cruz— with a cross at its altar considered miraculous ever since marauding Indians were struck by lightning when attempting to burn it. There also is a worthwhile Colonial Museum, in which many relics of the old days have been collected and attractively displayed.

Rosario, with its half-million-plus population, and a humming harbor on the Paraná River, is Argentina's third city—modern, industrial, and with but a minimum of attractions for the visitor. These would include, besides the University of Rosario, a pair of museums (Municipal and Historical), a far from outstanding cathedral (if one makes comparisons with so many others in Argentina), a sprinkling of skyscrapers, and the usual private clubs.

Paraná and Santa Fe are sister-cities separated by the Paraná River. Both are provincial capitals, the former of Entre Ríos province, the latter of the province bearing its name. Paraná served for a dozen years as the Argentine capital, in the mid-nineteenth century, during the period when the federalists were mad at the centralists in Buenos Aires. Around and near its graceful Plaza San Martín are a lovely cathedral with an elaborate sanctuary; the Museum of Fine Arts, in the Bishop's Palace; and Urquiza Park, dotted with historical statuary and affording splendid views of the countryside and Santa Fe across the river. The two towns are joined by ferry service. Santa Fe—about 230,000 population—is the larger, and the older, its first residents being settlers who came south from Asunción in 1573, when that city was still the chief town of southern South America. It was in

Santa Fe's Cabildo that Argentina's 1853 constitution was adopted. Beside the Cabildo, highlights include the venerable San Francisco Church, with a noted altar, the University of the Litoral, and a number of colonial buildings on the handsome Plazo Mayo.

The Andean cities of the northwest: While Buenos Aires was a struggling, neglected community bypassed by the colonial brass in the viceroyalty of Lima, Spaniards from Peru followed the ancient Inca roads leading through the passes of Chile into what is now northwest Argentina. The towns they founded throve during their early centuries, by trade with Lima, through which all of southern South America's produce then passed on its way to Spain. Until the Indians of the Pampa to the east were exterminated in the latter part of the nineteenth century, all of these towns were isolated from Buenos Aires and the east, and their development was along the insular Colonial pattern of their founders. It is only in recent decades that they have become modern and expanded; even so, their Colonial façades are far more in evidence than those of the eastern cities. And an Argentine visit that does not include a sampling of them is incomplete.

Mendoza, the farthest south, the closest to Chile, and—thanks to earthquakes—the most rebuilt and most modern, is in the center of the rich vineyard region of the republic. It was from here that José de San Martín led his troops across the Andes to help the Chileans—and later the Peruvians—free their countries. An immense monument in the park on Gloria Hill tells of the preparation for the hazardous journey and of the trip itself, and there are belongings of the Liberator in the Historical Museum. Not far from town are a number of handsome excursion points in the mountains, including the thermal resort of *Villavicencio; Cacheuta,* also with hot springs, and *Potrerillos,* a ski center.

Tucumán lies at the foot of the dizzying peak of the Sierra de Aconquija, in a region of sugar plantations irrigated with the waters of streams flowing down from that mountain. A city of a quarter of a million, it is nearly four centuries old, and it was here that the Congress of the United Provinces of the Río de la Plata convened in 1816 to draft the Declaration of Independence of what is now called Argentina. They met in the Casa Historica, which still houses the chair used by the presiding officer of the congress, and some other original furnishings, as well. Other highlights: the cathedral, among whose interior treasures are the cross used in the ceremony at which independence was declared; the Plaza Independencia, with orange trees landscaping it, and the San Francisco Church and Government Palace flanking it.

Salta and Jujuy are a pair of living museums, just a few miles apart. Salta, the larger of the two towns, is by far the more interesting and one of the loveliest Colonial cities in Argentina. Set in a verdant, hilly valley, with a four thousand-foot mountain as a backdrop, it contains both original and neo-Colonial architecture, its present inhabitants continuing their building in the style of their forefathers. Outstanding among the originals is the cathedral, dominating the main plaza, with its pride a pair of statues, one of the Virgin of the Miracle, the other of the Lord of the Miracle, commemorating what is believed to be the miraculous cessation of a disastrous earthquake in 1692, more than a century after the town was founded. The ancient Cabildo, or town hall, is now a charming historical museum, with unusual displays of folklore from the surrounding countryside. Jujuy is a young upstart in contrast to Salta. It was founded a full decade after its neighbor—in 1593. Here, too, history was made—the first Argentine flag was designed and sewn in Jujuy, and is still on display in Government House, which is more than anyone can claim for the flag supposed to have been made by Betsy Ross in Philadelphia. Jujuy's cathedral is virtually a museum of eighteenth-century painting and sculpture, and its adjoining chapel houses a gem of a pulpit. Yavi and San Francisco churches are also venerable; and not far from town, in the mountains, is the thermal resort of *Reyes.*

Córdoba: Despite its half-million population, Córdoba retains the personality of a far more intimate place. It has grown with the times but its modernity has not displaced its Colonial flavor— and for this the visitor can be grateful. By the time its San Carlos University (Argentina's first) was founded in 1613, Córdoba had had four decades of existence, and there are many evidences of its proud past still extant. Besides many old houses with flower-filled tile patios and wrought-iron grillwork, these include the cathedral, with a quartet of towers, each of which is embellished with a circular staircase; the house of the viceroy, whose mellowed interior makes an ideal setting for the Colonial-Historical Museum— one of the country's finest; the old Cabildo, or Town Hall; Obispo Chapel—the town's first, erected in 1593; La Compania Church, with its stark but stunning façade; Santa Maria Church, whose exquisite Altar of the Virgin dates to 1592; La Merced Church, distinguished by a gem of a hand-carved pulpit and superb candelabra, the lovingly-tended Sarmiento Park, replete with a waterfall of its own, a zoo, and a promenade affording superb views of this sumptuously situated city. The Plaza San Martín is the core of the old town, through which runs the Río Primero. The backdrop: rugged mountains extending in three directions, with the flat Pampa in the foreground.

Worth noting, too: Córdoba's industrial boom, generated principally by the great Kaiser and Fiat factories. Skilled workers at the former average more than $140 a month—high wages by Argentine standards.

Córdoba, eminently visitable in itself, has another touristic virtue: in its neighborhood is a quite spectacular mountain range— the *Sierra de Córdoba*—which is dotted with resorts filled with holidaymakers who take advantage of diversions ranging from golf and swimming to hiking and hunting. The climate year-round is mild, sunny, and bracing, hotels range from good to luxurious, transport from the city (bus and train) is convenient, and there is a surprisingly wide choice of destinations. These include *Carlos Paz* on *Lake San Roque, La Cumbre, La Falda, Asochinga,* and *Jesús María*—all to the northwest of the city; *Mina Clavero* (with thermal baths), *Yacanto, Las Rabonas,* and *Nono* are to the southwest, and due south is *Alta Gracia,* popular year-round with Argentines, and with a rich Colonial past. Not far distant is a curious salt lake, not unlike that of Utah's. Its called the *Mar Chicquita* (Little Ocean), and is ringed by resort hotels.

Falkland Islands (*Islas Malvinas*): Discovered in 1592 by an Englishman, taken later by the French, ceded by the French to Spain, retaken by the English, who were almost immediately driven out by the Spanish, who were in turn beaten off by the British, abandoned for a period of decades, resettled by the Argentines, who were attacked by an American warship presumably because an American was being held captive illegally, later reconquered from the Argentines by the British, still British owned and populated, but to this day recognized by the Argentines as Argentine territory. *That,* in a nutshell, is the tumultuous history of this group of islands which are some three hundred miles from the Strait of Magellan, and are populated by some twenty-three hundred hardy souls, most all of whom are sheep farmers. The climate, while rarely ever frigid, is rainy, and the winds—often very strong—are incessant. *Stanley,* on East Falkland, is the capital and chief town, with about half of the islands' population; a modern town hall which is also a museum, post office, and library; a fine harbor, and minimal accommodations, there being no great demand for hotel space. Most visitors, aside from Colonial officials out of London (the islands are a colony, administered by a Crown-appointed governor assisted by a partially-elected Legislative Council), are whaleboat crews, and passengers on occasional cruise ships seeking out-of-this-world ports of call. The Falklands fill the bill: lonely, desolate moors—mostly of rock and peat—stretch as far as the eye can see, and the winds, even in summer, rarely cease. One marvels at the way in which the islanders—many of whom know no other part of the world, not even the South American mainland—carry on, chins up, in true British tradition. As for Argentina, it has never even recognized the Falklands' Anglo-Saxon *name,* let alone its occupiers. To Argentines, these islands are the Malvinas. So complete is this lack of recognition that communication between the islands and the outer world is via the port of Montevideo, in Uruguay; from which ships sail monthly. Seaplanes connect the islands of the group, but there is no air service to the mainland.

WHAT TO BUY

Prices in Argentina have increased appreciably in the last half-decade, and the shops are not the bargain bazaars they once were. But there is still considerable treasure to be yielded in a number of categories. And accompanying the rising prices has been a tremendous improvement in both workmanship and design. Argentine shops, despite the country's economic difficulties, are laden with articles of great style and taste. There is no city in eastern South America which can hold a candle to Buenos Aires in this respect, and the visitor who does not allot a substantial period for strolls along Calle Florida (closed to vehicular traffic most of the day and evening, for the benefit of ambulatory shoppers), Calle Santa Fe, and the adjoining streets is quite likely to regret it.

Leather is, of course, the great feature. Alligator bags range from $30 (and if one looks hard, some at this price are quite good and would cost $60 in the United States) to $80 and more. There are lesser items—men's billfolds, passport cases, women's wallets, compacts, manicure sets, and belts among them—which are more reasonable and most attractive. Not to be overlooked by any means are counterparts of the above—and brief cases and suitcases as well—in other leathers, particularly the fine, supple calfskin and durable cowhide. Then, too, there are gloves for both men and women, hand-made shoes, antelope suede jackets and coats, and fur coats and jackets of Argentine nutria. In *Buenos Aires,* Lopez y Cia (Charcas 640–58 and a small Plaza Hotel branch) is my favorite shop, with an immense selection of all the foregoing, and then some. Others include Pisk (Santa Fe 774), Mayorga (Florida 394, Florida 777, and Sarmiento 648), plus Rossi and Caruso, Angelo Marsar, L'Umbrella, and Mattaldi. Ricardo and Guante specialize in hand-made shoes.

Men's causal wear—particularly sports shirts of cotton lisle, hand-knitted flax, and fine wool—are among the most handsome in the Americas. The two shops with the most distinctive models are Grant (Galleria Santa Fe) and Dott (Calle Florida). Others include Giesso (Santa Fe 1557 and Corrientes 930), Rhoder's, Warrington, Brighton, James Smart, Spinelli, and Iotti. High-style women's wear—sweaters, dresses, accessories—is best found at such shops as La Scala, Vittorio, Hermes and De War—all in the Florida-Santa Fe neighborhood. Casa America is good for recordings of Gaucho folk music; along with many other small stores—most in the immense arcaded shopping *galarias* in the main districts—they feature folk souvenirs, such as maté gourds and silver sippers, *bombachas* (the baggy Gaucho pants), small items of hand-wrought silver, hand-woven ponchos and blankets which are considerably higher in price than those found in Bolivia, Peru, and Ecuador. Antiques are found in a number of shops, but are rarely cheap. These include Vetmas, Verstar and Saudades on Calle Libertad, and Apollinaire and Cluny on Calle Parera. Leading department stores are Harrod's (related to the London Harrod's), Gath and Chaves, and La Piedad. All are good for general browsing, particularly in the lugguge, small leather-goods, clothing, and clothing-accessory departments, and all have English-speaking salesmen on tap. The same is true in the other shops; there is rarely any language difficulty. Branches of a number of leading Buenos Aires shops are found in *Mar del Plata,* with prices about the same. The Llao-Llao Hotel in *Bariloche* has a huge shopping arcade whose merchants occasionally offer bargains in soft wool stoles and other local handwork. There are, of course, shops of all sizes and varieties in every Argentine city, and one does well to browse everywhere. But Buenos Aires is the shopping as well as the political capital of the republic, and by the time one leaves it, one's Argentine buying-budget is pretty well exhausted. So are one's feet.

CREATURE COMFORTS

There is no country in South America where creature comforts are better attended to. It is difficult to find a bad Argentine hotel or restaurant, and night life—*boîtes,* cafés, theater, movies—is in-

variably pleasant. Two or three dollars buys a good restaurant meal
in Buenos Aires, and fifty cents a sandwich lunch in a *confitería*.
Prices in the smaller cities are less expensive. Hotel rates run a
wide gamut, and conventional night clubs are expensive.

HOTELS—**Buenos Aires:** The Plaza has all of the elegance of
an Old World hotel. Overlooking lovely Plaza San Martín and
minutes from the shopping and theater districts, it is at once attractive (the bedrooms are among the most tastefully-decorated
on the continent), convenient, and with a wonderfully luxurious
ambiance. Service is impeccable. Food—particularly in the urbane
Grill, which is one of Buenos Aires' major congregating places—
is superb (if expensive). The bar is congenial and the main dining
room perfect for leisurely dining. Shops, airline branch offices,
travel agencies are on the premises. All rooms have bath and are
air-conditioned. From $10 single—not expensive when one con-
siders that this is one of the world's great hotels. Considerably
less convenient, but in a lovely old residential neighborhood, is
the Alvear Palace, with a smart bar, restaurant, and supper club,
and the kind of décor one would expect at a luxe hotel in Paris.
From $10 single, with bath. Smaller, but modern and well-run,
is the Sussex; single, $5, with bath and air-conditioning. The Cali-
fornia, with a popular bar and restaurant, is also good. The City
is large, efficient relatively colorless, and moderate-priced (from
$7.50). The Claridge is pleasantly mellow, and with a fine, but
expensive restaurant. From $11 single. Others: Continental (from
$8 single), Crillon (from $7 single), Lancaster and Castlelar
(from $4.50 single), Nogaro, Richmond, Monumental, Dora,
Argentino, Carsson, Regent, and Royal. Advance reservations
are a good idea; there are often not enough rooms to go around.
Luján: Espana and La Paz are the leaders. **La Plata:** City,
Marini—take your choice. **Mar del Plata:** There are well over
two hundred hotels to choose from. Among the luxury group, my
favorite is the charming, attractive, and central Hermitage, from
$7 single. Also good is the Nogoro, from $7 single. The Provincial
contains the leading casino but is ugly and enormously massive;
from $5.50 single. Others in the top category include the Horizonte,

Tourbillon, and Royal. Reservations, even if made by phone or wire from Buenos Aires, are advisable during the season. **Miramar:** Golf-Roca, with golf course; Atlantico, Normandie, Gran Rex, and at nearby **Mar de Sud:** Atlantic. **Necochea:** Royal, Atlantico, San Miguel, Trocadero. **Bahía Blanca:** Austral, Central Muniz. **Bariloche:** The Llao-Llao is unsurpassed by any resort hotel in South America; ingeniously situated on a peninsula between Lakes Nahuel Huapí and Moreno, with the views of snow-capped mountains, blue lakes, and broad green valleys fantastically beautiful; handsome public rooms and lounges, including a glassed-in gallery for sitting gaga while taking in the scenery; travel agencies, many shops, pleasant bar; from $7 single, European plan. Smaller, more intimate, but also with a glorious situation and splendid cuisine is the Tunquelen, from $7.25 single, American plan. Open all year, but the favorite during the skiing season is the Catedral, atop Cerro Catedral, with ski lifts and other winter-sports facilities at the door, and every luxury within; from $4.50 single. Others: Bella Vista, in town, very pleasant, from $6.50 single, American plan; Tres Reyes, Huemul, Cristal, Trio Gran. **Trelew:** Touring, Galicia. **Puerto Madryn:** Playa, Siguoro. **Comodoro Rivadavia:** Colon, Espana. **Río Gallegos:** Gran Paris, Argentino. **Ushuaia:** Motel Hotel—$5 American plan, no private baths: plans, though, for a luxury hotel to make Tierra del Fuego a tourist magnet. **Iguassú Falls:** Iguassú, on the Argentine side—modern and attractive; das Cataratas, on the Brazilian side—Portuguese Colonial-style décor, excellent dining room, overlooking the falls, and with a first-rate swimming pool. **Posadas:** Savoy, Plaza. **Corrientes:** Nacional de Turismo, Paraná. **Rosario:** Savoy, Italia, Majestic, City, Europeo. **Paraná:** Plaza, Atenas. **Santa Fe:** Ritz, Espana. **Mendoza:** Sussex—first-rate; Gran Balbi. **Potrerillos:** Potrerillos. **Tucumán:** Savoy, Premier, Coventry. **Salta:** Salta, Plaza. **Jujuy:** Bristol, Alto da Vina. **Córdoba:** Briston, Crillon, Plaza Windsor. **Alto Gracia:** Sierras, with golf course. **Stanley,** Falkland Islands (Islas Malvinas): Ship Hotel.

RESTAURANTS: The highly-touted fifty-cent-steak-dinner days are largely a thing of the past in Buenos Aires, but food is still relatively reasonable, and generally excellent. One eats no better in any other South American country, Peru possibly excepted. The Argentine staple is, of course, beef. It is served in a multitude of ways—most of them delicious. But there is a great deal else to choose from in this genuinely cosmopolitan capital. What follows is a selective capsulization for Buenos Aires. The leading hotels have fine dining rooms, particularly the Plaza (Grill), the Alvear Palace, the Claridge, and the California. Also good is the small restaurant of the little-known Hermitage Hotel. La Cabaña is justifiably famous for beef specialties of all kinds, and it is most attractive; the Shorthorn Grill and La Emiliana are in the same category. La Querencia, El Ceibal, and Corrientes 11 are notable for Argentine dishes, steak among them, of course. El Tropezon (The False Step) is open all night and an old favorite with *Porteños* after midnight; Puchero keeps the same hours, as does Zun Edelweiss, with its largely artist-writer clientele. Spadavecchia is the best of the Italian restaurants in the gay Boca district, with singing waiters *and* diners, as well as fine food. El Cocodrilo, also in the Boca, is Italian, too, and Ligure and Napoli are among the better non-Boca Italian places. Au Bec Fin and Le Coqhardi are a pair of excellent French restaurants in the Bario Norte (Northern Section) of town, which also is the site of many *parrillada*-type restaurants serving mixed-grill platters; La Tablita is among the best. The Papa Frita chain—all over town—is similar. Other national cuisines will be found at New China (Chinese), Casa Sirio-Libaneso (Middle Eastern), No Name (Swedish smorgasbord), Volga-Volga (Russian), Hotel Español (Spanish). Pill-Pill is excellent for seafood. Good for lunch are the restaurants at Harrod's and Gath and Chaves department stores, and the Comega Club, affording a panoramic city view from its twentieth-floor location in the Comega Building (as well as any *confitería* —see below) and the *carritos*—lunch wagons which line the river front and dispense succulent *parrilladas. Confiterías,* or tearooms, are often *al fresco* in summer and serve sandwiches and snacks and alcoholic beverages as well as tea, coffee, and soft drinks. They're popular for afternoon tea, at lunchtime—almost any

time of day, for that matter. El Aguila is the most famous—
wonderfully old-fashioned and atmospheric. Queen Bess is more
chic and streamlined, and with an Anglo-Argentine clientele, in
case the name did not give you your first clue. The Petit Cafe
is noted for its sandwiches; other better-known ones include
Roussilon and La Ideal, near the cinemas, and El Dandy (open-
air), near Palermo Park. The aforementioned department-store
tearooms and the twentieth-floor Comega Club might also be
included in the *confitería* category, and not to be neglected are
the hundreds of stand-up coffee bars to which *Porteños* repair
at odd moments throughout the day for instant-energy cups of
strong black *café*.

NIGHT LIFE: The aforementioned all-night restaurants—Zun
Edelweiss, El Tropezon, Puchero—double as round-the-clock
cafés, and are invariably lively and not overexpensive. More conventional night clubs include Kings, Embassy Casino, Jamaica,
Fascination, Amok, and Gong—all with dancing and entertainment, and Whisky a Gogo, with dancing only. In the Bario Norte
(Northern District) there are the Reviens, which emphasizes hot
rhythms and bongo drums; the Sunset, with its own swimming
pool and dancing, but no entertainment; Las Brujas, and Erwins.
Dinner is served in all of the night clubs, but one is better advised
to go after having dined; prices are steep.

PRIVATE CLUBS: Circulo Militar, in an opulent old mansion;
Strangers, American, American Women's, English, YMCA,
YWCA, and of course, Rotary. There are, as well, a number of
others, including many devoted to one sport or another. The
Hurlingham Club, in suburban Anglo-Argentine Hurlingham, is
the most elaborate; others are devoted to tennis, football, rugby,
hockey, basketball, and of course polo. The British community
carries on with cricket, and the Americans do likewise with baseball.

Argentine food specialties: Besides beefsteaks conventionally
broiled, the Argentines, particularly at outdoor barbecues, roast
their beef over open spits and call it *asada*. They occasionally
top it with fried eggs and call it *bife a caballo* (steak on horse-

back). The *parilladas,* mentioned earlier, is a platter containing broiled beef, sausage, kidneys, and sometimes other mysterious innards; it is delicious. The *empanadas*—those little meat-filled turnovers one sees all over South America—are particularly good and are frequently encountered. The spicy sausage, *chorizo,* is marvelous, and not unlike that found in Spain. *Puchero de gallina* is a mélange of chicken, *chorizo,* corn, and potatoes. In the liquid department, maté is the traditional nonalcoholic beverage, but a good deal of coffee is consumed, and tea is popular, too. Argentine beers are very good, and the wines of the country, while not as well known abroad as those of Chile, can be excellent. Choose, if you can, Casa de Piedra, Fond du Cave, Bianchi Cabernet, or San Félipe. And don't hesitate to drink a toast with the cheap but good domestic champagne—Monitor and Federico de Alvear being among the better brands. Leading bars in the big cities and resorts are familiar with American cocktails, but, appropriately enough, a martini is a San Martín in Argentina. *Buen apetito!*

BRAZIL

(Estados Unidos do Brasil)

Entry requirements: *A tourist card, obtainable through transport company or travel agent, for which passport, two photos, and return or onward transportation ticket is required; or a visa, obtainable from Brazilian consulates.* **Best times for a visit:** *The seasons are reversed. Winter (May–October) is a time of warm days and coolish evenings in central and southern Brazil, with temperatures lower in elevated places like São Paulo than in coastal cities like Rio. Brazilian summers are nearly everywhere hot. In the far north winter is more rainy than cool, and in the far south it can warrant topcoats. Generally speaking, winter is the best all-round visiting period.* **Currency:** *The cruzeiro, currently very inflated and averaging about 450 to the dollar, with frequent fluctuation.* **Film availability:** *Both black-and-white and color usually available in major cities, with the latter more expensive than in the United States.* **Language:** *Brazilian-accented Portuguese, localized as is English in the United States, is the universal tongue, except in the case of the Indian minority in the interior which speak the Guarani and Tupi languages.*

There is a good bit of English in major cities, and at transport terminals and hotels throughout the country. Brazilians are proud of their language (they are the largest Portuguese-speaking people in the world) and do not relish its being confused with Spanish. Italian is spoken in and around São Paulo, and some German in the far south. **Domestic transport:** *The airplane leads by far; Varig is the outstanding line, with routes covering most major regions of the country; there are a number of other lines, too. New superhighways lead from the central coast and the north into interior Brasília. Railroads, now undergoing extensive modernization with the aid of the Export-Import Bank, connect major cities on the coast and in the central and southern regions, but planes are invariably the best bet.* **Tipping:** *Hotels add about 10 per cent as a service charge, but employees who have served guests expect 10 per cent additional. Restaurant and taxi tips average 10 to 15 per cent.* **Business hours:** *Shops in the larger cities are usually open until about 7 P.M., and do not close for lunch.* **Further information:** *Brazilian Government Trade Bureau, 511 Fifth Avenue, New York; Varig Airlines, 634 Fifth Avenue, New York, and Rua Santa Luzia 827-A, Rio de Janeiro, Brazil; Rio de Janeiro Tourist Office, Rio de Janeiro, Brazil; Brazilian Embassy, Washington, D.C.*

INTRODUCING BRAZIL

I wish I had a dime for every traveler who flies to Rio, climbs Sugarloaf, swims at Copacabana, dashes over to São Paulo, and leaves the country quite convinced that he's seen Brazil. It's not that I blame anyone for concentrating a holiday in those wonderful cities. It's simply that it makes as little sense to visit only Rio and São Paulo in Brazil as it does to see only New York and Washington in the United States.

Brazil is, after all, half of a continent, with more than 50 per cent of South America's population and nearly that proportion of its area. It's not only larger than the continental United States, but it's also bigger than Australia. That's not only a lot of coffee, that's a lot of country: more than three and a quarter million square miles, stretching more than twenty-three hundred miles from north to south, and about the same distance from east to west.

Brazil borders every South American country save two. It has three climatic zones (tropical in the north, subtropical in the center, temperate in the south) and as many time zones. It has nearly one hundred times the area of its former mother country, Portugal, and its population of sixty million is seven times that of Portugal's. It is the only South American country which has been a sovereign monarchy as well as a colony and a republic. (And it is probably the only colony in the world whose capital served also, for a period, as the capital of the mother country.)

Brazil, which has never known an official color bar, is probably the world's most racially mixed country, with its population primarily a congolomerate of Portuguese, Negro, and indigenous Indian, with some Asians and other Europeans—mainly Italians, Poles, and Germans. At the beginning of the nineteenth century there were more Negroes in the country than there were whites or Indians, but today, after a century and a half of intense European immigration not unlike that which the United States experienced, Brazil is estimated to be about 60 per cent white, 20 per cent mameluco (mixed white and Indian) and mulatto, 15 per cent Negro, and the remainder Asian and pure Indian. The races have been mixing and mingling for four centuries; only the Portuguese aristocrats who came as settlers refrained from what was to become a widespread practice.

One should not infer from the foregoing that Brazil is a land of racial sweetness and light; the whites remain at the top of the ladder financially, socially, and politically, with relatively few exceptions. And the purebred Negroes, mulattoes, mamelucos, and Indians are in decidedly lower echelons. A comparison with the position of the Negro in the United States is difficult, but it would probably be safe to say that there are few Brazilian Negroes who have attained the fame and distinction which has come to a number of American Negroes, or the degree of education (particularly higher education) which is achieved by many American Negroes. On the other hand, there is no Jim Crow in public places—no part of Brazil where a Negro is denied a restaurant seat, hotel room, or waiting-room bench because of his color—but there is social and economic discrimination, as there is in the United States. The difference is that in the United States the laws of many states still make it legal.

At any rate, this unique "Brazilian race," as it has been called by sociologists, is not nearly as widespread as one might expect. There are more than three times as many Americans as Brazilians, although Brazil is larger than the United States and just as old. A number of factors are responsible for this phenomenon, and the tropical climate of large areas of the country is only one of them. Even more important is the pattern of development: the emphasis, by and large, has been the get-rich-quick approach. From the beginning, Brazilians have aimed for speculative wealth, and the only parts of the country which are heavily settled are those which the speculators exploited—first with the new sweetener, sugar from cane, which the world of the time had come to like; next with gold, which the world has always liked; lastly (and currently) with coffee.

Of recent years there have been efforts to diversify the economy (Brazil is now, for example, the largest steel producer in South America), and to open up the interior, which is largely jungle in the north and vast plain in the center.

Brasília, the futuristic capital smack in the middle of nowhere, was created just because it *is* in the middle of nowhere, with the hope that it will serve as a nucleus for the settlement and development of the great *sertão* which has been left largely untouched for four centuries.

A backward glance: The Spaniards—at least a shipload of them under Vicente Yáñez Pinzón—were the first Europeans to visit

Brazil, but they had other things on their minds, and never bothered colonizing. That was first done by the Portuguese, who, possibly to make it easy for students of history to remember the date, chose the first year of the sixteenth century (1500) to claim the land for their sovereign.

There being no gold paving the beaches, they set about to exploit *something* and what they came across were handsome trees with reddish-colored wood, which we now call brazilwood. They called them *brasa,* which means "glowing coal" in Portuguese, and it is from that term that the country is believed to have got its name.

Some years later, in 1532, the first permanent settlement was established, mostly by Portuguese from the poorer southern regions of the mother country, at São Vicente, near what is now Santos. Not long after, other Portuguese—these mainly aristocrats from Lisbon and northern Portugal—began to settle on the north coast, at Olinda, near the slightly newer Recife. Later, the first highland village went up on the site of what is now São Paulo. Rio de Janeiro was not founded until 1567—and then only as a military-naval base.

Almost immediately, sugar cane was planted on vast plantations, with the most successful in the northeast, around Recife and Salvador. In that area the rich planters thrived. They found the indigenous Indians unsatisfactory as slave laborers, so they imported vast numbers of Negro Africans—the west coast of Africa is closest to the Americas at Natal—who were not only good laborers and overseers, but also brought with them the iron-smelting techniques which West African civilizations had known for centuries before the Europeans did. Northern Brazil grew along feudal lines—vast plantations owned by a very few rich settlers and worked by thousands of Negro slaves.

In the south, around São Vicente, things were different. The poorer settlers there couldn't afford to import Africans and had to make do with the inefficient Indians, who were more trappers, hunters, and fishermen than they were farmers and in whose culture the heavy work was done traditionally by women. The

dissatisfaction which this situation engendered was to lead the
ambitious southerners on to greener (or at least hopefully greener)
pastures in their search for the wealth which had come so easily
to their northern neighbors.

Meanwhile, the Dutch and the French, attracted by the rich
sugar estates of the north, gave the Portuguese a run for their
money in Brazil, and for a while the Dutch controlled most of the
coast. The settlers themselves, not the Portuguese from home,
finally routed the Hollanders in 1654; it was their first joint effort
and the confidence they gained from it was to serve them well in
later years. They coveted for a good while the Spanish-held area
to the south (then called the Banda Oriental—now Uruguay) and
they fought over it with the Spaniards of Argentina, with the
Uruguayans themselves the ultimate winners.

Gold, and a new capital: In the seventeenth century the earlier-
mentioned gold rush transpired in the interior region known as
Minas Gerais; it led to the development of that area and it brought
Rio de Janeiro to the fore to the extent that in 1763 it became
capital of the entire colony. The gold discovery was the first truly
successful effort of the disgruntled southern settlers in the São
Paulo region. Not content with their unprofitable sugar farms, they
gathered themselves together in groups, known as *bandeirantes*
(which does *not* mean bandit), and roamed the uncharted interior looking for riches. What they found, more often than not,
were clusters of Indians, whom they proceded to enslave and
cohabit with, and later to marry. By the time they found gold at
Minas Gerais in 1698, they had pushed forward the frontiers of
Brazil to the west and south, occasionally founding villages and
vast ranches. The gold boom (supplemented by the discovery of
diamonds and other gems) saved Brazil from the financial ruin
which would have ensued with the demise of the sugar boom
which, by sheer luck, it followed.

By 1800 coffee as a beverage had achieved popularity in Europe,
and Brazilians, mainly in the São Paulo region, took to meeting
the demand. It is coffee that lured millions of immigrants to Brazil,
and it was coffee, and the wealth it provided, that was responsible

for the fantastic growth of the city and state of São Paulo. But that was to follow.

From colony to empire: Brazil, while going from one speculative product to another, was also evolving politically, in a way no other South American country had. The Colonial system had been neither as rigid nor as fanatic as that of Spain's. The Portuguese were more lax as administrators, to the colonists' benefit, and less concerned with superimposing their institutions, cultural and religious, in their colony. But still they took enough of their colonists' revenues, and gave little in return. By the time of Napoleon, a yen for freedom had already manifested itself in an abortive revolt. But in 1808, when Napoleon invaded Portugal, its king, John VI, fled to Rio de Janeiro, which became the temporary Portuguese capital. John returned in 1821 to Lisbon, leaving his son, Pedro, behind as regent. This the powers in Lisbon did not like, and they demanded that Pedro come home. But the Brazilians, by this time, had crystallized their thinking. They wanted sovereignty, and they prevailed upon Pedro to remain in Rio. In May of that same year—1821—he was designated "Perpetual Defender and Protector," in September he issued his famous challenge to the Portuguese on the banks of the Iparanga River: "Independence or Death." And in December he was crowned Pedro I, Emperor of Brazil. Freedom had come bloodlessly.

In 1831 Pedro I was forced to abdicate—there had been marital difficulties and dissatisfaction over his concern with matters Portuguese rather than Brazilian. His young son and successor, Pedro II, was to become one of the most popular monarchs of modern times. Dashing, attractive, intelligent, politically liberal, socially humane, he helped Brazil become a modern state through the establishment of schools, transport systems, emphasis on expanded agriculture, and encouragement of mass European immigration. It was in his reign that Brazil helped in the defeat of Argentine Dictator Rosas, and Paraguayan Dictator López. But his greatest accomplishment—the abolishment of slavery—was what led to his downfall, the end of the empire, and the establishment of the republic. During his time the slave trade had been declared illegal, and plans were under way for the gradual emancipation of those already slaves.

From empire to republic: While on a trip to Europe in 1883—during which time his unpopular daughter Isabel was taking his place—the government issued a decree completely abolishing slavery. Rich, pro-slave planters who had been given no compensation when their slaves were freed joined forces with pro-republican leaders, and a republic was proclaimed, without bloodshed. The imperial family was banished to Europe, where the emperor died two years later. He had reigned fifty-eight years. In 1922, on the centenary of independence, the descendants of the imperial family were allowed to return to Brazil, and the body of Pedro II was brought back and buried in the Petrópolis cathedral; the emperor's people, even if a little late, had shown their appreciation for his accomplishments.

From the birth of the republic until 1930 Brazil moved along rather placidly, with its participation on the side of the World War I Allies perhaps the most important event. But the global depression was disastrous to the one-crop coffee economy of the country, and unrest reflected itself in politics. Getúlio Vargas, deceptively mild-mannered governor of the state of Rio Grande do Sul, engineered a revolution and took over as dictator, substituting for the democratic constitution a Fascist one of his own, and ruling what he termed the *Stado Novo* (New State) until 1945.

Vargas to Kubitschek: It was to Vargas' credit that Brazil was the only South American republic to send forces abroad during World War II, and there is no doubt but that he was in part responsible for considerable economic development. But Brazilians had had enough of police-statism, and a coup ousted Vargas in 1945. Under General Eurico Gaspar Dutra, Vargas' successor, there came a new constitution, so adhered to that Vargas himself got to be elected president under it in 1950. Dissatisfaction with his administration was so intense by 1954 that he was "invited" by the government to take a three-month holiday; he agreed and committed suicide. He was succeeded by the vice-president, João Café Filho, and in 1955, Juscelino Kubitschek was elected president. His administration was one of intensive economic activity, with the high point the creation of Brasília, in the far interior, as the new federal capital. Kubitschek's supporters claim that the inflation which resulted as a result of the Brasília expenditures was worth the effort, and that the country, in the long run, will be the better for them. His detractors, however, prevailed, and young (forty-five) Jânio Quadros was elected president in 1960, as the candidate of the opposition.

The current scene: Quadros had performed brilliantly, both as mayor of São Paulo city and governor of São Paulo state—the country's richest and most booming area. He fired thousands of government employees and hangers-on who rarely appeared at work except on paydays. He cracked down on working schedules for civil servants, insisting that each work a full day—a novel regulation for many. Internationally, he envisioned Brazil as an India of the Western Hemisphere. Although he had termed Cuba's Castro a "nuisance," hindering Latin American development, he viewed U.S.-Cuban difficulties as negotiable and offered himself as a mediator of the Cuban question. He announced that Brazil would exchange diplomatic missions with the Soviet Union (as does the United States), and his country entered into trade negotiations with Communist China (as has Canada, and as do many other nations).

President Kennedy seemed to recognize Quadros' capabilities and Brazil's undeniable right to view foreign affairs as it wished. He also appreciated Brazil's importance, when he said, prior to the U.S.-sponsored $338 million loan to Brazil: "The future of Brazil is vital to the future of the Western Hemisphere. By identifying ourselves with the economic and social aspirations of the people of Brazil, we are identified with the hopes of half the continent." President Kennedy also took action on the need for drastic measures in northeastern Brazil, with unemployment rife, discontent widespread, and pro-Castro Peasants Leagues increasingly popular. He received the director of the Brazilian

Northeast Development Agency at the White House in July 1961, assured him that the United States would co-operate with Brazil in the $900 million, five-year development program for that region, and noted that "there is no area in this hemisphere in greater or more urgent need of attention than Brazil's northeast."

The colossus of the Southern Hemisphere seemed to be moving along with agility, hope, vitality. Lincoln Gordon, a Harvard professor with considerable government experience and a rich Latin American background, was appointed the new United States ambassador. Brazil had been a leading participant in the Inter-American Economic Conference in Uruguay, at which the Alliance for Progress was launched. But that conference, at least indirectly, was to change the course of contemporary Brazilian history.

One of the delegates to the Uruguayan meeting—Major "Che" Guevara, the Cuban finance minister—stopped in Rio de Janeiro on the way home, and was decorated by President Quadros, possibly as a political gesture to satisfy the many Brazilians of the poor northeast who are sympathetic to the Castro regime. But other, more powerful, Brazilians are not. Leading politicians criticized Quadros, and within a week he resigned the presidency, while the vice-president, João Goulart, elected independently of the president, was en route home from a visit to China. Goulart, at once immensely wealthy and militantly leftist, and with a background reputedly pro-Peronist, was a political enemy of the conservative powers-that-be in Brazil. Represented by the military chiefs of staff, they at once took steps to block his constitutional accession to the presidency. Civil war threatened, but within a fortnight Brazil had resolved its crisis without a shot being fired— much to its great credit. It did so, however, by means of a compromise, which in the long run may impede the desperately needed increase in standard of living, and opportunity, for the great majority of Brazilians. Congress passed an amendment to the constitution, stripping the presidency of most of its former powers, transferring them either to the newly-created office of prime minister or to Congress itself.

In other words, a European-type parliamentary system replaced Brazil's U.S.-modeled presidential system. The military went along, and Dr. Goulart took the oath of office as Brazil's twenty-fourth president. Tancredo Neves, an effective near-center-of-the-road politician, became the first prime minister. It appeared, at first, that Quadros' sweeping plans for much-needed tax and land reforms (which the United States supported) would fall by the wayside. But one of Premier Neves' first proposals to Congress was a program embracing tax-reform and anti-inflation measures designed to spur saving and offer incentives to foreign and local corporations to invest in Brazil. Brazil's friends are hopeful that the Goulart-Neves administration will realize that failure to carry out basic social reforms will leave the government vulnerable to the increasingly vocal discontent of the impatient mass of poor Brazilians, many of whom rarely live beyond the age of thirty-five, average fifty dollars income per year, and continue to be exploited by wealthy landowners, Brazilian and foreign.

Brazil is a big country with big problems. More than half the populace is illiterate. There is still a tremendous housing shortage, so much so that one out of four residents of Rio de Janeiro lives in a ramshackle mountainside hovel. Medical care is still far from adequate. The middle class, while substantial in many urban areas, is still overshadowed by the vast lower-income mass at the bottom, and the small wealthy class at the top. And it remains to be seen whether the new capital, Brasília, will expedite the settlement and development of the enormous, virtually uninhabited interior. Still, it must not be forgotten that this is a country with a rich, dynamic culture which manifests itself in such spheres as architecture, engineering, music, literature, painting, sculpture, and a warm, gay infectious *joie de vivre*.

Brazil has bounce, drive, and vitality in proportions which astound visitors from colder climes who believe the tropics are *mañana*-land. And it has, as Walter Lippmann observed after a

1960 visit, "an impressive capacity to govern itself." This is a tremendously exciting, immensely likable land, one about which we care far too little and of which, on visits, we usually see far too little.

YOUR VISIT TO BRAZIL

There are parts of Brazil still not easily accessible by surface transport, but virtually any place one might choose has an airport. It was in Brazil, one does well to remember, that the first commercial flight was made in 1927. Since that time, the entire country has been made smaller by the airplane, to the extent that flights between the big cities often appear as frequent as the shuttle subway trains which link Grand Central Terminal and Times Square in New York. This is the way air-minded Brazil travels, and the visitor is wise to hop aboard too.

For where? No matter how many alternative suggestions might be offered, the newcomer to Brazil will no doubt want to begin in Rio de Janeiro—as well he might. From there—and only the strong of character will not have need of a self-imposed time limit—branch off to as many places as there is time for—spanking new Brasília in the interior, lovely old Salvador de Bahia to the north, Belém and/or Manaus in the Amazon tropics, modern Belo Horizonte and venerable Ouro Preto in Minas Gerais; Pôrto Alegre, the great metropolis of Rio Grande do Sul, near the Uruguayan frontier; the magnificent falls of Iguassú, on the Brazilian-Argentine-Paraguayan border, and, of course, skyscraping São Paulo and its port-resort, Santos—both a hop and a skip from Rio. Brazil is the only country in the world I know of where departure announcements of plane flights without exception conclude with a *bon voyage* greeting for the boarding passengers. I wish the same for you: *Boa viagem!*

CENTRAL AND SOUTHERN BRAZIL

Rio de Janeiro and environs: The only person I've ever met who didn't fall in love with Rio at first sight was an Englishman who had taken ill on board ship before arrival, and spent the better part of a month in bed in a tacky downtown hotel some disreputable travel agent had booked for him from London. He couldn't wait to leave. But his experience was quite the exception to the rule. Invariably, one is enchanted with Rio before one disembarks from either aircraft or ship. I have known arriving camera enthusiasts so transfixed with the panorama that they were unable to so much as snap a photo.

One must give credit where it is due and there is no denying that the Portuguese are—and have been for many centuries— among the most ingenious town planners on the face of the globe. One sees the results of their handiwork in the homeland, in the cities of their African colonies such as Lourenço Marques in Mozambique and Luanda in Angola. Even Macao, on the China coast, now poor and deteriorating, must once have been lovely. But Rio is in a class by itself. And it is doubtful that any but the Portuguese, and their creole descendants, could have so combined the structures of man with the masterworks of nature.

Rio deftly tucks itself on a six-mile flank of lowland which separates its backdrop of moss-green rock mountains from the wide white beaches and the blue-green sea. Its great, sweeping Guanabara Bay is protected by two majestic sentinels—2310-foot Corcovado, dominated by a giant stone crucifix, and Sugarloaf, or Pão de Açúcar, that distinctive elongated mountain which is a thousand feet lower, but still tall enough to hover over a series of somewhat less stunning peaks which, en masse, convey a "Sleeping Giant," Sugarloaf's part in the anatomy being a bended knee.

Brazilians identify strongly with their home towns and their home states, and there is fairly strong rivalry between *Cariocas,* the residents of Rio, and *Paulistas,* those who live in São Paulo. But this regional chauvinism has its limitations. Rio, to all Brazilians—wharf workers at Salvador, farmers from Pernambuco, business executives of Belo Horizonte, ranchers from the expanses of the *sertão* in the interior, urbanized Indians of the Amazon—is a very special place, a city which every Brazilian rightfully claims as a Brazilian phenomenon.

And it is just that. I suspect Buenos Aires has the kind of ordered urbanity which would appeal to strangers intent on long-range residence. I have no doubt but that one can concentrate on business matters more easily in the commercial atmosphere of São Paulo. I have no quarrel with those who prefer the quieter beaches of Salvador, or even the jungly exoticism of the north. Rio has its limitations in all of these respects, and others. A quarter of its residents, living in hovels on the high mountainside *favellas,* have only the view of the harbor as compensation for the squalor of their existence. Many have never even trekked downward to the bays and beaches, except perhaps at Carnival, once each year.

But for the more fortunate *Carioca,* and the visitor, this city is at once cultural mecca, maritime terminus, industrial complex, beach resort, architectural museum, and fun-town. It is a divided city, in that the natural terrain tends to separate its component parts. Distances from one part to another—from downtown to the popular Copacabana area, for example—are fairly long. And it must be admitted here and now that buses are jammed more often than not, and taxis, particularly after three in the afternoon, are as rare as hen's teeth, though cheap when obtained. Travel agencies, though, are among the best in eastern South America, with imaginatively organized tours and knowledgeable managements and guides; Saturin is among the better ones, and is herewith recommended for introductory forays, along the palm-lined waterfront boulevards, through the maze of the luxuriant *praças,* or squares, in and out of the gleaming skyscrapers and the mellow old churches, up the mountain peaks for panoramic views, to the beaches and the harbor islands, and on delightful out-of-town excursions.

Formerly part of a federal district not unlike the District of Columbia in the United States, Rio, since it was succeeded by Brasília in 1960 as the nation's capital, constitutes the new state of Guanabara. (Neighboring Niterói is capital of the *state* of Rio de Janeiro.)

Since losing the seat of government, Rio has taken a close look at itself, and is undergoing a spectacular rehabilitation in many sections. But two areas of the city have most appeal for the visitor—the central or downtown section whose principal thoroughfare is the inordinately handsome Avenida Rio Branco, and Copacabana Beach. In both, leisurely walks of a morning or afternoon are the ideal sight-seeing method. The Avenida Rio Branco and its adjacent streets and squares is at once Business Rio, Cultural Rio, and Historic Rio. Copacabana has but two functions: its towering apartment houses serve as homes for the wealthier *Cariocas,* and its maze of hotels serve as headquarters for visitors, mainly South American, interested only in the sun and surf, and those, mostly from other continents, who want both the sea and the sights. (Copacabana with its famed mosaic sidewalks and its little-known early-morning fishing fleets, which head to sea in dugout canoes, is the most popular, but not the only Rio beach; others include Vermillion, Ipanema, Leblon—each with a personality of its own.)

It is sad but true that a great many of Rio's attractions get lost in the shuffle. Many visitors content themselves with cable-car rides up Sugarloaf, drives to the summit of Corcovado, shopping expeditions downtown, a night spot or two, and the understandably habit-forming beaches. This program in itself is an eminently satisfactory one, but it omits a great deal. For example:

Colonial churches: São Sebastião Cathedral dates from the mid-eighteenth century, contains the tombs of many noted men, including Cabral, the first Portuguese to see Brazil, and is named for the city's patron saint—for whom, incidentally, the city itself was originally called. Santo Antonio Church, adjoining a convent of that name, was completed in 1615, is decorated in lovely blue Portuguese tiles, and contains among its treasures a silver altar, an exquisite throne, fine old doors, and the tomb of Brazil's first empress. St. Francis of the Penitence Church, with a little museum attached to it, features handsome eighteenth-century gilded walls and a frescoed ceiling. Nossa Senhora da Gloria do Outeiro, adorned with local tiles, was often attended by the imperial family. St. Benedict Monastery, built in 1633, is as much Colonial art museum as place of worship, and has the advantage of a superb hillside, harbor-view situation. Others worthy of visits include Holy Military Cross Church (1811), founded by the order for which it is named; San Francisco de Paula, with carvings by da Cunha, who was born a slave; Our Lady of Candelaria, with its beautiful sanctuary, and small but charming Santa Lucia.

There are a number of important, and interesting, *museums*. The former palace of the Brazilian emperors now houses the most significant, the National Museum, and the interiors of the building, as well as the gardens of the surrounding Quinta da Boa Vista, are quite as intriguing as the varied displays which provide a graphic picture of Brazil. The futuristic Museum of Modern Art is a striking new showcase for representative exhibits of contemporary artists, who are quite as worth knowing as the architects, if one is to have a balanced picture of the vitality of current Brazilian design. The National Museum of Art houses a vast collection of paintings and sculpture, both traditional and modern. The National Historical Museum is appropriately housed in the handsome building which had been the War Arsenal during Empire days. Its highlights are furniture and *objets d'art* of the Colonial period. The National Library is home to a million volumes, many of them old, rare, and very beautiful. The Indian Museum tells, with great clarity, the story of the Brazilian Indian cultures. The Foreign Ministry, like most South American foreign ministries, is housed in a fine old mansion, Itamaraty Palace, which is chock full of priceless furnishings, tapestries, and other art objects. In-

terested visitors need special Ministry permission—not difficult
to come by—for admission. The Ruy Barbosa House, long the
residence of one of Brazil's most noted leaders, is a minor treasure-trove, and open to the public, museum-style. All museums
are closed Mondays, with the exception of the National and Indian
Museums, which are closed Saturdays and Sundays.

Other points of interest would include the ornate Municipal
Theatre, whose lines resemble those of the Paris Opera and at
which one would be wise to take in a performance; Guanabara
and Cattete palaces—the former an ex-royal residence, and the
latter an ex-nobleman's house, both now used as official government residences and not normally open to the public; the spiffy
Jockey Club Race Track, with races on weekends and holidays;
the Praça Mahatma Gandhi with its movie theaters, skyscrapers,
and pleasant gardens; the gracious Praça da Republica, a pleasant
resting place in the center of town; the immense and eye-filling
Botanical Gardens, with rows of stately palms, some seven thousand species of plants, an aquarium and museum; the zoo, with
Brazilian animals and birds the specialties; the verdant mountain
forest of Tijnca, for a day's outing; and many other greens, squares,
and parks, among which is the French-designed Praça Paris, with
its well-manicured formal gardens and illuminated fountains. All
about are the delightful *al fresco* cafés which are a major glory of
Rio, and at every turn in the busier sections of town are stand-up
coffee bars, to which *Cariocas* repair innumerable times each day
for a quick—and when I say quick I mean quick—little *cafézinho*
thick, black, heavily sweetened, and delicious.

I have left till last the two deservedly famous attractions which
most visitors head for first: *Corcovado,* the hunchback-shaped
peak with its great 125-foot, 1200-ton Christ statue, and which
is mountable either by car, bus, or trolley, as far as the base of
the summit, which is reached by train; and *Sugarloaf,* which offers
an equally breathtaking *boa vista* of the city, harbor, and surrounding isles and peaks; accessible by car, bus, or trolley, followed by
an aerial cableway ride to the very top, where there's a restaurant
and playground.

Carnival in Rio, without doubt the most famous pre-Lenten celebration in the world—and with good reason—takes place the four days preceding Ash Wednesday, and hotel accommodations for the period are booked months in advance (as are plane flights to the city). Visitors include Brazilians from throughout the country and holidaymakers from many other countries in South America, as well as the United States. The entire city is aglow. Everyone is everyone else's buddy. Samba groups from the hills, attired in splendid costumes—made with money they have saved for an entire year—compete with each other in open-air contests throughout the city. The confetti-strewn streets are jammed with colorful floats, gaily-bedecked visitors, carefree *Cariocas.* And there are a number of traditional indoor festivities: a dance at one of the leading hotels in Copacabana, another at the enormous hotel in Petrópolis, and—the most difficult to get tickets for—the Grand Masquerade Ball in the Municipal Theatre, where the highlight of the program is the awarding of prizes for the most magnificent costumes; the judges, as one can easily imagine, do not have an easy time making their decisions. In recent years the number of applicants for the seven thousand available tickets has averaged two million. But even if one is denied admittance to one of the gala parties, Rio at Carnival is never disappointing. And it does not celebrate alone: every city in Brazil is simultaneously up to its ears in mass jollity.

Outside of Rio: *Petrópolis* is the most headed-for of the towns in the Rio de Janeiro region, and with good reason. Nearly three thousand feet above sea level, and a beautiful mountain drive from Rio, it makes a delightful destination for either a one-day or an overnight excursion, or for a quiet vacation at its leading hotel, which served as the site of the 1947 Inter-American Conference. Petrópolis was for a time the seat of the court of Emperor Pedro I. His palace, later used as a summer residence by the royal family, is a charming, garden-encircled building which is now open to the public as a museum. (Visitors going through on Sundays and Thursdays may have a peep at the glittering crown jewels.) Also of interest is the cathedral, with its royal tombs; the many handsome villas, some of them country houses of the Rio gentry, and the nearby Serra dos Orgãos National Park, a massive forest with mountains as high as seven thousand feet. *Teresópolis* is primarily a mountain resort with much the same kind of natural setting as Petrópolis, but without its rich historic background. There are pleasant hotels, though, and superb views. *Nova Friburgo,* though at a higher elevation than the earlier-mentioned towns, serves much the same function. And so does the *Itatiaia National Park,* a reserve in the Mantiqueira mountains.

Niterói, the bustling capital of Rio de Janeiro state, is a city of some 200,000, with its fine beaches the chief drawing card for visitors, and an impressive complex of government buildings. Accessible by ferry from Rio, it is the home of a good many American and British families, and has its share of sporting and private clubs.

Something else again is *Volta Redonda.* Since 1942, when it was selected as the site of a steel mill, it has been transformed from a village of no consequence to a model city, housing a population of some thirty-five thousand, most of whom are connected with the steelworks, which are the continent's largest. To many, the town itself, with its handsome houses, gardens, and shopping areas, is of more interest than the mills. However, the latter—with permission secured from the company office (Cia. Siderugica Nacional) in Rio—welcomes visitors. Volta Redonda is one of the most exciting chapters in modern Brazilian history.

São Paulo and Santos: Call it what you will—the World's Fastest Growing City, the Wonder City of the Globe, South America's Blue Chip, the Chicago of the Southern Hemisphere—São Paulo is quite literally fantastic. With a population now estimated to be between 4,000,000 and 4,800,000, it is one of the largest cities in the world, and there seems no end to its growth. Brazilians from throughout the republic migrate to it daily in search of jobs and a new life, and they are invariably successful; the unemployment rate is reputedly about 2 per cent.

New buildings rise at the rate of almost one an hour, industrial production has increased some 30 per cent for each year of the last decade, the number of factories—now exceeding fifty thousand—has doubled in that period, and the city has stretched almost to the port of Santos, on the Atlantic, nearly thirty miles distant.

São Paulo might give the impression of being a brand-new boom town, but it has nothing to be ashamed of genealogically, thanks to its four-century history. A Jesuit priest, Rev. José de Anchieta, from the coastal settlement of São Vicente, is credited with being its founder. He and a small band of followers climbed the heights—following the same route as the modern superhighway—from the coast in 1554. But for three centuries São Paulo was never able to exceed a population figure of twenty-five thousand. Then it came: the coffee boom, in São Paulo state. Between then and the third decade of the present century, some three millions of immigrants from abroad and migrants from elsewhere in Brazil had settled in the state, and its chief city mushroomed.

Blessed with a bracing highland climate, populated by ambitious people who were anxious to succeed, São Paulo throve. With its coffee wealth as a base, and its adjacent port at Santos as a harbor, it went industrial with a vengeance. Today, it turns out well over 60 per cent of Brazil's chemicals, textiles, and pharmaceuticals, and almost all of the country's rubber goods, machinery, and electrical products. Foreign corporations have been drawn to it, a number of them American. Today the visitor will find handsome, park-enclosed factories of such firms as Squibb, Willys-Overland, General Electric, Westinghouse, International Harvester, and even Avon Products, makers of cosmetics. The Germans, French, Swiss, Belgians, and Italians have all invested in São Paulo, too. Wages are the highest in the country, and both the Brazilian and foreign employers treat their employees decently; labor-management relations are sound and healthy. São Paulo's family incomes average $2000 a year—more than twice the Latin American average.

Former President Jânio Quadros was São Paulo's mayor during the most spectacular years of its boom, and his administration saw to it that the city—which could easily have become corrupt during such an economic heyday—kept its feet on the ground. Corruption, understandably rife in Latin America, to a great extent because of absurdly low government salaries, was routed, and public works were constructed with diligence. In 1960 the city undertook a $700-million crash program of public works. It is doing its best to keep up with its unbelievable rate of growth—getting its newcomers out of slums and into decent housing as soon as possible, providing increased power, of which there are adequate sources, and additional public facilities.

As one might imagine, this is not a conventional sight-seeing city. Its most distinguishing characteristic is its superb skyline—in many ways as impressive as Manhattan's, and certainly the peer of any other United States city. It is the skyline that I love most about São Paulo—looked at from a hotel-room window, from the stands of the Jockey Club Race Track, from the air as one approaches on a one-hour flight from Rio (there are a hundred flights a day between the two cities), or from the train as one climbs the plain from coastal Santos.

Specifics? Well, the heart of the city—the downtown *Triangulo*—makes for stimulating walks. And throughout the central area is specimen after specimen of the exciting contribution of the Brazilians to twentieth-century architecture. Take a look at the fifteen-story public library, the State of São Paulo Bank Building, Casa Anglo-Brasíleira, the Companhia Brasíleira de Investimentos, the Pacembu Stadium with its seventy thousand capacity, the University of São Paulo, whose Science Building houses an atomic reactor; the ultra-modern Central Market, with its spic-and-span stalls, fluted pillars, and stained-glass windows, the outstanding Museum of Modern Art, the wide boulevards, the well-manicured parks like the Jardim da Luz, the striking Opera House—one of Brazil's best.

There are more conventional attractions, to be sure. The Butantan Snake Farm, on the outskirts, has a good many thousands of poisonous snakes in residence, used by scientists in their good works. The Ipiranga Museum, where Pedro I proclaimed the independence of the country from Portugal; the Botanical Gardens;

the great coffee *fazendas* beyond the city . . . But these, in a city of São Paulo's dynamism, are anti-climactic. This is a town where the over-all façade—that marvelous skyline, the brisk pace, and the energetic populace, the *Paulistas* themselves—are the attractions. And the *Paulistas,* it must be noted, are as cosmopolitan a conglomeration as you'll find south of Manhattan—Italians, Germans, Japanese, Brazilians from every state of the republic, and a number of Americans, too. They have brought their cuisines, as well as other manifestations of their cultures, with them, so that one can eat well, with the range extending from sukiyaki to *salsa di pomidoro.* One word of warning when you roam: mind the scaffolding; there are as many buildings going up as there are already constructed.

Santos, all too often skipped by travelers who reach São Paulo by air, is as different from its senior-city as night is from day. Despite its eminence as one of the leading ports of the continent (it handled twenty-six million tons of cargo in 1960, including half of the country's coffee exports), it remains, away from the piers, delightfully old-fashioned, architecturally and otherwise. After touring the coffee-loading and storage operations at the piers—and the warehouses are enormous—one is advised to linger awhile at one of the beaches, and perhaps stay over at a resort hotel, of which there are a couple of handsome, elderly ones, in the grand tradition. Trips might be made, too, to the charming resort of *Guarujá* on Santo Amaro Island; the ancient settlement of *São Vicente,* where Brazil had its beginnings; *Alto da Serra,* atop the surrounding mountains, for a superb panorama. São Paulo is linked with Santos by a good railroad and a masterfully-designed, spectacular six-lane superhighway, a ride on which is an experience in itself.

Brasília: Since April 1960, a new city on the plains of Goiaz, in the great underdeveloped *sertão* in the Brazilian interior, has served as the federal capital, replacing Rio de Janeiro, six hundred miles to the east. Brasília is still in the making, and it will be for some years to come. Its streets are as yet largely unpaved, their red dirt has a way of making its presence felt on the clothing of visitors, and it can become a rather unpleasant type of mud when it rains. This is a pioneer city in a pioneer region of an enormous country.

Former President Juscelino Kubitschek brought the new capital to reality. Provision for it has been in Brazil's constitutions for years. Many Brazilians, throughout the country's history, have envisioned a completely new city as the seat of government. Brasília is it at last. Preliminary grading and road-building began in 1955 on the site which was chosen after extensive deliberation among government and professional experts. The following year a nationwide competition was held for the best general plan of the city.

It was won by Lucio Costa, an engineer, who supervised the broad scheme of the new capital, although the principal buildings are the work of the pioneering Brazilian architect Oscar Niemeyer, who is responsible for many outstanding buildings throughout the country, and was a consultant for the United Nations headquarters in New York.

Brasília's basic shape resembles the outline of an airplane, with a residential section extending for some seven miles, at right angles with the public-building section, which includes the Plaza of the Three Powers (executive, legislative, judicial). The plaza contains a striking pair of slim skyscrapers, one for each of the houses of Congress; the Supreme Court of Brazil, and the Executive Department Office Building. This striking cluster, surrounded by a contemporary-style *praça* based on the traditional mosaic technique inherited from the Portuguese and prevalent throughout the country, is flanked by a wide boulevard lined by a series of eleven functional skyscrapers, each identical, and each the headquarters of a government ministry.

Still other parts of the planned city include the Bus Terminal Area, with an adjoining shopping center and a complex series of ramps, escalators, and platforms to expedite transport; the Commercial Areas, with banks, hotels, shops, restaurants; the Communications Area, dominated by a television center; and the residential sections, each of which is an eleven-block contained unit, with a population of five thousand living in sixty-unit apartment buildings, adjacent to their own grammar school, shopping center (including supermarkets), playgrounds, chapels, and cinemas.

Embassy row has been designated, but most of the embassies have still not moved to their headquarters from the buildings they now occupy in Rio; the Brazilian government is giving them a period of several years to do so. But already the location of each embassy has been determined.

Brasília, bordered by an immense artificial lake, considers its show place the president's residence, known as the Palacio da Alvorado, or Palace of the Dawn. There are several handsome hotels, and the temporary air terminal is being replaced by a magnificent permanent one. In addition there are new superhighways which lead to such distant cities as Rio and São Paulo to the southeast, and Belém and Fortaleza, to the northwest.

It is these highways, along with the shuttle-like airways, which give Brasília its reason for being. What the planners of the city envision is the settlement and the development of the interior, as a result of the situation there of the new capital. Some fifty thousand persons, from countries all over the world, live in the Free City—the workers' settlement just outside the new town's limits. Their community, more Wild West than contemporary, will be torn down as soon as adequate facilities are available in Brasília proper. Meanwhile, the Free City is the ideal starting point for a Brasília tour. (By writing ahead, one can arrange to be met at the airport, and guided about—knowledgeably—in as little as a day, if time is short. Address: Sr. José Furia da Silva, Caixa Postal 328, Brasília, D.F., Brazil.)

Reactions to the new capital? They are bound to be very personal. What is sadly lacking, understandably enough, is greenery, landscaping, paved streets, and sidewalks. These, particularly in as flat and physically dull a setting as Brasília's, will help immeasurably. There is, too, a kind of antiseptic quality, engendered, no doubt, by the meticulous section-by-section planning of the town, and one suspects that this stratification of residents, by profession and/or income, might rob the new community of a dynamism which it might otherwise have.

But, withal, there is a great deal that is aesthetically exciting about Brasília: the Palace of the Dawn has the elegance a chief of state's home should have, but none of the ostentation such buildings are frequently burdened with. The saucer-shaped domes which house the chambers of Congress—one inverted, one right-side up—are extremely imaginative, both from the outside and within. The care and detail that has been lavished on relatively minor items, which are so often neglected in new communities, is heartening to witness (I wish the Port of New York Authority would take a look at that bus terminal!). And the spirit of Brasília—the boldness of its conception, the rapidity of its execution, the enthusiasm of its builders, from laborer to architect—and the hope for its future, which epitomizes Brazilian nationalism at its most sublime—all these make one want to go, and afterward, glad one has gone.

Curitiba: Typical of the lesser-known, but nonetheless worth knowing, smaller cities of Brazil, Curitiba is a state capital (Paraná), and the commercial center of a thriving coffee and timber region. With a population exceeding a quarter of a million, heavily Italian, Slavic, and German in background, it is not without an attractive European air. The city center is an area of impressive skyscrapers, wide boulevards, and smart shops. Of interest are the University of Paraná, the Colonel David Carneiro Museum, mostly historical in theme, Ahu Park with its curious mineral springs, a handsome public library and theater, and the complex of buildings of the state government—legislature, courts, secretariat, and governor's palace. Curitiba is generally a stopover point on flights to Iguassú Falls, to the west. Most visitors see only the new air terminal, between planes, and proceed on, but a layover of at least a day and a night is not time wasted.

Iguassú Falls: These falls—and they constitute one of the great

natural wonders of the world—have already been dealt with in
the chapter on Argentina (pages 86–87); they are covered briefly,
as well, in the chapter on Paraguay (pages 170–71). They are
mentioned at this point because they are located where the frontiers
of all three countries meet. One's itinerary determines the approach
to them. For the traveler on a 'Round South America air tour, they
can be worked in conveniently on the way south from Brazil to
Paraguay and Argentina, for there is flight service to them from
Rio de Janeiro and São Paulo via Curitiba. For the visitor wanting
to see them while in Argentina or Paraguay, they are accessible
either by air or by a much longer, but more interesting, boat and
train journey.

The advantage of the approach from within Brazil lies in the
location of the principal hotel on the Brazilian side. One can
practically tumble out of bed from it into the rapids. The Argen-
tine-side hotel (near Puerto Iguazú) is not as convenient. There is
no hotel on the Paraguayan side, as anyone who knows Paraguay
might suspect. However, there are direct flights to and from
Asunción, that country's capital.

The Brazilian approach is via the small, poor, dirt-paved town
called *Foz do Iguassú,* easily seen by car as one drives through it
en route from the airport to the Hotel, a good forty-five minutes
away. Set amid unspoiled, untrammeled woodland, the falls make
Niagara pale in contrast, and for some visitors, they outrank even
Victoria Falls in Africa. (I am not taking sides on the Victoria-
Iguassú issue; *both* are magnificent to me, in their own ways.)
They are so broad that they cannot be seen all at once, except
from the air (and the airplanes I've flown in over them are not
at all co-operative about this, unlike those which fly to the African
falls). There is actually a series of falls, many with paths leading
down to them (some are quite steep), each lovely in its own way.
One simply walks about—a great deal can be accomplished in a
day or two—taking in the vistas of each, snapping away with one's
camera from each breathtaking new angle. Depending on the time
of year, the falls can be as wide as three miles, and as high as

250 feet. Surrounding them, on both Argentine and Brazilian sides, are Texas-size national parks. May to November is the preferred season; the rest of the year it can be uncomfortably hot—but still decidedly worthwhile if one is in the neighborhood.

Belo Horizonte and Ouro Preto, two cities which could not be more dissimilar, can easily be combined on a single visit. The former, a metropolis of half a million and the capital of the state of Minas Gerais, is the country's first planned town. It has, besides a pleasant climate, a pretty countryside and a bustling economy (cotton, mining, diamond cutting, to name three industries), a suburb by the name of *Pampulha* which is a show place of Oscar Niemeyer-designed buildings, among them a pavilion in marble and glass overlooking an artificial lake, the handsome Iate Golf Club, and San Francisco Church, whose murals (by painter Cadido Portinari) have not yet received the approval of ecclesiastical authorities—and the church has not yet been consecrated. Within the city proper the façade of modernity is again worth observing: the broad principal avenues radiate from the hub-like center *praça,* in wheel-formation. There is an interesting City Museum, an exhibition of locally-made products in the Feira de Amostras Building, and a congenial populace, heavily Italo-German descended.

Ouro Preto—Portuguese for black gold—is within excursion distance from Belo Horizonte, but is actually centuries removed from it. It is, more than anything else, a living museum of Colonial Brazil—so much so that the government decreed it a protected national monument in 1933. Now with a population of but ten thousand, its chief contemporary importance is as the site of a Mineralogy Museum and School of Mines. But the prime magnet for the visitor are the well-preserved old buildings, constructed along the hilly cobbled streets. In many of them are paintings of the noted and talented mulatto sculptor nicknamed Aleijadinho (The Little Cripple), because of his disabled hands and feet. All about are enchanting churches, graceful *praças* with fountains playing in their centers, gaily tiled towers, old houses with blooming gardens before them. There are other Brazilian towns with many remaining Colonial traces, but none so all-of-a-piece and cohesive as Ouro Preto. Also near Belo Horizonte, and also with still extant eighteenth-century façades are the beguiling little towns of *Sabará* and *Nova Lima;* wise excursion destinations both, but only after one has done justice to Ouro Preto.

Pôrto Alegre: The most important city in Brazil south of São Paulo, Pôrto Alegre (Gay Port, if you'd like a translation) is an energetic community of a half-million, a goodly percentage of German descent, and many still German-speaking. It's the proud capital of the temperate-zone state of Rio Grande do Sul, the region of Brazil with the highest proportion of literate citizens. And it's also an important industrial center with factories manufacturing a wide range of products, from chemicals to foodstuffs, with coal—mined at nearby *São Jerônimo,* with its model miners' village—providing the principal power.

Handsomely placed along a chain of hills and valleys, Pôrto Alegre is the northernmost point on the immense tidal lagoon known as Lagôa dos Patos. It is just beside a point where five rivers meet, converge into the bigger Guaíba River, and flow into the lagoon, so that one might call it at once a lake port, river port, and seaport, for the lagoon handles ocean-going traffic and itself drains into the Atlantic. Pôrto Alegre has done its best to justify its unique natural setting. Its central portions are a myriad of clean-lined skyscrapers, and its dominant landmarks, aside from these, are a distinctive Governor's Palace, the old Nossa Senhora das Dores Church, and a new cathedral. Beyond the town, there is a wealth of excursion territory—brief drives from the city along the hilly lakeside; bathing resorts along the Guaíba River, such as *Tirsteza* and *Belém Novo; Caxias,* in the heart of the vineyards which provide most of the grapes for Brazil's wines, and *Novo Hamburgo*—heavily German as one might deduce from its name. There are other spots as well—mostly resorts. And there is a road leading straight to the frontier and Uruguay beyond it. The climate is refreshingly mild.

NORTHERN BRAZIL

Salvador (Bahia): Before proceeding one step further with this city—and it is one of the loveliest on the continent—let's clear up its *name*. One hears it referred to as Salvador *and* as Bahia, and one knows also that there is a *state* by the name of Bahia. Here's the score: The full name of the capital city is Salvador-Bahia de Todos os Santos. The state is named just plain Bahia. For a long time the city was also called Bahia, but in recent years, in order to differentiate between the two, the preferred title of the town has become Salvador. However, some people *still* call the city by the name of the state, and there's nothing you or I can do about it, except understand. Chances are, though, when one hears of someone going to Bahia, he's going to the city of Salvador unless he designates a specific locale elsewhere within the state.

That out of the way, what's it like? In a word, it's a dream of a town. More than four centuries old, it was founded in 1549 and has the mellowness which comes only with great age. But it is at the same time perky, gay, and thoroughly engaging. It is a beach resort, a state capital (the name of the state has already been alluded to), a major port (lucky are the cruise passengers who call here), and it is rich in remnants of its Colonial heritage.

Salvador, the Brazilian capital until Rio took over in 1763, was one of the major towns of the northeast during the days when the Portuguese aristocrats throve as owners of the great sugar plantations. Their laborers were enslaved Negroes imported from West Africa—geographically very close to Brazil at this point. The slaves were freed many decades ago by Brazil's last emperor, but the population of Salvador is still predominantly Negro and mulatto. And an attractive, charming, hospitable populace it is. Many of the women still dress in typical Bahia costume, with full, long skirts and gay bandannas around their heads. There is no city in Brazil which appears more relaxed and thoroughly pleasant. And there is none where one feels more immediately at home.

Its African backgrounds impart an unusual tone to the city's folkways. A number of the festivals which earlier city fathers had condemned as "pagan" have managed to survive and indeed today are fostered by the authorities, who are anxious to revive them. *Yemanja* is one of the most important. Wives of the city's fishermen light candles on the beaches and pray to Yemanja—a vain sea goddess—to bring their husbands back from the sea without mishap, and they placate the goddess by offering gifts of combs and inexpensive toiletries which they toss out on the waves. The *capoeira* is a traditional dance, believed to be of West African origin, in which participants do handstands, turn somersaults, and fight each other in sham battle, the object being to not actually touch one's opponent or soil one's clothes. *Capoeira* demonstrations—open to the public—occur frequently, and the art, like judo, is taught by professionals. Tales dating back to slave days still persist. A now-abandoned church in the center of the city is still believed to be haunted by the ghost of a slave who died before it after a whipping, and many Salvadoreans are convinced that the cries of the slave's ghost still echo through the church each night.

Salvador is an upstairs-downstairs city. The lower (*baixa*) town contains the marvelously animate Central Market, near the Praça Cairu; the new harbor, much like great harbors anywhere along the coast, and a considerably more interesting old port, where small craft still tie up while their cargos are unloaded on the hefty backs of the stevedores.

Up above—and there's a modern elevator which takes one on a two-hundred-foot ride for a penny or two—is the upper (*alta*) city. Here, for one thing, is a glorious view of the water from almost any point; for another there are restaurants and hotels and shops and banks, and most appealing, there are the bulk of the hundred-odd churches and the myriad of houses and the exquisite tiled *praças*—many in bad repair, but all gay and beckoning with the sun shining overhead and bright gardens festooning them.

I should head, posthaste, to the recently-opened Museum of Sacred Art, operated by the University of Bahia in the seventeenth-century church and convent of the Descalced Carmelites of Santa Teresa. The edifice itself with its austere white stucco exterior, so typical of Brazilian Colonial churches, has been refurbished by the university. Its lovely convent rooms have been turned into tasteful display-chambers. Students from the university are on duty in each room, and delighted to explain the background of the exhibits. There is a glorious altar in carved, gilded wood; exquisite altarpieces in finely worked, jewel-embedded gold; the original doorways throughout, framed in heavy wood and embellished by gay overhead paintings; statues—*santos*—of all sizes and textures; paintings of saints and priests in the kind of frames which are now so difficult to come by, and the lovely cloister of the convent—quiet, simple, extraordinarily beautiful.

Number Two should be San Francisco Church and Monastery, which was founded in 1587, not too long after Salvador's first settlers set foot on Brazilian soil. Within the church are beams and decorative woodwork of hand-carved rosewood, splashed with gold leaf. The pulpits are considered among the finest in Brazil, and there are some unusually excellent tiles which depict religious scenes, as well as a fine statue of Saint Peter of Alcântara in one of the side chapels.

Other requisites: The cathedral, with its inlaid-wood furnishings, fine marbles, and brilliant gold sun-medallion with the Jesuit order's seal on the ceiling; Nossa Senhora de Carmo (1585) with an outstanding gold-and-silver altar, and a series of unusually massive chandeliers; Bonfim, hardly the most beautiful but by far the most popular of the Bahia churches, and most interesting on Fridays and Sundays, when crowds of worshipers pray at the altar of the Lord of Bonfim (Good End) while scores of vendors cluster about the vestibule, selling religious medals and lottery tickets; and Monte Serrat, where families pray that they will find homes in which to live, and after finding them, hang a duplicate key on the church wall, now a great mass of keys.

I should walk through the always-open gardens of the handsome old Governor's Palace, inspect the gracious House of the Seven Lamps, a mansion-turned-museum, and meander along Rua Chile, the main street, stopping perhaps for a cold drink in one of the many informal cafés. I should take the elevator down to the Central Market and browse for beads or trinkets or the famous Bahia dolls, which are prized by collectors. Or I'd take a bus and swim at the beach in the shadow of the ancient Barra Lighthouse, or at one of the many other beaches—they line the ocean all the way from the heart of town to the airport some twenty miles distant.

In the cool of the evening, just as the sun begins to set, a stroll through the quaintly old-fashioned Dois de Julho Park would be in order, with a rest-stop, perhaps, on one of its giddy wrought-iron benches, to watch swarms of laughing children at their end-of-day games, on the swings and slides. One could look, too, at the Museum of Modern Art in a pavilion which is part of the unconventional but pleasing new Municipal Theatre, at the end of the park, and conclude with a drink in the lounge of the spacious, new, very twentieth-century-Brazilian Hotel da Bahia. It is somehow difficult for the visitor to worry in Bahia, despite its poverty; I suppose that is what sets it apart from most other cities.

Recife and Olinda: The city which Portuguese Commander Henrique Galvao made famous—when the luxury-liner *Santo Maria* put into its port, while the eyes of the world were upon it in 1961—is one of Brazil's oldest, the capital of the state of Pernambuco, and a great seaport and air terminus. Despite its four-century background, it has an amazingly fresh and modern look. Currently it has been experiencing difficult times economically, but still it has had its share of post-World War II building, and is a bracing, alert, cosmopolitan place.

It is also rather peculiarly situated, with three distinct sections separated by water but connected by bridges: Recife proper, actually a peninsula; San Antonia, an island between the peninsula and the mainland, and the mainland itself, known as Boa Vista.

Though not as heavily Negro as Salvador, the proportion is high; total population exceeds 600,000.

Boa Viagem—lining the Atlantic—is the newest residential quarter, and the city fathers are attempting, and not without some success, to turn it into a small-scale Copacabana Beach. Color-accented new buildings—most of them apartments—are already beginning to line its ocean beaches. The visitor arriving by air is hard put to leave this area, so near the airport, for the heart of the city, which truly deserves consideration.

I should recommend a look at two museums—the State, principally because of the fine old mansion it's housed in, and the Popular Art, for its refreshingly unpretentious ceramics—most done by local nonprofessionals. There are a good many old churches. Heading my list would be San Francisco, Santo Antonio, Carmo, Madre de Deus, Pilar, Esprito Santo, and Capela Dourada. There are many more, but if time is limited for antiquities, I should prefer an excursion to suburban *Olinda,* where the Portuguese settled several decades before building Recife, in the sixteenth century, and where later the Dutch were for a while in control. They stayed long enough to leave some souvenirs, among them several churches which were converted into monasteries and convents by the Portuguese. The old portions of Olinda—astride a hill; small, intimate, most attractive—contain such monuments as the Viceroy's Palace, São Bento Monastery (a treasure-trove of furniture, painting, and sculpture), São Francisco Monastery (notable for its wood-carving), and a splendid fountain. Some of the ancient houses remain, too, pink-walled and heavy-doored. And there are good beaches below.

Fortaleza, Natal, Parnaíba, and São Luiz are a quartet of lesser northern cities. None is of exceptional interest to the casual traveler. Of the four, *Natal* is perhaps the most visited, thanks to the international airport, which is called at by many transatlantic services, bound for and coming from European and African points. It is the capital of the state of Rio Grande do Norte, a center for the manufacture of cotton goods, and a port dealing mainly in cotton and sugar. The population is less than 200,000. *Fortaleza,* a good bit bigger, is capital of the state of Ceará, and frequently a port of call for ships coming from Europe and the United States. *Parnaíba,* the smallest of the lot, is of interest mainly because it, too, receives frequent ships from Europe and North America at its piers. *São Luiz,* another state capital—this time the state is Maranhão—straddles a thickly forested region of often heavy rains, and is built upon an island flanked by two bays. Though a city of less than 100,000 population, it is respected throughout Brazil for the inordinate number of good writers and poets it has produced. Though poorish and on the shabby side, it is pleasant and *simpático.* There remain some fine old churches and houses from the much wealthier Colonial era, and the forest is just at the back door.

Belém: Belém is either liked or disliked intensely by visitors. I am among the former, although I will concede to a number of points made by the latter. It is hot and humid and it is falling apart at the seams in spots. But I maintain that it has all of the exotic quality which one should expect in the chief port of the Amazon River.

I think its old harbor jammed with river boats, teeming with the trade and traffic of their Indian occupants, and of Negro stevedores unloading cargoes of rubber and Brazil nuts, is one of the most exciting on the Atlantic coast of South America. I think its market—where one can buy Indian-cured snakeskins, Amazonian dried fish, gaily painted calabashes, and feather fans and alligator skulls—is not the kind of market one comes by too frequently. I love its white marble Paz Theatre—massive, garden-surrounded, formally elegant. And I know of no public park like the Bosque, which is simply a piece of uncleared jungle, *au naturel,* ideal for those travelers unable to get closer to the real thing upriver.

There are other attractions: the fort which remains from the days of the first Portuguese, now the palace of the governor and furnished with pieces of local forest woods; the eighteenth-century cathedral, and the equally old churches of Mercedes and Saint Alexander; the fascinating Goeldi Museum, and the zoo—

alive with caged animals from the adjacent jungle, rainbow-colored macaws, and parakeets in their giant houses.

Belém is not without one major eccentricity. The rainy season is every day of the year, precisely at three in the afternoon, until about four, when it becomes fresher and cooler. There is a great need for a brand-new, fully air-conditioned hotel, and there is a dearth of good restaurants. But everything else that the curious traveler wants abounds in this harbor city at the Amazon's mouth, ninety miles inland from the Atlantic coast.

Manaus: If Belém is an introduction to the Amazon, Manaus *is* the Amazon, or at least a small metropolis in the heart of it. It is 850 miles upriver from the near-coastal port. By boat this means four days; by plane, three hours—flying low over the incredibly wide, forest-bordered river. The boat trip offers compensation for its relative slowness: passage, at first, through the sod-clogged part of the river known as the *Thousand Islands,* past clusters of sleek Indian-paddled dugout canoes, armies of chattering monkeys, small red-roofed towns like *Monte Alegre* and *Santarém,* at whose ports Indians row alongside to sell parrots and their handicrafts; swarms of birds by day and moths by night; Óbidos—named for the still-lovely white city of central Portugal, but a far cry from it; and lastly, a switch from the Amazon proper to one of its tributaries, the Rio Negro—and the harbor of Manaus.

Everything is more up-to-date in Manaus than one might imagine. There's a modern (but poorly-operated) hotel, an opera house so opulent that one is awestruck at seeing it—surrounded by its magnificent mosaic-tile *praça*—in a town of 140,000 people in the midst of the Amazon jungle; a cathedral which is so large that one cannot imagine its ever being filled to capacity; an understandably authentic zoo; wide principal streets with modern shops; delightful residential areas whose streets are dotted with gaily-pasteled houses, their windows filled with curious youngsters' faces, smiling and welcoming; and a trolley line which was South America's first.

How did it all come to be? Manaus is a product of one of

Brazil's relatively minor booms: rubber, which was at its height in the 1800s—the time when the great opera house was constructed by the barons—just before other world markets opened up and the boom fizzled. Since then, the city has lived by its location. There are no roads leading from it, but both the Amazon and the Negro rivers, at whose confluence it lies, take their place, and to it come the products of an enormous region—cacao, rubber, Brazil nuts for the most part, carried by plodding freighters and dugout canoes.

Manaus has government status, too, as the capital of the biggest state in Brazil—a quarter of the state's inhabitants live right in the city. Fussy, turreted ex-villas of the rubber barons now serve as government offices. There are other amenities—a substantial public library, some modern schools and churches among them. But of the city's buildings, it is the opera house—known as the Teatro Amazonas—which stands out. Its great dome is of yellow, blue, and red tiles, and the interior—with a thousand plush seats—is quite as elaborate as counterparts in any great city; the rubber barons would not have had it otherwise. There are pitifully few performances these days, but the building is open to the public, as a monument of a vanished era.

Selvatours, the leading travel agency—which doubles as a civic tourist bureau—operates a variety of river trips, and one is not advised to leave, particularly if one arrives and departs by air, without having a look at the outskirts of the city (i.e., the Amazon jungle). Within a single day a powerboat (with guide) can cover a vast stretch of both the Amazon and the Negro rivers. A highlight would be the confluence of the two—the yellowish Amazon waters and the blackish waters of the Negro, which, like the "blue" and "white" waters of the Nile and like oil and water, do not mix. Beyond, the boat might chug to tiny Indian villages along the river, where visitors are at once made welcome by the entire populace, on hand at the pier. Congenial fathers will have their handsome children at their sides and in their arms; mothers invite strangers to have a look at their stilted, reed houses. Teen-age rubber-tappers explain the techniques of their operations. The school and the church will be thrown open; soft drinks will be served at the tiny store. And after a walk through the dense woods, an entire plot of rubber trees will be seen.

Longer stays permit even more remote trips, into areas where the inhabitants have had virtually no contact with the outer world. Or one may go aboard a ship for a river journey all the way to *Iquitos,* the chief Amazon port of Peru (pages 349–50), and from there head on to the Pacific coast.

Macapá: Often neglected in favor of better-known cities, Macapá is the capital of the virtually uninhabited but immense Amazonian territory of Amapá. It's a short air hop from Belém, and though small—less than thirty-five thousand inhabitants—it is not without interest; there is even a state-operated hotel, and there is also the equator. The town straddles it, exactly. It parallels the jetty just outside the hotel, and promenaders walking two by two find themselves one in one hemisphere, one in the other. Other attractions: old Colonial forts which appear large enough to defend Rio de Janeiro, and gold dust in the river.

WHAT TO BUY

There are lots of interesting things to buy in Brazil, but they're often not at all easy to come across. The one exception is the best buy of all—*semiprecious and precious stones,* Brazilian-mined and Brazilian-mounted. There are rings, brooches, necklaces, and other pieces of jewelry in amethyst, tourmaline (the Brazilian version of a diamond, but *not* a diamond), topaz, and other stones. The best-known firm, as you cannot help but realize after seeing it advertised every time you turn around in South America, is H. Stern; main store in Rio, branches all over the continent. R. Simon is the leader in São Paulo; he has a Rio shop, too, and others throughout Brazil. Both companies guarantee their work and welcome visitors in their workrooms, as well as their showrooms. There are innumerable other gem-dealers, many of them reputable and reasonable. One, with unusually high-styled designs is H. Burle Marx, in Copacabana. *Salvador* is probably the most challenging shopper's town: the Central Market offers hand-woven hammocks in a variety of sizes and striking color combinations, tiny-bead necklaces, pert little clay figurines, iron images of Exu, a highly regarded local spirit, all manner of good-luck charms. At the Agua de Meninos Market there are tremendous varieties of ceramic bowls, both plain and fancy; unusual wooden trunks, gaily paper-lined, and an assortment of baskets. You might find use for the elaborate candles sold before the churches (but mind that you're not going where they'll wither or melt). Genaro de Carvalho (with the aid of his beautiful wife) sells bold tapestries from his handsome studio-house (expensive), and if you are lucky, you'll find the kind of antique you might have use for at such shops as Jorge José Carrapp, David Musse, or Casa Moreira. Other possibilities: *Rio's* chic art galleries offer contemporary paintings, often very handsome (GEA, Julio Senno and Marko, all in Copacabana, are good sources). There is some fine work in lingerie and linen, on sale at such shops as Casa Helio Barki and Casa Veneza, both in Copacabana, and two good Rio antique shops are Casa Anglo-Americana and Henrique Liberal. Top Rio department stores include Sears Roebuck (where have you heard that name before?), Mesbla, and Casa Sloper. The small specialty and men's shops in Copacabana are good for men's swimsuits and sport shirts, and women's blouses. In *São Paulo* there are good buys in locally-made cottons and other fabrics by the yard, at Anna Madeleine, and at the department stores, which again include Sears and Casa Sloper, and Mappin Stores, as well. In the north, in cities like *Belém* and *Manaus,* one can buy folding fans made of exotically-hued bird feathers and plant fiber, alligator skins, decorated gourds, and sometimes-attractive Indian jewelry. Leather goods are sometimes inexpensive but cannot compare with those of Argentina. Air travelers do well to think twice before purchasing bulky, heavy items, for shipping abroad can be difficult and expensive.

CREATURE COMFORTS

HOTELS—**Rio:** The elegant Gloria, at Flamengo between downtown Rio and Copacabana, is perfectly located, with easy access to all parts of the city. It's a hotel of the Old School, in the grand manner, but with such amenities as air-conditioning throughout, a fine restaurant and bar, a handsome swimming pool, and unusually gracious service; Rio's best bet, in my mind. From $6 single. At Copacabana there are a number of hotels, and the only one I would *not* recommend is the highly overtouted Copacabana Palace, where the emphasis is on nasty service more often than not, and where very few rooms are air-conditioned. From $13 single. Others include the Excelsior-Copacabana, opposite the main section of the beach (from $10 single); the Miramar Palace, from $6.50 single; the California, from $7 single, and the Trocadero. Downtown hotels include the San Francisco, from $4 single; the Ambassador, and the Serrador. There are, of course, many others, at a wide price range.

Petrópolis: Quitandhina—enormous, palatial, with a variety of sports, a busy night life, acres of public rooms and gardens, handsome restaurants and bars, and rates starting at $5 single. **Teresópolis:** Fazenda da Paz, Pensao Pinheiros. **Nova Friburgo:** Central, Magnifico, Gloria. **Niterói:** Casino, Balneario. **Volta Redonda:** Bella Vista. **São Paulo:** Jaragua—250 rooms with bath, public rooms, bars, restaurants, and *boîte,* all atop a modern newspaper plant. Good but impersonal service; from $10 single. Othon Palace—about on a par with the Jaragua, but with slightly lower minimum rates; central and modern. Others: Lord, Comodoro, Excelsior, São Paulo, Esplanada, Danubio. **Santos:** Parque Balneario—wonderfully old-fashioned and spacious, on the ocean, and recommended. Also good: Atlantic, Martini, and, in **Guarujá,** Grande Hotel Guarujá. **Brasília:** Until the new Hilton Hotel opens, the Brasília Palace remains the Number One—150 rooms with bath, striking modern design, pool, bar. From $4.50 single. Others:

Nacional—400 rooms with bath, swimming pool, restaurants, bars; Imperial, Lido Palace, Motel Petrobuas. **Curitiba:** Grande, Johnscher. **Iguassú Falls:** Cataratas—attractively designed in Brazilian Colonial style, good food, pleasant rooms, swimming pool, within view of the falls, and with abysmally poor service, there being no competition, at least on the Brazilian side of the falls. Across the frontier in Argentina: Hotel Iguazú—new and pleasant. **Belo Horizonte:** Normandy, Amazonas. **Ouro Preto:** Grande, Tofolo. **Pôrto Alegre:** City—the leader, by far; Plaza Umbu. **Salvador:** da Bahia—handsomely situated, modern, with fine service, and but one drawback (which may only be temporary) —tasteless food. Withal, highly recommended, for one can eat well a block away. **Recife:** Boa Viagem—modern, attractive, and on the beach in the Boa Viagem district. In town, the best is the São Domingo—also new and handsome; followed by the Grande and the Guararapas. Good in a pinch is the Mar Motel, at Boa Viagem—small but new and clean. **Fortaleza:** Palace. **Natal:** Grande. **Parnaíba:** Parnaíba. **São Luiz:** Central. **Belém:** The Grande, one of the Intercontinental chain, is elderly and unprepossessing, but it has been modernized, many rooms have been air-conditioned, and there is now an attractive air-conditioned bar and a dining room. Spotlessly clean and with pleasant service and a central location. But come on, powers-that-be at Intercontinental in New York, how about a brand-new hotel? Belém deserves one! From $7 single. **Marajó:** Marajó—good and government-owned. **Manaus:** The Amazonas is a perfect example of how a hotel can deteriorate when it has no competition. This one, though modern, with many (but not all) air-conditioned rooms and with great possibilities, treats guests as if they were prisoners at Sing Sing; and the food, even on the attractive dining terrace overlooking the Amazon, is barely edible.

RESTAURANTS AND NIGHT LIFE—**Rio de Janeiro:** The hotel restaurants are invariably good; that at the Gloria becomes *al fresco* at night, with the cuisine excellent and the prices moderate. The poolside café and the Bife de Ouro at the Copacabana Palace are both good, the former at lunch. The Chalet, in Brazilian

Colonial décor, is excellent for national dishes, and so are Au Bon Gourmet and Cabeça Chata. Churrascaria Gaucho is tops for Brazilian barbecued meat specialties, and the Albemar for sea food, Brazilian style. There are a number of good French restaurants, including Le Bec Fin, La Crémaillère and Vendôme. Cantina Sorrento and Al Pappagallo are among the best Italian places. Mesbla, atop a skyscraper, offers a superb view of the harbor and good cuisine at the same time, and so does Sears Roebuck's Sky Terrace. There is an excellent restaurant, too, in the new Museum of Modern Art, and among the many restaurants of moderate price in Copacabana is the congenial Le Petit Club. Excursionists will enjoy Os Esquilos at Pico da Tijuca and the Gávea Restaurant, at Gávea. Generally, there is no need for trepidation: if a restaurant looks inviting, give it a try. Rio abounds in pleasant *confeitarias,* which serve alcoholic drinks and snacks as well as tea and soft drinks. Among the many: Colombia, Verde Mar, Cave, Manon, Americana, Brasileira. Among the better bars—these are in Copacabana, where most visitors spend most evenings—are Black Horse, Michel, and Scotch. Two more, these with dancing, are Drink and Arpete. *Boîtes* with entertainment include Fred's (which also serves good dinners) in Copacabana, and the Night and Day Room of the Serrador Hotel downtown. Others include Sacha's—very dark and very expensive; the afore- mentioned Au Bon Gourmet; and the Studium of the Copacabana Excelsior Hotel. **São Paulo:** There are, of course, dining rooms in all the leading hotels, with a standout that of the Excelsior, which features smorgasbord and many inexpensive entrées. A Baiuca is one of the best—very attractive and with a fine international menu; Ca d'Oro is also in the top bracket. Moraes is a good, inexpensive bet for steaks. La Casserole and La Popote are among the better French restaurants. Sino-Braseilero offers good Chinese cuisine, and Trastevere and Cantina Piemontese are among the better Italian restaurants, of which there are many. Almanara is Arabic; 707, Yugoslavian; Gourmand, Hungarian; Nova Tokiwa, Japanese. Zillerthal and Brahma both specialize in German dishes. São Paulo night spots include Michel's and the Oasis with entertainment; the Boîte African, Jardim de Inverno Fasano, and Captain's Bar. Fasano, Mappin, and the Viennese are among the many good *confeitarias*. This is an excellent town for all kinds of food. **Santos:** The Parque Balneario Hotel's dining room is among the best, and there is a night club in the hotel, too. Others: Atlantico Bar, Casa Hesperia, Ibicaba, Pioneiro. **Brasília:** The hotel dining rooms and *boîtes* are good, but inquire about new restaurants and cafés which are opening up all the time. **Salvador:** The Paris serves excellent lobster and other sea foods, and until the Hotel da Bahia dining room improves, it is an excellent substitute and just a block away. Others: Anjo Azul, Chez Bouillant. **Recife:** Besides the restaurants in hotels like the Boa Viagem and the São Domingo, there are a number of others, Leite being among the best. L'Hermitage and Sambura are top night spots. **Manaus:** There are no restaurants to recommend, but the Acapulco is the only gambling casino in all Brazil; drinks, too, of course.

PRIVATE CLUBS—**Rio de Janeiro:** Brazilian Press Association, American Chamber of Commerce and American Society, American Club, University Club (for alumni and undergrads of U.S. colleges), Lions, Rotary, both the YM and YWCA, Gavea Golf and Country Club, Yacht Club, Rio Country Club. **São Paulo:** Automobile, Jockey, Scandinavian, São Paulo Golf.

Brazilian food specialties: Brazilian cuisine is distinctive in South America, and shows influences from Africa and from the Brazilian Indians, as well as from Portugal and the other European countries. It can be delicious. *Feijoada* is the national staple. Basically, among the poor, it is generally black beans and rice, but added to it in most restaurants are such ingredients as sausage, beef, tongue, pork, vegetables, and a variety of spices. Don't leave Brazil without getting to know it. Also typical, and very popular, is *vatapa,* a kind of stew with either shrimp or fish as the principal ingredient, coconut milk or palm oil can also be included. *Empadinhas* might well be called shrimpburgers with a pastry shell, and often contain a Brazilian delicacy, heart of palm. The beef specialty, of southern origin, is *churrasco* —broiled fillet with peppers, onions, and sometimes manioc flour.

Sea foods of all kinds are invariably excellent near the coast. There is a great variety of fruit, both temperate and tropical, including pineapple, guava, and two uniquely Brazilian ones worth trying: jaboticaba and genipapo. Coffee is, of course, a national institution, and delicious when served strong, black, and with sugar in demitasse cups—then called *cafézinho*. The beer is cheap, and not bad, and the same can be said for Brazilian rum, gin, and wine. There are many soft drinks, most of them gooey-sweet, but the ubiquitous colas are, needless to say, everywhere available. Imported liquors are expensive. For an authentic, and charming, introduction to the cuisine of this country, consult *The Art of Brazilian Cookery,* by Dolores Botafogo (Doubleday, 1960).

THE GUIANAS

British Guiana
French Guiana
  (Guyane Française)
Surinam
  (Suriname)

Entry requirements: *For* British Guiana—*no visa, simply return or onward transportation ticket and proof of U.S. citizenship (passport or birth certificate). For* French Guiana—*no visa, simply passport and yellow-fever certificate. For* Surinam—*no visa, simply passport or other proof of U.S. citizenship, return or onward transportation ticket.* **Best times for a visit:** *This is a moist part of the world, but the rains are not incessant, even during the wet seasons, which are as follows:* British Guiana and Surinam: *Mid-November through January, April through July;* French Guiana: *November through January, April through June. Average temperature is about 80°, and humidity is high, but fresh trade winds do a surprisingly effective cooling job along the coast.* **Currencies:** British Guiana—*the British Eastern Caribbean Territories (ECT) dollar (formerly known as the BWI—or British West Indies—dollar), which equals about fifty-eight U.S. cents.* French Guiana—*the franc, equal to about twenty U.S. cents.* Surinam—*the guilder*

(also called the florin), equal to about fifty-three U.S. cents.
Film availability: *One is well-advised to have adequate supplies upon arrival, particularly of color film.* **Languages:** British Guiana *is the only South American country whose official language is English; this is replaced by Dutch in* Surinam *and French in* French Guiana, *although a good bit of English is spoken in both of these. Other languages of British Guiana and Surinam: Javanese, Hindi, and talkie-talkie—an English dialect.* **Domestic transport:** *Steamers ply between coastal ports, and upriver to interior regions; there are limited road and rail networks, mostly concentrating on coastal areas; and domestic airlines (British Guiana Airways, Surinam Airways, SATGA in French Guiana) serve major points of interest.* **Tipping:** *Ten to fifteen per cent, where service charges are not included.* **Business hours:** *Shops and offices usually open very early, about 7* A.M., *close from 1* P.M. *to 3* P.M. *and then again at 5* P.M. **Further information:** British Guiana—*British Guiana Tourist Committee, Georgetown, British Guiana; British Information Services, 30 Rockefeller Plaza, New York,* French Guiana—*French Government Tourist Office, 610 Fifth Avenue, New York; French Embassy Press and Information Division, 972 Fifth Ave., New York. Préfecture, Cayenne, French Guiana.* Surinam —*Surinam Tourist Bureau, 10 Rockefeller Plaza, New York; Surinam Tourist Development Board, Paramaribo, Surinam. Both British Guiana and Surinam are members of the Caribbean Tourist Association, 20 East 46th Street, New York, which is also an information source.*

INTRODUCING THE GUIANAS

The little-visited and long-neglected Guianas, even though one is internally self-governing and another is virtually independent, are all that remain of Colonial South America. Ironically, their colonizers—the British, French, and Dutch—lost out elsewhere on

the continent to the two powers—the Spanish and Portuguese—
whose New World empires (which constituted all the rest of South
America) revolted and became independent republics more than
a century ago.

The Guianas—whose name means "land mass surrounded by
water" and which are encircled by the Orinoco and its tributaries
as well as the Caribbean—were discovered by the Spanish, but
neither they nor the Portuguese concerned themselves with settlement. What they most coveted—gold (not chanced upon until
centuries later) and quantities of indigenous inhabitants whom
they could enslave to do their work—was lacking in the Guianas,
whose fortunes fell into the hands of other European empire
builders, one of which gave up its claim to the then profitable
colony of New Amsterdam (now New York) in exchange for some
Guiana territory.

It is only in recent decades, thanks to the influence of the post-
World War II independence movements in Africa and Asia,
that the European occupiers of the Guianas began to concern
themselves much with the human beings resident; until then these
countries had been considered little more than sources of valuable
natural resources and rich tropical crops by the British and Dutch,
while the French made additional use of its Guiana as a penal
colony—the most infamous in the world, and at long last defunct.

Today, the Guianas remain sparsely populated. Though about as
large in area as Sweden, they are home to fewer than 900,000
persons, the great majority of whom—this is another Guiana
anomaly—are of Asian and African descent. But their future is
brighter than it has ever been. Health problems, long a major
scourge of the region, are largely solved. Communications and
transportation challenges are being met. The literacy rate is higher
than in many neighboring republics. Towns and cities are being
cleaned up and modernized. Tourism is being developed as an
industry. Lost time—a great deal of it—is being made up for.

A backward glance: Alonso de Ojeda—a sailing mate of
Christopher Columbus—and Amerigo Vespucci first sighted the
Guianas on their voyage along the Caribbean coast of South

America in 1499, but the Spanish, who made feeble attempts at settlement, gave up by the latter part of the sixteenth century, leaving the field wide open for others. Sir Walter Raleigh, in 1595, sent back glowing reports to England and spurred on the arrival of countrymen, as well as some Dutch, who went ashore in what is now British Guiana in 1596. Within a couple of decades, the British were in what is now Surinam (Dutch Guiana), and shortly thereafter the French had founded Cayenne, one of whose earliest exports—a hot pepper—took the little capital's name and made it world-famous out of all proportion to its actual importance.

Colonization continued, and so did squabbling among the three powers, whose Guiana territories were swapped back and forth among them over a period of centuries, in the best tradition of imperial checker-playing. The British, in 1667, gave the Dutch what is now Surinam in exchange for New Amsterdam, which they promptly renamed after the Duke of York and which has prospered rather considerably in the ensuing years, though not entirely under British auspices.

At one point the Dutch held all three Guianas, and during another period the trio reverted to the British, with the French darting in and out of the game. It was not until 1817 that all three nations sat down like gentlemen and agreed upon the division which has persisted to this day.

During all of this period, the colonists attempted in several ways to alleviate the labor shortage which plagued them, there not being nearly sufficient native Indians to do their bidding. The first imported labor was from Africa—shiploads of Negro slaves who, it was expected, would do the trick, but who didn't. Many promptly proceeded, not long after arrival, to escape into the wilderness and set up villages much like those they had lived in at home. Many, to this day, are at the same stage of development as they were at that time, and to differentiate them from urban Negroes are designated by the unattractive appellation Bush Negroes, although whites who live in the country are never, for some strange reason, known as Bush Whites to separate them from others of their race who are town dwellers.

The Asian influx: Slavery was legally abolished in the mid-eighteenth century, by which time the British and Dutch settlers had taken a new tack on imported labor, India being the source. Still later, the Dutch colonies of the Pacific yielded many thousands of Javanese. Both Indians and Indonesians came as indentured servants and upon completion of their contracts chose, by and large, to remain in the cities. Their descendants, particularly in British Guiana and Surinam (together with descendants of Africans and creoles—persons of mixed blood) now make up the majority of the population. The indigenous Indians, a small minority, are for the most part unintegrated with the other racial groups. They, too, have been given a special name. So that they will not be confused with East Indians and their descendants, they are known as Amerindians (a contraction of American and Indian). Europeans are, of course, the tiniest minority, but in all three Guianas there is no offical color bar, although each racial group has retained most of its traditional ways, and lives, for the most part, independently of the others. The visitor today to the Guianas is greeted by the rich cultures of each, and at the same time, by the modern façades of the Guianas, each at a separate stage of political evolution.

French Guiana, smallest in area, by far the tiniest in population, and poorest in resources, is the closest to a colony, in the old-fashioned sense, although it has been officially termed, since 1946, an "Overseas Department," sending a delegate and a senator to the Parliament in Paris, and with the same technical status as a department of the metropolitan motherland. Its governor, called a prefect, is, however, appointed in Paris, although his powers are somewhat diluted by an elected General Council.

French Guiana's two most noted citizens of recent times—both Negro—gained their reputations abroad: Félix Eboué was governor of French Equatorial Africa during World War II, was instrumental in that colony's siding with the Free French forces and was host of the Brazzaville Conference at which General de Gaulle's government of the time planned for post-war reforms which led to independence for French Black Africa. Gaston Mannerville has been president of the French Senate since 1947, and is, as such, the second-ranking official of the Paris government.

Surinam has been the official name of Dutch Guiana since 1954, when The Hague government granted its people complete control of their domestic affairs, as well as representation in the Dutch Parliament. Foreign affairs, including diplomatic representation abroad, are still functions of the Dutch. The governor of Surinam, appointed by the Dutch government, is the offical representative of Queen Juliana, but Surinamese affairs are actually conducted by a Surinamese prime minister—or minister-president, as he is called—elected by the members of the Legislative Council, whose members are themselves elected by the people. The current minister-president is S. D. Emanuels, whose administration's chief program is an ambitious ten-year development plan, touching every facet of the country's economy.

British Guiana—largest in area, population, and wealth of the three—had been since 1930 (with the election of the first Legislative Council) on the way toward self-government, but very gradually, and by the time a new constitution was approved by the Colonial Office in 1953, a considerable segment of the Guianese community had become impatient at the long delays, and was in a hurry for needed change and reform. As a result of the election of a new House of Assembly, following the promulgation of the 1953 constitution, the majority was retained by the People's Progressive Party, headed by Dr. Cheddi Jagan, an independent-minded, progressive dentist of East Indian extraction, whose wife is American. Because of what the British termed in a disputed White Paper "a dangerous crisis in both public order and in economic affairs" and "to prevent Communist subversion," the 1953 constitution was arbitrarily suspended. The ministers of the new government—all PPP members—were deprived of their duties, the governor was given emergency powers, and an interim government ruled until 1957, when elections were again held, with Dr. Jagan's party once again the winners. An Amerindian, of another party, was elected to the legislature for the first time in the colony's history. Other parties became stronger at this time, two merging to become the People's National Congress, and constituting the chief opposition.

Dr. Jagan, who became Minister of Trade and Industry, and his colleagues embarked on a policy of co-operation with the then governor, Sir Patrick Renison, to the extent that in 1960, at a Constitutional Conference in London, the British government accepted the principle of independence for British Guiana.

Complete internal self-government was granted the colony in August 1961, following colony-wide elections at which the People's Progressive Party (mainly East Indian in its following) captured a majority of seats in the legislature, with Dr. Jagan emerging as the new prime minister. The People's National Congress, headed by Forbes Burnham, and dominantly Negro in its support, came out second, and the conservative United Force, headed by Peter d'Aguiar, a Roman Catholic industrialist of Portuguese descent, trailed far behind in third place. The pro-Communist label which was pinned on the American-educated Dr. Jagan earlier in his career still sticks. Segments of U.S. opinion seem determined to make of Jagan a South American Castro. Dr. Jagan, however, pledged himself and his party to the principles of parliamentary democracy, at the time of the election. He also made clear his desire to participate in President Kennedy's Alliance for Progress program, and he indicated that British Guiana wanted to align itself economically with the countries of the Western Hemisphere. In October 1961, he made a personal appeal for U.S. aid, in talks with President Kennedy, at the White House.

There is no doubt but that British Guiana's foreign policy will be one of active neutrality. Dr. Jagan is explicit, too, about his party's objectives: "It is," he said, "dedicated to the goal, to the ideal of socialism." But there still remains no reason why the United States should not welcome and support this little country as a friend, and provide aid for it just as it does other Latin American states (the Fascist dictatorships included). The New York *Times,* in an editorial just after the election, put it this way:

"If British Guiana is handled by the United States with some understanding, sophistication and sympathy, there is every reason to hope it will become a desirable member of the inter-American system."

YOUR VISIT TO THE GUIANAS

All three Guianas can be conveniently combined on a single visit, thanks to frequent air services which link their capitals, and connect the region to adjacent Caribbean and South American points. Of the three, tourism is at its most developed in Surinam, whose government has pioneered—along with that of Colombia— in encouraging foreign visitors through the opening of tourist offices both in its capital and in the United States, and through the organization of improved facilities—including a sleek new de luxe hotel and packaged itineraries—for visitors. The Guianas are as offbeat on South American itineraries as Paraguay, but they have the advantage over that pathetically impoverished dictatorship, of cultures which represent the peoples of four continents, close proximity to the United States, unusually exciting natural phenomena (including one of the great waterfalls of the world), comfortable accommodations, and peoples at last beginning to participate in their country's own affairs who are glad of the opportunity to dispense a unique hospitality which deserves to be much better known than it is.

BRITISH GUIANA

Georgetown: Home to nearly a fifth of the population of British Guiana (which has but half a million inhabitants), Georgetown is the capital, commercial center, and chief port of the colony, and while hardly an exciting metropolis, is at once friendly and attractive, with wide, tree-lined streets and a number of unusual public buildings. Its chief appeal are its residents—Asians from both Indonesia and India, Negroes, creoles, Amerindians, and, of course, the British, best seen in the colorful mass and organized confusion of the Stabroek Market, whose wares reflect the varied backgrounds of their makers.

Of Georgetown's two great attractions, one—the Guiana Museum—burned some years ago; its collections are now dispersed to several sites, the most important going to the Carnegie Free Library, where the displays include those which relate the story of the Amerindians, the country's first inhabitants. The second landmark is the Botanical Gardens, whose 180 acres, just outside of town, contain what are reputed to be some of the world's finest collections of palms, orchids, and lotus lilies, and there is a handsomely-designed zoo adjoining, with unique animals of the region. I should not miss, either, the curious Anglican cathedral, which also has an international distinction—that of being the tallest wooden structure on the globe.

Also on most itineraries are the well-kept government buildings housing the Legislative Council, the government offices, and the courts; the fairly modern Technical Institute (British Guiana still has no university of its own), the veddy British cricket clubs, whose grounds are said to be the finest for that sport in the tropics. Hotels are small, hardly luxurious, but pleasant and perfectly adequate for the short time most visitors need to get to know the city. If one's holiday is limited, part of it should be allotted to what lies beyond.

The sugar estates: Sugar being the country's chief crop, one would be wise to have a look at a sugar estate. There are twenty-one of them, of which twenty are controlled by only three companies, which also dabble in retail stores. Booker Brothers, the biggest, owns almost three-quarters of the estates and even operates its own shipping line. About a third of British Guiana's workers are employed by the sugar interests, and some eighty thousand of them live on the estates. Many are the descendants of indentured Indians who had been housed on the estates during the time they were workers, but who had no place to move when their contracts expired. They and their offspring have stayed on, rent free, and the government is only just beginning to undertake new housing schemes which will make it possible for them to be relocated. This housing situation is one of the country's most chronic problems, and the cause of a great deal of discontent.

Mackenzie: Bauxite rivals sugar as the chief income-producer for the country. The largest bauxite resources in the world are at Mackenzie, sixty miles up the Demerara River, at whose mouth Georgetown lies. The mines are operated by an affiliate of the Aluminium Company of Canada (Reynolds Metal of the United States is at another smaller site). Some ten thousand people live at Mackenzie, nearly twenty-five hundred of them employees of the mines. Cleared from the deep forest by which it is surrounded, the community is well-run, mostly Negro, with good labor conditions and decent facilities. Though not an incorporated city, Mackenzie is the second largest community in the country, after Georgetown.

New Amsterdam (not to be confused with the North American community which once had that name but is now called New York) is the chief town of eastern British Guiana, but I should not bother heading for it, unless business called me. *Bartica,* in the interior, is more remote but eminently more interesting. This is the departure point for miners en route to the country's diamond and gold fields. It's also the place to which many Negroes, employed in the mines and on the plantations, come for relaxation in between contracts, and it's situated handsomely at the confluence of the Mazaruni, Cuyuni, and Essequibo rivers, three streams whose waters are a brilliant purple-blue. This is sometimes a stop-over point for travelers en route to what is British Guiana's most fantastic natural attractions, Kaieteur Falls.

Kaieteur Falls: One can reach the falls by an overland route embracing boat, truck, and shoe leather, in a week—eminently worthwhile for the hardy and curious, but heavy going for many travelers. A more popular approach is via plane, leaving early in the morning from Georgetown and returning that evening, or staying over a night or two at the nearby Garraway Stream Rest House, and taking in the British Guiana Consolidated Goldfields at *Mahdia* before returning.

The falls are the highest of the "bridal" variety in the world, with an unbelievable drop of 741 feet, and a width—not inconsiderable for cataracts so high—of some 300 feet. The flight en route from the capital is over rugged, verdant jungle, and the plane lands after passing over a ten-mile gorge and the falls themselves. A flying boat, it puts down a half mile above the falls. There's a trail to the brink, and paths to other lookout points. On the one-day outing, passengers eat lunch picnic-style in full view of the tumbling falls (and their spray!) and after a leisurely two- or three-hour stay, return to the city. Kaieteur Falls are five times as high as Niagara, and rank right up there with Victoria, in Rhodesia, and Iguassú, a few thousand miles south, on the Argentine-Brazilian-Paraguayan border. To not see them, if one is in British Guiana, is to miss one of the major travel experiences of the continent.

FRENCH GUIANA

Though three times the area of Holland, French Guiana has an unbelievably tiny population: Excluding some Amerindians in the remote interior who have never made themselves available to census-takers, there are only about thirty thousand persons living in the country, and about half are in the capital, Cayenne. What it lacks in humans, French Guiana makes up for in rivers (some twenty of them, all of which drain into the Atlantic), magnificent forests in which there are superb species of rare woods, and, lying between the deep forests and the low coast, vast plains. There are, as well, half a dozen respectably high mountain peaks in the Tumuc-Humac range, and there are, of course, those notorious islands which served as penal colonies. Their name—ironically, Îles du Salut—translates as Islands of Salvation, but they were hardly that for their inhabitants, particularly the one known as Devil's (du Diable), where the prison was closed in 1945—thanks in part to the patient crusade of a French Salvation Army officer.

French Guiana has tremendous tourist potential—its Amerindian and Negro villages on the rivers of the verdant interior could be superb destinations for visitors if they were more easily accessible, and if there were facilities for overnight stays. Still, the country is so remarkably offbeat and underdeveloped that one does well to include it in a Guiana tour, if only to contrast it with its more prosperous and advanced neighbors.

Cayenne: Hardly a metropolis, even by the standards of the two other Guianas, Cayenne is a community of some fifteen thousand French, Negro, Chinese, and creole inhabitants, among whom live a scattering of ex-Devil's Island convicts. It has spruced itself up a bit in recent years, boasts a surprisingly good hotel, offers swimming at a fine beach, and has a rather pleasant central area. The core of the town is the Place des Palmistes, part of which is taken up, rather incongruously, by a group of tennis courts. There are also: an unusual and small but interesting museum, with displays arranged in the thorough, meticulous French style; the rather grand residence of the prefect, or governor, of the colony; the pretty Botanical Gardens, hardly of the caliber of those in Georgetown; and a fairly modern stadium. Water buffaloes can be seen pulling carts in the streets, and the foliage, even in the heart of the town, is lush and properly tropical, wild orchids embellishing some of the trees. Drives can easily be made to the jungle which borders the town, so thick that in certain parts the sun never penetrates. And there are other excursions available, most by water.

Boat trips: If arrangements are made a few days in advance, a voyage upriver to a gold-mine camp is an excellent outing, undertaken in less than a day. Still other river excursions can be made to villages on the banks, with motorboats and powerized canoes the means of transport. Once a month a government launch goes to the *Îles du Salut,* but not to *Devil's Island,* one of the group. The stop is made instead at *Royale Island,* which was a prison for the mentally ill. Still to be seen are the old chapel, commandant's house, bakery, and cell blocks.

Other points: *Saint Laurent,* near the Surinam border, is the

Number Two city, with some two thousand inhabitants and the ruins of the penal colony, which made its name a feared one as far away as France. It is a good departure point for Surinam and for expeditions into the interior, where destinations might be gold mines, rosewood forests, and Amerindian communities. Gold is the chief export, emphasized at the expense of agriculture and increased exploitation of the rich forests. Needed too: roads, roads, roads, a policy which would encourage immigration from abroad, and conditions which would make immigration attractive.

SURINAM

Surinam's flag—rarely seen beyond its borders because the country, though self-governing, is not sovereign—is one of the most imaginatively designed of the new nations. Five stars of different colors are unified by an elliptical band—the black star represents Negroes; the brown, the creoles or mulattoes; the yellow, the Asians; the red, the indigenous Indians, called Amerindians; and the white, the Europeans. Between them, they have evolved a workable, relatively harmonious society, considerably richer because of the cultural contributions of each. Fortunately for the visitor, Surinam has taken steps to make tourism a profitable industry. Hotel facilities are the best in the Guianas, and an astonishing variety of tours make an introduction to the country easier than in the other Guianas.

Paramaribo: Biggest of the three Guiana capitals, Paramaribo (population 105,000) manages to retain an unmistakably Dutch façade, its polyglot population notwithstanding. It is as well-scrubbed a city as one is likely to find in the tropics, but it has a great deal more to its credit than cleanliness, which by itself has never seemed to me the only criterion by which to judge a place. Minutes from the jungle, it manages to have a big-city sophistication, thanks perhaps to its white-frame houses (some pillared and Colonial, others turreted and Victorian); the soft green lawns of its Oranje Square, flanked by the handsomely-proportioned Governor's Mansion and the rambling secretariat of the government; and its wonderfully animated, multicolored market and waterfront, with erect Negro women (Kotto Missies they're called) wearing the great billowing costumes which are their proud trade-mark, East Indian ladies in vibrant saris and jewels, Amerindians, bronzed and minimally clad, Indonesians in the costumes of their native Java, and Europeans, the men in crisp whites, the women in casual cotton frocks.

There are other pleasant landmarks: a small but charming Palm Garden, a botanical park, streets whose pavements are taken up with both donkey carts and bicycles (the favored means of transport in Holland) as well as autos, and along whose borders are exotic mahogany and tamarind trees, brilliant poinciana, towering royal palm. To be noted also are the religious edifices of Paramaribo's residents—a Moslem mosque, a Hindu temple, a Roman Catholic cathedral, a Jewish synagogue, and many Protestant churches. The Surinam Museum should be a requisite for visitors, those who cannot see more of the country than the capital, as well as those about to embark for the hinterlands, choosing from trips like those which follow.

Excursions from Paramaribo: Cars, river steamers, dugout canoes, and airplanes, all are utilized for imaginatively-planned excursions from the capital, organized by the travel agencies, with dates and itineraries approved by the Surinam Tourist Development Board. A requisite should be a *boat trip up the Saramacca River*. In a half day one visits the Negro village named *Harlem* (its antecedent being the city by that name in Holland, not the great New York City Negro community), as well as contrasting East Indian and Indonesian settlements built in clearings along the jungle-bordered river. Still another half-day trip is through the *Commewijne District,* by ferry across the Suriname River, affording a striking view of the Paramaribo skyline and waterfront, and thence by car through the great plantations to *Nieuw Amsterdam,* at the confluence of the Suriname and Commewijne rivers. En route there are visits to a sugar refinery, rum distillery, and Javanese community. A car tour of about the same length can be made through the *Surinam District,* to the river port of Domburg, past bauxite mines, and to an Amerindian village with a most un-Amerindian name: *Bernhard Dorp.* With a full day at one's disposal the destination might be *Joden Savannah,* by car to Paranam, site of an important bauxite-processing plant, and then by boat along the Suriname River to Joden Savannah, and the ruins of the Berachaahve Salom Synagogue and its cemetery. Joden Savannah (*Joden* means Jewish in Dutch) was one of the first Jewish settlements in the New World; its original inhabitants were Sephardic Jews who came north to Surinam in the seventeenth century, after being expelled from Brazil. An exceptionally interesting overnight trip is to the *Marowijne District,* beginning with a flight from the capital to *Moengo,* a hundred miles up the Cottica River, and the headquarters for the bauxite-mining operations of a subsidiary of an American corporation. From Moengo one can continue to *Saint Laurent,* the former penal colony just over the border in French Guiana (see pages 155–56), and stop also at the Amerindian village of *Bigiston,* and at *Negro Creek,* whose residents are specialists at performing the so-called voodoo fire dance, the spectacular highlight of which is the immersion of the dancers in a bed of hot coals, after which they rub their bodies with flaming branches and, for good measure, anoint themselves with boiling water.

Nieuw Nickerie, the second city of Surinam, can be reached by plane in a few hours, or by boat in a day, and from it one can drive into the great surrounding rice plantations, or with more time, hunt for alligators in the irrigation canals. A more elaborate journey, requiring five or six days and a good-sized bankroll, might be made for sight-seeing or hunting-fishing purposes to a variety of points in the magnificent jungles of the interior and to *Stoelmans Island* in the Marowijne River. The streams are full of a variety of fish, and the forests offer to the hunter wild pig, deer, and wild duck in profusion.

Of special interest, particularly for travelers who would like to approach Surinam from the nearby Caribbean island of Trinidad and return immediately to it upon their departure, are the Jungle

Cruises operated by the Alcoa Steamship Company. The trip totals six days, Trinidad to Trinidad. From that island the ships—whose prime functions are to load up with bauxite ore at Alcoa's Surinam mines—sail up the Commewijne and Cottica rivers to Moengo, bypassing Paramaribo, or go via the capital, up the Suriname River, to the mines at *Paranam,* this latter trip embracing wilder, more remote country. Because these ships were constructed especially for river service, they are of shallow-draft design, which means they tend to roll a bit in the open sea, and the refreshingly candid Alcoa Line advises that elderly or physically disabled travelers are wise not to travel on them. For others, though, they can serve as a marvelous entree to Surinam and its interior.

WHAT TO BUY

The public markets of all three Guiana capitals, and those in the smaller towns and settlements, are shopping centers for a profusion of crafts, representing the cultures of the varied populations. **British Guiana:** Georgetown has a number of small shops run by East Indians who sell beaten brasswork, gold and silver jewelry, and a variety of smaller Eastern-design crafts. In Stabroek Market, outstanding wares are those of the Amerindians—beaded aprons, bows and arrows, blowpipes, basketry, and if one is lucky, brilliantly-plumed headdresses. Bargaining is the rule in the markets and small shops, as well as with the occasional itinerant peddlers one sees at hotel entrances. **French Guiana:** Here the Amerindian crafts, similar to those in British Guiana, are the most interesting buys, either from peddlers, at the Cayenne market, or from the source: villages in the interior. Look for inlaid boxes and trays of tropical woods, flowers fashioned of feathers, gold jewelry, and unusual items decorated with the blue wings of Morpho butterflies. **Surinam:** Paramaribo's marvelous market abounds in crafts similar to those of the other Guianas, with bargaining again the rule. Travelers visiting the interior will want to browse at village markets, too, where prices are often cheaper, and where artisans often double as salesmen, vending wares they themselves have made.

CREATURE COMFORTS

British Guiana: *Georgetown's* leaders are the Park and Tower hotels, both with some air-conditioned rooms, restaurants, and bars; the Tower has a new fully air-conditioned wing, and swimming pool. From $7 single. Others: Woodbine, Palm Court; there are a few fairly good pensions, as well. The Garraway Stream Rest House near *Kaieteur Falls* is the most comfortable place in the interior. In order to stay over, on a visit to *Mackenzie,* advance arrangements must be made with the operators, Demerara Bauxite Company, an affiliate of Aluminium Limited.

French Guiana: The modern Montabo Hotel serves excellent French food, and is suprisingly good, with a handsome situation two hundred feet above the sea on Montabo Hill; Devil's Island is visible on clear days. From $6 single. The second, and only other, Cayenne hotel is the definitely inferior Palmistes.

Surinam: Queen of hostelries in the Guianas is Paramaribo's spanking-new Torarica, a combination hotel-casino operated by the Condado Caribbean Hotel Corporation, which also operates a hotel on the Dutch island of Aruba. Opened in 1961, the Torarica has eighty rooms with bath and balcony overlooking the Suriname River, a swimming pool, *boîte,* restaurant, coffee shop, and, of course, a casino. From $13 single, European plan. More central, in the heart of *Paramaribo,* are the older and smaller Palace, on Oranje Square ($11 single, with meals), Vervuurt, in the business center and with a roof-garden restaurant ($8 single), and Kersten, atop a department store ($7.50 single). All have some air-conditioned rooms, good restaurants, and bars. There are also smaller hotels and pensions, invariably clean and well-run. Although food at Cayenne's Hotel Montabo is undis-

putably good French fare, there is considerably more variety in
Paramaribo. There, the Hotel Vervuurt's specialty is the twenty-
one-dish Dutch-Indonesian *rijsttafel,* and one also can find the
more traditional Netherlands dishes like pea soup with sausages,
plus Indian curries, Chinese cookery, and creole dishes, including
pom, served at the Palace Hotel, a unique kind of chicken pie
with a crust of *tanjer* meal. Local beer and rum are the most
popular alcoholic drinks in all three Guianas.

PARAGUAY

(*República del Paraguay*)

Entry requirements: *A visa, obtainable from Paraguayan consulates, plus a health certificate (smallpox) and—this is the only South American country and one of the few in the world where this is a requirement—a certificate of good conduct from your local police department, to prove, presumably, that you're not on the lam from San Quentin. Once you're in, you've got to get permission to get out: an exit permit; ask the transport company whose facilities you're using, or your hotel, for directions on where to stand in line for this absurd formality.* **Best times for a visit:** *The summer months, October through March, are, to be blunt, hot as hell, and there's little air-conditioning for respite. Remaining months are cooler, with touches of frost between June and September. Rainiest months: March and December.* **Currency:** *The guarani replaced the valueless peso some years ago. It is, of course, named for the country's original inhabitants and their still-spoken language. G117=$1.* **Film availability:** *It's safer not to count on anything being available in Paraguay; have plenty with you.* **Language:** *This is*

the only country in Latin America where the language of the indigenous people—the Guarani Indians—is widely spoken by the descendants of the European conquerors. Spanish remains the official tongue, however, and is universally spoken in bilingual Asunción; elsewhere, Guarani is more popular. English is understood in hotels, transport terminals, travel agencies, and shops, and by some educated Paraguayans, of which there are precious few. **Domestic transport:** *The river boats, hardly luxe; poor roads; venerable public bus systems; and a national air service, of sorts. Travel agents have fairly serviceable cars available for organized tours.* **Tipping:** *Ten per cent in hotels and restaurants.* **Business hours:** *7:30 to 11 or 11:30* A.M., *3 to 5:30 or 6* P.M. **Further information:** *Paraguayan Embassy, Washington, D.C.; Paraguayan Consulate-General, New York.*

INTRODUCING PARAGUAY

It is rare that a poverty-stricken country has not at least its pride to cling to. But not contemporary Paraguay. It appears to have had just about as much agony, in its gruesome, ghastly history, as it can take. It flounders today, under the corrupt rule of South America's last remaining dictator of the Old School, landlocked, poor, phlegmatic, miserably backward, pitied and patronized by its Latin neighbors, with an as yet ineffective antigovernment opposition, and—this is sad to relate—a regime propped up to the tune of approximately $20 million in aid, by the liberty-loving government of the United States of America. I know of no country in the world where hope for a decent future is more ephemeral, nor where a visit can be more depressing.

A backward glance: No one is quite sure what Paraguay is doing, existing as a sovereign state, hemmed in as it is by Brazil, Argentina, and Bolivia; the last-named the only other country on

the continent without a seacoast. Paraguay's birth could not have
been more arbitrary. It has been populated since the early sixteenth
century by Spanish settlers. Many came from the original Buenos
Aires settlement to the south; they decided to stop off and
settle down while en route to the west coast on a treasure-hunt-
ing expedition. The original Paraguayans were the Guarani Indians, who did not resist the newcomers, and, as a matter of fact,
tended to absorb them, rather than vice versa, as has been the
case elsewhere. Spaniards not only intermarried in great numbers,
and with Colonial-government encouragement, but also had no
compunctions about retaining the Indians' language as their own,
to such an extent that Guarani is more widely spoken today than
Spanish.

At the start of the sixteenth century the settlers in Asunción
broke away from the Madrid-directed Buenos Aires government
and became a separate colony.

In those days Asunción's location proved to be convenient, at
least for explorers and soldiers of fortune. It served as a center
for those rugged souls who went off to colonize much of south-
eastern South America, and eastern Bolivia, as well. It was from
Asunción, too, that settlers returned south in 1580 to the Buenos
Aires they had abandoned almost half a century earlier, to re-
found it. How could any have realized at the time that the city
they established would become the greatest on the continent, in
contrast to the town from where they came, which has become one
of the sorriest and most dilapidated of the world's capitals?

But that prescient no one can be expected to be. Asunción was
looking up, in those days, and lots of people had high hopes for
it, not the least of which were the travel-seasoned priests of the
militant Jesuit order, who selected Paraguay as the site of a unique
experiment, which was remarkably successful. The Jesuits arrived in 1605 and remained until they were impolitely asked to
leave, by an unfriendly government, in 1767. During that not inconsiderable period they went about converting the Guaranis by
means of a chain of thirty-two communities which they established
and operated under a credo which was at once newfangled socialist

and old-fashioned paternalistic. The result was a group of settlements inhabited by Indians who had left a subsistence forest society for a semiurban culture, where they built superbly decorated churches, carving with great skill in wood, plaster, and stone, and painting, as well. The Jesuits educated them, Western-style, in their schools. And Paraguay saw what was probably its most hopeful period, at least in terms of the welfare of its people, who never again were to have it so good. But after the expulsion of the Jesuits the settlements were largely destroyed (only a handful of those great churches remain, few of them intact). The Christianized Indians became the vassals of the Colonial masters.

Independence from Spain, and El Supremo: And so Paraguay went, Colonial and feudal, until 1811, when a group of aristocratic settlers got together for a huddle, drew up a document decreeing that the colony was free of Spain, and got away with it. What was spared in bloodshed on that occasion was to be more than made up for in later years. The first of the dictators, José Gaspar Rodríguez Francia, took over the new Paraguay almost as soon as it was born, and ruled, as El Supremo, until 1840. Not one to brook *any* interference, he simply decreed that Paraguay's doors were to be locked to the outer world: no foreign trade, no visitors from abroad, no escape to the outside for Paraguayans, and, of course, no education within. El Supremo was head of the government, civil head of the church, and chief butcher, terrorizing, murdering, imprisoning all the years of his rule.

His nephew, Carlos Antonio López, took over upon Uncle Gaspar's death and ruled until 1862. He opened up Paraguay to the rest of the world, but to little avail. His regime was simply a little less harsh and isolationist than Francia's. And it proved to be merely the lull before the storm: the regime of his son, Francisco Solano López, who almost ruined the country for eternity by madly plunging it into an insane war, for which he is now venerated as his country's greatest hero. Assailed by uncontrollable Napoleonic delusions, and abetted by an Irish mistress by the name of Eliza Lynch, Francisco Solano, in 1865, brought upon a situation which resulted in the catastrophic Triple Alliance War. Tiny Paraguay, thanks to its dictator's intrigues, found itself in the unbelievable position of fighting, single-handedly, Uruguay (whom it had started out to *help*), Argentina, and Brazil.

A land without men—almost: Possibly the stupidest war in history, the Triple Alliance fiasco ended in 1870, after López himself was killed in battle. The vain dictator did not die alone. By war's end only some 220,000 Paraguayans were alive, out of a total population of a little over half a million. Of the survivors, less than thirty thousand were male, and it is only in recent years, thanks to the concerted efforts of what is probably the world's most aggressive female population, that the ratio of the sexes has begun to achieve some balance.

In other ways, Paraguay has never really recovered. Since that time it has been occupied by foreign powers, and at war with one country or another over boundary disputes. It fought with Bolivia between 1929 and 1935 over a portion of the Chaco, the vast plains west of the Paraguay River, which divides the country geographically. It won most of the land it wanted, but its manpower was again depleted, its economy virtually ruined, and its victory hollow. The hero of *that* war was General Estigarribia, who later became president and then dictator. A new constitution in 1940 was replete with democratic trappings, but so far has been little more than a scrap of paper. President Roosevelt, despite the popularity of German Nazis in Paraguay during the early years of World War II, managed to get Paraguay to expel Axis diplomats and allow for the construction of a U.S. air base.

The current scene: After the war the army, never unimportant in the Paraguayan governmental structure, became dominant. In 1954 General Alfredo Stroessner played his hand and with one neat stroke took over as president-dictator, and set up a purely military regime, abolished all civilian political activity, and doled out half of the nations' budget to the army; much of the rest has been eaten up by graft, including, no doubt, a good proportion of the United States' generous contribution to Stroessner's police state. (Some observers insist that Stroessner is a puppet of the army; others that he controls the military; at any rate, the country is a military dictatorship, and it was to Stroessner that Juan Perón rushed, after being deposed in Argentina.)

The old political parties are virtually powerless. The Colorados, conservative and dominant, welcomed the Stroessner coup because it negated the work of the opposition Liberals and the revolutionary Febreristas. There have been abortive attempts from these smaller groups to take over, but they have met with little success. Paraguay is torpid, tired, spent. Many of its outstanding leaders—intellectual, political, monied—have bribed frontier guards with a few hundred dollars in guaranis and fled into voluntary exile. Those who remain are hardly encouraged by Uncle Sam, whose spanking new air-conditioned embassy in Asunción (with the only decent swimming pool in town) is virtually next door to the president's palatial palace, and whose diplomats' wives, banded together as *Las Amigas Norteamericanos del Paraguay,* issue a gushing publication called *Land of Lace and Legend,* designed to convince American visitors that this country is one of charm, beauty, and progress, under the leadership of a dynamic president who is a great buddy of the United States. One hopes that this kind of approach to a ruthless military dictatorship will not remain a part of President Kennedy's Alliance for Progress. Just why the United States deems it expedient to butter up this regime—and such others as that of the Somoza brothers in Nicaragua—is beyond the comprehension of informed Americans and Latins who, perhaps naïvely, like to see the United States on the side of representative governments.

A country to visit? By all means. There is no other country in the world quite like Paraguay. It makes the state of Mississippi seem enlightened-twentieth-century in contrast.

YOUR VISIT TO PARAGUAY

Unless you are on a special mission or are an exceptionally rugged tourist, Paraguay will probably not detain you for long. It is not big in area (about the size of Montana); thanks to those wars, it is the most sparsely populated of the South American republics (about 1,500,000); its climate, particularly during the long summer, is hardly conducive to comfort, and the first decent hotel in its history was a-building while this book was written; it just *may* be finished by the time you arrive.

There are two major regions, geographically: the Gran Chaco, the vast plains to the west of the Paraguay River; and the eastern region, on the other side of the river, containing the capital, the bulk of the population, some verdant forests, and a good deal of fertile soil, not much of which is under cultivation. The principal products are agricultural: yerba maté, from which maté (often known as Paraguayan tea) is brewed, and quebracho, the extract from which tannin is derived.

Asunción: Imagine the kind of Latin American capital you remember from the Grade-B movies of your youth: indolent, ramshackle, dirty, and with traces of a bygone charm (*really* bygone, in this instance). That's Asunción, at least in part. Astride a low plain along the Paraguay River, it barely ekes along. A modern water system was recently installed, but twentieth-century sewage disposal is a project which may well be projected into the twenty-first century. There are squares and parks, in the Spanish tradition, but they need tending and mowing and gardening. There is a tiny legislative palace near the river, which is going to pot for lack of use. There is the little Pantheon, Asunción's answer to Paris' Invalides, with the tombs of the hero-dictators; there is a cathedral, with its interior even more nondescript than its dull gray-columned façade. There are a pair of museums (one with a few European paintings, the other, usually closed, dealing with Indian lore), and there is the fussily-decorated Government Palace, heavily guarded by machine-gun-toting soldiers of El Presidente, and not, of course, open to the public. (At night soldiers have been known to shoot at visitors who prowl too close to the gates; these same soldiers man street corners with their Tommy guns, and they often point them at pedestrians with commands as to which way the pedestrian is to pass them, either from the front or the rear. The sensible visitor swallows hard and obeys, remembering that these are armed soldiers, impressed into service without salaries, with only pitiful uniforms and meals as remuneration, generally without any education, and little, if any, fluency in Spanish.)

In the newer part of the city is the luxurious, well-tended residence of the president (he does not live in the aforementioned Government Palace), just a few steps away from the streamlined, well-enclosed compound of the American Embassy. There are, in addition, the remains of what were once, no doubt, gracious old buildings in the Spanish and Italian tradition, and there are a couple of decrepit private clubs, one of which has a swimming pool filled with the filthy muddy water of the Paraguay River, which it lies alongside. Asunción women do their laundry in the river. Elsewhere in the city, particularly near the harbor, country people, including cigar-smoking ladies, clutter the streets, some transporting themselves on the backs of donkeys, others walking barefoot.

Refreshment may be obtained at any of a number of rather tawdry *confiterías,* where bottled Coca-Cola is the safest item on the menus, unless fly-specked pastries are preferred. A few business offices are blessedly air-conditioned; shops are tiny and with a minimum of consumer goods. Aside from the American Embassy and the new hotel, the most modern constructions in this incredible metropolis of a quarter of a million people are the ships in the harbor, all of them foreign, if one excepts the fleet of the Paraguayan navy—two tinny-looking gunboats. For a dictatorship, pictures are easily taken, although I wouldn't attempt a shot of one of those armed soldiers, except possibly from the rear.

Outside of Asunción: It is touch and go as to what shape they'll be in, but the Botanical Gardens, on the grounds of the former palace of the notorious López family, are more often than not in fair trim. The elaborate residence itself has been converted into a Natural History Museum, which is of considerably less interest than the décor of the house. There is a small zoo on the grounds, and for compulsive golfers who must tee off, even in Paraguay, a nine-hole golf course, not quite of tournament caliber. Locale:

near the village of *Trinidad,* four miles down the Paraguay River from Asunción.

A boat ride from Asunción harbor, on an island in the Paraguay River, is the government-maintained reservation of the Maca Indians, with several hundred in residence. Originally from the Chaco, these people are primarily craftsmen. Their hand-wrought wares are sold on the island, and they peddle them on the streets of the capital, as well.

Most visitors to Asunción are not content to leave until they've had a look at *San Bernardino,* highly touted by the Paraguayans as their leading "resort." Well, if you insist. San Bernardino is a thirty-odd-mile drive from the capital, on the shores of a fifteen-by three-mile body of brown water, exotically named Lake Ypacaraí. The water is usually near the boiling point during the summer months, and it is generally too muddy for a refreshing swim. Other San Bernardino inducements: a run-down hotel which stays in business only because it has no decent competition, and a private club for Asunción's aristocrats. The "season" (i.e., when the water is at its hottest and brownest) is from December through February. En route to San Bernardino is the village of *Itauguá,* center of the *nanduti*-lace handicraft industry. Mothers and daughters collaborate, making the lace on wood frames, and sometimes taking several years to complete a large piece. I've never understood all the fuss about Paraguayan lace; it is considerably uglier than Belgian lace, but at least *that* comes from the charming town of Bruges.

Villeta: An agricultural center for cotton and tobacco farmers of the region, Villeta is a town of about ten thousand inhabitants, about twenty-five miles south of Asunción, on the Paraguay River. Day-long excursions by launch are available. The town, while hardly notable, makes for an interesting destination on the river. Getting to it gives the short-time visitor an opportunity for a glance at river life.

Iguassú Falls: No denying it: the visitor to South America who misses Iguassú ranks with the visitor to Africa who misses Victoria Falls. I am still unable to decide which was the greater experience for me. The Iguassú Falls are situated where Paraguay, Brazil, and Argentina meet, and are accessible from any of the three countries. Plane service, for those who want to make the trip while in Paraguay, is available several times a week from Asunción; the flight takes a little over an hour. But for travelers who are flying around South America, down the east coast and up the west coast, a visit to Iguassú is best made while in Brazil, en route from São Paulo to Asunción and Buenos Aires. (See pages 86–70 and 125–26.)

Concepción and Primavera: The Queen City of the Chaco is even less notable than the capital, which is hardly a show place. Concepción, with about thirty-five thousand residents, is a good deal smaller than Asunción, and even seedier. It is, though, the commercial center of the north, and much of what enters the country from Brazil passes through its free port. There are few public buildings of any interest. Strangers in the town are mainly businessmen, occasional hunters en route to the Chaco, and residents of that region, including members of a number of the several Mennonite communities which are situated within its borders. There are flights from Asunción; but getting to Concepción by boat, while time-consuming, is a good way of seeing the country. The vessels follow the winding Paraguay River, never more than a quarter of a mile wide, full of alligators, nasty piranhas, and boats making their way south with the produce of northern Paraguay: cattle, hides, maté, lumber, tobacco, and the valuable quebracho. Boat passengers might want to go only as far as *Rosario,* a small town less than a hundred miles north of Asunción.

From Rosario, it is about fifty miles by road to *Primavera,* where the Society of Brothers (*Sociedade de Hermanos,* also known as the Hutterites), almost a thousand strong, run a thriving farm community embracing some twenty thousand acres. Founded just before World War II in Germany, the Society came to Paraguay at the outbreak of the war, when no other country would admit them because of their pacifist views. Although they marry, bear children, and are strong believers in education—

through the university level—they live in a number of closed communities throughout the world, sharing the wealth they acquire largely by communal farming and handcraft shops. Their precepts are those which they believe to have been practiced by the early Christians, and their program extends to medical missions and schools for their needy neighbors, particularly in Paraguay. The Society welcomes visitors to Primavera, which is also accessible by occasional planes from Asunción. They are hearty, hospitable, happy people, and I consider getting acquainted with them (either at Primavera, or at their retail craft shop in Asunción) a highlight of a visit to Paraguay.

Other Paraguayan destinations: South of Asunción, by river boat, is *Pilar,* a fairly substantial town by Paraguayan standards, situated at the confluence of the Bermejo and Paraguay rivers, almost two hundred miles from the capital. This is what might be called the country's industrial center: a couple of distilleries, a few cotton-ginning mills, and some sawmills. Nearby are orange groves and cotton plantations. At *Capiatá,* a fairly short drive from the capital, is a splendid old seventeenth-century Jesuit church, one of those remaining from the days of the *misiones,* when the craft-genius of the Guaranis flourished under the aegis of the priests. In the same general area is *Caacupé,* a religious shrine with its main landmark the charmingly-named Church of the Blue Virgin of the Miracles. Nearby are fine old churches, also dating from *misiones* days, at *Tobatí, Piribebuy,* and *Paraguarí.* Other old churches are at *Yaguarón* (here the Indian-made paint on the wood carvings is still as vivid as it was three centuries ago), *Jesús,* and *Tabarangué,* whose church is the *pièce de résistance* of all of those which remain from the Jesuit period. Way south, on the Argentine border, is the port town of *Encarnación,* second only to Asunción in population (about forty thousand) and from which boats sail all the way north to Iguassú Falls. Train travelers to and from Buenos Aires remember this city, for it is at this point that trains are ferried across the river from the Argentine town of Posadas.

WHAT TO BUY

Asunción's most interesting shop is that operated by the afore-mentioned Society of Brothers (*Sociedade de Hermanos*), where rare Paraguayan woods of many varieties are worked by hand into cigarette boxes, trays, salad sets, napkin rings (attractive, cheap, lightweight), and bowls, in both traditional and modern designs, and in both oiled and highly-polished finishes. Members of the Society act as salesclerks, and are experienced in shipping parcels to the United States; prices are fixed. Along the narrow streets which border the harbor are any number of small shops dealing in Paraguayan crafts: handsome, hand-woven sashes (those in the Paraguayan national colors—red, white and blue—are a knockout); basketry; silver *bombillas* (straws for sipping maté) and their companions, the maté gourds in which the liquid is placed; the immense straw hats worn by both men and women; poor-quality leather goods, and that tacky Paraguayan lace. Bargaining, at these shops and from street vendors with similar wares, is the rule.

CREATURE COMFORTS

The Stroessner dictatorship is building a luxury hotel in the center of **Asunción.** Just when it will be finished, and how it will be operated when that occurs, cannot be predicted. But, assuming it *is* finished and *does* open, it cannot help but be the best place in town. Otherwise, there is the unbelievably grim Gran Hotel del Paraguay (don't let that fancy name deceive you) with only a few air-conditioned rooms, no hot water, possibly one or two rooms with private baths, cockroaches, lumpy beds, virtually no ventilation, a swimming pool so biliously green that no one swims in it, and a dining room which was the grand *salon* of Madame Lynch, paramour of the notorious dictator López; it is about four stories high, illuminated by what seem like four three-watt bulbs, and ventilated by a tiny wall air-conditioner with power enough to cool a kitchen cupboard; there are no windows, and the dark walls are decorated with hideous murals of Madame Lynch's choosing. If there is a more revolting place to dine in South America, I have yet to see it. Not quite so bad is the dining room of the other so-called habitable hotel, the Terraza Caballero, with an outdoor terrace affording an enchanting view of Asunción's shantytown, astride the muddy riverbank. The best restaurant, and this is not saying much, is La Preferida. *Confiterías,* invariably delightful places all over South America, are appalling in Asunción, and the private clubs are not much better. You might try having a drink at one of the hotel bars (if the refrigeration is working and ice cubes are available) or at the Intermezzo or Ambassador "night clubs," which sometimes offer Paraguayan folk singers and guitarists, undeniably pleasant to hear. Cinemas, of which there are several, are not air-conditioned. The Del Lago Hotel at **San Bernardino** has the same management as the Gran in Asunción; 'nuff said?

Elsewhere—Iguassú Falls: No hotels on Paraguayan side; see chapters on Brazil and Argentina. **Concepción:** Frances. **Pilar:** Gardel. **Caacupé:** Victoria. **Encarnación:** Suizo. **Primavera:** Visitors interested in a trip to the Society of Brothers community may make arrangements for transport and accommodation through the Society's shop in Asunción.

PRIVATE CLUBS: American, Asunción Golf, Centenario, Deportivo de Puerto Sajonia; Union.

Paraguayan food specialties: Many local dishes, based on beef, are fairly similar to (though, needless to say, rarely as good as) those in neighboring Argentina; these include stews of the puchero type. A number of Italian style *pasta* dishes, utilizing noodles and spaghetti, are popular, and corn is a diet staple. On the whole, though, one does well not to count on being bowled over by the food in this country.

URUGUAY

(República Oriental del Uruguay)

Entry requirements: *Passport and smallpox vaccination certificate—no visa, no tourist card, and so far not a single tourist has attempted to overthrow the republic or abscond with the treasury.* **Best times for a visit:** *For sun-worshipers and beach-habitués, the ideal months are December through March, the Uruguayan summer. The remaining months, even those of midwinter, are mild, however; it never snows, nor does it go below 40°.* **Currency:** *The peso, equal to about ten U.S. cents, and written with a $ sign. Money-changing firms called* cambios *usually give better exchange rates than hotels and banks.* **Film availability:** *Black-and-white film is more easily found than color; more expensive than in the United States, of course.* **Language:** *Spanish, with the accent a peculiar one, similar to that of Argentina; there is a great deal of English spoken, some French and German, too.* **Transport:** *Good roads (and modern buses), good air service, and a good rail network link most towns of this small country. There is steamer service down the Río de la Plata to Buenos Aires, but the quickest connection with the nearby Argentine*

capital is via Causa Airlines' flying boat: an hour from the downtown harbor of Montevideo to the near-downtown Buenos Aires harbor. Regular planes make frequent flights but are more time-consuming, the Montevideo airport being forty-five minutes from the city center. **Tipping:** *Hotels add 15 to 22 per cent service charge; otherwise tip 10 to 15 per cent, including taxi drivers.* **Business hours:** *These vary, but in general there is a lunch-hour closing from noon to about 2:30 P.M. and closing hour ranges from 6:30 to 6:50 P.M.* **Further information:** *Oficina Nacional de Turismo, Montevideo, Uruguay; Varig Airlines, 634 Fifth Avenue, New York; Panagra, Chrysler Building, New York; Uruguayan Embassy, Washington, D.C.*

INTRODUCING URUGUAY

The trouble with Uruguay is that it is a country of so little unpleasantness that outside of Latin America it is virtually an unknown quantity. Newspapers, which rarely bother reporting the comings and goings of the smaller, stable nations, rarely carry a line about it. And even though the outer world did come to learn a little about Uruguay when it was the site of the 1961 and 1962 Inter-American Conferences, it would not be remiss to make clear that (1) it is *not* Paraguay, from which it is as unlike as is night from day; (2) it is at once the smallest and in many ways the most advanced of the South American republics, and (3) its remarkable development from strife-ridden buffer state to model republic has taken place bloodlessly, in the last half-century.

Though far from Utopia (as is, indeed, *any* country), Uruguay belies the clichés of the pessimists who look upon Latin America as an interminably hopeless, hapless proposition. Until recently the United States did little more than take it for granted, often sending to it inept diplomats, while simultaneously according VIP treatment to notoriously dictatorial neighbors. Uruguay is de-

cidedly worth knowing about, and knowing. How many countries, after all, have a cosmopolitan capital city which doubles
as a beach resort, and is the gateway to a Riviera, beginning on
its outskirts and extending two hundred beauty-filled miles?

A backward glance: Uruguay, in the manner of its South
American neighbor Argentina, and its North American neighbor
the United States, did a thorough job of killing off the great
majority of its original inhabitants, the Charrua Indians. But that,
of course, was long before Uruguay was Uruguay. The history of
this little land is so riddled with complexities as to make even
the United States appear relatively simple in contrast. I do not
envy Uruguayan schoolchildren having to learn about their republic's pre-twentieth-century past, which will be capsulized herewith as briefly as possible, with this prefatory comment: *everybody* got into the act.

But to get on with those Indians: the Charruas had the first
laugh, but hardly the last. They killed, with prompt dispatch and
understandable irritability, the first of the European invaders, the
Spaniard Juan Díaz de Solís, in 1516, and for a number of years,
none of the conquistadors gave much of a damn about the territory, it having been adduced (and correctly) that there was
no gold or silver to be had from it. Later, after Buenos Aires had
been properly established, some soldiers from there attempted to
do what Solís had been unable to accomplish, but the stubborn
Charruas repelled them, and it took some resolute missionaries—
Franciscans and Jesuits—to actually start the ball rolling, in 1624.
By the end of the seventeenth century the Portuguese had moved
in, setting up the town of Colonia on the Río de la Plata, opposite Buenos Aires.

A few decades later the Portuguese had got to the point of beginning to settle Montevideo, but before they had dug many excavations, in came the competition, and it was under the Spaniard
Bruno Marico de Zabala that Montevideo was actually put on the
map, in 1726. For a number of years thereafter, you couldn't
tell who was in control of Montevideo without a score card. It
was alternately Spanish and Portuguese, and even the ubiquitous

British took control for a very brief period, in 1806, during the time when they were also trying to fly the Union Jack over Buenos Aires. That failing, they departed from both places, but the plot continued to thicken.

Montevideo, in 1808, arbitrarily decided that it would be independent of the Spanish Colonial government in Buenos Aires, which governed it, but a few years thereafter, in 1811, the Brazilians began to feel expansionist, and attacked, quite unprepared for the fight they were to get from José Gervasio Artigas, the Gaucho who was to become Uruguay's most distinguished patriot, and who soon declared Uruguay independent of both Brazil *and* Argentina. Battles against these enemies continued until 1820, when Artigas had to flee to Paraguay, and the Portuguese took over Montevideo, which was a Brazilian province for the ensuing half-decade.

The Treinta y Tres: But the tide was about to turn, and decisively, at long last. Another brave Uruguayan, Juan Antonio Lavalleja, invaded his country from Argentina, at the head of a band of thirty-three fighters who have become immortalized as the *Treinta y Tres Orientales* (the Thirty-three Easterners—for Uruguay, in Colonial days, had been known as the Banda Oriental, or Eastern Region, of the realm administered from Buenos Aires; it has retained the *Oriental* in its modern appelation—República Oriental del Uruguay). At any rate, Lavalleja, at this stage of the game aided by Buenos Aires forces, defeated the Brazilians at the Battle of Ituzaingó in 1827. And after receiving the backing of the British, the Lavalleja forces were able to irrevocably declare the independence of Uruguay from both Argentina and Brazil, both of which relinquished their claims on the territory.

From then on, until the start of the twentieth century, Uruguay was pretty much bedlam. The two major political parties—the Reds (Colorados) and the Whites (Blancos)—feuded mercilessly with each other, intrigue followed intrigue, dictator-type president followed dictator-type president, there were civil wars of varying degrees of ghastliness, and at one point Uruguay found itself in the Triple Alliance War against Paraguay.

It was only in 1903 that blood stopped flowing. José Batlle y Ordóñez was elected president, serving until 1907, and for another four years beginning in 1911. A brilliant, reform-minded dynamo, he calmed down the antagonistic Blancos and Colorados, and impelled Uruguayans to work for the transformation of their country into a modern democracy.

The contemporary scene: Here's what has happened as a result of Batlle y Ordóñez' New Deal: Uruguay is now a country with nationalized waterworks, electricity, and railroad systems; the government controls key industries including chemicals and oil, runs insurance companies and banks, and even subsidizes the theater; it controls tourist-frequented casinos and has hotels of its own; it runs the telephone system and supports music and other art forms, and manages the state broadcasting service.

At the same time, it pioneered in protecting the workingman, with a forty-four-hour week, minimum-wage and vacation-with-pay laws, medical programs, pensions, and unemployment insurance. Women have long had the vote, and even though Uruguay is largely Roman Catholic, divorce is legal. Illegitimate children have inheritance rights and legal status.

Education is not only compulsory and free on the statute books—as indeed it is in virtually every Latin country—but it is a fact of Uruguayan life: the literacy rate of close to 90 per cent is one of the highest in the world. The press is free, respected, and widely read. And capital punishment has long since been abolished.

Uruguay has been attempting to diversify its economy; it wants to be as little dependent on the whims of the world wool and meat markets as possible (wool, sheared from twenty-one million sheep, is its chief export; almost the entire crop was exported in 1961, for the first time in a number of years). Factories have gone up, and there is now a considerable amount of manufacturing, although much of it is for domestic consumption. The more conservative of the two parties, the Blancos—in power since 1959, for the first time in ninety-three years—is meeting some success in its economic program, which emphasizes fewer imports, lessened expenditures on domestic welfare programs, and the first income tax in the country's history. Politically, the country insures stability by its decade-old pluripersonal executive. The presidency is held by the National Council of elected officials, who rotate the chairmanship among themselves during their terms of office. Faustino Harrison became the leader in March 1962.

Welfare state? By all means, but one in which private enterprise still functions and where the government is literally democratic and actually representative. There are no strong men, and the atmosphere is far from one of smugness or self-satisfaction. Uruguayans are aware of both pluses and minuses in their national life, and they can be counted on to evaluate and adjust them, as responsible citizens of a broadly-based government in which everyone has the Right to Gripe.

YOUR VISIT TO URUGUAY

Uruguay resembles Denmark in a number of ways: they are both small countries, they are both pioneers in social welfare, both are low countries surrounded by a great deal of water, and in both, the capitals are home to an abnormally large percentage of the population—about a quarter in the case of Denmark's Copenhagen, and about a third, with Uruguay's Montevideo.

In both cases the visit of a traveler from abroad revolves around the capital, and again in both instances the welcome to the stranger is warm, spontaneous, and hospitable. But there the similarities end. Indeed, aside from certain resemblances to southern Brazil and Argentina, which it borders, Uruguay is a distinctive country, even in a Latin American context. It is also a very pleasant place to visit. A hundred thousand Argentine vacationers make for it every year, and with good reason.

Montevideo: Magellan, on his historic trip around South America, through the strait named for him, is supposed to have meandered by what is now Montevideo, and though undoubtedly apocryphal, the story of the lookout on his ship who named Montevideo continues to be told, and it might as well be repeated here just once more. The sailor said, as the ship passed by the rather unprepossessing hill which overlooks the bay behind which the city now stands, *"¡Monte vide eu!,"* which translated from the Portuguese means, "I see a mountain!" That bit of folklore dispensed with, shall we have a look at this hardly mountainous but very attractive city?

Even for a walker without the faintest sense of direction (like me, for example), Montevideo is amazingly easy to get about. Its principal street cuts through a great chunk of it, and is interrupted every so often by rather grand plazas. From the harbor onward until it hits the Plaza Independencia, this artery is called Calle Sarandi, and beyond that plaza it is the Avenida 18 de Julio, named for the 1828 day on which independence was proclaimed ("18," by the way, is *dieciocho* in Spanish, and that *J* in *Julio* is pronounced like an *h;* this free Spanish lesson is included here only because you may have occasion to pronounce this street's name and it is difficult for non-Spanish speakers). The Plaza Independencia is, more often than not, the visitor's home territory. Flanking it are the town's finest hotel, the sky-scraping Victoria Plaza; the relatively small, unpretentious but beautifully-proportioned Government Palace, guarded by a pair of traditionally-uniformed soldiers, who are perfectly happy to pose for pictures; the lovely old Teatro Solís (which also houses a splendid landmark of a restaurant, the Aguila), and the Museum of Natural History.

Nearby is Montevideo's maddest and tallest building, Palacio Salvo, quite obviously the work of an architect who had satisfied what must have been a lifelong urge to build a medieval castle, even if it be twenty-six stories high; and just beyond, down the aforementioned Avenida, the shops and more conventional sky-scrapers (many of them quite attractive, in the best South American tradition). The cathedral, distinguished chiefly because of its age (it was finished in 1804) and its not inconsiderable height, dominates the oldest square of the city, the Plaza Constitutión, on which also faces the similarly-aged Cabildo, originally the city

hall and now the Foreign Affairs Ministry, and the quite-posh
Club Uruguay.

Not too far away from this area—but hardly walkable—is the
Legislative Palace, like the Palacio Salvo, another ambitious but
aesthetically ghastly landmark, into which went more than three-
score varieties of Uruguayan marble and granite, a great deal of
money and effort. Once inside, while hardly inviting, the interior
is at least impressive, and contains, among other things, elaborate
mosaic floors, the chambers of both houses, a good many enormous
historical murals of the kind so often seen in state houses north
of the Rio Grande, and the Uruguayan counterpart of Washington's Library of Congress.

Aside from the beautifully-tended parks of which it is justifiably
proud (one, the Prado, has a rose garden with 850 varieties of
that flower), and the historically important monuments which
pay homage to early covered-wagon settlers and the Gauchos,
there is not a great deal of unique interest. This is not to say that
Montevideo is without impressive hospitals, excellent museums,
modern government ministries, schools and playgrounds, an excellent university, a myriad of cafés, including many outdoor ones,
a highly rated Planetarium, and delightful residential sections.
It is simply that given the modernity of Uruguay and its relatively
high standard of living, these are the features of its capital which
one would expect.

What does come as a special bonus, especially during the
months of the Uruguayan summer, are the beaches. Off-season
they can only be looked at wistfully by the sun-worshiper. But
during the summer months they come alive, each with a personality
and flavor of its own. Of the eight of them which straddle the
city's waterfront, these stand out: because it is the nearest to
downtown Montevideo, *Playa Ramirez,* while crowded, is the most
convenient. Beyond it by a couple of miles is *Playa Pocitos,* which
in the past five years has become the city's most fashionable. Tall
apartment houses, on the order of those at Rio's Copacabana
Beach, flank its shores, which are dotted with restaurants, cafés,
and snack bars. Here, too, is the city's Trouville swimming pool,

frequently the site of international contests. Beyond is *Puerto Buceo,* with the nine-story Montevideo Yacht Club and the Oceanographic Museum, a beach off whose waters regattas are held frequently. *Playa Malvin* is next in line, and up the road a piece—one of a cluster of smaller beaches, is the *playa* which honors the intrepid English—the *Playa de los Ingleses,* just beneath a bluff which is the setting of the lovely Virgilio Park. Way at the end of the twelve-mile network is *Playa Carrasco,* understandably enough the most unspoiled, least crowded, and most attractive beach, backed by a little forest, and with its chief amenity a huge hotel-casino.

All of the beaches are easily accessible by the public city buses which traverse the waterfront Rambla Sol. (Simply wear your swimsuit under your clothes, and disrobe at the beach.) For the visitor who is unfamiliar with the Uruguayan pronunciation of Spanish, I might point out here that the Spanish word for beach, *playa,* is here pronounced *plaja,* the *j* being soft, and the end result coming awfully close to *plaza,* which can be confusing to the uninitiated.

A further word, before heading out of town: two annual Montevideo events are worth noting in planning your itinerary. The first is *Carnival,* usually held in February. Though without the international reputation of Rio de Janeiro's, and without the Rio setting, it is still a fete to be reckoned with: masked balls, elaborate parades, much merriment, *al fresco* and otherwise. In March comes a truly distinctive Uruguayan festival: *Creole Week* (*Semana Criolla*), when the national folk hero—the Gaucho—is honored by his countrymen. On the program, aspects of which are not unlike the rodeo of the U. S. West, are horse shows, riding exhibitions, and evening festivities which feature entertainment by the Gauchos themselves, mostly folk-type songs and wonderful guitar-playing.

It is always easy, regardless of the time of year of one's visit, to not only see the Gauchos, but to see and meet them on home ground. Travel agencies in Montevideo conduct half-day excursions from the capital to nearby *estancias,* and they are not, believe me, especially "rigged" for *turistas,* but bona fide working ranches where the visitor is received warmly and shown about. Near the *estancia* headquarters, Gauchos—with wonderfully weather-beaten, wind-blown (and often handle-bar-mustachioed), sun-tanned faces topped by broad-brimmed hats, and with hand-rolled cigarettes dangling from their lips—round up steers for mass-production weighing on immense scales, to determine the amount of tax due the government, which computes by weight. Inside, other Gauchos can be found relaxing at the *estancia* bar, over midmorning maté, or possibly a short snort of grappa, the cheap, popular, and plenty-potent national bracer-upper. What's it like? Don't ask: step up to the bar and sample the stuff yourself!

En route back to the city, the car will pass by lonely mounted Gauchos rounding up cattle on the plains, or Gauchos in groups, riding back to the *estancia.* These are friendly men, and they are invariably obliging about posing for photographs. Few speak English, but Spanish-speaking visitors find them pleasant to chat with, if they've a free moment. The Gaucho, industrialization not-withstanding, remains the economic backbone and the folk hero of Uruguay. It was his forebears who stubbornly led the fight for independence. He's very worth becoming acquainted with, if one would know Uruguay.

Punta del Este: "You haven't been to Punta?" Residents of Montevideo are as crestfallen when they learn of visitors who miss their leading resort as are New Yorkers with tourists who never quite make it to the tower of the Empire State Building. Punta del Este (it means East Point, and is usually shortened to just plain Punta) means a great deal to Uruguayans. They are quite aware that there are more elegant resorts in southern South America; they know, too, that there are holiday spots with more physically spectacular settings, and they quite realize the Punta's accommodations are, for the most part, considerably less opulent than those of other beach communities.

Why, then, this almost patriotic affection? It is difficult to give a reason which appears valid to anyone who has not experienced at least a weekend on the scene. Perhaps the explanation lies in the town's unpretentious conviviality, the swimability of its waters, the breadth and whiteness of its vast quantity of beach strips, the pretty houses—some fairly grand, many less elaborate—and perhaps most important, the air of relaxed informality which is so prevalent, so immediately pervasive, even to the just-arrived visitor.

Men never wear neckties in Punta, even in the two casinos, perhaps the most delightfully casual in South America. The center of the town draws vacationing shoppers who will break their afternoons or mornings with stops at one of the open-air cafés. The beaches, in many sections gay with striped canvas cabanas, cater to the surf-lover and the serious swimmer; for the former, the Playa Brava (replete with mountainous breakers) is ideal, and for the latter, there is the Playa Mansa (on the bay, calm and inviting). In the environs of the town and its satellite summer-house communities are uninhabited woods shaded by eucalyptus and pine, scented with mimosa, and bordering the sea. They make fine picnic locales; the fare—crusty bread, wine, local cheeses and sausages, and possibly the excellent pasteurized milk—is easily procured at the town's groceries and dairies. Available, too, are a fine yacht club, the facilities of a country-and-golf club, which often lets rooms to nonmembers (including delegates to the 1961 and 1962 Inter-American Conferences), and deep-sea fishing as well as angling in nearby lakes. Populating the scene are great numbers of Argentines. The visitors from the land across the Río de la Plata come in great numbers because there is no resort within their own country with quite the informality of Punta, and the transport companies make it easy for them, wisely enough, by providing direct plane service from Buenos Aires.

Punta has many competitors, both within Uruguay and in neighboring countries. But it is like no other South American resort, completely invalidating that oft-true maxim, "If you've seen one, you've seen 'em all." A one-day excursion from Montevideo is hardly adequate to get Punta's flavor. A weekend, or better yet, of course, a fortnight, is far preferable. But even a brief peep, particularly if one's visit is a summer one, is better than none at all. Both road and railroad follow the sea en route from Montevideo,

passing through or alongside one resort after another, set among
beaches and bays, backed by wooded hills, animated by holidaymakers who are quite obviously having such a damned good time
that one is impelled to pop out of the car (or jump out of the
train) window and join in the fun.

Other beach resorts: Punta del Este is about the halfway point
in the two-hundred-mile chain of Atlantic resorts extending from
Montevideo to Chuy, on the Brazilian border. *Between Montevideo
and Punta,* the most important of these are *Atlántida*—only thirty-
five miles from the capital, verdantly wooded, with fine beaches,
gold links, and a "suburb"—the even smaller and more *intime
Las Toscas.*

Continuing a few miles up the coast is *La Floresta,* where a
special diversion is horseback riding in the surrounding woods. Beyond is *Solís,* noted for its fishing, both in the ocean and in the
river at whose mouth it is situated. *Piriápolis,* the next major town,
comes second to Punta in size and facilities, with a score and a
half of hotels, including the immense hostelry operated by the
Uruguayan Government Tourist Department, with an adjoining
casino. The volcanic hills behind the town are, by Uruguayan
standards, towering peaks, rising as high as a thousand feet. There
is a good yacht club, auto racing, and for variety, mineral springs.
The last of the major resorts, west of Punta, is *Maldonado,* which
is one of the few Uruguayan towns with any considerable remains
of the Colonial period; these include a still fine watchtower, a
church, and ruins of walls on an island in the harbor. Maldonado
doubles as both resort and capital of the Maldonado Department. It
has the dubious distinction of having been sacked by the British
in 1806. They were not to return to the area, at least in a warring
mood, until 1939, when they defeated the forces aboard the Nazi
battleship *Graf von Spee,* at Punta del Este.

Between Punta del Este and the Brazilian frontier—a hundred-
mile stretch—the beach-resort network continues. These include
(in order of distance from Punta) *Rocha,* a pretty town of thirty
thousand not far from the restored Colonial *Fort Santa Teresa,*
which is the focal point of a national park whose facilities include

swimming pools and a bird sanctuary; *La Paloma,* with a harbor for yachts, and both fresh- and salt-water fishing; and, on the frontier, *Chuy,* near which is *Lake Mirim,* which straddles the boundary line, part of it in Brazil, part in Uruguay, on which side stands venerable Fort San Miguel, now a museum. Not far are seacoast beaches, and one of the *paradores,* or inns, operated by the Uruguayan government, at *La Coronilla.*

Other Uruguayan towns: Though rarely visited by Americans, there are a number of eminently visitable towns and resorts west of Montevideo on the Río de la Plata, northwest of the capital on the Uruguay River, which defines a part of the frontier with Argentina, and in the interior.

One of the most unusual is *Colonia Suiza,* which, as its name implies, was settled by the Swiss, who to this day stubbornly carry on traditions of the old country, including the manufacture of music boxes. Not far from the town are *Nueva Helvecia,* also with a Swiss façade, and the colony of the *Waldensians,* a Protestant sect. *Colonia,* though founded in the seventeenth century by Portuguese traders to compete in commerce with the Spanish in Buenos Aires, is now little more than a pretty pleasure resort and sight-seers' goal, with a number of Colonial buildings (including the Viceroy's House) and an exceptionally handsome plaza. *Mercedes* welcomes both cattle to its corrals (it's the livestock center of the region) and tourists to its hotels. Situated on the Río Negro, it is popular with fishermen and small-craft sailors. *Salto,* in the north on the Uruguay River, is a substantial town of sixty thousand, making its livelihood on cattle, oranges, and both beet and cane sugar, and with its principal embellishments a river promenade, and the nearby Salto Chico rapids and Salto Grande waterfalls (on the Uruguay River) which attract both sight-seers and fishermen. Away from the rivers, in the interior, are towns which serve as good departure points for visits to *estancias,* and which typify that large portion of pastoral Uruguay. These would include *Minas,* where the early hero Lavalleja was born and where a unique industry is the mining of the kind of marble and granite used to construct the Legislative Palace in

Montevideo; *San José,* a cattle center with little to recommend a visit to it; *Treinta y Tres,* named for the famed thirty-three followers of Lavalleja but not otherwise significant, and *Rivera,* one of whose streets constitutes the Uruguayan-Brazilian frontier, the town across the road being the Brazilian city of Santa Ana do Livramento.

Facts for fishermen: This book is not a sportsmen's guide, but it would not be remiss to emphasize here that Uruguay is particularly fertile fishing country, with the dorado the most sought-after specimen. Colorful (gold, green, and purple in hue), frisky (not easy to catch!), and multisized (some weigh as much as forty pounds!), the dorado is a fresh-water fish, and best caught (or, at least, sought after) at Rincón del Bonete on the Río Negro, a 160-mile bus or train ride from Montevideo, at the Fray Bentos Fishing Club, and at Salto Grande, on the Uruguay River. Deep-sea fishing is popular at all of the coastal resorts, including Punta del Este and La Coronilla, near the Brazilian frontier. One's catch might include shark, pompano, black corvina, sea bass, bonito, and bluefish. There are government-operated *paradores* and/or pleasant inns at all of these fishing centers.

WHAT TO BUY

I wish I could report that the copious stocks of Uruguayan leather goods were quite as fine as those in neighboring Argentina, but they are not. Neither, as a matter of fact, are many of the other items which might tempt the tourist: footwear, knitgoods such as sport shirts and swim trunks, and even the specialty handbags and jackets made of unborn calf. None of it can compare with what is obtainable in the shops of nearby Buenos Aires, prices are no cheaper, and design and workmanship are inferior. The only exceptions to the rule are *bombillas,* the silver or tin straws through which maté is drunk when served in the gourdlike maté containers, both being purchasable as a set; and *possibly,* coats, jackets, and furpieces of Uruguayan nutria; these are considerably cheaper than in the United States, but once again, the quality, design, and workmanship are often disappointing. In Montevideo, have a look, if you like, at such shops as the Pan-American Leather Factory, the Montevideo Leather Factory, and the Casa Schiavo. There are a number of modern department stores, including the London-Paris, which are pleasant for browsing, and many attractive shops on the Avenida 18 de Julio and the Calle Sarandi, where salespeople are invariably friendly and courteous, and where bargaining is *not* the rule. Punta del Este has branches of many of the better clothing and accessory shops in the capital, where during the season their smartest merchandise is featured. But the traveler visiting Buenos Aires, as well, will be far better satisfied with the shops of the Argentine capital.

CREATURE COMFORTS

HOTELS—**Montevideo:** Uruguay's capital is the site of one of South America's finest hotels—the modern, fully air-conditioned, twenty-two-story, four hundred-room Victoria Plaza. Operated by Intercontinental Hotels Corporation of New York, it is centrally located on the lovely Plaza Independencia, with handsome rooms (all with bath, of course), service unsurpassed anywhere on the continent, an excellent restaurant (which doubles as a night club), and a delightfully informal bar-lounge which is the city's chief congregating place. From $12 single. Considerably less expensive is the elderly Nogaro, with the minimum, single rate $6. Others downtown include the new, inexpensive Crillon, and the Alhambra. At **Ramírez Beach:** the cavernous but unexciting Parque, with casino; at **Pocitos Beach:** the Ermitage, plus the Gloria and Bulevar; at **Carrasco** (the most distant beach from town): Hotel Casino Carrasco (open only from December 8 through March 24), the Bristol, and the smaller Cottage; and, at **Malvín Beach,** the Playa Malvin. **Atlántida:** the Atlántida, the Casino Golf Palace, and the Rex are the poshest; more modest: Remanso, Mi Cielo, Los Angeles, Chalet. **Solís:** Alcion, Solís. **La Floresta:** Oriental,

Parque; **Piriápolis:** The immense Hotel Argentino-Casino, oper-
ated by the government's tourist department, is the undisputed
leader. Smaller hotels include the Rex, Juvencia, Italian, Atlántico,
Perla, Rambla, and Embassy. **La Paloma:** Cabo Santa Maria.
Punta del Este: The Cantegril Country Club (site of the annual
Cantegril Film Festival) is primarily a private club, but often
takes nonmembers in its four-person bungalows, where rates are
$20 daily with meals for all four, and at the adjoining Cantegril
House and motel, where accommodations are let on a conventional single- and double-room basis. Facilities include a swimming pool, tennis courts, *boîte,* and two golf courses. Cantegril
is a few minutes' drive from Punta del Este proper, whose hotels
include the San Rafael, with casino, from $8 single, American
plan; Playa—catering to families, friendly, informal, clean, and
cheap, $5 single with meals; Floreal, Biarritz, Cigale, and many
others—modest and inexpensive. **Rocha:** Arrarte, Roma. **La
Paloma:** Del Cabo, Barcelo. **Chuy:** Parador San Miguel. **Colonia
Suiza:** Nirvana, Del Prado. **Colonia:** Esperanza, El Mirador.
Mercedes: Brisas del Hum. **Salto:** Salto Grande Hotel (in town),
Salto Grande Paradore (at the falls). **Minas:** Parador Salus (eight
miles out of town, cheap and charming), Minas (in town).
Rivera: Casino. **La Coronilla:** Parador la Coronilla, Costas del
Mar.

RESTAURANTS AND NIGHT LIFE—**Montevideo:** The Victoria
Plaza's restaurant, *boîte* and lounge-bar are Montevideo's leading
rendezvous, and justifiably so. The Aguila, in the venerable Solís
Theatre building, is the most famous of the old eating places, with
typically substantial Uruguayan dishes including the noted *pavesa*
soup. Cichilo's offers Italian cuisine quite as authentic as that
found in Rome or New York. Steak, sea food (including corvina),
and convivial informality are Moroni's specialties, while the Gold
Club is at the other end of the gamut, elegant and fashionable,
particularly for a lunch of partridge, and a view of the Río de la
Plata. Others: Gaucho, for beef dishes; Forte di Makale,
Stradella, La Paloma, and Tasende, for Uruguayan favorites;
Hungaria, Hungarian cuisine; Sancho Panza, sea food; Ding-Jo,

Chinese; El Pollo Dorado, Grand Hotel España grill room, El Rincon, Catari. The many tearooms or *confiterías* serve stronger stuff as well as tea, and snacks, as well. Best known are El Telegrafo, Conaprole, Babulu, El Ateneo, and La Americana, but don't hesitate to sample any that look inviting, and linger as long as you like. After-dark haunts, besides the aforementioned restaurants, some of which provide music and dancing, are the Club de Paris, Ermitage, Pygmalion, El Patio, and Intermezzo night clubs, all with floor shows and all in town, plus La Cabana; Marecchiare, with entertainment, at Carrasco Beach; Cavillini's for dinner and *al fresco* dancing in season, also at Carrasco; El Retiro, similar to Cavillini's, but at Parque Rodo, and, of course, the casinos at Carrasco and Ramírez beaches, during the summer season. There are a number of midnight-and-later bars which cater to students, writers, artists, and journalists—casual, cheap, fun; hotel desks will know the currently popular ones. Restaurant rates, in general, are modest: $2–$3 will usually buy a first-class dinner, but imported European and American whiskies are very expensive, in contrast to reasonably priced native wines and beers, which are good. Outside of Montevideo, hotel dining rooms are the principal restaurants, except at the larger resorts like Punta del Este, Atlántida, and Piriápolis, where there is a profusion of bars, cafés, and restaurants, many of them open-air, which vary in quality season by season and which are best learned about on the spot.

PRIVATE CLUBS: In Montevideo, the Golf, Automovil, and Yacht clubs are open to visitors, the first two being exceptionally pleasant for lunch. The Jockey and Uruguay clubs, with restaurants, are for members and their guests. Rotary and Lions welcome foreign members. Punta del Este's Cantegril Country Club, open to visitors, is listed in the Hotels section.

Uruguayan food specialties: As in Argentina, beef is the staple of the Uruguayan diet, prepared in a number of ways, most all of them good, and worth sampling. *Asado,* spit-roasted beef or veal, is very popular. Otherwise, again as in Argentina, the food has Italian and Spanish accents. There is a great deal of sea food,

too, fresh and imaginatively prepared. Specialties you might try:
the aforementioned *pavesa*—thick and a meal in itself; *parrillada*—
a mixed grill; *carbonada*—an unusual ragout whose ingredients include rice and a variety of fruits; and *puchero,* another type of
stew, this with sausages and beans. Milk is pasteurized, tap water
potable, green salads safe. Tea-like maté is worth knowing. Of the
Uruguayan wines, Cabernet, Santa Rosa (red), and Chablis
(white) are among the standouts, and even the champagne (Faraut
and Fond de Cave) is quite good. Beers come *rubia* (light) or
negra (dark). The Gauchos' favorite, *caña,* is rum—very cheap
and very result-producing; *grappa,* a grape brandy, has a similar
effect.

VENEZUELA

(República de Venezuela)

Entry requirements: *The time-consuming, cumbersome red tape for so long required by Venezuela for entrance has been replaced by a simple tourist card, obtainable through transportation companies and consulates—quickly and effortlessly.* **Best times for a visit:** *In Caracas the temperature is about 70° year-round, with sunny days and cool evenings; it is pleasant even during the wet season, June–December, when rains are far from incessant. The coast and Orinoco River regions are hot and humid, and the higher mountain regions are always cool.* **Currency:** *The bolívar (known colloquially as the "B"), equivalent to about thirty U.S. cents; 4.58 bolívars equal one dollar; Bs. 1 equals two reales, or four medios, or twenty centavos.* **Film availability:** *Black-and-white and color film on sale, but it's expensive.* **Language:** *Spanish, with a fair amount of English in the cities, particularly at hotels, transport terminals, and major restaurants.* **Domestic transport:** *Modern highways connect the main coastal and near-coastal cities with Caracas, and intercity bus service is good. There is also a fairly extensive domestic air network (LAV, Avensa, and*

Ransa) and Orinoco River steamer service—slow but scenic.
Tipping: *Hotels add 10 per cent service charge; additional tipping is expected but optional. Restaurants add 15 per cent service charge to bills.* **Business hours:** *Generally 8* A.M.*–12 noon, 2* P.M.*–6* P.M. **Further information:** *Venezuelan Embassy, Washington, D.C.; Venezuelan Consulate General, New York; Dirección Nacional de Turismo, Ministerio de Fomento, Caracas, Venezuela; Caribbean Tourist Association, 20 East 46th Street, New York.* **Trinidad:** *See pages 209–10.*

INTRODUCING VENEZUELA

That Vespucci man would have been the envy of Madison Avenue today. Not only are the Americas named for the intrepid Amerigo—and this long before the days of Hollywood-type press agents—but it is *his* name for Venezuela that has stuck—or so the story goes. For reasons which were clear only to himself, he detected a resemblance between the *grande palazzos* on canal-filled Venice and the simple Indian houses atop stilts on Lake Maracaibo. "Ah," said he upon first glimpse of the lake, "Venezuela —Little Venice." And so it has been. Venetians probably wish there were more resemblance between their canals and Maracaibo, whose waters cover untold petroleum wealth. And there may well be Venezuelans—possibly some of the more recent Italian immigrants, of which there have been many—who are still looking for resemblance between the "Little Venice" and the original.

Be that as it may, this republic—nearest in South America to the United States, with great natural riches, with a past more discordant than democratic, and a current government which is conscientious, liberal, and intelligent—bears firsthand acquaintance. The only stumbling block for most Americans is that it is not cheap. The dollar, very often, goes no further than it does in the United States. Still, a trip to this country can have its rewards.

A backward glance: Two peaceful groups of Indians—the Caribs,

for whom the Caribbean Sea is named, and the Arawaks—were
the original Venezuelans. It was they who constituted the reception committees for the first European tourists, among whom were
one Christopher Columbus, who happened along the coast in 1498
(on his third New World cruise), and, a year later, the aforementioned Signore Vespucci and Alonso de Ojeda, a Spaniard to
whom some attribute the "Little Venice" appellation.

But two decades were to elapse until the Spaniards could make
permanent settlements, the first was at Cumaná in 1521, and the
second, a few years later at Coro. Together with German gold-
diggers—Nikolaus Federmann among them—the Spanish went
about conquering the Indians, enslaving them to mine gold and
tend farms. By 1552 Barquisimeto was a thriving little agricultural
community. Valencia followed in its footsteps in 1555, as did
Caracas in 1567.

The New Granada period, and Bolívar: Venezuela, during this
Spanish Colonial period, was a part of the domain of New
Granada, along with what is now Colombia. For nearly a century,
the settlers relentlessly spread themselves about, gradually working
their way into the interior, intermarrying with the Indians, importing Africans to work as slaves on their sugar plantations, developing the towns into South American miniatures of their Spanish
homeland. All the while, British buccaneers were raiding and looting the coastal towns in the best derring-do tradition, and at the
same time independence winds began to blow, with the first anti-
Spanish effort (valiant but ineffective) in 1796, and two more,
led by Francisco Miranda, in 1806 and 1811. These last were
abortive but important in that they gave impetus for additional
tries. Simón Bolívar, the Young Man of Caracas (he was born
there in 1783), took over where Miranda left off.

It was not until he captured Angostura in 1817 (now called
Ciudad Bolívar, in his honor) that he began to make inroads on
the Spanish forces; joined there by Orinoco Valley cattlemen and
British troops, he undertook a fantastic march over the Andes
which culminated in victory at the Battle of Boyacá and the
capture of Bogotá. The declaration of independence of the republic

of Gran Colombia ensued, even though the Royalists had by no means been entirely routed; they were not to make their final surrender until 1823, at Puerto Cabello.

Bolívar died in 1830, and that same year, Venezuela seceded from the republic of Gran Colombia to become an independent state on its own, thanks to the dominance of José Antonio Páez, the separatist *caudillo* of the influential cattlemen, or *llaneros,* and the hero of that decisive 1823 victory battle.

The republic, and Gómez: From that time onward Venezuela was controlled by the conservative landowning classes, with one dictator or another at the helm; the only exception was the brief liberal presidency of Juan Falcón in the 1860s. But it was not enough to turn the country on the road to representative government, and things were to get worse before they got better: the reign of Juan Vicente Gómez as president lasted from 1908 until 1935, and although he brought a measure of modernity and prosperity with the help of foreign oil concessions, he was one of the most brutal, vain, corrupt, and tyrannical of the South American dictators.

Venezuela, although mildly sympathetic toward the Allied cause, did not get around to entering World War II until just before it was over, in 1945. By that time its oil revenues had begun to bring fabulous riches to the government and the already wealthy upper classes, but abject poverty remained the lot of the vast majority. The first postwar government was that of a junta headed by the man who is today's Venezuela's president, liberal Romulo Betancourt. Under his first administration Venezuela's constitution was changed so that for the first time in history, the president would be elected by direct popular vote. A distinguished writer, Romulo Gallegos, was the first man to be elected chief of state in this manner. But his 1948 victory was short-lived.

The bloody Pérez Jiménez regime: That same year a military coup, under the leadership of Colonel Marcos Pérez Jiménez, took over the government. Pérez Jiménez was to remain dictator for almost a decade, and in the gruesome fashion of the earlier Gómez he kept Venezuela in his clutches, spending vast amounts of money on grandiose public works in the neighborhood of the capital, virtually neglecting the rest of the country, offering even less education than was the case before his advent to power, tolerating fantastic corruption (in which he, his family, and his cohorts were dealt in, to the tune of millions), blacking out, with the aid of his secret-police torturers, anything resembling civil liberty, turning Caracas into what at the time looked to be an armed camp with as many machine guns as people, vulgarly amusing himself in a two-million-dollar mansion he built on a private island, to which his private planes transported bevies of young girls for the entertainment of himself and his cronies, and leaving the country in debt by half a billion dollars.

The American business community in Caracas, enriching itself on Venezuela's phony prosperity, acclaimed Pérez Jiménez as Venezuela's modern savior, and the American government considered him a warm friend, awarding him the Legion of Merit in 1954, and later naming him "Honorary Submariner" on the occasion of an admiral's visit.

But among his own people there was not this enthusiasm. He was overthrown in January 1958. Just after he had himself "re-elected," the tide turned.

An uprising in which hundreds were killed or wounded, supported by the navy, many army leaders, the politically active university students, and the population at large, forced the pudgy, gaudily-uniformed dictator to resign and flee to exile in the Dominican Republic, then the estate of a brother-dictator, Trujillo, and thence to Miami, where a court in 1961 held him to be extraditable. Less than eleven months after his ouster, the military junta which had taken power held the elections it had promised, and the attractive, competent admiral who had been the junta's head—Wolfgang Larrazabal—lost out as a candidate to Romulo Betancourt, who returned to the Presidential Palace, this time as head of a coalition administration made up of his own Democratic Action party and the two other major parties.

Betancourt—attacks from right and left: President Betancourt has not had an easy time of it; the extreme left has attacked him as not being liberal enough, and for the extreme right, he has been too liberal. His government put down an attempted coup in late 1960, which was believed to have been planned with the aid of the late Dictator Trujillo's Dominican Republic government, whose forces had earlier attempted to assassinate Betancourt. The Organization of American States, with the United States concurring, voted sanctions against the Trujillo regime as a result, and the United States even withdrew its ambassador from Santo Domingo.

Domestic crises notwithstanding—and these have included a vacillating policy toward Castro which crystallized in late 1961, when Venezuela severed diplomatic relations with Cuba—the Betancourt administration is attempting a democratic social revolution, with increased education, agrarian reform, more housing, and essential public works as its goals, and additional oil revenues from foreign exploiters providing the wherewithal. There is a long way to go: 1.7 per cent of Venezuela's families own 74 per cent of the land, and forty per cent of the population is responsible for six per cent of the gross national product.

Venezuelan-U.S. relations are good. Betancourt was among the first of the Latin leaders to endorse the Alliance for Progress, and he was the first South American president to receive Adlai Stevenson on his mid-1961 tour. The Stevenson welcome was warm, in contrast to that of the then U.S. vice-president, Richard Nixon, a few years earlier. And the reception for President and Mrs. Kennedy, in late 1961, was ecstatic.

What Venezuela needs are understanding friends and a patient populace to offset the minority of pro-Communists and reactionary soldiers and aristocrats. It must have time on its side, too, and a peaceful atmosphere in which to work out its own problems, and acquaint itself with the ways in which representative governments work, for this is a land which has known precious few years of freedom since it made such a bright and hopeful start under the aegis of its native son Simón Bolívar.

YOUR VISIT TO VENEZUELA

Venezuela is big in area (a third larger than France, and the sixth in size of the South American republics), sparsely populated (New York City exceeds it by two million), with an immense Caribbean coast line (two thousand miles) and four distinct regions (the Andean highlands in the center and northwest, the lowlands around Lake Maracaibo, the Guiana region of the east—fully half of the country's area—and the central *llanos,* or plains, of the Orinoco). The most populated, and important, of the areas is the central highland region. It contains, among much else, the capital, which for most travelers is not only the focal point but the *only* point of a Venezuelan visit. Time and budget permitting, there is no reason, however, for not going beyond Caracas. Towns you've probably never heard of have spanking new hotels, many of them part of a government-sponsored chain, the likes of a number of which, other South American countries could do with.

At the same time these towns are, for the most part, in great contrast to the capital, which the Pérez Jiménez regime modernized and glamorized, confident that the majority of foreign visitors would think it typical of the country at large. All too many did, but the Betancourt government, with nothing to hide, encourages the foreigner to have a realistic look at Venezuela as it is, with an unbelievably poor mass populace living amid the great riches of a petroleum economy. Tourism is, at long last being encouraged officially, under a program inaugurated at the end of 1961, by Development Minister Godofredo Gonzales, with the support of President Betancourt, in order to "stimulate trade, to show off our new democratic Venezuela, and particularly to contribute to greater inter-American understanding"—to quote Minister Gonzales. His first step was to simplify tourist admission procedures, so that only an easily-obtainable tourist card is now needed—and for this act alone the good minister deserves a private oil well of his own!

Caracas: Though it is almost four centuries old, Caracas is about

as Colonial in façade as Manhattan. There are some remnants
of the old days, to be sure, but in the main this metropolis of
nearly two million people is bouncy and vigorous, with a mercurial
boom-or-bust personality, skyscrapers which take your breath
away, slums near which it is better not to breathe at all, and, all
about, purple-green mountains out of whose passes are ingeniously-
chiseled superhighways leading to the nearby sea.

Caracas is not easy to love. It takes knowing, and knowing, in its
case, takes lots and lots of bolívars. The quickie visit, while always
better than none at all, leaves a lot to be desired, for this is a city
in which the populace is an intrinsic part of the picture. *Caraqueños*
are far from difficult to know, but the formerly high cost of eating
and lodging in this city—lower now, with a better dollar-exchange
rate—has prohibited far too many friendly foreigners from having the opportunity. One must be more uninhibited than usual,
and speak up!

With all of its evils, the Pérez Jiménez regime remains responsible for a good bit of the new Caracas. The moon-faced little
colonel cut himself in on the profits of every major construction
job he commissioned, and there were a good many, some serving
a useful purpose, many absurd, ostentatious, and bordering on the
vulgar.

In a country where many people are illiterate and hungry, is
there *really* a need for a cable car carrying one from the seaport
of La Guaira *directly* to the top of Mount Avila in the capital,
which itself is connected with the lower city by still another aerial
railway?

Well, that gives you an idea. There are other contemporary
facets of Caracas worth a look, too: the glitteringly ostentatious
Circulo de las Fuerzas Armadas, which Pérez Jiménez built for the
army officers he pampered, in order to maintain the loyalty which
they withdrew after a decade; the University City, with its remarkably handsome auditorium, or *aula,* and an eleven-hundred-
bed hospital; the twin towers of the Centro Simón Bolívar with its
underground arcades of shops, in the heart of town; the Military
Academy, where no expense was spared to produce a strong officer

corps; the quite striking low-rent apartment houses, which have begun to displace the revolting shack-communities on the mountainsides fringing the city; new residential areas, often overelaborate in the style of the Latin American rich, with too-well-tended gardens, always wall-enclosed.

More elderly, but hardly Spanish Colonial, are the Presidential Palace, more heavily guarded by Tommy-gun troops than are most in South America; the lush and lovely Country Club; the pretty parks and plazas, statue-filled, crisscrossed by neat, bench-lined paths, animated by children with all of the appeal of park children in any great city; and a not-bad Fine Arts Museum which borders Los Caobos Park, itself near the elaborate Botanical Gardens. There are manufacturing zones which may or may not be of interest, and busy downtown streets more interesting for strolling than shopping, Venezuela being a land virtually devoid of bargains.

Of more traditional significance are the bits and pieces of Old Caracas which remain. I should not leave the city without a pilgrimage to the Casa Bolívar, the charming house built around a tiled patio where the Liberator was born and which is now a national shrine and museum. I should want to see, too, the Pantheon, a church-turned-mausoleum, where Bolívar and other Venezuelan heroes are buried, and the still-lovely Plaza Bolívar, with an equestrian statue of its namesake behind which is the gracious and properly aged cathedral.

And I would have a look at the urn containing Venezuela's Declaration of Independence in the Elliptical Salon—a kind of historical art gallery in the National Capitol. *Caraqueños,* convinced as are *Bogateños* (the residents of Colombia's capital) that Americans feel cheated without views-from-on-high, will be disappointed if you don't take a cable car to the summit of Mount Avila (where, by the way, Pérez Jiménez had a hotel erected—hardly the most convenient location in town, the summit being 4000 feet above the city, which itself is 3136 feet high). There is not too much else for rubberneckers, except for a pair of Colonial buildings: one, the eighteenth-century Casa del Anauco, recently achieved museum status, and deservedly so; the other, San Francisco Church, has an eminently viewable golden altar. Three Caracas sports deserve special mention: U.S.-style baseball at the mammoth Caracas stadium, Spanish-style bullfights on winter Sundays, and Venezuelan-style "bull-tossing," a rodeo-related madness.

The aforementioned *La Guaira,* chief passenger-ship port of the republic, is less than a half-hour distant, via the *autopista* which was hacked through the mountains. Maquetia Airport, which serves Caracas, is about midway between the capital and the port. The latter's most impressive landmark is a big new passenger terminal. Otherwise, one need not linger there, but nearby are a number of pleasant beach resorts, at least one of which might be a pleasant day's outing. These include *Laguna Beach, Macuto, Carabelleda,* and *Los Caracas,* which has been quite extensively developed by the government as a wage-earner's vacation haunt, but which welcomes even the laziest loafers regardless of occupation or nationality.

What then? Where to, after the Caracas-La Guaira region has been explored? There are many alternatives. One can drive over the well-paved Pan-American Highway through the Andes into Colombia, by way of a chain of interesting cities each of which is also accessible by plane. One can make a flying excursion to Angel Falls, the world's highest. One can get away from it all on an Orinoco River trip, or soak in the sun on the Isle of Marguerita. Consider the possibilities which follow:

West to the Colombian frontier: The first of the major cities encountered on a westward journey from the capital, via air or Pan-American Highway, is *Maracay.* Of note primarily because of its military bases, it was the playground of the notorious dictator General Gómez (see pages 196–97). Now a town of about a hundred thousand, Maracay regards its Gómez monuments as Las Vegas does its casinos: they're simply part of the landscape. Venezuelans as well as others are among their inspectors. To be seen: the fountain-filled park of the once-luxurious Hotel Jardin which Gómez built for his guests; the Gómez mausoleum, with its enormous arch; the Gómez opera house, which he didn't quite finish building; the *small* Gómez town house—relatively modest;

the *large* Gómez town house (now Hotel Moro); the Gómez country house (where he died of old age) with the adjoining Gómez zoo; Rancho Grande, the palace Gómez was building at the time of his death; and not far away, straddling the Turiamo Naval Base, the road Gómez had constructed for emergency use as a getaway artery to the sea.

Valencia: A mite larger than its neighbor, Maracay, four-centuries-old Valencia lies on the bank of the Cabrioles River, near Lake Valencia, in the heart of a rich farming area, with a fine moderate climate, some lovely old cobbled streets, narrow and venerable, and an Andalusian-style plaza flanked by a fine cathedral and an animated market place.

Mérida: Still small—there are less than forty thousand *Merideños*—Mérida is Venezuela's loveliest Colonial gem: no industry has come to destroy the façade which conquistadors and their creole descendants gave it, and not even Pérez Jiménez attempted to glamorize it for visiting press junketeers. The rain still falls, violently and electrically, every afternoon for a brief period. The streets are still twisting and largely cobbled; the houses, though aged, stand proudly, and behind high walls are the convents of orders whose earlier members came as missionaries to convert the resident Indians of the area, whose descendants still come into the weekly Monday markets.

Mérida, for many years, had been the educational and spiritual center of Venezuela. The University of the Andes, opened in 1785, is still going strong, and the old cathedral, though rebuilt, continues to serve the faithful. Not far away, and visible from the town, is Venezuela's highest and proudest mountain, Bolívar Peak, reaching some sixteen thousand feet into the skies. There are other mountains, too—the Sierra Nevada, whose valleys are dotted with fishing lodges and ski chalets. And the most startling piece of modernity is an eight-mile cable railway, running from the town to Espejo Peak (just a little lower than Bolívar Peak), and stopping en route at a chain of five stations, each with its own restaurant and inn.

Maracaibo: The lake whose stilt-supported Indian houses re-

minded Amerigo Vespucci so much of Venice that he called it
Venezuela, is still to be reckoned with, and not because of quaint
thatch huts on poles. Oil—one billion four hundred million dollars'
worth of oil—is pumped from beneath the waters of hundred-mile-
long Lake Maracaibo every year; the hundreds of wells produce
two million barrels *per day.* The sleepy Colonial town surrounding
the lake and named for it has, since the discovery of that oil in
1917, grown in the way only oil towns can grow—like mad. It's
now a city of half a million people, with its due share of twentieth-
century appurtenances, a humid climate at its hottest during July,
August, and September, a mitigating sea breeze which blows in
blessedly each evening, an excellent hotel, a respectable quantity of
churches and parks, an interesting university, a polyglot international population drawn by the oil industry, and some Indians—the
Motilones—resident in nearby swamps; they would have nothing to
do with the white man when he arrived four centuries ago, and still
won't. The Motilones live near the Catatumbo River, above which,
virtually every evening, there is a natural fireworks display in the
form of lightning; no one has ever yet figured out its whys and
wherefores. Maracaibo's oil is piped to refineries on the not-far-
distant *Paraguaná Peninsula,* from whose ports much of it is
shipped abroad.

Puerto Cabello: Frequently a port of call for cruise ships, his-
tory-steeped Puerto Cabello is Venezuela's Number Two port after
La Guaira. It is about a ten-mile detour from the Pan American
Highway connecting Caracas with Colombia, and its main attractions are palm-fringed bathing beaches (particularly Playa
Ganango), a busy harbor, and some traces of the Colonial era,
including La Libertadora Fortress, the Plaza Flores, and a sprinkling of handsome old houses.

Ciudad Bolívar: In the days when this city was known as
Angostura, three events occurred which gave it a lasting claim to
fame: the least-known but most important of the three was re-
organization by Bolívar of his forces here, and the preparation for
his ultimate victories. The second was the inauguration of Bolívar
as president of the short-lived republic of Gran Colombia, and

the third was the invention of Angostura bitters by a physician. Visitors today need not worry about being forced into visiting the Angostura bitters factory; it was moved some decades ago to Trinidad. There remains much else of interest, though.

Ciudad Bolívar is the most significant of the Orinoco River towns; it is the trade center for that vast, sparsely-populated, still-neglected portion of tropical Venezuela. Though small, with a population of about fifty thousand, the city which bears the Liberator's name is far from languid. To its wharves and warehouses comes the exotic produce of the region: chicle and tonka beans, diamonds and gold, skins and hides. River boats, sleek and hand-crafted, and ocean-going cargo vessels crowd its harbor. Nearby are the government's immense Matanzas steelworks, and smaller ports of shipment for the iron ore and other metals mined in the region.

Ciudad Bolívar is unlike any of Venezuela's other major cities, those either in the mountains or on the Caribbean coast. Its modern airport makes it just a brief hop from Caracas, and it is the starting point for *cruises up the Orinoco*. One can, with five days at his disposal, go by fairly modern steamship all the way from Ciudad Bolívar to *Puerto Ayacucho*, capital of the Venezuela's Amazonas Territory (175,000 square kilometers in area, and with a population of but fifteen thousand, more than half of whom live in Puerto Ayacucho). The return to Ciudad Bolívar can be made in another five days, or one can fly directly to the capital. *Another river trip* worth considering takes one along the Apure River (a tributary of the Orinoco, commencing at *San Fernando de Apure,* a small but thriving cattle and oil center reached by air from Caracas) to Puerto Ayacucho. Along the way: authentically Hollywood jungle, steamy and verdant; still-unassimilated Indian communities; and a profusion of wild life, which hunters can have a go at if arrangements for permits and firearms have been made in advance.

Margarita Island: Pearl-diving, anyone? The waters of Margarita Island are the source of most of Venezuela's fine pearls. They are also swum in and fished in by an increasing number of vacationers, still mostly mainland Venezuelans. Though by no means minuscule—it is twenty miles broad at its widest point, and forty miles long—Margarita is home to only seventy thousand year-round residents, most of whom make a living fishing, pearling, weaving fiber hammocks and straw hats, and catering to visitors. *Porlamar* is the chief town and port, and *La Asunción,* the capital, is the seat of a cathedral whose Virgin's robes are pearl-studded. The beaches are wide, white, and smooth, the waters are blue and inviting, the people are delightful, and both principal towns—plus tiny *Pampatar,* another port—are charming. Best months: January through March, during which time the pearling fleets are at their busiest. There are daily flights from Caracas to Porlamar.

Angel Falls: The world's highest waterfalls, believe it or not, are a twentieth-century discovery. Named for an American flyer who happened over them in 1937, they are 3212 feet high—almost eleven times the depth of Africa's great Victoria Falls. Though considerably narrower than Victoria, and even Niagara, they are quite something to see, and can be reached in one-day excursion flights from Caracas, over the mountains to *Canaima,* near the site of the falls, which lies between the Orinoco and Amazon rivers. There's no guarantee that the falls will be visible on such a trip, for the plane flies over them for something like half an hour and fog is not infrequent. For pessimists who are convinced that a quickie trip will not yield a view, there's a simple camp near Canaima, where one may rough it for a day or two, interrupting the daily schedule by constant peeps at the cascading torrents.

WHAT TO BUY

If your budget is anything like mine, the answer is: very little. There are, however, a few fairly tempting items in Caracas, including flower-shaped *cochano* gold brooches, with pearl insets, beginning at about $15 and going up—*way* up. Rings and charms of the Venezuelan *asabache,* a black, stone-like mineral, can be had for as little as $5; you may, or may not, find them attractive.

Jewelry shops include Panchita, on Sabena Grande, the main shopping avenue, Peters Brothers, and Junin. Varied handicrafts, not a true bargain in the lot but sometimes attractive, are on sale at the government's shop, and at the Hotel Tamanaco's gift shop; artisans include Orinoco forest Indians. Margarita Island's little shops offer locally-retrieved natural pearls, mother-of-pearl items, and a variety of straw stuff, of the kind found all over the Caribbean.

CREATURE COMFORTS

HOTELS—**Caracas:** The modern, strikingly-designed, four hundred-room Tamanaco is one of the continent's finest. Part of the Intercontinental Hotel chain, it features excellent service, a honey of a swimming pool, handsome bedrooms (all with bath), a coffee shop, bar, dining room, and *boîte,* and splendid views of the city from the mountain on which it is situated, in one of the city's newer residential sections. From $15 single. Others: Not on Mount Avila, but in still another residential section, is the Avila, whose facilities include a pool and 120 rooms-with-bath; the Humboldt *is* atop Mount Avila, is often encircled by clouds, contains only suites, starting at about $20 per day, and is accessible only by cable car; the El Conde, all of whose rooms have showers but no tubs, is downtown, as is the Potomac, also tubless. Cheaper hotels include the Mara, Anauco, Tiuna, Comercio, and Savoy. **Macuto,** 20 miles from Caracas, and near both La Guaira and Maiquetia (the capital's international airport) is the site of the glittering new Macuto-Sheraton, operated by the Sheraton chain, built at a cost of $20 million, with 410 air-conditioned rooms, 2 pools, a 1500-foot Caribbean beach, golf privileges, deep-sea fishing facilities, and a number of restaurants and bars—including a rooftop nightclub. **Maracaibo:** Here, the leader is another Intercontinental hotel—del Lago—air-conditioned, sleek-lined, with a fine pool, excellent dining room, *boîte,* friendly bar, even private bungalows; from $13.50 single. Number Two is the Detroit. Others:

Granada, Shamrock, Fitzwater, Peters. **Maracay:** The Maracay is one of the newest and handsomest of the Conahotu chain. **Puerto Cabello:** Los Banos, in town; Rivera, Balneario Cumboto, on the beach. **La Guaira:** No hotels. **Valencia:** Carabobo—central and modern; Victoria, Gran Hotel Valencia. **Barquisimeto:** Neuvo-Segovia—modern and with pool; Rex, Lara. **Mérida:** Prado del Rio—modern and with pool; Sierra, Tinjaca. **San Cristóbal:** Tama—new and unusually handsome, with pool; Bella Vista. **Ciudad Bolívar:** Gran Hotel Bolívar—modern and attractive; Piscina. **Puerto Ayacucho:** Amazonas. **San Fernando de Apure:** Apure. **Porlamar** (Margarita Island): Bella Vista—new, charming, all rooms with bath and balcony, swimming pool, $10 single with meals; Bahia. **Trujillo:** Trujillo—new and pleasant. **La Puerta** (near Maracaibo): Guadalupe—extremely good.

RESTAURANTS AND NIGHT LIFE—**Caracas:** Eating well is expensive—an orange-juice, toast, and coffee breakfast in a hotel coffee shop can cost $1.25. With that as a guide, and bearing in mind that Caracas is generally more expensive than the smaller cities, here goes: Besides the excellent restaurants of the Tamanaco, there are the Avila and El Conde hotel dining rooms; Tony's—elaborate and with international cuisine; Hector's—expensive (figure $6 for dinner) but delicious; Chez Abadie, La Cremaillere, Montmartre, Monseigneur—all with French food; El Palmar—Chinese; Centro Venezuelano-Americano—foods of both nations; Tarzilandia and the Steak House—both good for beef specialties; El Campo—for fine Venezuelan food; Pergola, Chicote, Antatoe, Tyrol, Dragon Verde, Rincon Bavaria, Casa Italia, and, if you're really set to splurge, Belle Epoque. For dining, dancing, and mostly-imported entertainment, the Montmartre, listed above, is pleasant, as is the Naiguiata Room of the Tamanaco. Others— and I warn you, they're *all* expensive—include a Caracas institution called My Vaca y Yo (My Cow and I), which features an itinerant cow, wandering at will from table to table; Ali Baba, Bagdad, Mazot, and the aforementioned Tony's and Hector's.

PRIVATE CLUBS: Those in Caracas include Caracas Country, Valle

Arriba Golf, Paraiso, and Venezuela. Rotary and Lions are found in major cities throughout the country.

Venezuelan food specialties: *Sancocho*—a chicken-meat-vegetable stew; *hallucas*—tamales wrapped in banana leaves and containing a mixture of meat, eggs, corn, and olives; also good: *mondongo* soup; oysters and clams served with lemon juice are typically Venezuelan snacks, at the beaches. The country's own rums and beers are good, and a beverage specialty is eggnog known as *ponche crema*. It should go without saying that imported whiskies are expensive.

TRINIDAD

Though not a part of South America, Trinidad, a member of the British Commonwealth, lies just a few miles from its northern coast, just a stone's throw (seven miles) from Venezuela. It is frequently included as a stopover point in air travelers' South American itineraries, and is a port of call, as well, for certain ships which ply the continent's Atlantic coast. Exuberant *Port of Spain* is the capital. Nearly fifty miles long, and some thirty-five miles wide, Trinidad is lushly tropical (January–May is the driest season) and has a wonderfully conglomerate population. Asia is represented by descendants of East Indians and Chinese, Africa by Negroes, Europe by Portuguese, Spaniards, and of course British Colonials. There are Hindu temples, Moslem mosques, Christian churches, intriguing bazaars, cultures and customs which run the gamut of nationalities and religions. And in addition there are splendid bathing beaches, and a bonus in the weather department— cool evenings.

Besides the attractions of the capital, centered around Woodford Square and including the Queen's Park Savannah and nearby Botanic Gardens, there are any number of excursion possibilities into the countryside. Just twenty minutes distant by air is the island of Tobago, a dependency of Trinidad and a bird-filled, beach-dotted paradise, reputedly the locale of Defoe's *Robinson Crusoe*.

The spanking new Trinidad Hilton, in Port of Spain, is one of the finest hotels in the West Indies—elegant, luxurious, strikingly designed, and highly recommended. From $11 single. Others in the capital are the Queen's Park (from $10 single), Bretton Hall (from $10 single), Bergerac, Normandy, and Coblentz, as well as a guest house and small hotel (BelAir) at the airport. Tobago's leading hotels—all American Plan—include the Arnos Vale Beach, Bluehaven, Robinson Crusoe, and Bacolet. There is, of course, calypso music unlimited, and there are a number of restaurants in Port of Spain; most interesting are those with Chinese and East Indian cuisines, the Lotus and the Kimling among them. The unit of currency is the West Indian dollar, worth about sixty U.S. cents. *Further information:* Trinidad and Tobago Tourist Board, 48 East 43rd Street, New York, and Port of Spain, Trinidad; Varig Airlines, 634 Fifth Avenue, New York.

W E S T E R N
South America

BOLIVIA

CHILE

COLOMBIA

ECUADOR

PANAMA

PERU

WESTERN SOUTH AMERICA

*Drawing his sword, he traced a line with it on the sand from
East to West. Then, turning towards the South, "Friends and
comrades," he said, "on that side are toil, hunger, nakedness,
the drenching storm, desertion and death; on this side, ease and
pleasure. There lies Peru with its riches; here, Panama and its
poverty. Choose, each man what best becomes a brave Castillian.
For my part, I go to the South." So saying, he stepped across the
line.*

—Pizarro *to his followers, in* The Conquest
of Peru,* *by William H. Prescott* (1847)

Two factors set western South America apart from the eastern
portion of the continent: the Andes, which parallel the entire
length of the Pacific coast, rising to sometimes staggering heights;
and the Indians—substantial parts of the populations of Bolivia,
Ecuador, and Peru, minorities in Chile, Colombia, and Panama.

The ethnic make-up of the community—the presence of the
Indian in large numbers in the countries which are the core of
western South America—is quite as responsible for the region's
special flavor as is the terrain. The Spaniard, when he arrived and
for long after, came close to being a fanatic in his zeal to transplant
his civilization to the New World. He succeeded in many ways,
among his own people and among the enormous mestizo class
which he was largely responsible for creating. But among the
indigenous peoples he has been successful in injecting little else
besides his religion. The way of life of as many as half of the inhabitants of several of the western South American republics remains quite as it has been for many hundreds of years.

There is change in the air now, more than ever before since the
colonies became republics a century and a half ago. But before the

* Now available in a paperback edition, with a fascinating introduction by
Victor W. von Hagen (New American Library, 1961) and recommended
pre-trip reading.

Indian and European communities of such lands as Bolivia, Ecuador, and Peru are integrated, the traveler has the opportunity of
observing them as they co-exist, particularly if he will wend his
way from the capital cities into the countryside.

The handiwork of the European and his descendants embraces
the entire region, from the southern tip of Patagonia to the
Isthmian highlands. And it runs a wide gamut: German-settled
agricultural communities, British-built railroads, the American-
designed and engineered Panama Canal, and most of all, the architectural genius of the Spaniard: great churches in Quito and Cuzco,
still dazzling baroque towns including rarely-visited ones like
Potosí in Bolivia, La Serena in Chile, Cuenca in Ecuador.

Here, too, are those vestiges of the Old Spain of the aristocrat—
the gentleman-farmer with near-feudal domains, the social structure in which a middle class is only beginning to emerge, the caste
system held together for centuries by the force of tradition, and
only just beginning to weaken.

Western South America is that region of the continent where
the blacks are very black, the whites very white, the middling grays
only just beginning to appear perceptible. Here things are felt
strongly, by the visitor as well as the resident. The purples and
browns and whites of the tremendous mountain ranges are clearly
and crisply delineated. The ponchos and *rebozos* and petticoats
of the Indians are vivid and indelible. Tiled plazas, towered cathe-
drals, low green valleys, Inca and Aymara and Chibcha and
Araucanian relics—all impart a durability and timeliness which
convey history in terms of eras rather than generations or even
centuries.

Perhaps like no other part of the world, western South America
brings one into contact, at once sobering and joyous, with the
glories and the shames of civilizations so diverse that not even
half a millennium has fused them.

BOLIVIA

(*República de Bolivia*)

Entry requirements: *No visas or tourist cards required of U.S. tourists, just a valid passport and health certificate.* Best times for a visit: *Western Bolivia (the most-visited area, which includes La Paz) is pleasantly cool year-round, about like October in the northern United States; the lower eastern regions are semitropical—hot and humid. The wet season (December–March) is not incessantly rainy by any means, but roads and the airports in lesser cities are often closed at this time. The dry season—April to November—is ideal: clear skies, and with transport at its best for trips out of La Paz.* Currency: *The boliviano, about 15,000 to the U.S. dollar. Notes come in large denominations (1000, 5000, 10,000), however. Still, a simplified system is under consideration by the government. The inflationary boliviano has made Bolivia one of the cheapest countries on the continent for travelers with dollars.* Film availability: *It's advisable to have an adequate supply of your own, particularly color.* Languages: *Spanish is the official language, but Indians, who are by far the majority of the population, speak either*

Quechua or Aymara, plus Spanish if they're city-dwellers or with some education. English is spoken a good deal in La Paz, Cochabamba, and at air terminals and hotels. **Domestic transport:** *Lloyd Aereo Boliviano, the national airline, is the best bet for trips to major centers, except for excursions by car in the La Paz region, and the Yungas. Roads are generally poor, particularly during the wet season, and provincial airports are sometimes closed when rains are heavy. Railroads are narrow-gauge and can be grimy; interesting, though, from La Paz to Lake Titicaca, for passengers en route to Peru, from the lake, via steamer.* **Tipping:** *Hotels add 10 per cent service charge; taxi drivers are not tipped; otherwise, 10–15 per cent.* **Business hours:** *9 A.M.–12 noon, 2 P.M.–6 P.M.* **Further information:** *Bolivian Embassy, Washington, D.C.; Panagra, Chrysler Building, New York, and La Paz, Bolivia; Dirección Nacional de Turismo, La Paz, Bolivia; Dirección Nacional de Informaciones de la Presidencia de la República, La Paz, Bolivia; Turbol Travel Agency, Sucre Palace Hotel, La Paz, Bolivia.*

INTRODUCING BOLIVIA

Readers of gossip columns know of the Patiño family, one of the most opulently wealthy in the world; they are Bolivians. Bolivian, too, are the great mass of Indians and mestizos who constitute 95 per cent of the population, and who are, for the most part, poor and illiterate. The Patiños and the Indians (there is not much in between) have virtually nothing in common except their little-known country. Paraguay excepted, it is the least-visited of the South American republics, and at once fantastically beautiful and generously hospitable, with an intriguing past, a dynamic present, and tough sledding notwithstanding, a hopeful future.

Here, after all, is a land without a seacoast, with the world's highest capital (as well as the world's highest golf courses *and* the world's highest ski run), with an area twice that of France and a population smaller than Chicago's, with a quarter of the world's supply of tin, potentially wealthy lowlands which are virtually uninhabited in contrast to the dramatically bleak *altiplano,* which is the population center. Bolivia's history records, since independence, nearly a dozen constitutions, more than three-score revolts, and a half-dozen presidential assassinations, and it is in Bolivia that the last half-decade has seen a vigorous, idealistic, and young-spirited revolutionary government set itself the task of transforming an isolated, feudal barony into a modern twentieth-century state, with the help of recently-pledged, large-scale U.S. aid. How did Bolivia come to be? What brought the Spaniards to settle in its mountain fastness? And what did they find when they arrived?

A backward glance: This is as good a place as any to emphasize, in loud, clear tones, that the Incas are not the *only* Indians of western South America. *Other* Indians, from which the Incas are believed by some archaeologists to have derived a part of their culture, are largely lost in the shuffle. I refer to the Aymara group, many of whose descendants still inhabit the Lake Titicaca area of Bolivia and adjoining Peru. Except for the ancient language which they still speak, little is left of their greatness. The Incas were later to conquer, but not to absorb, them, and the Spaniards and their descendants were then to become the bossmen for several centuries; they are still in neighboring Peru and Ecuador.

But we are getting ahead of the story, which should begin with at least mention of the Tiahuanaco civilization, whose ruins are still the goal of today's Bolivian sight-seers. Standing at the southern tip of that great inland sea in the clouds, Lake Titicaca, are the monuments of the Aymaras' early skills: a sobering monolithic gateway, and remains of houses and other substantial edifices, built of massive stones weighing up to a hundred tons, and brilliant specimens of masonry at its most ingenious. Without using mortar, stones were fitted to a precision in squaring, cutting, and notching equaled in no other early society on the continent, the Incas included—all in a region of the world thirteen thousand feet above sea level. The dates of construction? Archaeologists vary in their estimates. Some say they go back five hundred years before Christ. Others say they were begun about A.D. 600, and that building continued through 900, with an additional spurt two or three centuries later. Carbon-14 tests place construction at the beginning of the Christian era.

There is little doubt, though, that their culture excelled not only at structural architecture, but at finely wrought bas-relief carving in stone, ceramics, weaving, and work in metals. The zenith of the Aymara civilization had already been reached, and they were in their descent, by the time the Incas came east from Peru to conquer them in the thirteenth century. A hundred-odd years later even the powerful Incas came under the thumb of Pizarro's forces, which, ignoring the dizzying heights of the harsh *altiplano,* came in force.

The silver rush: Their mission was treasure, and they found what they were after—mountains of silver. Sucre was founded in 1538, and within two decades Bolivia had become the Audiencia of Charcas, functioning as a division of the viceroyalty of Peru. A few years later Potosí began to thrive as a silver-mining center, and it became, quite rapidly, one of the finest of the Spanish cities on the continent, as even today's visitors will bear witness.

As early as 1661, unrest against the rigid Spanish regime began to manifest itself, when the mestizos of La Paz revolted—the first attempt at freedom in Colonial South America; pure-blood Indians followed suit on a number of occasions, and even held La Paz for a very brief period in 1780. It was at the University of San Francisco Xavier, in Sucre—one of the oldest in the Americas—that the first formal declaration of liberty for all of the Spanish colonies was made, in 1809, but it was not until the forces of José de San Martín and Simón Bolívar gained strength that Bolivia became free, at the Battle of Ayacucho in 1824, when Bolívar's general, Antonio José de Sucre, was victorious. On August 25, 1825, the Republic of Bolivia was decreed sovereign and given its name, some say by Bolívar himself.

Unhappy republic: Independence did not prove to be Utopia.

The social structure remained unchanged—Spanish aristocrats and their descendants, known as creoles, exploited the Indian majority in the mines and on the great estates. The rich got richer, and the Indians barely eked out an existence. Bolivia, which had a seacoast at birth, lost it to Chile in the War of the Pacific, which raged for four years from 1879 to 1884, and emerged the loser, with nothing gained but a railway which Chile built from Arica to La Paz. Later, the pattern repeated itself: Argentina annexed some of Bolivia's Chaco territory, and gave it in exchange another railway. But the greatest loss was that of the latest, and most horribly devastating, war, against Paraguay, lasting from 1928 to 1930, and revived again in 1933 for two more years. Paraguay gained three-fourths of the immense Chaco plains; its lowland troops were on home ground and slaughtered those of Bolivia, mostly from the rarified atmosphere of the *altiplano,* and unable to breathe well near sea level.

And so it went. Absolutely nothing seemed to work in Bolivia's favor, geographically, socially, economically, politically. Presidents came and went—some by old age, some by assassination, at least one by suicide. Constitutions were scrapped and replaced, of little more value than the paper on which they were printed. By the time World War II rolled around, influential pro-Nazi Germans had settled in the cities; even the national airline was German-run. The government which took control in 1940 expelled the German minister, and relations with the Axis powers were broken off. In 1943 Bolivia entered the war with the Allies; it became later a charter member of the United Nations. The current president, Dr. Victor Paz Estenssoro, first came into the limelight as Minister of Finance during the Villaroel administration after the war. Villaroel was hanged but Paz Estenssoro, one of the most militant members of the Movimento Nacionalisto Revolucionario (MNR) fled to Argentina.

The revolutionary government: The MNR was outlawed, but it vainly attempted to overthrow the regime which succeeded it in 1949. In 1951 it was again voted into power, with Paz Estenssoro the president. But before he could return from his Argentine exile, a military junta took over, remaining in office until May 1952, when a popular, but harsh, revolution succeeded in overthrowing the junta, and bringing Paz Estenssoro to La Paz and the President's Palace. He was succeeded by Herman Siles in 1956, but was re-elected in 1960. His government—a coalition of the MNR and the Labor Party—is attempting, and not without success, to completely change the fabric of Bolivian life, through a policy, still barely attempted in other largely-Indian Latin countries, of universal suffrage with no literacy requirements (thereby giving the vote and participation in government to all the Indians, for the first time in modern history), expropriation and nationalization of the tin mines, and land reform through redistribution of the immense, feudal estates. Full democracy has not been achieved, by any means, but the ordinary Bolivian realizes that his government is at last concerned with his welfare and is actually doing something about it. A new MNR-written constitution went into effect in August 1961. It incorporates the reform policies of the government, strengthens executive power, separates the Catholic church from the government, makes possible the re-election of a president, and ends capital punishment.

The United States, in an unprecedented move, announced in mid-1961 that it was aiding the Bolivian government with a $10-million loan, part of which would assist the recently activated government-operated oil monopoly and the government-run tin mines as well. This was the first U.S. grant to a nonprivate industry, and indicated a measure of flexibility and realism in the Kennedy administration's Latin American program which had not been in evidence during the Eisenhower years. Additional help came in 1961 from the Inter-American Development Bank, which proposed a plan to save the nationalized mines, by means of $38 million in foreign credits.

The wealthy Bolivian whom the American visitor meets today in La Paz or Cochabamba will no doubt moan and groan about the current govenment, and understandably enough. His status has been tampered with. His wealth may be reduced. His children may have to go to school one day with Indian children—still virtually unheard of in Bolivia. But he, the rich Bolivian, is part of an infinitesimal minority. What counts in the long run is the great mass, who want an education, a decent house, a good job, and hope for their children's future. If Bolivia's antagonistic internal factions can resolve their differences, it may just be that all these are in the offing.

YOUR VISIT TO BOLIVIA

Bolivia, at first glance, simply doesn't make sense. Eye-opener Number One: Approximately three-quarters of its four million citizens live in an area which constitutes but a tenth of the total land mass of some 425,000 square miles. (Only four South American countries are bigger.) Eye-opener Number Two: That populated 10 per cent of the country is pretty close to the clouds, the altitude of the *altiplano* region hovering about thirteen thousand feet. Eye-opener Number Three: The country itself is hemmed in by the Andes, which separate it from the sea, to the west. And its two great divisions, the lofty *altiplano* and the tropical lowlands, are also separated by a mountain range, with but minimal communications connecting the two.

It is in Bolivia that the Andes are at their widest—about four hundred miles. Dividing Bolivia from Chile is the near-arid western Cordillera, with peaks approximating twenty thousand feet in elevation, and some volcanoes, for variety. The *altiplano* itself, lying to the east of the western Cordillera, embraces almost forty thousand square miles, and is over five hundred miles long, with the northern part the more liveable and the more occupied, and the southern part mostly desert. Eye-opener Number Four: Lake Titicaca, the most unlikely of the world's inland seas, is at an altitude of twelve thousand five hundred feet, with an area of thirty-five hundred square miles.

Eye-opener Number Five: The Bolivians themselves—the great majority Quechua and Aymara Indians, whose traditional cultures impart a special and appealing flavor to the country, and the Euro-

pean-descended minority, which embodies graciousness and hospitality. The social revolution their government is attempting to
achieve makes Bolivia the most politically exciting of the South
American republics.

In no other republic on the continent is a government attempting such sweeping changes, in no other country is the challenge
greater or the gap between haves and have-nots more divergent,
in no other country is the setting—physical and cultural—more
fantastic, and in no other country can a visit be more rewarding.
The question, Is this a land to visit?, answers itself. It's time that
the Bolivian "detour" sign be removed from the itineraries of
South American travelers. And it's time, too, that the oft-repeated
bugaboo about the unhealthful quality of Bolivia's *altiplano* altitude be dispensed with.

The only travelers who need concern themselves with the lofty
heights are those with heart conditions, and I have friends so
afflicted who have not been bothered. Others need only take things
easily during their first few days—walking slowly, resting at midday and late afternoon as well as at night, and eating (and drinking!) moderately, at least during the first days after arrival. (The
near-avoidance of solid foods for the first twenty-four hours is
often recommended, and a Bolivian friend at the United Nations
in New York advises travelers to his country to take a Dramamine
pill just before arrival in La Paz; if you like, query your physician,
in advance of departure, for his counsel.)

La Paz: No matter how the visitor arrives, by air, or by train
from coastal Chile, or by boat-train combination from Peru, his
first headquarters in Bolivia is undoubtedly Nuestra Señora de La
Paz—La Paz—the unofficial (but actual) capital, the business
mecca, and the cultural headquarters of the republic. (The official
capital is Sucre, where the Supreme Court sits.) I hope that on
your first visit you reach La Paz by air, because landing at its airport is one of the great experiences of international travel. Even
the dramatic flight over the Himalayas from Patna, India, to Kat-
mandu, Nepal, pales in contrast to the landing in the Bolivian
capital.

The La Paz airport, it must be noted, is even higher than the city itself—on a plain of the *altiplano,* nearing fourteen thousand feet in altitude, which is nearly two thousand feet higher than the town. As the aircraft approaches the airport (assuming the passenger is on the right-hand side of the plane), the view is of the barren, windswept landing field, over which looms the jagged, snow-covered peak of Mount Illimani, soaring 21,185 feet upward.

As the plane touches down, and the passenger alights, he is whisked through customs, and more likely than not, the vista that greets him is modern Bolivia in miniature: the twentieth-century modernity of the air terminal and the aircraft themselves, in contrast to a phlegmatic-appearing llama or two tied to a hitching post in the terminal garden, not far from a family or two of *altiplano* Indians, squatting on the ground, babies peering from papoose-like containers on their mother's backs, ambulatory youngsters clustered about baskets of food (in which are interspersed bottles of Coca-Cola).

Into a taxi you go, for the descent to the city, unprepared (unless you've had warning) for the glories of the journey. And look sharp, for just yards from the air terminal, the car makes a swift turn, and before you, set in a cavernous, almost circular valley, lies La Paz, built on steep tiers, with the town center at the bottom, and that magnificent Illimani peak towering over it all. If the day is fine, with the sky a vivid blue, the outline of the mountain sharp and white, and the beige skyline of the town clear, you are almost justified in believing that what is to follow will be anticlimactic. But approached the right way, you will not be disappointed.

La Paz, a city of a third of a million people, is very special—not without its share of modernity, to be sure, but with an *ambiance* which gives South American capitals their own special flavor. In this case, the recipe is a delicious mélange of Indian and Spanish Colonial, with judicious dashes, in just the right proportion, of the accoutrements of this century.

In no other capital on the continent is there such a high proportion of Indians. In Lima and Quito, the Indian is evident, but not in quantity. In Santiago and Bogotá, he is virtually nonexistent, and in the eastern capitals, he is less in evidence than he is in Washington or New York. But the Indian and the *chollo,* or mestizo, *is,* to all intents and purposes, the backbone of La Paz. The poorer he is, the higher up he lives. (La Paz is just the opposite of most cities, in this respect; here the richer folk live down below, where the altitude is not quite so rarified, the climb to one's home not so steep.) The lower the street, the more fashionable it is, and the suburbs, unlike those "in the hills" of so many other cities, are even closer to sea level, with Obrajes, for example, sixteen hundred feet below the city center.

If he is male, the city Indian's costume is likely to be western— blue-jean trousers, work shirt, sweater, and jacket or topcoat. But the distaff Indians have, for the most part, clung to their traditional dress—bright-hued wide skirts under which there are a quantity of vivid *polleras,* or petticoats, gaily embroidered blouses covered with hand-woven *rebozos,* or shawls, of varying shades, over which still additional *rebozos* carry either merchandise or infants, under the protective brims of derby-type hats covering black, pigtailed coiffures.

The Indians are, of course, all about the town, but they may be seen en masse on any day at the Central Market, and on Sunday at the Plaza San Francisco Market, when they sell, among other things, the superb products of their own making—ponchos, *rebozos,* vicuña and alpaca cloth by the meter, blankets, and all manner of silver goods. In addition, and here the customers are largely Bolivians who like bargains, there are contraband bottles of Scotch, imported sport shirts, and other items of clothing for both men and women, as well as toiletries, pots and pans, bits and pieces of furniture, and although I have never spotted one, I'm sure there must be a kitchen sink or two.

The silver-hunting Spaniards selected the site of La Paz over four centuries ago, to afford them some protection from the winds of the higher plateau. And though it cannot be denied that they must have been just a little mad to have had the courage to build a town in so remote and so elevated a part of the world, the location they chose is not without its advantages. The temperature hovers

about the 50° mark all year long, with nights invariably cold, and
days, at least during the dry season, bright, crystal-clear, and sunny.
Snow is virtually unheard of, and even during the wet months the
rain falls no more than a few hours of each day, and some days
not at all.

Bisecting the town, at its lower extremities, is the La Paz River,
to the northeast of which is the main district, with the Plaza Murillo
(named not for the painter but for a Bolivian hero) its focal point.
Pleasantly landscaped, the Plaza is bordered by a huge, modern,
and not terribly attractive cathedral whose chief attribute is a
seating capacity of ten thousand; the good-looking President's
Palace, which is not open to the public; and the interesting Legislative Palace, where guards are delighted to escort visitors about,
particularly to the elaborate, portrait-dotted chambers of the upper
and lower houses.

Aside from the Plaza Murillo, the high point of a La Paz stroll
is the Prado, its most imposing thoroughfare, and, like many
South American streets, with two names, the other being Avenida
16 de Julio. This is promenade territory. Wide, with carefully-
tended boulevard-like gardens in its center artery, it is at its most
interesting at sundown of each day, and before noon on Sundays,
when the strollers have music to walk by, courtesy of the municipal and military bands.

More serious sight-seeing highlights of the Bolivian capital
would include the National Museum (also called the Tiahuanaco
Museum) with superb exhibits of relics from Tiahuanaco, as well
as other memorabilia of Bolivia's past, and the Tiahuanaco Outdoor Museum, with still more of the curious remnants of that
early civilization. I would have a look, too, at the sixteen-story
skyscraper University of San Andrés, whose students are glad to
talk with visitors and show them about; San Francisco Church,
the city's principal Colonial building, with a fine façade, starkly
simple and impressive, and a dark but pleasant interior, with the
congregation dominantly Indian; and the old Santo Domingo and
San Sebastian churches, with Indian designs in the interior of
the former. For a handsome view of the town and the mountains

which encircle it, an excursion to Monticulo Park is recommended.

Otherwise, La Paz is a town in which to relax—informal, un-guided walks, shopping expeditions, possibly a movie, play, ballet, or concert at the pleasantly ornate Teatro Municipal, and after a few easygoing days, during which time the altitude has been ad-justed to, excursions to nearby points in and around the *altiplano,* the valley city of Cochabamba, and, for the hardy traveler, other parts of the country.

Excursions from La Paz: *Lake Titicaca,* that wonderfully-named inland sea, is, of course, the largest navigable and closest-to-the-clouds body of fresh water in the world—120 miles long, 40 miles wide, and as much as a thousand feet deep. It is not far from La Paz, and it can be visited via a number of schemes. Some travelers come upon it en route to the capital from Peru, via train from Are-quipa or Cuzco to Puno—the lake's principal port, in Peru—thence by overnight steamer across the water to *Guaqui,* from which La Paz is three hours distant via either car or train. This is a worthwhile journey and it can be, and often is, made in either direction, both to and from Peru.

But for the visitor who is traveling from one country to the other by plane, Lake Titicaca is easily approached by excursion car from La Paz. The outing can be for as little as a single day, depending upon the time available and the particular lake destina-tions chosen, some being more distant and time-consuming than others, on a body of water so enormous.

If I were a visitor with but a single day to devote to the lake region, I should head for *Huatajata,* a pleasant village on the shores of the lake, with Indian farms bordering it on either side. Lunch and/or tea can be had at the club's little headquarters; there are powerboats available for fishermen with a yen for im-mense lake trout, and there are the apparently limitless craft of the immense balsa fishing fleet, which provide a livelihood for men of the many families whose little farms border the water. The balsas are ingeniously-designed little rowing boats, made now as they have been for many centuries by the lake's Indians, out of the *totona* reed which grows in the lake's marshes. On some, even the sails are made of the same material as the craft itself. Seating capacity is limited to two, and the boats have short lives, water-logging limiting their hardiness. But they ride with the waves, serve the fishermen amply, and are equaled aesthetically—at least in my view—only by the kayak of the Eskimo and the pirogue of the African. Don't hesitate to board one yourself; there are always a number moored at the Yacht Club landing, and the skippers are not unlike captains of larger vessels elsewhere—friendly, hospitable, and delighted to have you aboard, to pose for a photo with you, or give you a sample ride, not without charge, of course.

On your way back to the city, drive slowly, and look sharply to right and to left. The route is scenically lovely—the mountains reflecting themselves on the surface of the blue lake, the balsas silhouetting themselves on the horizon, the neat sod farmhouses of the Indians, whose land is worked mostly with the same tools, and on the same pattern, as it was before the arrival of the conquistadors. Stop, here and there, at a farmhouse and ask permission to take a photograph of one of the ladies of the family at work on her loom, or of the youngsters in hand-woven costumes which are exact replicas of their dads', or of the family's livestock—ducks and ducklings, geese and goslings, pigs and piglets, cows and calves, goats and kids. Take a good look at the superb ponchos and *rebozos*. And consider, too, while in the midst of this rooftop of the world, the magnitude of the task before the Bolivian government, which wants to bring these people a measure of the blessings of a technology which most have yet to become acquainted with.

Some twenty miles from Huatajata and the Yacht Club is *Tiquina,* an interesting little town worth a stopover on the way to *Copacabana*. At the Strait of Tiquina cars are floated across the lake on boats, and from the other side of the lake *Copacabana* is thirty miles distant. It has been a center of pilgrimages for the Indians of the region for some five centuries, ever since the Indian Tito Yupanqui carved a small but lovely "dark virgin" for the local church. The Yupanqui virgin is now encased in gold and silver in the church, which diminates lovely Copacabana Bay—part of it in Peru, part (including the village and shrine) in Bolivia. Though the beach named Copacabana in Rio is considerably more famous, at least in the United States, the Copacabana in Bolivia is the original. It is an Indian name, not a European one, and it means "Beholder of the Sacred Stone."

The Indian who carved the statue within the village shrine attempted three earlier versions, none of them a success, each in a different material. The final gilded carving is little more than a yard high, and the church in which it is housed dates from the seventeenth century. It was honored at a special ceremony, authorized by papal decree, in 1925, and it has become one of the most important shrines in South America, so famous is its Virgin of the Lake, and so credited is it with miracles. Visitors in the region on February 2 or August 5 do well to be in Copacabana on those days, when the Virgin's coronation is celebrated. Copacabana, even without its unusually interesting shrine, is exceptionally lovely, and is fortunate in that it possesses a good restaurant and a tolerable little hotel, the trip from La Paz almost necessitating an overnight stay.

For the visitor who enjoys extensive motorboat rides, a trip to the *Islands of the Sun and of the Moon* can be a pleasant excursion, with the departure point the Yacht Club at Huatajata. The islands, according to legend, are the birthplace of the Inca civilization. Some Inca ruins are still visible, but the islands need not have a priority on any itinerary.

Deserving of priority is, however, *Tiahuancaco* (see pages 217–18), the great pre-Inca ruins which border Lake Titicaca and are but a three-hour trip by car from the capital. The trip can be a one-day excursion, and I should not miss it, even though some remnants of the Tiahuanaco culture are on view in La Paz. There is nothing comparable, in town, to the great Puerto del Sol, or Gate of the Sun, and it should be seen in its own setting to be viewed in proper perspective. Worth viewing, too on the site: The Acapana Hill pyramid, fifty feet high and some six hundred feet in length.

For skiers and golfers: Not far from La Paz are *Chacaltaya,* which the Bolivians modestly but honestly bill as the world's highest ski run, and *Mallasilla Valley,* which is the site of the highest-elevated golf course in the universe. Though the Mallasilla is hardly a sight-seeing requisite for nongolfers, Chacaltaya *is* for nonskiers, like me, who, skis or no, are advised to board the ski lift for a ride to the top, and be rewarded with one of the most glorious vistas imaginable—on a clear day one's eye can encompass an area one hundred square miles in breadth, embracing the heart of the Bolivian Andes. Chacaltaya, about fifty miles from La Paz, is inexpensively reached by train, and its new pride and joy is a ski lodge which does not require credentials from nonskiers come for the view.

The Yungas valleys: A quick change from the *altiplano?* By all means. Your destination should then be the Yungas valleys, colloquially known simply as "The Yungas," visitable in as little as a day, and worthy of a spot on any Bolivian itinerary. Leaving La Paz early in the morning, one ascends before descending, and within an hour the car is at an altitude of some fifteen thousand feet, driving through an area where it snows more often than not. The land is bleak and white, the only ways to look are down, into valleys on the grand scale, or straight ahead, on to pastureland alive with llamas and alpacas darting through the snow, their offspring following close behind. At intervals a solitary Indian farmhouse breaks in upon the quiet solitude of the area, and before one knows it, the road descends rapidly, into considerably warmer and greener territory, temperate-zone for a while, and then semitropical, with lush foliage, and farms and orchards which make the Yungas the breadbasket of much of Bolivia. *Coroico* is the most popular destination, thanks to its passably good hotel for those staying over, and a dining room for those wanting only lunch before the return to La Paz that afternoon. *Tip:* If undertaken during the wet season, take along a box lunch; road conditions may preclude arrival at Coroico and the car may have to turn back; it's good to have some food along.

Cochabamba: The favorite city of foreigners resident in Bolivia, largely because of a mild climate and an elevation almost four

thousand feet lower than that of La Paz, Cochabamba is the pleasant Second City of Bolivia, in the heart of a fertile region of farms
and orchards. A good bit smaller than La Paz—its population
hovers around 100,000—it is also considerably less dramatic a
place than the capital. The highlights of a visit would be the
admittedly dazzling Municipal Market (here the women wear
white, flat-brimmed hats, in contrast to the brown derbies of La
Paz; each region has its own women's headgear); the Cancha
wholesale market; the vista of the city and surrounding area from
San Sebastian, a conveniently-placed midtown hill; the charming
Spanish-style houses and public buildings, and the gracious Plaza
14 de Septiembre. Cochabamba is Patiño territory, abounding with
stories from residents who "knew Simón Patiño when," meaning,
of course, during the days before he became the Tin King and one
of the richest men in the world. Los Portales, the copper-roofed
mansion of the Patiño family just out of town, is now the University Museum, and near *Vinto,* even more distant, is Pairumani,
the family's five thousand-acre country estate, which may, upon
special request, be opened for visitors. Worth seeing too, in the
surrounding region, are the towns of *Qillacollo* and, if one would
make a longer excursion, *Arani,* some forty miles from Cochabamba, in the Punata Valley.

Potosí: Once a rich and elegant metropolis of 150,000, Potosí
is now a town with one-third of that population, and not so much
as a single decent hotel, or an all-weather airport runway. It has,
in other words, seen better days, but a great deal of its opulent
past remains to excite the rare visitor who journeys to it today.
More than four centuries old—it was founded in 1546 by silver-
seeking Spaniards who found what they were looking for—it is,
in many respects, a living Colonial museum, older than La Paz by
three years, and higher by a thousand feet. Its oldest streets are
winding, and barely wide enough for autos to pass through. Its
Plaza 10 de Noviembre remains great, flanked by the ex-Cabildo,
the former Royal Treasury, and the lovely cathedral. Nearby is
the Casa de Moneda, dating from 1572, and used for many years
as a mint, in which the silver gleaned from Cerro Rico Hill, just

outside of town, was transformed into coins. Churches? There are a score and a half, the bulk of them exquisite examples of Romanesque and Renaissance architecture. Potosí flourished as a silver city for its first two centuries, until its lodes began to run out and silver mines began to operate in Mexico and Peru. For a while, this proud city was a ghost town, but it made a comeback with tin, the metal which the Spaniards ignored, but which the modern world clamored for. Prosperity, at least in limited form, returned gradually, and now besides tin, miners are once again extracting silver from the hills, although in small quantities, and copper and lead as well. Of a thousand travelers to Bolivia, nine hundred and ninety-nine inevitably miss Potosí; La Paz travel agencies fail to promote it, as facilities are so minimal. But I hope that this city, from which so much of the wealth of Spanish America derived, will make a comeback, not only economically, but touristically, spurred on perhaps, by a reader of this book!

Sucre: Smaller by a few thousand, older by a few years, and until the advent of the railroad in recent years, even more isolated than Potosí, Sucre retains the charm of its Colonial past, and a good many of its monuments as well. It is still the legal capital of Bolivia, and although the legislative and executive branches are headquartered in La Paz, where the diplomatic corps is also resident, Sucre retains the Supreme Court of Bolivia, which meets in the modern Santo Domingo Palace. Nonetheless, it was in the old Legislative Palace—still open to visitors and with swords of Generals Sucre and Bolívar displayed proudly—that the country's Declaration of Independence was signed. Other principal buildings are the handsome four-century-old cathedral with its golden, bejeweled virgin; Junin College, the striking Consistorial Building, and the venerable university, which was established in 1624. The principal touch of modernity, besides the seat of the Supreme Court, is a relatively new government secretariat. But in a city with so many fine old public buildings, and a quantity of mellow, white-towered Colonial churches, the twentieth-century façade is of little consequence. Have a look, if you can, just before Lent, when every resident with even a smidgen of silver shows it off to his neighbors in the annual Silver Parade, which culminates in a mass *al fresco* blessing.

Oruro: A mostly-Indian mining town—silver, tin, tungsten— Oruro hugs the slopes of a hill, at an altitude of over twelve thousand feet, 150 miles south of La Paz. It is of little interest for 364 days of the year, the exception being a pre-Lenten festival, on the Saturday before Ash Wednesday, when hundreds of superbly costumed and masked dancers enact an elaborate processional drama, their own variation of the good-evil theme. The ceremony, dating from Colonial times and traditionally participated in by Indian miners, ends in the Chapel of the Virgin del Socavon (Virgin of the Mine), at which point the dancers remove their masks, kneel, sing a hymn in Quechua, and pray for pardon.

Santa Cruz: The chief town of the vast, largely undeveloped semitropical region of Bolivia, east of the eastern Cordillera of the Andes, Santa Cruz, though three and a half centuries old, is still a town of less than forty thousand population. The government, in trying to remove it from its isolation, has had a good bit of success, thanks to fairly frequent air services (including international flights en route to Lima and Rio), good roads, and new railways. Still, age notwithstanding, Santa Cruz has a frontier look: largely unpaved streets, poor water supply, limited accommodations. But this is one of Bolivia's most hopeful cities, its New Frontier, with Mennonite settlers being imported from Paraguay, and still others, including Indians and their families, from the *altiplano*. Natural riches are being exploited: fertile soil for all manner of agricultural products, iron deposits, and oil, oil, oil.

WHAT TO BUY

The crafts of Bolivia are among the finest in all South America, and, it must be added, among the cheapest. This is the country for silver purchases (handsome cigarette boxes in a variety of sizes, tastefully decorated with adaptations of ancient Tiahuanaco designs; jointed silver fish, a good luck symbol of the Indians of the

Lake Titicaca region, in various sizes), gold (amazingly cheap— rings, bracelets, compacts, cigarette boxes, etc.), *retablos* (miniature altars made by Indians for their homes, sometimes blending Christian and Inca religious themes), woolen goods (brilliant-hued blankets, ponchos, and *rebozos* in lambs wool, as well as shawls and scarves for both men and women in fine alpaca and vicuña; rugs and throws of white, brown, and black alpaca fur), and— don't leave Bolivia without one!—reproductions of Ekeko, the happy domestic god of good luck, smiling and overloaded with pots and pans, in silver, gold, or ceramic, in various sizes, and for bracelets, pockets or with brooch-clasps. Possibly because she gave me a tiny silver good-luck piece (worth all of four cents) after my second visit, possibly because she inserted the cigarette I offered her in the mouth of a jumbo Ekeko and left it there, possibly because I liked her merchandise, her warm, shrewd, businesswoman's face, and her black derby, I found Signora Flora's shop, Casa Flora, excellent; address: Calle Sagarnaga 251. Also recommended: Joyería Sucre, Calle Loayza 215, for its excellent silver and gold items, and occasional *retablos;* Peleteria Santiago, Calle Mercado 1329, for vicuña cloth, alpaca fur rugs, and other woolens and furs; and King's in the Hotel Sucre Palace, for silver, gold, and other handicrafts. Bargaining is the rule in the shops, as well as at the stalls in the public markets of La Paz and the other towns. And don't be afraid of the stern-visaged Indian merchants; smile and they'll smile right back.

CREATURE COMFORTS

HOTELS—**La Paz:** The Crillon, La Paz' newest, is by Bolivian standards a skyscraper, and by any standards one of the friendliest-staffed hotels in South America; pleasant rooms with bath, fine food in a rooftop dining room, congenial bar; my favorite in the capital. Others: Copacabana, also modern, with a good dining room, bar, and adequate rooms with bath; Sucre Palace, oldest of the big three, still good, busy, friendly. Rates at the aforementioned trio average about $6 single, with bath. Lesser choices: La Paz, Paris, Austria. Pensions include the Ormachea (quite new and comfortable), Brecker, Cuellar. **Cochabamba:** Cochabamba, with swimming pool and tennis courts; Beverly, also with pool; Capitol, Colon, Ambassador. **Chacaltaya:** Club Andino, new ski lodge. **Chulumani:** Hamburgo, adequate for a night or two. **Copacabana:** Copacabana. **Sucre:** Colon, Londres—chins up, stiff upper lip for both. **Potosí:** Londres, Central—don't expect the Ritz. **Oruro:** El Oruro—well. . . . **Santa Cruz:** Austro Plaza, Vienna.

RESTAURANTS AND NIGHT LIFE—**La Paz:** The dining rooms and bars of the top three hotels—Crillon, Copacabana, Sucre Palace—are all good, and there is dancing nightly at the Copacabana's El Prado Room. Interesting restaurants include the Gallo de Oro, Maracaibo, Italia, Austria Inn, Torino, and, for a most unusual evening, the China, operated by a delightful Chinese recently arrived from Hong Kong, who with his wife, attempts to speak Spanish; their Chinese accents are quite as absurd as our American ones. The 21 is the newest, swankiest *boîte,* for wee-hours drinks and dancing; I suggest you refrain from dancing until you've been in town at least twenty-four hours—I wish I had. Also popular in this category are the Gallo de Oro, the Daiquiri, the Maracaibo, and the Hotel La Paz roof garden. For rests while shopping or sight-seeing, pop into any *confitería* which looks pleasant, for tea, coffee, a Coke, or a drink, as well as sandwiches and pastries. **Copacabana:** Club Princesa—good food and after-dinner drinks.

PRIVATE CLUBS: Anglo-American, La Paz, La Paz Tennis, La Paz Golf, Yacht (in Huatajata), Rotary, Lions.

Bolivian food specialties: Spice is the keynote in Bolivian cookery, sometimes liked and sometimes not by visitors. Among the popular dishes are a Bolivian variation of the *empanadas,* or meat-filled turnovers—always good with drinks; a dish based on the native corn of the Indians, combined with potatoes, beans, and cheese and known as *plato paceno;* and *picantes*—diced chicken in a hot sauce. Beer is Bolivian-brewed, tasty, and cheap, but other alcoholic drinks are fairly expensive.

CHILE

(República de Chile)

Entry requirements: *No visa or tourist card necessary; just a valid passport and health certificate. Bravo for Chile!* **Best times for a visit:** *The seasons are, of course, reversed, and the central region (which includes Santiago, and the principal lake, mountain, and beach resorts) has pleasantly warm summers and relatively mild winters; swimmers enjoy the former season; skiers the latter. The far north is always hot and sunbaked, while the extreme south is cool and rainy. Best all-round months: October through April.* **Currency:** *The new escudo, which is worth about one U.S. dollar but fluctuates in value, is replacing the old and inflated peso, of which there are about one thousand to the dollar. Both currencies are still used concurrently, but the peso is on its way out.* **Film availability:** *Both black-and-white and color available, the latter being fairly expensive.* **Language:** *Spanish, peculiarly Chilean-accented, with a good bit of English in the cities and resorts. A few hundred thousand people are bilingual in Spanish and Araucanian, an Indian language.* **Domestic transport:** *An extensive, and often good, railway system which includes the* *fantastic Trans-Andean route to Argentina; air service, via the national line, LAN–Chile, and two smaller lines, to important points throughout the country; and a road network at its best in the central region. Santiago taxis are cheap and in fairly good supply.* **Tipping:** *Hotels add a 10 per cent service charge (plus 25 per cent tax) to bills; many restaurants add a service charge, too, and when this is the case, there's no need for more than a token tip, if that; cab drivers don't expect tips. Otherwise, tip 10 to 15 per cent, for minor services.* **Business hours:** *8:30 or 9* A.M. *to 12 noon, 2 or 2:30* P.M. *to 7* P.M.; *half-day Saturday.* **Further information:** *Servicio Nacional de Turismo, Santiago, Chile; Panagra, Chrysler Building, New York, and Carrera Hotel, Santiago, Chile; Latour Travel Agency, Carrera Hotel, Santiago, Chile; Chilean Embassy, Washington, D.C.*

INTRODUCING CHILE

Yes, Chile's name *does* derive from an Indian word roughly translated as "chilly." No, Chile is not always chilly, only sometimes and in some places, and then not very. Yes, it *is* "delightful down in Chile," as the song lyric says it is, but only for a still too-small proportion of the generally poor population. No, the wealth of the country, from copper and nitrate and wine grapes, has not yet spread itself as thin as it might, within the country, and a good deal of it ends up in foreign (i.e., U.S.) hands. Which leads to the next contradiction: No, Americans are *not* lumped together as capitalistic villains by Chileans, who happen to be exceptionally warm, gracious, and hospitable, and who, moreover, have a somewhat more democratic tradition than certain of their Latin neighbors.

A backward glance: Contradictory Chile confounded its very first foreign visitors, the Inca Indians of neighboring Peru, who in the fifteenth century were able only to occupy the northern districts, but were repelled from further advances by the indigenous Araucanians—not as clever culturally as the invaders but brave and stubborn defenders of their homeland.

A century later the Araucanians were less successful. Pizarro sent down his conquistador colleague, Almagro, from Lima with a band of fellow Spaniards and a few thousand Inca troops. They managed to traverse the parched northern desert and succeeded in getting through to the fertile central regions. But they were to consider their efforts a waste of time and manpower: there was not an ounce of gold to be found.

Back they marched to Peru, probably gallumphing right over the rich copper and nitrate deposits which were later to form the basis of Chile's wealth.

It took the gold-hungry conquistadors more than a decade to simmer down in Lima, before giving Chile another chance to yield them the gold they were after. Finally, in 1541, Pedro de Valdivia led another army south and founded Santiago, populating it with settlers from both Peru and the Spanish motherland. Still, there were the fierce Araucanians to reckon with. Valdivia made some inroads beyond the capital, but in 1553, the Indians lost patience with him and tortured him to death. It was almost a hundred years before they would sit down over a conference table with the still unwelcome invaders, and an agreement was made whereby they would keep all lands south of the delightfully-named Bío-Bío River. That did not stop the colonists from fighting their way into that area, and only in 1777 were the Indians subdued sufficiently to acquiesce to white settlement.

Aristocrat and "inquilino": All this while, the social fabric of Chile was in formation, and although attempts have been made to alter it, the pattern persists in far too many ways. What happened was that the aristocratic conquistadors and their descendants parceled out great chunks of the land among themselves. And although there was intermarriage and cohabitation between white and Indian to such an extent that a mestizo class was produced almost overnight, the great landlords farmed their estates with Indian slaves, who were only gradually replaced with mestizo laborers known as *inquilinos*. Though actually free men, the *inquilinos* were little more than serfs, bound for their lifetimes to their *estancias* by unwritten laws, paid virtually nothing at all, without rights or recourse. It was not until more recently that many Chileans like to admit that any improvements were made in the lot of the *inquilino*, and the selfishness of the rich few is at the root of the discontent, still chronic, of the great mass.

All manner of phenomena, much of it physical, made progress difficult. There were tidal waves and earthquakes to contend with, and European pirates, looting coastal cities, as well. Virtually all trade was with Peru and Spain, for Chile was a province of the viceroyalty at Lima, and its rich, powerful leaders began to chafe at the bit.

O'Higgins, and independence: Bernardo O'Higgins—a general in the Spanish forces, with a Chilean-born mother and an Irish father who had been a Peruvian Colonial official—proclaimed Chile independent in 1810. With Juan Martínez de Rosas, he led forces against the Spanish troops, and might have been successful, at the Battle of Rancagua four years later, had not his rivalry with José Miguel de Carrera (another Chilean patriot) been so consuming. Not until the Argentine hero José de San Martín arrived with reinforcements in Chile in 1817, after an unbelievable march over the snowy Andes, was there a decisive victory.

O'Higgins, the following year, established Chile as a sovereign state, and it was, for nearly two decades, a military autocracy, with O'Higgins the first "supreme director." The new country was off to a start as a kind of oligarchy run by aristocratic, and hardly democratic, creoles—descendants of the Spanish founders. A new constitution was fashioned in 1833, with some representative provisions; it was the handiwork of Diego Portales, who though never president was the founder of the Conservative party and the leader who brought order to a country where stability had not come easily. Later, from 1841 to 1861, under the administrations of Presidents Manuel Bulnes and Manuel Montt, there was considerable material progress, a good bit of governmental reform, and Chile obtained the rights to mine nitrate in the desert north, which was then Bolivian territory.

But Bolivia did not remain content with the arrangements and the two nations fought over that valuable land in the War of the Pacific (1879–84), in which Chile came out the victor, Bolivia losing access to the sea—something it has never recovered. Later, Chilean-Argentine border troubles consumed much Chilean energy which might have been better expended in other directions. The famous Christ of the Andes Statue, on the Andean frontier, was erected in 1904 to commemorate the settlement of that dispute.

The current scene: The early twentieth century saw little improvement in Chile's government structure (indeed, for the first twenty-five years, Congress ruled rather than the presidents, until another new constitution was adopted), but railways were built, industrial activity commenced, and U.S. capital began to exploit the rich copper deposits. Miners and factory workers began to press for social reform, and were not completely unsuccessful, but Chile—which was not without its Fascist elements in the '30s and '40s—remained neutral during World War II, and its more recent presidents, including the near-perennial and onetime pro-Fascist José Ibáñez, and the current Jorge Alessandri Rodrigues, have been essentially conservative. Chile, though one of the most industrialized of the South American nations, has not yet faced up to the kind of reforms within its society which will bring a better life for the great majority of its seven and a half million people. Many of the *inquilinos* are now small farmers on their own, there are strong labor unions, there is a quite considerable social-welfare scheme, the government has embarked on much-needed low-income housing (over 80 per cent of working-class families still live in one room) and there are a free press and civil liberties. Still, the old aristocratic families and the American-owned copper interests retain a great deal of influence, and even though extensive United States aid, both technical and financial, was greatly appreciated after the disastrous earthquakes of 1960, many Chileans look to their rich northern neighbor for more imaginative leadership and the kind of help which, instead of perpetuating the old structure, would help more of Chile's riches be beneficial to more—many more—of Chile's people.

By late 1961, rumblings of discontent were disrupting the national façade. A mounting wave of strikes made serious dents in the economy, covering, as they did, the national railroads, the American-owned copper mines, the steel plants, and the coal mines—all of which were demanding increased wages. In order to strengthen his government and give it a broader base to meet domestic crises, President Alessandri brought the opposition left-of-center Radical party into the cabinet, thereby giving his administration a majority in Congress for the first time and a major land-reform scheme has been proposed. Chile's friends hope that the newly constituted government and the help that will come from the Alliance for Progress program will be sufficient to set it on a more progressive, dynamic, and viable course.

YOUR VISIT TO CHILE

Toothpick-shaped Chile—2800 miles long and never more than 110 miles wide—is one of the smallest of the South American countries, but it would still hold its own in, say, Europe, since it far exceeds a major country like France in area. Straddling a sliver of land between the Pacific and the Andes, half of it is mountainous (with altitudes over twenty thousand feet), portions of the north are flat, bone-dry, and rich in copper and nitrate, and the deep south is almost eternally moist and with a Norway-like fiord landscape.

In between are the central regions—the heartland—with the great majority of the population, the major cities and lush agricultural valleys, and the Lake Country—a paradise of blue waters, white volcanoes, and green forests which is one of the most beautiful parts of the world. To the south, stretching from Puerto Montt to Cape Horn, is archipelagic Chile—few people, much rain, and a maze of islands and channels complementing the myriad of fiords. Sound like a country worth knowing? It most certainly is. The hub of the country is Santiago, the capital, from which the visitor may easily fly, drive, or entrain to the nearby beach and ski resorts and the only slightly more distant Lake District. The far south, while a good many miles away, is only a few hour by air, as is the arid north. Ideally, every portion of Chile should be on a traveler's itinerary, but the most essential are the most convenient—the capital, the coast, the mountains, and the lakes.

CENTRAL CHILE

Santiago: The sun makes a bigger difference in Santiago than in any other South American capital, Bogotá possibly excepted. In fall and winter, covered by gray clouds, it can be one of the gloomiest cities on the continent. It was under such circumstances that I was introduced to it; not until I was fortunate enough to return in the summer did I come to like the capital: at that time of year, the jagged, pristine Andean peaks which guard the town are clear and white. The days are warm but unhumid, the nights are fresh and pleasant, and the Plaza de Armas—the one major remnant of old Santiago, in the center of the city—is dotted with strollers and shoppers and sun-lovers on the benches.

The Civic Center—almost all of it surrounded by colorless undistinguished skyscrapers—is where most visitors headquarter. But it should be the Plaza de Armas to which they beeline upon arrival. On its south and east flanks are shops artfully protected from the elements by gracious arcades; on the northern border stand the city hall and post office, and on the west is the quiet, graceful cathedral—cool and proud, despite the indignities which it has suffered by rebuilding and redecoration through the years. Visible from its great doors is the garden-encircled Congress, quite the least prepossessing and at the same time the most charming government headquarters in South America.

Number Two, in my book, after the Plaza de Armas, is Santa Lucía Hill—again barren in the winter, thoroughly delightful in the summer. A mass of rock jutting up some 230 feet in the heart of the city, Santa Lucía is approached by the Caupolican Espalanade, named for an Indian leader, a statue of whom dominates a nearby platform. Santa Lucía does duty as a park, a promenade, a historical monument, and the setting for a small but fine museum of antiquities. There is, to be sure, a view of the long, well-proportioned Catholic University directly below, and of much else of the city's façade. And there is a fat old cannon which announces the arrival of noon every day of the year. But it is the gardens and pathways of Santa Lucía that distinguish it, interspersed as they are with tiny pavilions, deftly placed benches for lunch-hour and late-day strollers, and on one side of the hill, the miniscule Plaza Pedro de Valdivia, with a statue of the city's founder and a little waterfall.

Of the aforementioned Civic Center there is but one important aspect (if one discounts the Carrera, the city's leading hotel, of which more later) and that is the Moneda Palace (1805), one-time mint, and now containing the President's Offices and a good many old paintings and sculptures. Visitors are welcome to amble through its patios and public rooms, and many wisely make it a point to be on hand at 10 A.M., on at least one day of their visit, to watch the changing of the crack, nattily-uniformed Presidential Guard.

Avenida O'Higgins, known colloquially as the Alameda, is Santiago's main boulevard, and though Chileans must be forgiven their enthusiasm, it bears little resemblance, other than width, to Paris' Champs-Élysées, with which it is all too often compared. Still, one does not go wrong in getting to know it, with the National Library—South America's largest, and containing the Chilean archives—a good walking destination.

Other diversions: a view of the city (for lovers of views not content with the vistas afforded by Santa Lucía) from the more distant thousand-foot-high San Cristóbal Hill (yes, it *does* have a cable car for access, as well as a restaurant, a trio of observatories, and at its foot, a zoo); the paintings and sculpture in the Palace of Fine Arts, on the lovely grounds of Forestal Park; the frenetic Central Market; the government-operated University of Chile (it and the Catholic University are the nation's top institutions of higher learning); the venerable San Francisco Church and Monastery (the city's oldest), and the Union Club, the city's most opulent establishment, with one of the longest bars in the world (closed to women, sorry!) and any number of ornately decorated lounges.

There are several impressive new residential districts (the United States Embassy is moving into one of them), *confiterías* quite as inviting as those in the other leading South American cities, an elaborate and properly mellow Municipal Theatre, and a surrounding countryside offering more excursion possibilities than most visitors have time or energy for. Excluding Valparaíso, Viña del Mar, and the ski centers—which should have priority—these would include such little resort towns as *Apoquindo,* half a dozen miles from town at an elevation of twenty-six hundred feet; *Penalolen,* a bit more distant and affording a handsome view of the city and valleys; *San José de Maipó* and nearby *Melocotón,* in the mountains and with a pleasant hotel; *El Volcán,* at a forty-six-hundred-foot elevation and with a magnificent situation—an excellent day's train excursion. *Mendoza,* Argentina, is 250 miles from Santiago, through the Aconcagua Valley and the Andes, and can be reached by car most times of the year. Beach resorts frequented by residents of the capital, but little known to foreigners—more's the pity—include *Cartagena, Llolleo, Maipó,* and *Santo Domingo;* all have hotels, with the most and best at Santo Domingo. A number of haciendas, some of whose main crop is wine grapes, are open to visitors through travel agencies.

Valparaíso: A few hours by train or car from Santiago—and the routes (two different ones, for autos) are most interesting—is Valparaíso, second city of Chile and the greatest port on the Pacific coast of South America. Though by no means an unpleasant city, Valparaíso (it has been given the ugly nickname Valpo by British sailors) is by no stretch of the imagination a Chilean San Francisco, its well-meaning publicists notwithstanding. What the two cities do have in common are similar climates, a common ocean on whose shores they are both built, and—here is why the two are often compared—similar terrain, both towns dramatically straddling hilly slopes which lead to the sea's edge.

But there the similarities end. Valparaíso, while not without its more attractive sections, is a visibly poor, down-at-the-heels port, most of whose inhabitants live in wretched clusters of huts on its steep hills. Its tempo is, to be sure, quick and pulsating and gay—the kind which lovers of sea towns (myself included) take to almost at once. There is a slightly British flavor to the atmosphere, which gives it additional flavor, for this is the head-quarters of the Chilean navy, largely officered by Anglo-Chileans ever since the days when Lord Cochrane and his forces helped the insurgents win Chile's freedom.

Though they constitute a much smaller community than the Anglo-Argentines of Buenos Aires (Valparaíso's total population is less than 300,000), the Anglo-Chileans of Valparaíso are quite as much of an anomaly: they, too, are completely bilingual in both English and Spanish, and give the visitor the impression of being British Colonials resident in a Crown Colony rather than citizens of a South American republic with roots, and loyalties, as old as many whose only language is Spanish. I hope you get the opportunity to meet some; they are most curious.

The bay of Valparaíso is its greatest blessing: sweeping, backed by those fantastic hills, with the white-peaked Andes in the far background. Travelers approaching the city by sea are usually the most appreciative of Valparaíso's situation, but those who have come by air can get almost as good an impression by taking a funicular railway car, or *ascensore,* up one of the hills for a birds-eye view. The finest for this purpose is Cerro Artilleria, with a bench-lined promenade, and just yards away, the Naval Academy.

Plaza Sotomayor is the heart of the lower region of the city, with the Government Palace, amusingly ornate but still impressive, its landmark; and jutting out of it are a number of the principal streets, the Calle Prat (later called the Calle Esmeralda) the most important, and with the major shops, few of which have anything of interest for the selective shopper. The piers, also a step from the main plaza, are worth a glance, too, their berths occupied by ships—both passenger liners and freighters—from all over the globe. Precious little remains of Colonial Valparaíso. Earthquakes, fires, and plunderers have robbed it of most evidences of its four-century history, the only exception being the little neighborhood known as The Port, with its highlight the venerable Matriz Church.

There are a fair number of restaurants and cafés, a not-bad new hotel, and a number of private clubs, but the visitor will be wise to not linger overlong. Only minutes from the city center is Viña del Mar.

Viña del Mar: At once a suburb of Valparaíso, a substantial town in its own right (population 115,000), and the chief resort of the Pacific coast of South America, Viña del Mar—or Sea Vineyard, if you would be so crass as to translate—is the only Chilean town which might properly be called elegant. It draws the wealthy not only of Chile, but from neighboring Argentina as well, its magnets being a palatial, garden-encircled casino, replete with restaurant and bars; a lovely setting on the rocky coast, which is enhanced by brilliant flowers at every turn; wide beaches and casual cafés; some very good hotels and restaurants; a profusion of fussily-designed villas (one of which is the president's summer house) and newer sleek-lined apartment houses; and a heavenly summer climate—sunny days and cool, cool evenings.

If one is a swimmer, there is a slight drawback: the water is quite close to frigid, and although Americans who vacation on the Maine coast might like it, I find that getting into it requires more bravery than I am capable of, at least as frequently as I should like.

But you may be hardier, or you may be more interested in sun-bathing and gambling than in swimming. In any event, Viña has something to offer. Just driving to it and strolling through it is a visually exciting experience. And excursions might well be made from it to smaller resorts like *Las Salinas,* whose beach is protected by two massive rock crags; *Concon* and *Quintero.* The route is a coastal one—one of the most scenically breathtaking on the continent—and if there are photographers in the group, sufficient time for picture-stops will have to be allowed for; this is country which shutterbugs find irresistible.

The ski resorts: Skiing is a new sport in Chile, developed less than a quarter of a century ago. In that period some of the world's finest ski centers have evolved, and an estimated forty thousand Chileans are avid skiers, with the number increasing yearly. In a country with as tiny a leisure class as Chile's, and with a still-small middle-class, this is a not inconsiderable figure.

The great thing about Chile's ski resorts is that even nonskiers (i.e., the writer) get a tremendous bang out of visiting them, and even ascending the peaks on the mechanized lifts. We nonskiers are not the only supporters of these spots, however. Within the last decade Chilean slopes have attracted top U. S. Olympic skiers and champs from a number of other lands, including Norway, which is hardly without facilities of its own.

The season runs from May to October, with July and August the top months in the Central Region resorts, near Santiago. In the south, September and October are the ideal months. For Americans, this means skiing during the summer-vacation period, and to accommodate the fans, Panagra Airlines runs special all-expense ski tours during that period, allowing travelers to transport a set of skis, bindings, and poles for only $7 from Miami, and $10 from New York.

Special tour or no, skier or not, the visitor does well to visit at least one of the ski spots. My favorite is Portillo, a magnificent five-hour train ride through the mountains, from Santiago, and with one of the handsomest lodge-hotels on the continent. But here's the lineup:

Near Santiago—Portillo, 9450-foot elevation, modern Hotel Portillo, night club, movies, and even a skating rink for us nonskiers. The world-championship ski grounds include one slope with a 5000-foot drop, and another, with a little climbing, of 6000 feet. There are gentler slopes for novices, and the aforementioned chairlift, which *any* visitor is advised not to miss. Instructors are on hand to teach the uninitiated, who may, or may not, want to budge from the wide-open terrace which is ideal for the acquiring of a mountain tan. Excursions: One of especial interest is to the *Christ of the Andes statue* on the Argentine-Chilean border; especially rugged travelers may ski all the way back to the hotel—

but this is not compulsory, I hasten to add. *Farrelones:* Considerably closer to Santiago (just a little over thirty miles by car), Farrelones is at an altitude of seventy-three hundred feet, adjoining a delightful village. Its two *refugios,* or lodges, accommodate 350 devotees, and there are private lodges, too. The longest run is three miles, and there's an exciting chairlift seven hundred feet long with a vertical drop of seventeen hundred feet. *La Parva:* Just two miles from Farrelones (where visitors must stay), La Parva is relatively new, with a double chairlift more than a mile long, and exceptionally fast slopes and downhill trails for experienced practitioners of the craft, plus some additional ones for us beginners. *Lagunillas:* The Club Andino de Chile, and other ski organizations, maintain lodges at this center, 6550 feet high and thirty-seven miles from Santiago.

The South—Chillán: Less than sixty miles from the town of Chillán, this resort centers around some surprising hot springs, at an altitude of fifty-nine hundred feet; there's a lodge maintained by the Club Andino de Chile. *Llaima:* Almost five thousand feet above sea level, Llaima is fifty-six miles from the city of Temuco, and its lodges are those of the Llaima and Cautín Andean Ski Clubs. *Choshuenco:* Near Valdivia, and reached by both road and rail from that city, Choshuenco is particularly scenic—near the shores of a mountain lake, and with a large *refugio* for visitors. *Antillanca:* Near the Lake Region town of Osorno, this one is forty-six hundred feet up, and with a *refugio* operated by the Osorno Andean Club. A visit to it might well be tied in with a trip through the Lake District. Facilities at the more central ski centers near Santiago are more extensive than those of the South.

THE LAKE DISTRICT

The traveler bound for Argentina from Chile, or Chile from Argentina, is faced with a difficult choice in routing: one can fly over the Andes from Santiago to Buenos Aires (or vice versa) in a few hours and on a route which is one of the most excitingly beautiful in international aviation. Below will be the Christ of the

Andes monument, lonely and impressive in the snowy passes of the frontier which divides the two countries. And not far from the plane's path will be the peak of Mount Aconcagua, hovering 23,081 feet above the level of the sea. There will be, too, forests and pampas and cities and towns. No flight in South America, except possibly the approaches to La Paz or Rio de Janeiro, is more rewarding. But there still remains the question: is there a better route? Better? The adjective is not quite the proper one. But there is an alternative route which takes much longer, is more costly and more enervating. From Santiago, it takes one south by plane or train to the Lake Country, through the Chilean lakes by bus and boat into the Argentine lakes, from which one proceeds north by train or plane to Buenos Aires. Roundabout? It certainly is. Worth it? I've never yet met a traveler who hasn't thought so.

But I should point out that should one elect to make the trans-Andean flight, there is no reason why the Chilean lakes cannot be visited on an excursion from Santiago. And the same would obtain for the Argentine lakes, which can be visited from Buenos Aires. In both cases the traveler is returned to one or the other capital, to continue his journey by air, if he wishes.

Should the Santiago-lakes-Buenos Aires itinerary be selected, the traveler must allow himself a *minimum* of four days to get from one capital to the other; this can be, and very often is, stretched into a fortnight or three weeks. And there are, of course, Argentines and Chileans who spend entire vacations at the lakes.

American travel agents who know South America can prepare a lake-trip itinerary, and so can travel agents in Chile and Argentina. There is probably no other trip in South America where an agent's services are more helpful. The traveler is forced to make his journey by so many varied conveyances that to do so on his own, particularly in a matter of a few days, would confuse even the most veteran voyager. When planned by a travel agent, the traveler's lot is an easy one: he departs with a coupon-book and timetable-itinerary in his pocket, chronologically dispenses coupons for meals, hotel accommodations, boats, trains, planes, and buses, and aside from keeping an eye on his baggage to see that it follows him on schedule, has little else to do but enjoy himself. Though the trip can be made at any time of year, the most ideal months are September to March, the Chilean summer, although winter-sports fans are drawn to the region during that season.

A typical Santiago-lakes-Buenos Aires itinerary: Pucón, with a stay at its luxury hotel on trout-filled Lake Villarrica; Osorno, in the shadow of a perfect conical volcano; Ensenada, amid a region of farms and flowering fields; Lake Llanquihue; Petrohué, on the shore of Lake Todos los Santos, perhaps the loveliest of all the lakes; Peulla, a tiny lakeside village at the foot of a waterfall-embellished mountain, and then through customs at Casa Pangue into Argentina and the resort center of Bariloche, from which departures can be made by fast plane, or slow (and rather dull) train, to Buenos Aires.

Many travelers fly from Santiago all the way to Puerto Montt, and from there proceed to the lakes. However, there is train service, particularly good during the summer months when the extra-fare "Rapido" covers the 650-mile run from the capital to Puerto Varas (near Puerto Montt) in a single day. Other trains take longer, and involve an overnight stop at Concepción. *What follow are the highlights of a rail journey, in order of distance from Santiago.*

The railroad traverses some of the most beautiful countryside on the face of the globe, with white Andean peaks running roughly parallel to the tracks. The first major towns are *Rancagua,* important mainly because its streets are the site of the 1814 battle fought under O'Higgins, and because of a big copper mine some miles to the east; *San Fernando,* a provincial capital with a faintly Colonial façade; and *Talca,* with a population of some eighty thousand, and a New Look, thanks to the unfortunate necessity for rebuilding following the disastrous 1928 earthquake, and surrounding countryside which grows most of the grapes for Chile's great wine industry and through which runs the Maule River, whose ports include the pleasant resort town of *Constitución.*

Farther south is *Chillán,* twice destroyed by earthquakes (it was last rebuilt in 1939), the birthplace of O'Higgins, and the site of thermal springs and an already-noted ski resort on the slopes of Chillán Volcano.

Concepción: Though little known beyond Chile, this is the third city of the republic and the chief city of the south, with close to 170,000 inhabitants. Its port, *Talcahuano,* is ten miles away on a wide bay of the Pacific which provides the best harbor in the country, its climate is mild and agreeable, and its recently-constructed university is one of the most modern and progressive in Chile. Also of fairly late vintage (thanks to earthquake damage in 1939): a massive cathedral and an imposing law-courts building. Worth ascending is Caracol Hill, for a vista not only of the city, but also of the Bío-Bío River, a number of neighboring lakes, and of course, Talcahuano and the Pacific Ocean. Excursions from Concepción might be made to such destinations as *Tomé,* with its sandy beach and wooded hills; *Dichato,* a quiet seaside village; *Coronel,* a coal port in a picturesque, verdant area; *Lota,* a port and coal town not far from the huge Cousino mines; and *Laraquete,* a fisherman's haven offering species from both the sea which it borders and the river which flows through it.

To the south lies the **Lake Country,** stretching roughly from Concepción to Puerto Montt, and including—besides a baker's dozen of lakes, some blue, some green, some atop mountains, some astride valleys—snow-capped volcanoes; a complete variety of waterfalls, short, squat, and powerful, or tall, slim, and graceful, take your choice; a selection of rivers, and land which runs the gamut from thick green forest to open, brilliantly-hued fields of wild flowers. Hotels, some luxe, others old and plain, are nearly all well-operated and pleasant, and the resident Chileans—including a good proportion of the Indian minority—are so friendly that they give the impression of never having seen a tourist before. Strangely but blessedly absent: bothersome bugs. *Highlights—*

Temuco: Aside from interesting schools operated by American Baptists and the South American Missionary Society, Temuco, a town of about 115,000, is of note mainly because of the access it provides to such excursion points as *Carahue,* in the heart of

Indian country, and *Villarrica,* four centuries old and perched on
the bank of a wooded lake by that name—one of the most beautiful
of the region, thanks to the backdrop of Villarrica Volcano, always snow capped, and more than ninety-three hundred feet high.
From Villarrica it is a short drive around the lake to *Pucón,* another gem of a Lake District town, with one of the finest resort
hotels in Chile, a lovely setting which seduces many travelers into
tarrying longer than they had planned, fishing, idling in the sun, or
exploring the countryside on horseback, with perhaps a ride up
the slopes of Villarrica Volcano, or trips to *Lakes Caburgua* and
Colico, or to the thermal baths at *Menetue.* One may go from
Pucón directly into Argentina and its Lake District, via the Argentine village of *Junín de los Andes,* on a road whose attractions include *Lake Quilleihue* and the *Quetrupillán Volcano,* on the
Chilean side, and Lake Tromen and Lanín Volcano, on the Argentine side, from which one can continue to Bariloche and thence
northward to Buenos Aires.

Valdivia is the town named for and founded by Pedro de
Valdivia in 1552. In the mid-nineteenth century it was bolstered
by settlers from Germany who developed it industrially and
aesthetically and farmed the fertile area surrounding it. Here, too,
is the new Austral University. Excursion possibilities are limitless—to smallish seaside resorts, along rivers flowing into the interior, and to a quantity of lakes, with such intriguing Indian
names as Panguipulli, Calafquén, and Pirehueico.

Osorno: Like Valdivia, Osorno is old (1558), and with a German community dating only a century back. Few traces of its
Colonial past remain; modern architecture is the keynote, and it
seems to blend well with the crisp, bracing setting: the tower of the
great Osorno Volcano in the background, and two rivers, the
Damas and Rahue, whose junction delineates the town's original
boundaries. From here one can drive, via Lakes Todos los Santos
and Laguna Verde, to Bariloche, Argentina, or, if there's time,
linger a while, and by means of excursions, take in the countryside.
Possibilities: a car trip to Lake Llanquihue (which, as every
English-speaking Chilean quickly advises, is pronounced *yankee-*

way) via Ensenada and Puerto Varas; a visit to Pilmaiquén Waterfall and the thermal waters of Termas de Puyehue on Lake Puyehue; and, if one is a winter visitor and a skier, a go at the slopes of the Antillanca ski fields, near Puyehue.

Puerto Varas: A port resort on the shores of the huge and magnificent Lake Llanquihue, Puerto Varas is also near Lake Todos los Santos, which with its clear green waters and the mountains encircling it is the favorite of most visitors, and justifiably so. Lake Llanquihue has not quite the serenity of its competitor, its waters are blue rather than green, and from it one has a superb view of the 8790-foot Osorno Volcano. You have to pick your own favorite! At any rate, I should not leave the area without having explored both. *Lake Todos los Santos,* just east of Llanquihue, has ports at both *Petrohué* and *Peulla* (pronounced *pay-ool-ya* in Chile and *pay-ooja* across the border in Argentina). Visitors entering the Chilean lakes from Argentina usually spend their first Chilean night in Peulla, and those bound for Argentina frequently leave the country from there.

Puerto Montt: Indians on the street selling handsome handwoven ponchos and blankets, smallish but neat public buildings and houses, garden-lined streets, a good bit of rain when one least wants rain, and at its feet, the massive Reloncaví Sound. Puerto Montt is only sixteen miles, by bus or train, from Puerto Varas, and visitors from Argentina concluding their lake visits at Puerto Varas often motor over to Puerto Montt by modern bus, spend a day and a night, and head north for Santiago by either train or plane, or, if they'd like a taste of rarely-trodden archipelagic Chile, proceed south.

THE DEEP SOUTH

Fully a third of Chile is to the south of Puerto Montt, and yet there are less than 150,000 persons living in the entire area, largely because of more rain than even an Englishman would like to cope with. The extreme north and extreme southern tip of the region contain most of the population; the center is mostly impenetrable forest. The coast line is a complex jumple of fiords, inlets, and bays, with its chief landmark *Chiloé Island,* mostly dotted with wheat fields, potato farms, fishing hamlets, and the fair-sized towns of *Castro* and *Ancud,* both with less than twenty-five thousand inhabitants and neither particularly cheery places for prolonged visits.

Punta Arenas: Way south—bypassing that uninhabited center chunk of the region—is the world's southernmost city, Punta Arenas, astride the Strait of Magellan, just about equidistant from the Atlantic and Pacific oceans, and with a population of about fifty thousand. Aside from its neat but monotonous low buildings, mostly frame but with newer ones of stone and concrete, and a museum whose exhibits tell the story of the local Indian cultures as well as regional flora and fauna, and an interesting British community, there is not a great deal else within the town. But beyond are the heavily Scottish sheep farms, and about seven hours distant by car is the town of Puerto Natales in the district of *Última Esperanza* (Last Hope, in English) whose superb fiords rival those of Norway in beauty and majesty, and whose waters are loaded with frisky fish. The Punta Arenas Touring Club is especially helpful to visitors, who should know in advance that this is a region of great winds and much rain, even during the summer season.

Tierra del Fuego, is, of course, the island just across the Strait of Magellan from the mainland. The larger portion of it is Chilean, the remainder belongs to Argentina. *Porvenir* is the principal Chilean town on the island, with less than two thousand inhabitants, most of them for some strange reason of Yugoslavian descent. Tierra del Fuego's glaciers and fiords are exceptionally beautiful. (For Argentine Tierra del Fuego, see page 86.)

THE FAR NORTH

Bleak, dusty, hot desert—the far north of Chile is another world from the overmoist forested area of the deep south. Both are difficult to live in, and were it not for the copper and nitrate deposits of the north, it would probably be almost completely uninhabited. As it is, the population is less than half a million, and its needs, including water and food, are largely imported from the green valleys to the south. The casual air-tourist rarely visits the north and the traveler by ship is sometimes more impatient than he might be to get under way for greener pastures. Not even its stanchest supporters would say that northern Chile is conventionally inviting, but it is not to be ignored by the curious traveler.

Arica: Bordered by sand dunes on all sides except the sea side, Arica (population forty thousand) is the most northerly port of the republic, eternally rainless, but with pleasant bathing beaches, a church of iron designed by none other than the Monsieur Eiffel of Paris, a railway connection with its sister city twelve miles to the north, Tacna, Peru, and another railroad leading to landlocked Bolivia's capital, La Paz, on which is transported fully half of the exports and imports of the mountainous republic in the interior. Excursions can easily be made across the border to Tacna, which dates to Colonial days, into the bleak but nonetheless dramatic desert, and even to the not-far-distant Andes.

Iquique, a hundred-odd miles south of Arica and with about fifty thousand residents, not nearly as intriguing as its name would imply, is kept alive by commerce at its port in nitrates and iodine, and is not far from an honest-to-goodness oasis town called Pica, and a thermal resort (needless to say the waters are naturally hot) called Mamiña, which boasts a good hotel. There is fine swimming at the beaches and excellent deep-sea fishing.

Antofagasta: Closest of the major northern ports to the heartland of the country, and the largest of the northern cities (population about eighty thousand) Antofagasta is important because of its harbor, through which is exported both copper and nitrates. Though hardly a city of beauty, Antofagasta has its share of amenities—a number of hotels, *confiterías,* clubs, bars, and beaches. The climate is surprisingly comfortable (at its best between May and September), and it is from Antofagasta that many travelers depart by train for Bolivia, via the oasis community of *Calama* (where the Smithsonian Institution has a solar observatory) and the spectacular

Atacama Desert wastes, and for Salta and Buenos Aires in Argentina, the Argentine capital being five days' journey from the coast.

Probably the most interesting excursion from Antofagasta is to *Chuquicamata,* thirteen miles distant, and the site of one of the world's biggest copper mines, at an altitude of 10,435 feet. The operators, the Chilean Exploration Company, welcome visitors, have a guest house for their convenience, and show the step-by-step details—mining, leaching, electrolysis, smelting, and drawing. Near Chuquicamata are a cluster of tiny Indian settlements in oases bordering the Andes; visitors able to get accommodation at the mine's guest house might well head for them before returning to Antofagasta.

Chañaral is small (twenty thousand population), and of significance only because it contains the head office of the Andes Copper Mining Company, whose principal mine is now at El Salvador, about a hundred miles distant; it employs about fifteen thousand workers. About 150 miles south by rail is another substantial copper town, *Copiapó,* a little larger than Chañaral and more modern and attractive, but still, unless one is doing a doctoral dissertation on copper towns, hardly worth detouring for.

La Serena is by far the most attractive of the cities which lie in the relatively small zone separating the arid desert from the fertile central heartland. By the time the Chilean declaration of independence was signed there in 1818 it had been—since its founding in 1544—razed by Indians, reconstructed by conquistadors, and looted by British pirates. It is calm today, with pleasant gardens, a notable cathedral, some venerable monasteries, good beaches (Peñuelas, with a casino, is understandably the most popular), exhibition grounds which are the site of agricultural fairs and rodeos, and a Chamber of Commerce which is intent on turning the city into a second Viña del Mar. La Serena is the major city of the Elqui Valley, where Gabriela Mistral, who won the Nobel prize for her poetry, was born. Recommended: Car excursions through the valley villages to *Vicuña,* the chief town in the little-visited but charming interior.

WHAT TO BUY

Chile's chief product, copper, is made into some of the ugliest objects imaginable by this country's artisans, and they're by no means cheap. The only shop in all Santiago which has truly attractive pieces is in the dining room of a private house in a remote, down-at-the-heels residential area, but I suggest you beeline for it, and keep your taxi waiting. The owner-designer-manufacturer is an elderly gentleman named Fortunato Riveros, address: Sargento Adlea 941, Telephone 53784. Señor Riveros' daughter speaks good English and acts as saleslady. Available, in both copper and brass, are beautiful candlesticks, chafing dishes, trays, platters, bowls, coffee spoons, ash trays, and whatever else Señor Riveros happens to feel like creating. Don't be tempted by his copper demitasse cups and saucers; they're very handsome but conduct the heat so efficiently that it's impossible to drink coffee from them until it's turned cold; I speak from experience. Otherwise, the copperware on sale in Santiago, without exception, is tacky and not worthy of the five-and-ten. What the Chilean copper and tourism industries need are a few good designers. The aforementioned material excepted, there is a good selection of crafts at Chilean Art, Agustinas 1169, probably the leading shop of its kind in Santiago, far from cheap, but with its important articles in good taste and of good quality. On hand are beautiful *choapino* rugs, the *mantas,* or half-ponchos worn by the Chilean *hausos,* some interesting ceramics, including black-and-white Quinchamali, carved wooden stirrups, pottery. Imaginative hand-crafted products with a contempory flair, the work of inventive modern weavers, ceramists, and painters, is the specialty of Til-Til, Providencia 2138. Los Gobolinos is good for vicuña and alpaca cloth, Bel (Huerfanos 618) has interesting hand-blocked fabrics. Otherwise, browse at the Central Market and at the tiny shops in downtown Santiago. The *Lake District,* particularly towns like Puerto Montt and Puerto Varas, is cheaper than Santiago for *choapinos,* often sold on the streets by itinerant Indian merchants. In *Viña del Mar,* Reynares (Calle Valparaíso 418) is good (but not cheap) for leather goods and wood-carved specialties, and Siboney (Calle Valparaíso) specializes in imaginative straw articles.

CREATURE COMFORTS

HOTELS, IN AND NEAR THE CAPITAL—**Santiago:** In the Civic Center, next door to the Ministry of Finance and across the plaza from the Palacio Moneda, the President's Palace, is the seventeen-story Carrera, unquestionably Santiago's finest. Operated by Hilton Hotels International, it is modern, with fine service, big rooms all with bath, a rooftop swimming pool around which drinks, lunch, and dinner are served in the summer, the town's most popular bar, a restaurant-*boîte,* a good, inexpensive coffee shop, airline ticket offices, Latour Travel Agency headquarters, and a slew of shops; highly recommended, $12 single minimum. Others, all less expensive: Crillon, older, with a popular teatime lounge, restaurant, and bar; Panamericano—smallish, but modern; Santa Lucía, and Emperador. There are also a number of smaller, even cheaper hotels, none outstanding. Good hotels at nearby resorts include the Millahue in **Melocotón,** and the Valdes in **El Volcán;** the Club Rocas in **Santo Domingo,** and the Continental in **Cartagena. Valparaíso:** The Prat is the newest and the leader. Others: Lebell, Lancaster, Paris. **Viña del Mar:** The Miramar, hands down—all rooms (each with terrace) face the sea, natural-rock swimming pool, superb situation, outdoor terrace for drinks, ocean-view dining room, charming décor, and pleasant service; $7 minimum single. Larger, but away from the beach, is the O'Higgins, also with pool; $7 minimum single. Others: San Martín, Alcacar, Embassy, France, Hispaño, Victoria. At nearby **Concón:** Gran Hotel Concón, Asturia; and ten miles distant at **Quintero:** Pacifico, Case de Piedra, El Refugio. SKI RESORTS: **Portillo:** Gran Hotel Portillo—one of the finest in South America, with three hundred attractive rooms, handsome public rooms, bar, restaurant (with fine food), night club, cinema, infirmary, open terraces for drinks and sunbathing, a ski lift at the door, professional ski instructors, and a fantastic mountain setting. From $9.50 single, with meals. **Farrelones:** Posado Inn, pleasant and comfortable, plus two *refugios* for skiers. **Lagunillas:** *Refugio* operated by Club Andino de Chile. **Chillán:** Club Andino de Chile *refugio,* at ski resort; Espana, in town; hot springs. **Llaima:** *Refugio.* **Choshuenco:** *Refugio.* **Antillanca:** *Refugio.* CENTRAL CHILE AND LAKES: **Rancagua:** Santiago, Ducal. **San Fernando:** Marcano (in town), Termas de las Vegas del Flaco (at thermal springs). **Talca:** Plaza, Claris. **Constitución:** Gran, Playa. **Concepción:** City, Ritz, Gran. **Talcahuano:** France. **Tomé:** El Morro, Durdos (summer only). **Dichato:** Playa, Dichato. **Temuco:** Frontera, Central. **Carahue:** Sol. **Villarrica:** Yachting Club, Central, Parque. **Pucón:** Pucón—one of the best in the Lake District, with golf course; Antumalal—away from town, small but expensive, exceptional fishing facilities; Playa Malbrich. **Valdivia:** Pedro de Valdivia, Schuster; at nearby **Niebla** resort: Mira-Mar, Riechers; at **Carboneros** resort: Vila Lucia; at **Amargos** resort: Schuster Amargos. **Osorno:** Gran—one hundred rooms, all with bath; Waeger, Czaya. **Puerto Varas:** Gran—modern, attractive and most comfortable; Playa, Heim, Bellavista. **Puyehue:** Gran Hotel Termas de Puyehue. **Petrohué:** Petrohué—small, simple, clean. **Peulla:** Peulla—very old, but clean and with a superb setting, plus the Chilean customs in the basement, for the newly-arrived from Argentina. **Puerto Montt:** Club Aleman, La Bomba, Central; Hosteria Hoffman—on **Tenglo,** a nearby pleasure island. DEEP SOUTH: **Ancud** (Chiloé Island): Residencia Ancud. **Punta Arenas:** Cosmos, Savoy, France. FAR NORTH: **Arica:** Hostería Arica, Grand, Tacora. **Inquique:** Prat, Ingles, Phoenix. **Antofagasta:** Antofagasta Prat, Plaza, Splendid. **Chuquicamata:** Guest House. **Chañaral:** Residencial Malina. **Copiato:** Carrera, Tourist. **La Serena:** Francisco de Aguirre, Berlin, Londres, Bahia. **Vicuña:** Hosteria.

RESTAURANTS AND NIGHT LIFE—**Santiago:** Except for occasionally good sea-food dishes, the food is not wildly exciting, but it can be very good. The Carrera Hotel Empire Room restaurant, Copper Room coffee shop, and poolside café are excellent, and serve both international and Chilean dishes, including the wines of the country. Other interesting spots: Crillon Hotel dining room and lounge, the latter for afternoon tea; the Pollo Dorado, for Chilean specialties in a gay setting, with lively *hauso* entertainers; Waldorf, French and American foods; Chez Henri (French); Bahia; Feroni; Danubio Azul (Chinese food in a Spanish patio setting); El Escorial; Nuria; Mandarin; Parron—beef specialties, most attractive, away from the center of town; Sarao—a charming Colonial farmhouse twenty minutes from the city, with Chilean dishes and *al fresco* service in summer; Chiaranda, also with tables outdoors in summer; Casino, on San Cristóbal Hill, is pleasant for lunch; Las Perdices and Las Brujas are both in the foothills of the mountains. *Confiterías* are numerous and invariably good for tea, drinks, sandwich lunches, and snacks. Among them: Cuba, Goyescas, Nurias, Astoria, and Oriente; but try any that look inviting. *Night clubs* in the capital include the stylish Boîte at the Hotel Carrera and its congenial bar, the Tap Room, and a number of the aforementioned restaurants which feature music, dancing, and entertainment, such as Pollo Dorado (particularly recommended), Waldorf, Goyescas, El Sarao, Las Perdices, and Las Brujas. **Viña del Mar:** The restaurants of the Hotels Miramar and O'Higgins are both very good, and so are those of the handsome Casino. Others—none in this town are cheap—include the Cap Ducal, Chez Gerard, Virreina, and Los Lilenes, near Concón. Viña night life centers around the Casino, where besides gambling (the roulette tables are huge!) there is dining, dancing, and entertainment in the various dining rooms and bars. **Valparaiso:** Besides the restaurant of the Prat Hotel, there are the Monico, Nave, Vienes, and for sea food, Altamirano and Castillo, on the waterfront. Elsewhere, the hotel dining rooms are generally the best bets, although independent restaurants appear and reappear in some of the bigger towns and more populated resorts; hotel desks are always up to date on the latest good ones.

PRIVATE CLUBS: **Santiago,** besides Rotary and Lions, has such private clubs as the elegant Union, Club Hipico (racing), Los Leones Golf, Prince of Wales Golf, and Polo (with pool and tennis courts). In **Valparaíso,** clubs include British-American, Valparaíso, and Naval. **Vina del Mar's** is the Sporting. **Antofagasta:** English, Union, Spanish, Nautic, and Auto, which serves good lunches on its seaside terrace.

Chilean food specialties: Sea food, particularly at coastal towns and in Santiago, is invariably good, and includes dishes of shrimp (*camarones*), crayfish (*longostinos*), and crab (*jaibas*). *Caldillo de congrio* is a typical fish soup-stew, and *chupe de mariscos* an assorted sea-food platter. Tasty fish include corvina and *congrio*. Steaks are generally above average, but a specialty which you may *not* like is roast kid—tough and tasteless. Other popular dishes: *cazuela de ave*—a chicken-potato-green-vegetable stew, usually with whole ears of corn and rice as well; *pancho villa*—a bean-based casserole, with corn and poached eggs thrown in; *papas rellenas*—potato patties stuffed with chopped-meat or cheese fillings, and the ubiquitous *empanadas*—little turnovers with a variety of fillings, invariably delicious, and often served as canapés accompanying cocktails. Fruits, especially avocado pears, are excellent. Chilean wines, as many Americans know from specimens purchased in the United States, are probably the finest in South America. Of the many, leaders are Aconcagua, Lontue, Cachapoel, and Maipo, from the vineyards of central Chile. There are, of course, red (*vino tinto*) and white (*vino blanco*) varieties, as well as surprisingly good champagne, not-bad gin (which makes gin and tonic a cheap and tasty drink), fair brandy, and even crème de menthe. Imported whiskies are as expensive as the local wines are cheap. Worth remembering: bottled wines are graded by quality: best is *gran vino*.

COLOMBIA

(*República de Colombia*)

Entry requirements: *A tourist card, a health certificate (smallpox), and a transportation ticket indicating that passage out of Colombia has been paid for.* **Best times for a visit:** *In the lofty interior, particularly in Bogotá, December, January, and February are the driest and pleasantest months; the year-round temperature in the capital averages 57°. On the Caribbean coast, the dry season extends from October through March, but the remaining period is far from incessantly rainy; all year-round temperatures are hot (75° to 80°), but there are cooling trade winds during the dry season.* **Currency:** *The peso, of which there are about eight to the U.S. dollar, each peso equaling about twelve and a half U.S. cents.* **Film availability:** *Black-and-white, and generally color, available in the larger cities, at prices higher than in the United States.* **Language:** *Beautifully-spoken Spanish, with a fair amount of English at hotels and major shops but a minimum of English at transport terminals.* **Domestic transport:** *Avianca and other Colombian airlines, with safe but often tardy and indifferent service, by means of which the* *principal towns and cities are linked; relatively few paved roads, poor railroads, and slow but scenically interesting Magdalena River steamer tours.* **Tipping:** *Ten per cent is the general rule.* **Business hours:** *9* A.M.*–12:30* P.M., *2:30* P.M.*–6* P.M. **Further information:** *Colombia National Tourist Board, 424 Madison Avenue, New York; Empresa Colombiana de Turismo, Bogotá, Colombia; Panagra, Chrysler Building, New York, and Cali, Colombia; Caribbean Tourist Association, 20 East 46th Street, New York; Colombian Embassy, Washington, D.C.*

INTRODUCING COLOMBIA

Colombia is a country that one wants to be enthusiastic about. Its government, at least for the last half-decade, has been one of the most conscientious, best-led, and most socially-conscious in Latin America, under a president who has for long justifiably commanded international esteem. It is a country which has long honored the scholar, the writer, the poet, the painter, the journalist, and the architect. It is one of the closest of the South American republics, geographically, to the United States, and one of the most accessible. It is, after all, the land which the conquistadors were convinced was El Dorado, where indigenous mountain people had worked in gold and mined emeralds long before the arrival of the Spaniard, where pirates and buccaneers looted and battled, where the terrain ranges from Andean peaks to the coast lines of two oceans, and where, to become topical, the United States Peace Corps set up its first Latin American operation.

Withal, Colombia, at least for this visitor, is approached with reservations. That portion—the interior—which is most traversed by the tourist is, in at least one tourist's opinion, aloof, minimally hospitable, and lacking to so great an extent the graciousness and warmth of so many other South American countries, that those of its attractions which deserve knowing seem not always worth the effort.

On the other hand, the least-visited part of Colombia—the Caribbean coast—is something else again: poorer, without the aristocratic hauteur of the inland regions, but gay, relaxed, and populated by thoroughly delightful people. The traveler who takes in only Bogotá—and there are many such—is quite likely to wish he hadn't bothered. I hope he gives himself the time and opportunity to meet the *Costeños* of the Caribbean, who are, of course, descendants of the first Colombians to come from abroad.

A backward glance: Of Colombia's original inhabitants, the most outstanding were the Chibcha Indians of the mountainous interior, who, without the influence of coastal peoples, developed on their own a quite remarkable culture. Though mainly farmers living in permanent communities and working their corn and potato fields, they were, as well, miners of and artisans in gold, emeralds, and copper. They were talented weavers and ceramists, with a well-organized political system. Their rigidly autocratic leaders—the Zipa, in what is now Bogotá, and the Zaque, in what is now Tunja—were quite as ceremonial-minded as politicians are anywhere. They evolved an elaborate ceremony, upon taking office, during which they were quite literally rolled in gold dust. Word of this glittering immolation was to hasten their downfall.

But that is getting ahead of the discovery of Colombia. Its first known visitor from abroad was Ponzo de Ojeda, who landed at what is now Cartagena on the Caribbean, in about 1500, only to be rather rudely repulsed by the Indians already resident. Some twenty-five years later another group headed by Rodrigo de Bastias put into Santa Marta, and stayed. A few years later, in 1533, Cartagena was actually settled, and by that time word had got around in conquistador circles that the interior of Colombia was El Dorado, the gold paradise. In 1536 Gonzalo Jiménez de Quesada, who proved to be the most doughty, durable, and long-lived of the early Colombians, decided to have a look, and set sail up the Magdalena River until he came upon the distant Chibchas, whom he lost no time in conquering. By 1538 he had established Bogotá, which he named Santa Fe, and within a decade his forces had secured a great part of what is present-day Colombia, calling it New Granada, after Quesada's home town in Spain.

Meanwhile, some other would-be gold diggers were entering the scene. From Ecuador came Pizarro's lieutenant, Sebastián de Belalcázar, who established Cali, Popayán, and Pasto in 1536. And from Venezuela came the German Nikolaus Federmann. As a child of three might have foretold, an unsettled period followed, but by 1550 the various conquistador factions went along with the establishment of the Spanish Audiencia of Santa Fe, and in 1564 it became the more impressive presidency of the Kingdom of New Granada, which embraced all of Colombia (except the area claimed earlier by Belalcázar, around Popayán), Ecuador, Venezuela, and Panama, as well. Later, in 1718, ties with the viceroyalty of Peru were severed and Colombia (along with Venezuela) achieved separate viceroyalty status. Development along rigid, authoritarian Spanish Colonial lines ensued, in an atmosphere largely tranquil, the pirates and buccaneers storming Cartagena being the exceptions.

The fight for independence: Abortive attempts at independence came later in the eighteenth century, but it was not until 1808, when Napoleon gained control of Spain and replaced the king with a Bonaparte brother, that things really began to pop. A revolutionary junta was set up in Bogotá in 1810, Bolívar landed at Cartagena in 1814 from Venezuela and, the following year, attacked that country from Colombia, destroying five armies in half a dozen battles, none of them decisive enough to make Caracas his. The Spanish, Napoleon out of their hair in Madrid, then retook Cartagena, but in 1819 Bolívar again entered the scene, and after a valiant three-day battle, he and his forces took over Bogotá from the Spanish loyalists. Later that year, the Republic of Gran Colombia—combining Colombia, Ecuador, and Venezuela—was born. Bolívar headed the forces for centralized government, whose descendants are the Colombian Conservative party, and Santander became the leader of those in favor of a federation of states, now the Colombian Liberals. Those two parties, born with the country, were at odds—often violently—until half a decade ago, when they joined forces to oust a dictator-president.

But Bolívar's Gran Colombia was short-lived; Venezuela went off on its own in 1829, and Ecuador followed suit a year later. Colombia itself again started life as the United States of New Granada (it did not take the name Colombia until 1863). The remainder of the nineteenth, and indeed the first five decades of the twentieth, century saw considerable friction between the conservative, pro-Catholic-hierarchy Conservatives, and the progressive, anti-clerical Liberals, and in 1889 the two parties' forces came to blows, with a civil war ensuing for almost three years, at a cost of a hundred thousand lives.

Panama secedes: At this point Panama—still a part of Colombia—with United States aid and encouragement revolted and declared itself independent. Colombians were understandably enraged at the United States, which finally, in 1921, paid Colombia $25 million for its Panamanian loss, but refused to apologize for its complicity in the affair.

Even without Panama (but no doubt with the aid of the canal which came to be built there) Colombia made tremendous economic and industrial progress, and its major cities have become modern metropolises. Oil has enriched the coffers a great deal, facilitating modernization, and the airplane has brought formerly antagonistic and isolated regions together. Governments were stable and representatively elected between wars, but the tranquillity was not to last. In order to oust a ruthless post-World War II dictator, Laureano Gómez, the Liberal and Conservative parties acquiesced in the *coup d'état* by which an army general, Gustavo Rojas Pinella, became president in 1953, ostensibly to make conditions suitable for free elections. Actually his regime was one of the most ruthless, corrupt, and bloody in Colombian history. It came to an end in 1957 when Rojas Pinella attempted to have himself "re-elected" by his rubber-stamp legislature to a second four-year term of office, fully a year in advance of the expiration of his first term.

Unity through revolution: This was more than Colombians could take, and Liberals, Conservatives, and the military collaborated in a swift but not entirely bloodless revolution which ousted the dictator. They supported the election of a distinguished Liberal, Dr. Alberto Lleras Camargo, as president under a National Front Administration (half Liberal, half Conservative). Both parties agreed that the president, in the succeeding four administrations, is to be alternatively Liberal and Conservative. The 1962 elections were looked upon as a test of the strength of the National Front coalition, for both the Liberals and the Conservatives had split into two factions. (During the visit, in December 1961, of President and Mrs. Kennedy, they were, however, solidly united as hosts. The Kennedys, who visited both Colombia and Venezuela to inaugurate Alliance for Progress projects, were enthusiastically welcomed.)

Dr. Lleras Camargo had once before served briefly as president of his country, and was Secretary General of the Organization of American States from 1947 to 1954. He has been, as well, a journalist and a teacher, and did as well as he could in a country which, though once again with a representative government, has many problems, most of which revolve around the tremendous divergence between the tiny, aristocratic wealthy class and the great mass of twelve million Colombians—a third white, 40 per cent mestizo, nearly 20 per cent mulatto, 5 per cent Negro, 7 per cent Indian—mostly all poor, and half illiterate.

Despite opposition from Conservative factions, the Lleras Camargo government cut military expenditures, putting the money into enlarged health, education, public welfare, and agricultural projects. Even so, Colombia—the only South American country with coasts on two oceans, the fourth largest on the continent—is having a difficult time.

Symptomatic of conditions are the continued killings by bandits in back areas of isolated farm districts, where life is at its toughest. This rural violence has taken 300,000 lives in the last thirteen years. It began as a form of political warfare, manifesting the antagonisms of the Liberal and Conservative parties, in 1948, when politicos would often incite illiterate country people to homicide in the cause of their party. By the time the Lleras Camargo government took over in 1958, politics was no longer a reason for the killings. Banditry had simply become a lucrative trade, particularly in those areas where land is dear and money scarce. The coffee harvest—twice annually—still sees terrorism in the remote regions, as poor, jobless laborers attempt to drive coffee farmers from their lands and steal their crops. There are no more than a few hundred full-time *banditos* in the hills, according to the Colombian Ministry of War, but they are believed to receive help from some thirty thousand part-time terrorists. The average visitor is not likely to travel in those remote mountain regions where the *banditos* ply their trade, but the existence of this Colombian phenomenon is worth knowing about, and indicates the complexity of a land where poverty is so great that murder has become a rural industry.

YOUR VISIT TO COLOMBIA

Even though three-fifths of Colombia is uninhabited, there is a good deal more to the country than its capital, Bogotá, which is about all that many visitors bother seeing. Others are misled into wasting valuable time on relatively dull cities like Medellín, at the expense of the beguiling Caribbean coastal area; hardly any at all ever get to such places as Popayán, with its venerable Colonial façade, or Buenaventura, the Pacific port which borders on thick jungle, and virtually none take the time to cruise leisurely along the Magdalena River, Colombia's principal waterway.

The fault is not only that of the time-pressed tourist. It can be laid, too, to some of the travel agencies operating within the country, which often have a knack for steering visitors to the republic's least interesting spots, and to the well-meaning but unprofessional national tourist board. We should all be grateful that Colombia was the first South American republic to boast a truly functioning tourist department, with an operating budget for promotion, advertising, and publicity, liaison with regional and municipal tourist offices throughout the country, and—wonder of wonders, for a South American republic—a branch office in the United States. Tribute must be paid for this pioneer beginning, but at the same time, fingers must be crossed that the Empresa Colombiana de Turismo, now that it has organization, money, and the support of both the government and the travel industry, will come to realize that to do a fine job, as do so many similar organizations in Europe, Asia, and Africa, it must be managed and staffed not by professional politicians and men from other fields of endeavor, but by people who know tourism, and who are not under the impression that American tourists are interested only in skyscrapers, country clubs, views from the tops of hills reached by cable cars, and assorted gimmicks. For that, at present, is the emphasis on sightseeing in Colombia, and it is a great pity, for there is a great deal more to be seen than Bogotá from Monserrate Hill, and the opulent retreats of the very rich. And while a cathedral carved out of a salt mine is impressive and unusual, so are four-century-old churches and streets and houses, and indeed *towns,* which the powers-that-be seem to feel would not interest Mr. and Mrs. John Jones of Cedar Rapids, or Jack Jones, Stamford '63, or Susie Jones, on two weeks with pay from Marshall Field's. In no other capital of South America do authorities in the field of travel take the patronizing attitude toward the American mentality that seems so prevalent in Bogotá.

That preface to tourism in Colombia behind you, here is the republic, in brief, beginning with the too-neglected Caribbean coast.

Barranquilla: Except for the aforementioned Medellín, there is probably no other major city in Colombia with fewer sight-seer's musts than Barranquilla. What it lacks, though, in one department, it makes up for in others. Barranquilla, though established in 1629, is substantially a twentieth-century town, full of factories and offices, and with the greatest harbor on the Caribbean coast

of Colombia. It is hot, and at times humid, and many of its people are poor. Possibly because I have never been rich, or anywhere close to it, I am not under the illusion that one must be
poor to be happy. Nonetheless, much of Barranquilla's population,
predominantly Negro and mulatto, *is* poor, and if not happy,
eminently able to convey a conviviality and charm which, while
typical of the whole Caribbean area of Colombia, is worlds
away from that evident in much of the Andean interior.

I suppose that is Barranquilla's chief asset—its *joie de vivre*
atmosphere. To become acquainted, one need only wander about
—down the wide and handsome Paseo Bolívar, the principal
boulevard; along the wharves of the harbor on the Magdalena
River (which, by the way, is twelve miles inland from the sea);
through the public markets, noisy and gay and earthy and without a great deal of merchandise that you'll want to carry home;
in the pretty tropical parks, particularly the one named 11 de
Noviembre; at *futebol* matches in any of the trio of modern
stadiums, and, of course, in the cafés, bars, and nearby beaches
of *Puerto Colombia* and *Pradomar*.

To be seen, too, are the School of Fine Arts, which embraces
painting, sculpture, and music; the University of the Atlantic;
the contemporary-design Civic Center, and, for acquaintanceships
with the city's minority of affluent residents (who are quite as
personable as the less well-heeled majority), the private clubs,
boîtes, restaurants, and hotels, one of which—El Prado—is the
loveliest in northern South America.

It is from Barranquilla that the hunter (or photographer) of big
game can set out on a South American version of the African
safari. Colombian Safaris, Limited, of this city, offers fourteen-
day package tours to the Central Magdalena Valley and Amazon
Basin, for about $1000 per person, Barranquilla to Barranquilla,
with deep-sea fishing off the coast included, as well as dry-land
opportunities for such trophies as jaguar, puma, ocelot, tapir,
wild boar, and crocodile. Tailor-made safaris, lasting up to thirty
days, can also be arranged. Camps in the bush are quite as
luxurious and comfortable as those in East Africa, and like them,

are under the supervision of professional hunters. (Still other safaris can be undertaken from Bogotá, where the Touring Club de Colombia offers ten-day packages (eight in the bush, two in the capital, for less than $700). Safaris should be booked well in advance, and the nonhunting angler is reminded that he can deep-sea fish to his heart's content in and around Barranquilla, where arrangements can be made upon arrival.

Cartagena: It would be unfair to say that Cartagena lives entirely in the past. Barranquilla has taken over from it as the major port and industrial center of the coast, but the 170,000 Cartageños—mostly Negro and mulatto like their Barranquilla neighbors—are far from idle; their city is still not without commercial importance. But it is not matters of trade that should highlight Cartagena on tourist itineraries. Two other factors do: the past, and the beaches. No other city on the Caribbean combines still-extant souvenirs of a glorious history with the trappings of an informal sun-and-surf resort as does Cartagena. Given this combination, to which must be added the relaxed *ambiance* which its handsome and thoroughly charming residents engender, one is hard put to leave. Even during one's stay there is conflict: which shall it be, the remains of the Spanish greatness, or the inviting sands and the calm blue surf? The ideal is a combination of the two, but for the visitor without time for both, it is Old Cartagena which must have priority.

And old it is—*very* old. A conquistador by the name of Pedro de Heredia is credited as its actual founder. He was leader of the first permanent settlement in 1533, although an earlier abortive attempt had been made. Before long, Cartagena found itself a rich port. The wealth of the Colombian interior had been exploited, and through the Cartagena harbor, en route to Spain, went gold and tobacco and cacao and emeralds and indigo. Word got around that the warehouses, churches, and palaces of this new town were worth looting, and the pirates and corsairs of the Caribbean lost no time in doing just that. The first sacking was in 1543, French professionals being responsible. An Englishman, John Hawkins, later bombarded the town from the harbor but was unable to go ashore, as did Sir Francis Drake in 1586, with the aid of a thousand-odd assistants. He was followed by the notorious Henry Morgan and some ten thousand sackers and looters in 1597, and in 1741, one Sir Edward Vernon (a friend of George Washington's family, for whom, some say, Mount Vernon is named) made a hardly minor attack, aided by more than twenty-five thousand men, and persisting for almost three months, but in vain. They had not reckoned on the strength and persistence of Cartagena's commander, the famed Blas de Lezo, who did not let his infirmities—lameness, a missing eye, and an absent arm—deter him.

It was not only pirates that figured in this town's history. It played an important role in the independence movement. After it had decreed itself sovereign in 1811, Bolívar used it as the take-off base for his first antiroyalist campaign in Venezuela. Its men fought so valiantly against the Spanish that the Liberator himself gave Cartagena the title *Ciudad Heroica,* even though it was re-taken by the Spanish in 1815, not to become free again until six years later.

This bit of background in the picture, Cartagena's fantastic battlements are more understandable to today's visitor. Old Cartagena dwells imperiously upon an island in the Caribbean, a series of bridges its links with the mainland. In its heyday, seven ingeniously constructed fortresses (put together by Negro slaves whose descendants today constitute the bulk of the town's population) protected it from the sea. Philip IV of Spain began erecting them in 1634, and they were finished a century later, when Ferdinand VI was king. There was no stinting, as there is in so much of today's building. Walls, in places, are sixty feet high and seventy feet thick, and ramps on them are wide enough for cars to drive along today.

Most powerful and imposing of the battlements was, and is, the Fortress-Castle of San Félipe. A hundred and thirty-five feet above the sea, it commands a superb view of town and coast, and after its inner passages, secret tunnels, and thick-walled chambers have been inspected, an *al fresco* café, wisely installed by the local authorities, awaits. Within, the old town is a place of arcaded plazas and narrow streets lined by thick-walled white houses and palaces, enclosing gardened patios, with superbly embellished gates and doorways. I would make it a point to start out from the Plaza Bolívar, dominated by the Palace of the Inquisition—now a museum but once a dreaded house of torture, and still a brilliant building, with the royal coat of arms an impressive label over its immense wood-paneled doors.

Cartagena's other Colonial edifices bear the brunt of the pillaging of centuries. Most are now devoid of the treasures which constituted their furnishings, pirates having made off with them centuries ago. And in some instances, garish modern décor provides an unwelcome jarring note. Colonial interiors cannot compare with those of Quito, Cuzco, or even of some in Bogotá.

Still, there are a few which the curious visitor will want to inspect; the University of Cartagena, housed in the former San Augustín monastery, built in 1580; the cathedral; the churches of La Trinidad, Santa Clara, and San Pedro Claver. The last-mentioned dates from 1603 and contains the remains of the saint for which it is named, a Spanish-born Jesuit who became known, even during his lifetime, as "the slave of the slaves," devoting his life to the welfare of the Africans who were brought to Cartagena, meeting them at the harbor as they arrived, nursing them while they were ill, begging money in the streets to help ease their lot, interceding with the authorities on their behalf, and at the same time, converting them to Christianity. He died a weak, sick man—and the Jesuits who still maintain the church carry on an admirably extensive welfare program. They also station one of their number at the church entrance who is armed with English-language literature on the church and the saint, and who attempts to cajole money out of visitors by selling them the literature before they've even had a chance to see the church. The procedure is a little too high-pressure for my tastes and is not at all typical of other Catholic institutions in South America, but the local tourist authorities are powerless to modify it. Once past the priest at the door, the church, while sparsely furnished, is architecturally massive and impressive, with a lovely cloister, and a fine view from the easily-climbed towers. San Pedro Claver, who lived in the church's monastery, died in 1654, but was not canonized until 1888. His remains are in a gold casket beneath the high altar of the church.

Lucky is the traveler who finds himself in Cartagena on November 11, when the anniversary of the city's independence is quite wildly celebrated, with costume balls and pageants and dancing in the streets, or on February 2, the Feast of Candlemas, when the townsfolk climb five hundred-foot-high La Popa Hill to worship in the ruins of Santa Cruz church. Still, the hill can be, and is, ascended by visitors at any time of year, and even on a nonfeast day the waterfront market of Cartagena is a carnival by itself. So, in their ways, are the streets, plazas, and arcades. Quieter, of course, are the wide beaches in the new city; the sands are smooth and white, the water is warm blue and just the right temperature, and the surf is rarely so powerful that it precludes swimming.

Hotels are a notch below those of the more glamorous Caribbean islands, but a number of them are spanking new, clean, and comfortable. Cuisine in their dining rooms, and in the restaurants, runs, naturally enough, to sea food—fresh, well-prepared, and usually delicious. And the local drink is the Colombian version of a potent liquid consumed as well in Central America—fire-hot *aguardiente,* each sip taken with a squeeze of fresh lemon and a few grains of salt.

Also hot, but not in the manner of *aguardiente,* are a chain of twenty pint-sized volcanoes, constantly erupting, at *Turbaco,* fifteen miles from Cartagena, and an interesting excursion point, should one want a change from the life of that town, which is hardly likely.

Santa Marta: Just coming into its own as a resort—it came into its own as a town when it was founded in 1525 as the first settlement in Colombia—Santa Marta has had a history not unlike that of its bigger and better-known neighbor, Cartagena. It has been sacked and ransacked through the centuries by pirates and soldiers, Sir Francis Drake among them, to the extent that relatively few of its Colonial appurtenances remain. What makes it outstanding today, aside from the fact that it is a port, mainly for United Fruit Company bananas, are (1) its superb beaches, (2) the Quinta de San Pedro Alejandrino, the hacienda just out-side of town where Simón Bolívar came to die, and (3) the al-ways snowy peaks of the Sierra Nevada de Santa Marta, almost nineteen thousand feet high and so close by—twenty miles—that one sees them while sunbathing on the beach.

Several new hotels have gone up in recent years, at Rodadero Beach, in the newer part of the city, which itself flanks a lovely crescent-shaped bay, bordered by the palm-lined Avenida Rodrigo de Bastidas. The Quinta Pedro Alejandrino has become a museum of Bolivariana. It was there that the Liberator died a poor man on December 17, 1830, aged forty-seven. His body, after an initial burial in the Santa Marta cathedral, was taken to the Pantheon in Caracas, his birthplace. The bedroom in which he died is now viewable to sight-seers, furnished as it was over a century ago, and elsewhere in the house are other momentos of his career and his era.

While most visitors are content with an excursion to the Bolívar memorial and a leisurely stay at the beaches, excursions into the nearby mountains—there are no others anywhere so high and yet so close to an ocean—are easily undertaken, with the village of *Cincinnati* a convenient destination. The fishing village of *Taganga* is a two-mile spin from town, and nearby, too, is *Villa Concha,* a tiny resort on a handsome bay, with small pen-sions, and facilities for wonderful deep-sea fishing. Barranquilla is but twenty minutes distant, by air, and Bogotá is but a couple of plane-hours away. The new and much-needed Atlantic Rail-road, largely financed by the World Bank, began to carry freight in late 1961 from Santa Marta through the Magdalena Valley to *Solgar,* in the interior, several hundred miles distant. The rail-road, whose construction involved the conquest of near-impene-trable jungle and swamp, shortens transportation time from ten days, by Magdalena river boat, to twelve hours, and will be a great boon to the Colombian economy.

San Andrés Island: Two hours by air from Cartagena, and just off the coast of Nicaragua, is the Colombian island of San Andrés, and its dependency, Providencia Island. Seven miles long and sea-horse-shaped, San Andrés does a thriving tourist business with its clientele largely Central American and Colombian, and its lures free-port merchandise (there is no other free port in Colombia), wide beaches, exceptional water-skiing and skin-diving, good fishing, and the balmy scenery which typifies Caribbean isles. The population is small—about eight thousand, mostly Negro, and bilingual (English-Spanish), thanks to former British stewardship of the island. Aside from tourists, the island deals mainly in coconuts. There are no particularly lush hotels, but the atmosphere is pleasant, relaxed, and attractive.

By steamer from the coast to Bogotá: As admirable as is Colombia's new Atlantic Railroad (see above), the Magdalena River journey—for the traveler, if not for freight—from the Caribbean coast to the Andean capital remains very much worth making. There are package tours offered by travel agents which include a river journey, but the trip can be made independently, starting from Barranquilla, at the mouth of the Magdalena River, and continuing to Bogotá—some seven hundred miles distant—via steamer, and embracing also train and car for those portions where the river is not navigable. The time involved is usually four days; it may be as much as a week, however, if schedules become altered because of river conditions. Though hardly luxurious, the boats—old paddle-wheelers—have been refitted in the first-class section and contain a number of cabins with private shower, and occasionally air-conditioning. Food ranges from fair to good, and there are mosquitoes aplenty on deck at night.

One hardly makes the trip because of the opulence of the ship's accommodations, but because of the route it follows, meandering along a river bordered by market towns, tiny impoverished villages, immense stretches of farmland, verdant jungle, mucky swamp, and, very often, in the distance, Andean peaks. There is no better way to get a bird's-eye view of the country, from the tropical coast to the elevated plateaus. And assuming one is lucky enough to come upon some congenial shipboard company, the journey can be a lot of fun.

Here is the breakdown on the schedule: From Barranquilla to *La Dorada,* about 560 miles, via steamer; from La Dorada for twenty miles by rail to *Honda;* from Honda one can fly directly to Bogotá, or approach it more indirectly but more scenically, by car and train, via *Fusagasugá,* a mountain resort town, the *Zipa-quirá* salt mines and cathedral, and the *Bogotá River Falls.* Cost of the steamer voyage can be as little as $55 first class.

Bogotá: Colombia's capital, at an elevation of 8563 feet, and with a population exceeding one million, is chilly in more ways than one: its atmosphere is the unfriendliest of any of the South American capitals, and there is not a great deal to compensate for this decidedly unappealing aloofness. But this is not to say the city is better avoided. It is interesting to see how an isolated capital has become a modern skyscraper-filled metropolis in little more than a few decades—for such has been the case with Bogotá. And there are some eminently visitable landmarks, a number of which are either skipped entirely, or swiftly driven by, on guided tours. Though it prides itself on its cultural achievement and continues to call itself the "Athens of South America," Bogotá is rarely able to put its cultural foot forward with visitors. Travel people emphasize on tours the view of the city from the peak of Monserrate, reached by cable car, where there is an undistinguished new church; the museum of Chibcha Indian gold-work, which is admittedly important, and an emerald collection in the same building; the unusual, and immense, cathedral hacked out of the salt mine in suburban Zipaquirá, and the not particularly dazzling Tequendama Falls, also out of the city. If there is a bullfight scheduled for a Sunday, attendance at it will be suggested, rightly enough. There just might be a zoom past the cathedral and the Capitol on handsome but somber Plaza Bolívar, and if one is lucky, he might be taken to the Quinta Bolívar, the gracious Colonial house in which the Liberator lived and loved for some years.

But Colonial Bogotá, otherwise, seems virtually unknown to the travel agencies, and I heartily suggest you see it on your own, or insist on being introduced to it. Besides the interior of the cathedral—cold, massive, but with a fine choir and an exquisite silver altar in the Chapel of El Tupo—I would not miss the El Sagrario Chapel, with its seventeenth-century turquoise-inlaid columns; the exquisite ceiling of inlaid wood in La Concepción Church; the even more beautiful interior of San Francisco Church, with mid-sixteenth-century altar and choir, and a Moorish-type ceiling; Veracruz Church, originally constructed in the sixteenth century, since rebuilt several times, and now the official Church of the Republic and National Pantheon; and, if there's time, other notable old churches including Las Nieves, Spanish-Moorish in décor; small but lovely Santa Clara, Santa Inés, and San Ignacio. I would not miss either, if I had the slightest interest in Colonial art, the Colonial Art Museum; though without the charm of Quito's, it is quite as well-stocked with superb paintings, religious objects, and furniture.

And I would make it a point to take in the National Museum, which graphically tells the story of Colombia, from Indian days onward, beautifully complementing the aforementioned display of Chibcha goldwork in the Banco de la República. It is worth noting that the Chibchas worked, not alone by simple hammering, but by the highly complex "lost-wax" process, also used by early West African civilizations.

Unless you take the initiative, you'll not get to the new, modern, and stimulating University City, nor will you more than drive by San Carlos Palace, once a home of Bolívar and now the Foreign Ministry. Even if it is officially closed, I would try and have a look at the wonderfully ornate Colon Theatre, the Mint, which dates back to 1720, and the *interior* of the colonnaded Capitol, the seat of the legislature.

There are a goodly number of first-class restaurants, most of them rather stiff and elegant, but with good food. Night life fol-

lows the same pattern, and shopping is limited, unless one wants
an emerald (hardly cheap in Colombia, but cheaper by a good
deal than at home) or a *ruana*—the handsome wood poncho-
type cloak of the Andean Colombians. Assuming the sun is shining
(and this happens little during the nondry months), strolls about
town can be interesting. But *Bogateños* seem so intent on their own
business that they have little charm to exude and the *ambiance*
is far from being one which impels the visitor to linger on. The
only thing which might delay one's departure from the strikingly
handsome and enormous new El Dorado airport is the almost
complete absence of direction markers, in any language, telling
one how to get through the terminal to one's plane. For the
traveler who does not speak Spanish, little help can be expected
from the almost entirely unilingual personnel on duty. I suppose
the airport typifies Bogotá—big, impressive, and not the least
bit *simpático*.

Manizales: A new Colombian city—it dates back only to 1846
—austere Manizales is 7063 feet up in the Andes, and capital of
the Caldas Department, a region which produces almost a third
of the nation's crop of fine-quality coffee. Skiers, though, are
attracted by its always snowy slopes on nearby Nevada del Ruiz,
where there is an attractive hotel, among whose attractions are,
incongrously enough, thermal baths. There is plane service direct
from Bogotá, but many visitors fly only as far as *Pereira* and from
there go on by car for a quite spectacular thirty-five-mile journey
through the mountains to Manizales, the last portion of which is
via aerial cableway. Principal sights within the town, most of whose
buildings are of dull concrete: a quite striking State House, a
modern bull ring, and the republic's biggest cathedral. Way below
the city is the flower-filled village of *Santa Maria*.

Medellín: A few thousand feet lower than the capital, and
smaller in population by half a million, Medellín is a progressive
industrial city in a mountain valley, with a pleasant climate (it's
usually about 70°); some orchid farms at which the flowers are
in bloom at only certain times of year; a hectic and refreshingly
lively cattle market; slews of factories, many of them making

textiles, which is the major industry; a few universities; an ugly modern cathedral which is presumably the biggest all-brick building in the world, if that means something to you; and a large but decidedly mediocre hotel with barely edible food and steep rates. Once again, don't follow the travel agents' advice; it's not worth the effort, unless, of course, you're on a business mission, or are visiting friends.

Cali: About the size of Medellín, and similar also in that it is largely industrial and in the interior, Cali has, however, a certain verve and lightness in its personality, possibly because of its relative nearness to the Pacific. It is the commercial center of the Cauca Valley. Its central district is buoyant and bouncy, and the principal square, Plaza de Caicedo, is dramatically flanked by towering royal palms, a bevy of sleek skyscrapers, the Government Palace, and an undistinguished cathedral. There are pleasant views from Cristales Hill, which is dominated by a tall Christ statue, and from Three Crosses Hill, on which there are, you might have guessed, a trio of crosses.

Little remains of Colonial times, but from this era there is San Francisco Church, with an unattractive modernized interior, a still lovely old bell tower, and some fine old paintings of long-since departed Franciscans who lived in the adjoining monastery; San Antonio Chapel, still charming although without the beauty that it no doubt had when it was built in the seventeenth century; and the handsome three-century-old Hacienda Cañas Gordas (six miles from town), open to the public as a museum. An hour's drive through sugar-cane plantations makes for a pleasant excursion, with *Buga* the destination, for lunch or overnight at its attractive hotel and swimming pool.

However, if I had a choice of but one sight-seeing destination, it would be the new clubhouse and grounds of the Club Campestre. Now, as any visitor to Colombia will tell you, *every* city is distinguished by at least one magnificent country club and any number of elegant urban clubs. This is a class-conscious republic and the well-to-do set great store by the number of their club memberships, and the quality of them. Every city attempts to outdo every other

city in the opulence of these palaces, and while none that you are
likely to see anywhere in Colombia will come close to being uncomfortable, the new Cali building is a standout. It was designed
by a team of Colombian architects, who belong in an international
architects' hall of fame, if such there be; their names, which deserve mention are: Rafael Borrero Vergara, Fernando Borrero
Caicedo, Alfredo Zamorano Pizarro, Dario Mejia, and an Italian
colleague, Renato Giovanelli.

The building and its grounds, which are beautifully blended into
a harmonious whole, are starkly contemporary and at the same
time warm, inviting, and ingenious. There are surprises wherever
one turns: waterfalls cascading from beneath rock gardens, a
swimming pool deftly hidden behind a miniature cabana colony,
handsomely-furnished lounges overlooking green landscape,
mosaic-floored terraces, cozy bars, properly formal dining rooms.
The club is open to members only, but if you are interested in seeing what is quite likely the most exciting example of modern architecture in western South America—and there is nothing, for that
matter, in Brasília which is any better—I suggest you try and
arrange permission for a visit through the Cali office of Panagra,
or a knowledgeable travel agent. That is, unless you know a member, or have access to one: there are twelve hundred of them.

Popayán: South of Cali, near the Pacific, not a great distance
from the Ecuadorian border, and in that region of Colombia which
has the largest Indian population, Popayán has been largely content
to let time pass it by. All too many tourists have done likewise,
which is a great pity, for this is one of the loveliest of Colombia's
cities. The early Spaniards, attracted by its relatively pleasant climate—it has an altitude of 5774 feet—retreated to it from their
money-making endeavors on the hot and humid Pacific coast.
They built lavishly, and their handiwork survives, much of it in the
authentic rococo style of Andalusia.

The town's founder was no less a personage than Pizarro's
lieutenant, Belalcázar, who arrived in 1536. By 1640 a university
was in operation, and the town had become a city in its own right.
As in Cartagena, many of the old buildings have been near-ruined

by grotesque modern interior-decoration jobs, but a great deal of the original beauty remains. Most outstanding are San Agustín, with its handsome carved doorway and elaborate monstrance; San Francisco, with a finely detailed pulpit and the clearest and most resonant bell in its tower of any in the city; Belén Chapel, in a lovely setting atop a hill overlooking the city; the old houses of Calle Proceres; a pair of treasure-filled museums; and the university, housed in a venerable Dominican monastery, near which are a fine stone fountain and a three-hundred-year-old church.

Popayán's Holy Week celebrations are regarded by Colombians as the South American equal of Seville's, in Spain. They begin on Palm Sunday, when a pair of images is carried from the hilltop Belén Chapel to the cathedral in the town, and they continue, with elaborate processions (one, at night, is by candlelight) of splendidly-garbed marchers, both lay and clergy. Spectators include Indians from the countryside, and their women in gay, homespun wool skirts and black shawls. Nearby is *Puracé,* a tiny town practically astride the Puracé Volcano, which can be climbed. And not far, in a wooded valley, is *Silva,* most of whose inhabitants are Guamba Indians, among the most curious, and independent, of the Colombian tribal groups.

Buenaventura: The principal Colombian port on the Pacific, Buenaventura straddles Cascajal Island, ten miles inside Chacó Bay. Despite its importance, it is still small, with considerably less than 100,000 residents. It is also hot, humid, rough, and rugged, with a great deal of rain, and a harbor through which pass such exports as coffee, sugar, gold, and platinum. Mostly populated by mulattoes, who come to see very little of the wealth which gives the town its reason for being, Buenaventura is a far cry from the other principal towns of the republic. Its streets are still largely unpaved and its houses dried-mud huts. There is probably no other important port quite like it on the Pacific coast; still, it has the friendly zip characteristic of harbor towns, humidity notwithstanding. I shouldn't recommend an overlong, or even an overnight, stay, but a brief visit is revealing, and the town can serve well as a base for a launch trip up the Agua Dulce River (translated, that means "sweet water," but I wouldn't substitute it for Coke) into the steamy jungle. Buenaventura can be taken in in a single day, from Cali, by leaving that city in the early morning via the five-hour electric train (*autoferro*) through the verdant jungle, and returning by small, six-passenger plane in the late afternoon.

WHAT TO BUY

Colombia is hardly a shopper's paradise, unless one is in the market for native-mined emeralds, which are among the finest in the world. Decent-sized stones range in price from a little over a hundred dollars to a couple of thousand dollars, with prices reputedly less than half of what they are in the United States. Jewelers with good collections include Kling, Carlos Bauer, Bauer (not to be confused with *Carlos* Bauer), and Fox. Within the reach of more travelers are *ruanas,* the poncho-like cloaks of Colombia —of wool when worn in the Andes, of cotton when worn in the warmer regions. Martha Bauer's shop and Dagmar, in the Hotel Tequendama, stock them, as well as other minor Colombian craft items (none exceptional) and antiques, including brass stirrups. Try also Cansino (next to the cathedral) and Medina. Three good silversmiths (tea services, trays, etc.) are Arturo Medina, Gutierrez Vega, and Orfabria Florentina. Outside of Bogotá, there is even less really worth buying. Medellín features unbelievably ugly leather bags which coffee farmers keep their cash in, and which women are supposed to find attractive as handbags. Cartagena and the coastal towns feature straw products, much like those elsewhere in the Caribbean. My most treasured souvenir of Colombia is a lump of rock salt, which I picked up on a road leading into the Salt Cathedral outside of Bogotá, for free; it's a fine paperweight. Almost as cheap: matches in handsome boxes which feature the flags of the South American republics.

CREATURE COMFORTS

HOTELS—**Bogotá:** The Tequendama, operated by Intercontinental Hotels Corporation, of New York, is the more important
of the top two in the capital. Modern, functional, clean, with a
good coffee shop, restaurant, *boîte,* shops, attractive bedrooms, all
with bath; from $9.50 single. The Number Two Bogotá hotel is
the Continental—modern, but smaller than the Tequendama, with
a good dining room and a central location. Cheaper are the San
Francisco, and the Santa Fe and Steves pensions, or *residencias.*
Barranquilla: El Prado is one of the most beautiful and best-
operated hotels in South America, and a member of the Intercontinental Hotels group. Though not old, it is designed in Spanish
Colonial style, with a swimming pool and terrace filling its immense
gardened patio, golf and tennis, a new coffee shop, a handsome
Andalusian-style dining-room, *boîte,* charming rooms, some with
balcony, all with bath, and most with air-conditioning, and perfectly splendid service. In a pleasant residential section of town,
El Prado is a resort in itself, and one of the chief attractions of
the city; from $8.50 single. In-town hotels: Genova—new and with
swimming pool; Central—older but good; Astoria, Victoria,
Alhambra, Luxor. **Cartagena:** The del Caribe is the biggest and
best-known but it is not as good as it is reputed to be, although
it has a lovely pool, a seaside location, and all rooms are with bath.
Smaller but newer are the Playa and the Bahia, all on the beach
and all with rooms with bath, some with air-conditioning. Near
the beach is the brand-new Quinta Avenida. Under construction is
the Hotel Casino, with adjoining casino. The San Félipe is the best
downtown hotel; all rooms with bath and air-conditioning. **Santa
Marta:** The Tamaca is brand-new, on Rodadero Beach, $7 daily
for room, bath, and three meals. Others: Barque, Miami, Tyrona.
Going up: El Rodadero. **Medellín:** The Nutibara (with swimming
pool) is the best—modern, but with tasteless food, and so jammed
with businessmen who have no place else to stay that the manage-

ment doesn't exert itself to extend good service. Others: Europe, Normandie, Veracruz. **Cali:** The Alfarez Real (with swimming pool) and the Aristi vie for top billing, which is not saying a great deal; poor food, mediocre service. Others: Los Angeles—small but very good; Melendez, New York, Europa, Balkanes. **Manizales:** Ski Lodge; in town: Escorial, Europa. **Popayán:** The Lindbergh and the Europa are the top two, both adequate. **Buenaventura:** Estación—poor, but there's none better. **San Andrés Island:** Casa Blanca, Abacoa.

RESTAURANTS AND NIGHT LIFE—**Bogotá:** Aside from the hotel dining rooms and coffee shops there are a number of good restaurants, including Gran Vatal (Luxembourg-Belgian-French cuisine, in a lovely old house); Temel, sea food; Koster, French; Meson de Indias, Spanish; La Pampa, Argentine beef specialties. For both dinner and after-dinner entertainment, there are the Montserrate Room of the Tequendama, Grill Europa, Sahara, Casbah, Leon's, and Grill Colombia—all fairly expensive. **Barranquilla:** The attractive, Moorish-style dining-room-*boîte* of El Prado Hotel is the Number One spot; the hotel's coffee shop and several bars are also very pleasant. In town: Metropole, San Blas, Brandes restaurants; many cafés and bars. **Cartagena:** Fishermen's Club (Club de Pesca)—fine for sea food, harbor view; Del Caribe Hotel's *boîte* for late dinner-dances, entertainment, casino adjoining. Meson del Pirata, Capilla del Mar (French food), Barrachina, plus many other cafés and hotel dining rooms and bars. **Santa Marta:** The restaurants and bars of the Tamaca and other hotels. **Medellín:** The Grill of the Nutibara Hotel is more expensive than the dining room but the food is a little better and the atmosphere not so grim. La Fonda Antioqueno is lively and serves interesting Colombian foods; Salvator and Piemonte, both Italian; La Hosteria, good for chicken and Continental European dishes; Tom's—bar and international menu; Chino, Chinese; Don Ramon, Spanish. **Cali:** The hotel dining rooms are dull, uninspired and mainly populated by lonely traveling salesmen. Don Carlos is the town's best restaurant, and it is excellent. Other interesting eating places: Bella Napoles, Hosteria Madrid, Los Gauchos, and La

Tablita for delicious Argentine-type beef specialties; Club 20–50, a new and fashionable *boîte*. **Manizales:** The Ski Lodge and the hotel dining rooms. **Popayán:** Lindbergh and Europea hotel dining rooms. **Buenaventura:** Nothing recommendable.

PRIVATE CLUBS—Class-conscious Colombia is a country of country clubs. In the larger cities where there is little else to see, visits to the top clubs are invariably included in city tours. Finest in the country, and one of the best examples of South American contemporary architecture, is the already-described Club Campestre in Cali. Others: **Bogotá:** Jockey, Gun, Anglo-American, Medico, Lawyers, Bogotá Country, Los Lagartos, San Andrés Golf, Military, plus the ubiquitous Lions and Rotary. **Barranquilla:** Country, Barranquilla, Anglo-American, German Centra Israelita. **Medellín:** Union, Campestre, Medellín, El Rodeo, Profesionales. **Cali:** The aforementioned Campestre, Colombia, de Tennis, San Fernando.

Colombian food specialties: A *piquete* is a popular all-inclusive meal, including well-seasoned potatoes, meats, and vegetables, served with *ají,* a peppery sauce. Sea food is excellent in the coastal cities. In the Medellín region, *mondongo,* a thick vegetable-meat soup-stew combination, *frijoles* (beans), *arepa* (corn bread), and *bocadillos* (oversweet candies) are typical. All over the country the most popular (and cheapest) strong drink is *aguardiente.* Colombian rum is good, and imported whisky is available in better bars; it is, of course, fairly expensive.

ECUADOR

(República del Ecuador)

Entry requirements: *A tourist card, obtainable from Ecuadorian consulates, directly or through travel agents and airlines; health certificate (smallpox) also required.* **Best times for a visit:** *June–October, the dry season, is the ideal period. Mountainous Quito, almost on the equator, is cool and spring-like the year round, with an average temperature of 55°; the coastal area, including Guayaquil, is tropical, hot, and humid, but even there (as well as in the mountains) rains during the wet months are far from incessant.* **Currency:** *The sucre, named for the great general-president, is divided into one hundred cents, and equals about six U.S. cents.* **Film availability:** *Both color and black-and-white available, but not as inexpensively as in the United States.* **Language:** *Spanish, although many Indians speak only Quechua. English is spoken in hotels, leading shops, major transport terminals.* **Domestic transport:** *Planes connect the major cities and there is a convenient charter "air-taxi" service (Atesa, Quito); fair to poor roads; the fantastic roller-coaster railway connecting Quito and Guayaquil is hardly luxe, but gets you there,*

eventually. **Business hours:** *8:30* A.M. *to noon, 2 to 6* P.M.
Tipping: *Ten to fifteen per cent in hotels and restaurants; taxi drivers are not tipped.* **Further information:** *Ecuadorian Embassy, Washington, D.C.; Panagra, Chrysler Building, New York, and Quito, Ecuador; Metropolitan Touring, Quito, Ecuador; Dirección Nacional de Turismo, Quito, Ecuador.*

INTRODUCING ECUADOR

Next-to-the-smallest of the South American republics (Uruguay is *el mas pequeño*), Ecuador is a microcosm of western South America. A good bit less than half the size of Alaska, it is a polyglot of peoples, terrains, and cultures, all far from perfectly blended, but cohesive enough to allow even a relatively brief visit to encompass a great variety of sensations, visual and otherwise. What it lacks in riches, natural and per capita, Ecuador compensates for with inordinate charm. But this is not to say that it is a completely carefree, happy land, much as it might so appear to the visitor, for its burdens are not unlike those of neighboring countries with great Indian populations, except, of course, that Ecuador's are peculiarly Ecuadorian.

A backward glance: An extensive Pacific coast line assures Ecuador adequate ports and contact with the world, but the Andes, running from the Colombia border in the north to the Peruvian frontier in the south, divide the little republic into two distinct regions, geographically, economically, and ethnically. And Bigger Neighbor Peru has played a major role in the drama of Ecuador for centuries; an apparently interminable boundary dispute (of which more later) keeps the two from approaching the intimacy which might be expected of two states sharing a common heritage.

Ecuador's earliest recorded invasion came in the mid-fifteenth century, when the aggressive, superbly organized Incas decided, at their capital in Cuzco, to enlarge their empire. They subjugated, without great difficulty, the Indians already resident in Ecuador (although they were not completely successful in imposing their culture on all groups), and as Incas will—or would, in those days—set to work on a road-building job which staggers many of today's technologically superior engineers. They ran a highway from Cuzco to Quito. Two Inca brothers—co-Incas they might be called—named Huáscar (who lived in Cuzco) and Atahualpa (who lived in Quito) took turns ruling the area, until the start of the sixteenth century, at which point another brother-act wrote itself into the script: the advance-men for the Pizarro boys (of whom there were four, with Francisco, of course, rating top billing) entered the country, beginning at Esmeraldas, on the coast, going south to the Gulf of Guayaquil, and a few years later taking over the interior Kingdom of Quito as well, after Huáscar and Atahualpa began to spat with each other. Atahualpa came out the victor, but not for long. Pizarro killed him off in 1533. So ended the Inca Empire, and so began the occupation of the interior of Ecuador by the conquistadors.

Pedro de Alvarado moved in with troops to claim what Pizarro had already decreed was *his* territory, and Pizarro, not content to let *that* happen, sent two lieutenants, Belalcázar and de Almagro, north to take over from Alvarado, which they did. Lima became capital of the whole area in 1535, and in 1539 the eldest Pizarro sent his brother Gonzalo into Quito to take charge. More interested in gold than politics, Gonzalo promptly dispatched a colleague, Francisco de Orellana, on a prospecting expedition, and by the time he returned, he had drifted down the Napo River to the mouth of the Amazon. He was the first white man to make the trip, and Ecuadorians remain proud of him to this day, as well they might.

Colonial Ecuador: The gold, of course, was never discovered, there being none, and back in Quito life was hardly tranquil. Assorted forces—conquistadors, the Spanish Crown, and even a priest (who had Gonzalo Pizarro executed)—kept things lively, until at last Quito became an *audiencia* of the viceroy of Peru. Things were relatively quiet for almost three centuries, during which time the Spaniards made the mountain city one of the most beautiful in

Colonial America. Priests put the Christianized Indians to work building and decorating churches and other public buildings which to this day surpass any other remnants of that age in the Americas in opulence, design genius (often a blend of Hispano-Inca), and craftsmanship. Negro slave labor began to be imported in the eighteenth century for work on coastal plantations, and Ecuador today has the biggest Negro population of any of the west-coast republics. The Spaniards had a going thing; their colony was thriving, at least for the privileged, powerful minority.

Sucre, and a new republic: But independence fever was in the air. The first attempt at freedom, in 1809, was a flop, but in 1821 General Sucre moved troops north from Guayaquil, defeated the Spanish in a fierce battle on Mount Pichincha, and took over Quito, which the mountain overlooks. Bolívar soon came to support him, and talked the Sucre forces into joining the Gran Colombia federation (with Venezuela and Colombia). Ecuador stayed in only until 1830, when it opted for complete sovereignty. Its first president was a harsh dictator with the deceptively gentle name Juan Flores. No flower was he, however. The ensuing century saw the conflict of the Flores-founded Conservatives—who supported entrenched privilege for the tiny ruling class and dominance of the Roman Catholic church—and the Liberals, among whose leaders have been President Vicente Rocafuerte (who was exiled after his term of office expired, so fearful were the aristocrats of his influence with the Indians and mestizos whose cause he championed), and Flavio Eloy Alfaro, president at the beginning of this century, until he was murdered by a gang of thugs. Still, the administrations of Rocafuerte and Alfaro were not in vain. To a certain extent, their reforms had an effect, to the extent that the aristocratic minority, when in power, was at least somewhat aware of how far it could exploit the mass of the people. By the time World War II ended, governments began to approach stability, and came into office as the result of ostensibly democratic elections.

Literacy remains a requisite for the ballot, nonetheless, and only half the population can read or write. What amounts to an oligarchy, with the support of the military, has run the country to all intents and purposes, with the most perennially popular president Dr. José Maria Velasco Ibarra. A president may not succeed himself, but Dr. Velasco—now seventy-three, gaunt-visaged, very much the demagogue—has popped in and out of the Presidential Palace with amazing regularity.

His most recent inauguration—the fourth—was in 1960, when he succeeded Dr. Camilio Ponce Enriquez. The wealthy but independent and liberal vice-president, a member of an old Guayaquil banking family, Dr. Carlos Arosemena Monroy, was visiting the Soviet bloc in 1961, while Adlai Stevenson was in Ecuador; shortly thereafter President Velasco accepted an invitation from President Kennedy to visit the United States, but he did not have a chance to accept. Discontent with his economic policies—particularly new taxes on consumer goods, in a country with a tremendously poor mass populace—led to riots and a demand that President Velasco step aside—which he did, by flying to exile (for the second time in his career) to Argentina, his wife's homeland. Vice-President Arosemena assumed the chief executive's office, and appointed a coalition cabinet—heavily moderate, it should be noted—with a program aimed at reducing the cost of living and implementing much-needed tax and land reforms.

Ecuador today is almost 50 per cent illiterate, 40 per cent pure Indian, 40 per cent mestizo, 10 per cent Negro and mulatto, and 10 per cent white, with the Negroes and mestizos mostly coastal, the Indians and whites mostly in the interior. In recent years the two areas, so long separated geographically and ethnically, have begun to eradicate regional differences, thanks to improved communications and transportation, a very gradual improvement in the economy, and the shrewd politics of Ecuadorian presidents, particularly Dr. Velasco, who gained popular support through emotional appeals for return of Ecuadorian territory granted to Peru in 1942, as the result of the Protocol of Rio de Janeiro.

Ecuador claims that because it was small and defenseless, it had no choice but to accept the decision of the Rio treaty, which was forced upon it. Peru claims the decision was perfectly aboveboard, according to the precepts of international law. But Ecuador is not buying this. It is sensitive, understandably enough, to the gradual whittling down of its territory through the centuries, and it points out that when it became sovereign its area was roughly the size of United States' eastern seaboard, while today it is nearly two-thirds smaller.

Friends of both Peru and Ecuador are hopeful that their arguments will be resolved around a conference table. Meanwhile, the government goes about its task of domestic improvement. Attempts are being made to diversify the economy, by exploiting the as yet largely untapped maritime riches of its Pacific coast in co-operation with the United Nations Special Fund. But until the waters take over from the land, bananas will no doubt remain the country's top export. Ecuador is, indeed, top banana, leading all nations of the world in international trade in that fruit. Other top exports: coffee, cacao beans, and rice. Of the imports, tourists—at least at this stage of this chapter—are the most important. And those who go, export themselves with understandable reluctance.

YOUR VISIT TO ECUADOR

I suspect I would be a rich man if I had a sucre for every visitor who enters and leaves Ecuador via Quito, and sees very little else of the country. In an attempt to rectify this situation, this section of the chapter will commence with the coastal area, easily seen, but too often skipped over, by the traveler en route to the appealing capital.

Guayaquil: Ecuador is not without surprises. Its largest city is not the capital, but the port of Guayaquil. And Guayaquil is not on the Pacific, as most major west-coast ports are, but thirty-five miles inland, on the Guayas River. It is not, to continue in the negative, a Pacific version of São Paulo with a streamlined, sky-scrapered façade. A great deal of the wealth that has made it into a metropolis of half a million population, seems to leave almost as soon as it arrives, and until very recently Guayaquil was little more than a sprawling collection of near-shacks—unhealthy, unappeal-

ing, un-air-conditioned, and unattractive to even the most soci-
logically-inclined of visitors.

Time, particularly a brief span, does not heal all wounds, and
Guayaquil has a long way to go before offering any competition to,
say, Buenos Aires. But it has cleaned and spruced itself up considerably, and the visitor who doesn't give himself a chance for at
least a brief acquaintance is denying himself a taste of the heart and
soul of half of Ecuador. Almost all of the republic's imports pass
through Guayaquil, more than half of its exports are shipped from
it, and something like 40 per cent of the Ecuadorian population
lives in the area it dominates. Its residents have that open, hearty
quality which is common to residents of harbor cities, and the
visitor can not help but enjoy himself as he wanders about.

Life in Guayaquil revolves about the quite marvelous harbor,
which is bordered by extensive Malecon Drive, into which the
principal thoroughfares converge. The Malecon is animated with
river steamers, and the stevedores who load and unload great stems
of bananas aboard them. Plaza Centenerario is the principal square,
dominated by a bulky, ornate, and not particularly handsome
monument which reflects the gracelessness of the turn-of-century
period when it was erected. There are countless other smaller
squares, and a number of parks, and all are embellished with
statuary of one sort or another.

Most interesting of all, in this department, is the monument
commemorating the strange but historic meeting of Simón Bolívar
and José de San Martín, the greatest of the continent's heroes,
which took place in Guayaquil during the pre-independence period.
It was after this meeting that San Martín, who had been responsible
for liberating an immense chunk of South America, relinquished
whatever glories remained for him in the Pacific regions of the continent, and shortly thereafter disappeared into the oblivion and
anonymity of a Paris pension, where he died a poor man some
years later. Why he bowed out of the picture after the Guayaquil
meeting has never been definitively explained; neither he nor
Bolívar ever reported on their deliberations.

But enough of statues and the stories behind them, one excepted—that of Darwin, who explored the Galápagos Islands, Ecuador's Pacific "colony." His statue is on the grounds of the University of Guayaquil, itself worth a stroll, particularly if it can lead to conversations with students and professors. Good chitchat locales, too, are the sidewalk cafés, always a welcome haven in between bouts of rubbernecking and shopping. There is an immense, gleaming-white cemetery just outside the city which is considered eminently worth visitors' inspections—assuming visitors like looking at cemeteries; this one doesn't. There is an absolutely enormous cathedral, and there are some fairly well-proportioned public buildings in the center of town, the gingerbready Municipal Palace and the much plainer Government Palace among them. Most interesting, at least for this traveler, is the district known as Las Peñas, oldest of Guayaquil's neighborhoods, with Santo Domingo, a fifteenth-century church, and a curious street, Numa Pompilio Llona, curving, narrow, authentic Colonial, paved with great flat stones and lined by houses as old as the thoroughfare itself—balconied affairs on one side, bigger houses, overlooking the river, on the other. Above looms the summit of Santa Maria Hill, to which every visitor is taken, at one time or another, for a vista of town, harbor, and verdant countryside.

Travelers arriving in Guayaquil by air miss the approach to it via the Gulf of Guayaquil, up from the open sea and the island of Puná, where larger ships tie up, transfering passengers to smaller craft for the interesting four-hour journey to the city. En route, on either side, the jungle hugs the water's edge, and plying back and forth are all manner of craft—barges loaded with bananas and cacao, sailing vessels of local fishermen, modern cargo ships flying foreign flags, sleek little canoes on shorter runs between river villages.

For air travelers, the river can be traversed by means of tourist cruises originating at the yacht club; the direction on such journeys is inland from the city, through even less-developed areas than that between the sea and Guayaquil. And for visitors with no time for any sort of river trip, there are the balconies of the bedrooms in the town's newest hotel, which look out on the river and its never-ending activity.

The coastal resorts: Ecuador is only just beginning to fully exploit the marine riches of its Pacific coast industrially, but it has not lagged in taking recreational advantage of those blue waters and white sands. The visitor who has spent as little as twelve hours in Guayaquil will have heard about Salinas and Playas.

Playas, the closer to Guayaquil of the two, is fifty-eight miles from town, via paved highway; travel agents make arrangements for transport via private boat or plane from Guayaquil. Besides a first-class hotel, country club, casino, golf course, and deep-sea fishing facilities, Playas is blessed with the Humboldt Current, which is responsible for bringing cool winds from the Antarctic to air-condition the equatorial Ecuadorian coast. From May through November the weather averages 78°, and sweaters and wraps are evening necessities.

Salinas is ninety-six miles from Guayaquil, along the same paved highway that leads to Playas. Delightfully situated on a crescent-shaped bay, this resort has quite the same sort of appeal as Playas—fine beaches, and a modern hotel; it is lacking only in a casino, a facility which is more attractive to some vacationers than a room with a sea view, and white sands. Compensation, for those with a gambling urge, is horse racing, from February through April. Salinas is the site of the spanking-new Ecuadorian Naval Academy, inaugurated in 1961 by Admiral Arleigh A. Burke, chief of U. S. Naval Operations, and built with U.S. aid.

Other coastal river towns: *Esmeraldas* goes back to conquistador days, but has grown little through the centuries. Still a town of less than twenty thousand population, it is a quiet banana port, in the northwest, at the mouth of the Esmeraldas River, in a region whose produce runs the gamut from gold to rubber. *Babahoyo, Daule,* and *Vinces* are small Guayas River communities, of no special interest, except that they serve as good destinations for visitors to Guayaquil who would like to sample life along the tropical river. Boats ply between them and the city in as little as a few hours, and the route makes for an offbeat introduction to flora and fauna of the area. *Montecristi* and *Manta* are known principally for the manufacture of the misnamed Panama hats, which have become so expensive that they've about priced themselves out of business; the hat industry is now a dying one in Ecuador, and unless you plan on reviving it, these last two towns need not concern you.

Cuenca: Ecuador's third largest city (its population hovers around fifty thousand), Cuenca is barely known to the non-Ecuadorian, and is perhaps for this reason a dreamy Indo-Colonial town, rarely intruded upon by even the most intrepid of tourists. And more's the pity, at least insofar as the tourist is concerned. The altitude is nearly 8500 feet, which makes for spring-like sunny days, and cool nights. The atmosphere is easygoing, slow, eye-filling: cobbled streets, venerable houses and public buildings constructed of native marble, enchanting churches, a vibrant Indian community whose Thursday market is one of Ecuador's most interesting, and a population which sees outsiders so rarely that it can't do enough for them.

Regardless of how brief your visit, have a look at Concepción Church, which is just a few decades newer than the town itself, which was founded in 1557 upon the site of an ancient Indian town called Tomebamba; Carmen Church and its cloister, with its superb pulpit; the richly-decorated San Francisco Church; and three treasure-troves of museums: the Municipal, the Archaeological (which includes a picture gallery of Colonial art), and the Konanz Archaeological, outside of the city, with the finest collection of its kind in Ecuador, particularly of the Inca and pre-Inca periods.

Last but not least (if you're not to offend the proud citizens of the *"noble y leal ciudad de Cuenca"*— so termed in pre-independence days), there is the so-called New Cathedral, which has been a-building for close to eighty years and is still not quite completed.

By roller coaster to Quito: I had always thought, before traveling to Quito from Guayaquil by train, that the most spectacular railroad in the world was that connecting Oslo, Norway's capital, with Bergen, on the Atlantic. Now, I have my doubts, and I suspect that even the most chauvinistic Norwegian would at least put the Ecuadorian route on a par with that in his own country. Before the railroad was opened in 1908, it took two weeks to reach Quito from Guayaquil, or vice versa. Now, that journey takes from twelve to eighteen hours, depending upon how healthy the train is on the day selected.

The Guayaquil–Quito Railway is the result of the engineering genius of two Americans, Archer and John Harman, who began the job in 1896; the job took both their lives, but it is a great memorial to them, traversing on its near-three-hundred-mile route some fifty miles of low, swampy delta, shortly thereafter climbing to an altitude of more than 10,000 feet in the course of fifty miles, chugging onward to the highest point, 11,841 feet, subsequently weaving upward or downward in the 8000–11,000-foot category, and at last descending to Quito, at a little over 9300 feet.

There are switchbacks and zigzags galore, and stops at towns and villages—most pathetically poor—all along the way, at which food peddlers come aboard with exotic-looking, -tasting, and -smelling Ecuadorian specialties, including cheese pastries wrapped in immense green leaves, roast pig, and a strange beverage known as Pepsi-Cola. There are views of snowy peaks, magnificent valleys, well-tended farms, and, all along the way, the people of Ecuador—Negroes and mestizos on the low, tropical coast, Indians in the mountain villages, whites in the larger towns.

There are two types of service. Most popular with visitors from abroad is the *autoferro,* a one-car diesel coach which is advertised as modern and comfortable, but which is actually neither. The trip by *autoferro* is *supposed* to take twelve hours; it took me eighteen, leaving at six in the morning and arriving at midnight. There is no food aboard; one is advised to take a box lunch from a hotel in Guayaquil (or Quito, if going in the opposite direction, which is often faster, thanks to the terrain). Picture-taking on the way is difficult. The windows of the car are too dirty to shoot through and it is impossible to open them, or even to stand still while the train is moving; when it stops—which can be often—the subject matter is not always what the photographer has in mind.

Still, undertaken in the right spirit, the *autoferro* ride can be a memorable experience, providing a graphic, honest picture of life as it is lived by the ordinary Ecuadorian. Regular trains make the run, as well as the *autoferro,* but are supposedly slower; this is not always the case, however, and if you chose to leave on a day when the *autoferro* is not running, don't hesitate to book first-class passage on the regular train. Fares, either way, are cheap, (about eight dollars) and the trip is well worth making, even if your air ticket covers this portion of your itinerary.

The Guayaquil–Quito itinerary is extensive and involved, and I'm not going to attempt to name every town, village, and mountain on the route. I will mention, though, the most exciting part of the journey—the climb up *Devil's Nose*—Nariz del Diablo—which begins after the train (coming from Guayaquil) has left *Huigra,* at forty-eight hundred feet. From there the railroad traverses the Chanchán River, continues along a ledge with the canyon directly below, and then starts *really* climbing, via a series of weird zigzags, Devil's Nose being a perpendicular ridge protruding a thousand feet upward from the river's gorge.

Both the *autoferro* and the passenger train make a stop of an hour or so at *Riobamba,* a sixteenth-century town of some thirty thousand population—moderately industrial, poor, dirty, with no good hotel accommodations, and only its bustling Saturday market, which takes place in a trio of separated plazas, to recommend it.

Before reaching Quito, both train and *autoferro* also stop at *Ambato,* which is best visited on Monday, market day. (From Quito, Ambato is two and a half hours by daily *autoferro*.) Ambato is one of the most flavorful of Ecuador's towns. Its market is the biggest in the republic, with sellers from all over the country, and neighboring countries as well, vending wares. Together with buyers and prospective buyers from the surrounding countryside, they virtually double the town's rest-of-the-week population of thirty-five thousand. The market is a day-long bazaar, commencing at nine in the morning and continuing until sunset. Its participants arrive mostly by means of open trucks, moving-van size, each named in the manner of the Mammy Wagons of Ghana and Nigeria, except that here the connotations have a local, or at least Western Hemi-sphere, flavor (*Asi es la Vida,* Such is Life; *Domador de Suegras,* Mother-in-law Tamer; and *Caryl Chessman No. 2* are among them). Merchandise for sale includes textiles; handsome ponchos and blankets; cereal grains; livestock; vegetables and fruits, among them luscious strawberries and *chirimoyas* (difficult to describe, but they *look* like artichokes); more varieties of banana than you ever imagined existed; woven fiber products—mats, hats, sandals, and rope woven of *cabuya* fibers; and, as a final touch, dogs, cats, and the Ecuadorian species of guinea pig which, roasted, is the culinary *pièce de résistance* of the mountain people. The daily take? It's estimated to be the equivalent of some $600,000 every Monday—quite a tidy sum to any Chamber of Commerce.

Except in its residential sections, and the market on Monday, Ambato has little of special interest to offer. Its more affluent homes are pleasant though, the more so because of their vivid, well-tended gardens. And the town, unique for smaller places in Ecuador, has a pair of good hotels, both of which serve more-than-just-edible meals. Tourists, incidentally, are about as rare as they are in Cuenca; one's welcome is warm.

Baños: A kind of Ecuadorian Vichy, Baños can be reached from Riobamba or Ambato—although it is closer to the latter—or, of course, from Quito. The trip by car, mostly downhill through the mountains, makes for a magnificent journey, but planes fly to this little resort, too. It might be an ideal resting point for the tired South American traveler—replete with both cold *and* hot thermal springs, walking trails laid out in the tradition of the British hiker, bus trips to nearby beauty spots like *Mera* and *Topo,* and—not to be taken for granted in rural Ecuador—two tolerably good hotels.

Latacunga and Machachi: These are the last two towns on the route of the Guayaquil–Quito railway, before one reaches the capital. Many of Latacunga's buildings are constructed of gray lava rock which has tumbled down volcanic Mount Cotopaxi (19,344 feet) less than twenty miles distant. With luck and clear weather its peak is visible, and so are the cones of nine satellite volcanoes. Machachi, just twenty-five miles from the capital, lives on its great natural resource, mineral springs, whose water is bottled, labeled with the name of the town, and consumed throughout the republic. *Quiteños* frequently come on weekends, for sips from the source.

Quito: Of the great cities of the Americas, Quito is the most enchanting. Many capitals are larger, many more cosmopolitan, many richer, many perhaps more intellectually stimulating and more abounding in entertainment facilities; many, even, with *more* remnants of the Colonial past. But Quito is very special; those handiworks of the conquistador, the early creole, the padre, and the Indian he Christianized, are the most sparkling of the diamonds in the tiara of pre-independence South America.

I have winced, overhearing tourists speak disdainfully when being informed of Quito's attractions. "Oh, more *churches?* We've seen lotsa churches." Very true, no doubt, but I'll wager no one can name churches anywhere in the world more glorious than La Campañía and San Francisco in Quito. I challenge anyone to produce a square which is lovelier than this city's Plaza Independencia in late afternoon, just before the sun slides behind the mountains which stand as sentinels over this equatorial city. And I have still to find a more idyllic cloister anywhere than that of the San Francisco Convent.

The equator is actually fifteen miles distant, but it is thanks to it and the ninety-three-hundred-foot altitude that with the exception of periods when it rains with some frequency, Quito is a one-climate city, spring-like all the year, with the sun rising at six and promptly setting just twelve hours later.

Completely old? Not by any means. Newer sections of the city are quite as modern—although on a scale befitting a town of 300,000—as any Latin capital. There is a spanking new Legislative Palace, quite as intriguingly contemporary as many of the master-works of Brasília or São Paulo. There is a knockout of a new hotel, one of the most handsome, and handsomely situated, in South America. There are pleasant residential sections (in contrast to most unpleasant slums and near-slums) and there is a sprinkling of near-skyscraper office buildings.

But it is Old Quito that calls the visitor. It is to the Plaza

Independencia that he will go first. Flanking its green, carefully-manicured lawns, which are intersected by inviting bench-lined sidewalks, are a quartet of handsome buildings: the gleaming white, many-columned Government Palace (headquarters of the president) with its gardens and patios open to the public; the Palace of the Archbishop; the Municipal Palace, adjacent to it; and the cathedral, with its unusual and immense stone porch, a bevy of shiny tiled domes, and an interior—anticlimactic in contrast to the outer façade—which is stark and massive, its chief attractions the tomb of General Sucre and an elaborate altar.

Due west of this plaza—and the visitor does well to return to it before leaving town, possibly just to sun himself on a bench and watch Quito walk by—is the Plaza San Francisco, named for the great church and monastery which dominates it. San Francisco (1534) was more than a century in the making; most of its artisans were skilled and highly talented Indians, working under the direction of priests whose art-genius is responsible for one of the great religious edifices of the world. The great pity is that the guide to the church is out of print, with no plans to republish. I hope that when you make your visit, you'll remember to ask the monk on duty if Padre Samuel Calvo, curator of the art treasures of the church, monastery, and museum, is available to show you about. Sprightly, Spanish-born, English-speaking, he is a walking encyclopedia of Quito Colonial art; he had lived in the monastery for more than three decades when I last saw him, with time out a few years previously for a return visit to his homeland—via the United States—on the twenty-fifth anniversary of his ordination. He knows, and loves, every painting, sculpture, window, door, arch, and decorative embellishment in the San Francisco complex, and he enjoys showing them off to sincerely-interested visitors.

Behind the twin towers of the church, and within its sanctuary, you'll see, among many other treasures, a dozen painted wood statues executed by Caspicara, one of the Indian artists of the church. You'll stand entranced before the magnificent altar, elaborately carved in gold. You'll marvel at the fantastic carved ceiling, at the many paintings, including a group by the mestizo master, de Santiago, and, throughout, décor, much of it in gold and gold-leaf, which is elaborate but not jarringly so, with the over-all effect one of tremendous beauty.

Adjoining the church is the Franciscans' monastery (or *convento,* as it is called in Spanish), with what is probably the loveliest enclosed cloister in South America. Venerable paintings embellish the stone walls of its two-story gallery, stone paths crisscross its gardens, brown-robed monks and priests of the order walk about in silent meditation, and a great fountain marks its center. The cloister is open only to men visitors, but women may peek quickly through the entrance door, and await their male companions' return in the reception room where the members of the order receive family and friends on visiting days. Both sexes are welcome to visit the Franciscan Museum, in the convent. Though little publicized, it contains one of the greatest collections of Colonial paintings and sculpture on the continent, and the visitor with even a sprinkling of interest in art is a fool to leave Quito without seeing it.

Not far from San Francisco is Quito's other religious masterpiece, the Church of La Compañía, with a truly great, sculptured front façade, nearly a dozen side-altars of superbly-embellished gold, gilded balconies, walls and ceilings and an unimaginably exquisite high altar of gold, with diamonds and rubies inset in its tabernacle.

There are fifty-five other churches in Quito, a great many of them old, well-preserved, art-filled. The curious visitor does well to look in, when he comes across one that appeals to him. At the top of the list, after San Francisco and La Compañía, are San Agustín (with a cloistered monastery), La Merced, and Santo Domingo. The last, on a square of that name, is but a short walk from the Plaza San Francisco. Santo Domingo embraces a treasure-filled church, a fine chapel, and a museum of Colonial religious art within its monastery. Centered in the square it dominates is a noteworthy statue of General Sucre, his arm extended toward Mount Pichincha, which overlooks the city and was the site of the victorious battle against the Spanish forces that led to the creation of the republic.

Still another requisite for visitors even mildly interested in art and architecture is the Museum of Colonial Art, not the biggest on the continent, but assuredly the most charming, thanks to its setting in a not-overlarge but wonderfully well-preserved ex-mansion. The exhibits of paintings and sculpture are handsomely displayed in the rooms of the house which encircle a tiled patio-garden. Here, as in the Franciscan museum, the curator —in this case an elderly Ecuadorian gentleman—is delighted to show visitors about and explain to them in English the stories behind the exhibits.

Quito remains proud of its art. It was the Colonial art center of Spanish America, and it is today a center of contemporary art in South America. Modern works are on view at the School of Fine Arts, the Nacional Museum of Fine Arts (in the baroque Sucre Theatre), and the Casa de la Cultura Ecuatoriana, a multifunction institution which displays art, publishes all manner of books on matters cultural, and as a side line, offers visitors a unique exhibit of musical instruments from the world over.

Quito lends itself to casual walks, and to viewing-from-on-high. The six-hundred foot-high Cerro Panceillo, or Little Bread Loaf Hill, is the most celebrated locale for a bird's-eye glance at the town and its mountain-volcano setting. Strolls along such old streets as Rocafuerte, La Ronda and 24 de Mayo can be rewarding; the Indian market takes place on the last-named every Tuesday. More conventional shopping is centered on the Calle Guayaquil.

Excursions from Quito: The aforementioned *Ambato* and *Baños* (often visited by travelers while en route from Guayaquil to Quito) are earlier described. Both can be excursion destinations from Quito, and Ambato, if not otherwise explored, is highly recommended in this category. But there are other eminently worthwhile journeys. The important thing is that the traveler whose Ecuadorian headquarters is Quito, hie himself out of the capital

during part of his stay, with at least one Indian market on his
itinerary. There are markets and fairs in one or another Ecuadorian
town virtually every day of the year, but here is the timetable for
the principal ones:

Santo Domingo de los Colorados	Sundays
Ambato	Mondays
Saquisilí	Thursdays
Otavalo	Saturdays

Of these, Ambato and *Saquisilí* can be visited conveniently without
staying overnight. The trip to Saquisilí is via the towering Cotopaxi
volcano, through inordinately beautiful countryside, and the Thursday fair in the village of Saquisilí is one of Ecuador's most colorful, thanks to the stalls on woven woolenwork, much of it utilizing
the brilliant hues which only Andean Indians seem capable of
achieving, and which they combine so skillfully.

Otavalo is something else again. To reach it in time for the
Saturday fair one must either leave Quito in the middle of the night,
in order to arrive at the market place by the crack of dawn, when
things start popping (and where they last only until 9 A.M.), or one
must leave Friday afternoon (the preferable arrangement) for a
leisurely drive through the mountains to the fair-sized town of
Ibarra, dine and spend the night in that town's small, madly-
decorated, ancient but clean hotel, retire early, arise at 5:30, and
drive to the fair in time for the arrival of the Otavalos themselves.
This Indian group, of pre-Inca origin, never allowed itself to be
absorbed either by the Inca conquerors or the conquistadors.
Otavalos have retained their culture—one of the most advanced of
any Indian community in South America—and their identity; there
has been little intermarriage with whites or other Indians. Short of
stature, handsome-featured, personable, these people are farmer-
artisans. Their farms are among the most prosperous of any
Ecuadorian Indians, and they mostly own their own land. At the
same time they weave, within their homes, blankets, ponchos,

scarves, and shawls, both in the traditional manner and with a twentieth-century touch, which gives some of their work the appearance of Scottish-type tweed.

They have been helped along in that respect by United States technicians, and I'm not at all sure I see the advantage. Their centuries-old styles and designs are distinctive and beautiful. Their "contemporary" wares are purchasable at any dry-goods counter in the world, and I wonder how they can compete in that field. At any rate, they themselves are far from twentieth-century. The men, as they have for centuries, wear their hair in pigtails, and dress in clean, starched, bell-bottom trousers of white-duck-type material, covered by a navy-blue poncho. The women, in multicolored costumes, are considerably less somber.

Many hundreds of Otavalos walk to market, some of them from a good many miles away, carrying with them in great baskets the handwork they want to sell. Within the small village are two separate markets. Most interesting—and indeed like no other in all South America—is the *exclusively* Otavalo bazaar, where the only vendors are Otavalos themselves, the only merchandise on sale, hand-crafted goods made by the sellers. This is undoubtedly the quietest market in the world. Sellers place themselves in long lines, in which they stand silently and erectly before their merchandise, on the ground. Prospective buyers, equally as speechless, walk down one line and up another, looking over the displays. Vendors make no sales pitch whatsoever. If a looker is interested, he asks the price, and is given it, in a low tone. He either buys, or walks on and comparison-shops. The only aggressive dealers are a handful of ambulatory mestizos who sell interesting pieces of Otavalo craftsmanship, on commission of the owners. These might include brass-decorated wooden riding crops, silver necklaces, and other pieces of personal jewelry. The Indians themselves sell mostly textiles, of which ponchos and scarves are of the most interest to visitors. Also available: raw wool, in great white mounds; household pottery, all of it hand-crafted; woven basketwork, in varied shapes and sizes.

From their own market the Indians move along to a great plaza in the town where non-Otavalo-made merchandise is on sale, much of it by mestizo merchants—soap, combs, blue jeans, pots and pans, and other factory-made requisites of the kind handled by five-and-tens and variety stores in the cities. By noon the town of Otavalo is virtually deserted, with the Indians well on their way back to their farms, and the visitor well on his way back to Quito. Otavalo merchants, it should be added, are often seen on the streets of Quito, and travel, by foot, as far north as Bogotá, Colombia, with their textiles. I hope, though, that you have the opportunity to meet them on home territory.

Santo Domingo de los Colorados: This village is the heart of the Colorado Indian region, some eighty miles from Quito, in the western lowlands. The Indians are most easily seen at their market in the town on Sundays, and during their festivals in August they paint their bodies, most parts of which, for both males and females, are unencumbered by clothing. The trip can be made in one *terribly* long day, beginning with a drive from the capital before dawn and ending late that night. It is considerably less hectic, and more interesting, if stretched over a two- or three-day period.

Two lesser excursions from Quito, both of them considerably more popular than they have reason to be, take one to the *Valley of Chillos* (an hour's ride; site of a pair of thermal swimming pools, with some villages, farms, and pretty countryside en route) and the *Equator Monument,* fifteen miles north of Quito, marked, as out would expect it to be, 0°00′00″, and probably the most photographed spot in Ecuador. Although European geographers located the line in the sixteenth century (and Indians, some say, before then), the pink granite marker, of little aesthetic quality, went up in the 1920s and tourists have been flocking to it ever since. (There is a smaller version of same, down the equator a piece, on the road to Otavalo.)

The Jivaro Indians, a small tribal group whose head-shrinking ancestors have led countless travelogue-viewers to believe South America is a continent of head-shrinkers, may be encountered by means of a four-day trip from Quito, by air, to *Sucúa,* a small jungle settlement. This junket is expensive, but for travelers interested in acquainting themselves with one of the few truly primitive groups on the continent, well worth while.

The Galápagos Islands: One of the strangest archipelagoes in the world, this island group—numbering in the hundreds—is a dependency of Ecuador, with but two thousand inhabitants, and an official (but rarely used) Ecuadorian name, Archipiélago de Colón. *Galápago* is, of course, Spanish for tortoise. The name was given the islands when discovered by a Spaniard, Tomás de Berlanga, in 1535. Though mostly a collection of barren lava piles, with an infinitesimal population, no hotels, and a rather inconvenient location—650 miles off the Ecuadorian coast—people have been going out of their way to get to the Galápagos ever since Charles Darwin made a visit in 1835 to study the incredible wild life. Whalers, later in the nineteenth century, greedily killed a good bit of it off (their specialty was the giant tortoise, for food and fat).

But the government has decreed the entire archipelago a wild-life sanctuary, and though poachers remain, a good bit of incredible fauna still is to be seen: the land tortoises (which weigh as much as five hundred pounds) and giant lizards, or iguanas, of both sea and land varieties; a profusion of land and sea birds, including the bizarre flightless cormorant, the frigate bird, and the swallow-tailed gull; plus quantities of sea lions and penguins. More than 95 per cent of the reptiles in the islands, more than a third of the shore fish, and almost half of the plants exist nowhere else in the world. The twelve major islands of the group have English names—no doubt taken from the buccaneers who visited them—by which they are familiarly known, and once again, official Ecuadorian names, in Spanish, which are rarely used.

Albermarle (or Isabela) is the biggest island, some seventy-five miles long; Chatham, a onetime prison colony, comes next. The Compañía Ecuatoriana de Turismo, of Guayaquil and Quito, operates tours on its two ships, *Ancón Trader* and *Cristobal Carrier,* one of which leaves Guayaquil every twenty days for a fourteen-day cruise that includes stops at the five most important islands, with shore excursions at each, and the ship serving as a hotel. The all-inclusive rate is about $130.

WHAT TO BUY

For the traveler who will visit Peru and Bolivia, Ecuador is considerably less appealing, at least insofar as crafts are concerned. It is more expensive than Bolivia, and its work is often less imaginative than that found in Peru. Ecuadorian Indians' color and design skills, while most admirable, fall a little short of their Peruvian neighbors. The cheapest sources of Indian crafts are, of course, the Indian markets in the villages and smaller towns of the country. Quito's shops are generally overpriced, and there are relatively few with worthwhile merchandise. The top two are Folklore (Avenida Colón 274), whose specialty is unattractive but good-quality hand-woven rugs, designed not by Indians but by the European owner, and ridiculously expensive; and Akios (Gorivar 236), whose price range and stock runs a considerably wider gamut. Most appealing wares include textiles of great variety— ponchos, stoles (*rebozos*), scarves, belts and sashes, and other items; basketry—including nests of twelve Otavalo-made baskets, one inside the other, with the largest fitting in the palm of one's hand; dolls of varying materials; silverwork—mostly bracelets and rings, inferior to that of Peru and Bolivia, and more expensive; and Colonial antiques, terribly steep in price. Before buying in either of these shops, browse through Quito's Indian market stalls. Bargaining is the rule, but it won't get you far in the top two emporiums; they're too spoiled by free-spending tourists who don't take the time to look elsewhere. *Note:* Panama hats, made in Ecuador as you well know by now, are of course available. There may be some women who might be interested in using them as a basis for a hat, but I don't know what appeal they would have currently for American men, so badly styled are they, and so expensive. There is little of distinctive interest in Guayaquil shops, except perhaps some rather poor-quality alligator goods. Concentrate on the Indian markets in such places as Otavalo, Saquisilí, and Ambato, as well as Quito.

CREATURE COMFORTS

HOTELS—**Guayaquil:** The Humboldt International is the easy winner, facing the always-animated Guayas River, modern, clean, with air-conditioned rooms, a swimming pool, a pleasant bar, and rooftop dining room and terrace which is at least attractive, even if the food is mediocre. Also new and with forty of its eighty rooms air-conditioned is the Palace, with a good dining room. Others: the not-bad Metropolitano, with rooftop swimming pool and bar; Continental, Majestic, Crillon. **Playas:** Humboldt, same management as the Humboldt in Guayaquil, swimming pool, seaside location, ocean bathing, pleasant bedrooms and public rooms, and a casino; from $6 single. **Salinas:** Miramar—new, air-conditioned. **Cuenca:** The Crespo is the better of the top two, with the Majestic following. **Esmeraldas:** Europa—hardly reminiscent of the continent for which it is named. **Riobamba:** Metropolitano—only if you must. **Baños:** Villa Gertrudis—good. **Ambato:** Villa Hilda—good; Florida, Number Two. **Quito:** The new Hotel Quito, operated for the Ecuadorian government by the Hotel Corporation of America (whose other establishments include the Plaza and Roosevelt in New York), is one of the most beautiful in South America. Situated in the new residential section of the city, with a superb mountain-and-valley view from many rooms, and from the terrace of its swimming pool (midday is warmest and the best time for a dip), it is a resort hotel in a capital city. Besides the lovely pool and Cabana Club, there is a striking rooftop restaurant and cocktail lounge; a *boîte,* with nightly dancing and entertainment; an inexpensive but good coffee shop with authentically-costumed Indian waitresses; splendid rooms, all with bath and terrace; a casino absolutely jammed with slot machines (including one-sucre ones for Big Gamblers like me), and pleasant service. From $7.50 single. I can't conceive of staying elsewhere in this city, but if you must, the Humboldt, downtown, is the next most modern hotel, with but fair meals in its restaurant. The elderly Colón, near the

Quito, is noted for its superb food, although few rooms have bath. Others: Embajador, Majestic, both with a high proportion of private baths, and the Lutetia, a first-class pension, cheap and friendly. **Ibarra** (near Otavalo): Turismo—madly-decorated and decrepit, but clean and adequate for overnight.

RESTAURANTS AND NIGHT LIFE—**Guayaquil:** You might try the Palace Hotel dining room, a vast improvement over that of the Humboldt. Independent restaurants, none out of this world, include the Fortich, Wivex, Salon Rex, Melba (with a Yankee-type soda fountain), and an enterprise known as the Bim Bam Bum which embraces a restaurant, casino, and swimming pool. The sidewalk *confiterías* are good for drinks and snacks. **Quito:** Hotel Quito's aforementioned rooftop restaurant offers a superb view and fine cuisine, its coffee shop serves good, inexpensive table d'hôte dinners as well as breakfast, lunch, and short-orders, and its bars and the Cabana Club terrace are all congenial. There's always entertainment and dancing in the *boîte,* and additional diversion in the adjoining casino, with a bar of its own. There is also the famed Hotel Colón dining room, the Normandie for French food, the Wonder Bar, with American-accented menus, and the Rincon de Sicilia, for Italian specialties. Here, too, the *confiterías* are inviting.

PRIVATE CLUBS: **Guayaquil** has several: Tennis, Yacht, English-American. **Quito's** include the ubiquitous Rotary and Lions, plus the Golf y Tennis Club for those activities, plus bridge for sedentary sportsmen.

Ecuadorian food specialties: *Locro*—a cheese or potato stew, with avocados; *humitas*—tamales not unlike those of Mexico; *llapingachos*—a cheese-potato combination; variations of the Peruvian *ceviches*—raw marinated fish and shrimps; roast guinea pig; and the juice of a delicious Ecuadorian fruit called the *naranjillada*—a kind of citrus-peach combination. Ecuadorian beer is excellent and very popular, and whisky drinks are moderately priced. Wine, though, is fairly expensive.

PANAMA

(República de Panamá)

Entry requirements: *A tourist card, obtainable through trans-port company or travel agent, with onward or return trans-port ticket a requisite for issuance. Proof of nationality, ideally—but not necessarily—a passport, is also required.* **Best times for a visit:** *Except in the cool mountains, one can count on temperatures hovering about 80° all year round. Panama's weather is mostly pleasant; there is no specifically rainy season, although October and November are generally the moistest months, with January through April the driest period.* **Currency:** *The balboa, at par with the U.S. dollar, and used interchangeably with it. Indeed, there is no Panamanian paper money to be used; only coins of one balboa and smaller denominations, along with which U.S. currency is also circulated.* **Film availability:** *The best place in Latin America to stock up; both black-and-white and color film is often cheaper than in the United States, many imports being duty-free, or* almost *duty-free.* **Language:** *Spanish is the offical language, but there is a great deal of English, thanks to the influence of the great number of*

Americans resident in the Canal Zone and the not-incon-siderable Negro population, mostly of British West Indian origin and bilingual in Spanish and English. **Domestic transport:** *Well, there's the Panama Canal, if it can be called domestic; rail and road routes which nearly parallel its course; highways, including the 287-mile Inter-American Highway from Panama City to David, and air service (via Copa and Talsa airlines) to major points.* **Tipping:** *Ten per cent.* **Business hours:** *Early openings, to compensate for two-hour midday closings.* **Further Information:** *Panama National Tourist Commission, Panama City, Panama; Panagra, Chrysler Building, New York, and El Panama Hilton Hotel, Panama City, Panama; Panamanian Embassy, Washington, D.C.*

INTRODUCING PANAMA

It is geography which has been at once the bane and the blessing of Panama for as long as white men have known it. A number of nations have involved themselves in its destiny—Spain, whose conquistadors shipped their gold through it; Colombia, of which it was once a province; England and France, who coveted it as a canal site, and, of course, the United States, which constructed the great waterway across the isthmus, wiped out malaria and yellow fever as a prerequisite for its construction, alienated Colombia and deviously brought about the birth of the Republic of Panama in order to bring the canal into being, condoned rulership of the little country by a revolving circle of the aristocratic minority (there have been twenty-nine presidents in little over a half century and a number did not exit gracefully), and in so doing, gained Uncle Sam the epithet "Yankee Imperialist."

It is only in relatively recent years—since one Roosevelt's Good Neighbor policy attempted to dispel the ill-will created by an earlier Roosevelt's Big Stick policy—that the stigma has shown

signs of disappearing. But so long as the United States has rights
"in perpetuity" to the Panama Canal and the zone of land which
borders it, the United States leaves itself wide open for Latin
criticism. The contrast between the Americans in the Canal Zone
—well paid and with a high standard of living; living on an
antiseptically spotless reservation amid the still-general poverty
of the great majority of Panamanians—does not always go
down well locally. Panamanian nationalists begin to draw parallels
with the British in Suez, to the extent that even their government's
leaders, upper-class and rich though they are, have begun to
articulate the shortcomings of the situation.

The boon to the Panamanian economy created by the Canal
becomes relatively unimportant, and the time may come when the
United States will have to alter its Canal arrangement with the
Panamanian government, which may find it more expedient to
change Canal policy than attempt to raise living standards by
energetically solving local problems in a society which is superficially democratic, but in actuality not without sizable remnants
of that peculiarly Spanish feudalism which the conquistadors
bequeathed to so much of Latin America.

A backward glance: A Spaniard, Rodrigo de Bastidas, sighted
the Panama coast in 1501, and a year later, Columbus dropped
anchor at Portobelo, but neither realized what a freak of terrain
he had come across. It was not until 1513 when Balboa trekked
across the isthmus from the Atlantic to the Pacific that the glory
of Panama—the short distance over it from one sea to another
—became known.

Panama City was founded shortly thereafter, by a Spaniard so
grateful to Balboa that he had Balboa executed. Before long,
Panama became the take-off point for Pizarro's discovery of Peru,
and convenient it proved to be: the gold plundered from the
Incas was shipped to Spain via the isthmus, and Panama thrived
as part of the new viceroyalty of Peru, until 1740 when New
Granada (Colombia) took it over. In between, some Scots had
attempted to settle as agricultural colonists, but in vain. The area
which had started off as a roadway for gold continued in that

fashion, interrupted in its progress only by the forays of such distinguished pirates as Sir Francis Drake and Henry Morgan. The latter in 1671 reduced the original Panama City to ruins, compelling the Spanish to rebuild a new town a few miles distant, fortifying it so effectively that no further attacks were made directly upon it.

Still, the buccaneers remained a threat, so much so that the Spanish rerouted traffic around Cape Horn in 1746, and for nearly a century there appeared to be little convenient about conveniently-located Panama. Ironically, it was America that changed all that. Masses of forty-niners trekked to the gold fields of California via Panama, many dying en route, so disease-ridden was the isthmus at that time. The traffic was great enough to warrant a railroad across the country and Americans built one, completing it, after seven years' work, in 1855.

By that time the dream of a canal—originally envisioned in the seventeenth century but turned down as too costly by Charles II of Spain—began once again to stir in men's minds. While the United States and the British were dickering over which of them should go into the canal business, a French company, headed by Ferdinand de Lesseps, the man who built the Suez Canal, began construction. The project ended in disaster. Many lives were lost because of yellow fever and malaria, and much money went down the drain, literally. Another French firm under Philippe Bunau-Varilla retained the canal rights.

The United States and the Canal: By 1901 the United States and Britain had agreed, in the Hay-Pauncefote Treaty, that the former would operate the Canal. Bunau-Varilla and his French colleagues began negotiating to sell their construction rights to the United States. President Theodore Roosevelt and Congress favored Panama as the site, rather than Nicaragua, which some experts preferred, and the United States set out to buy the necessary land from Colombia, of which Panama was still a province. But the Colombian Congress would have none of it, and shortly thereafter, on November 3, 1903, Canal proponents (including the shrewd Bunau-Varilla), in collaboration with certain Panamanians, engineered a Panamanian revolt against Colombia. The United States sent a warship to prevent the Colombians from quelling the outbreak, and three days later, the Republic of Panama came into being, setting a record among the nations of the world in the briefness of its struggle for independence.

A bare fortnight after its birth the new country, represented by none other than Monsieur Bunau-Varilla, promptly signed an agreement with the United States, giving it rights "in perpetuity" to the Canal Zone, for the same price which the United States had offered the Colombians—an initial payment of $10 million, and $250,000 annual rent, which since that time has been considerably increased; it now amounts to $1,930,000 each year, but the Panamanian government wants it substantially raised. It was not until 1921—eighteen years after its shabby role in aiding and encouraging the detachment of Panama from Colombia—that the United States finally indemnified the Republic of Colombia for its action, by a payment of $25 million. Only then did Colombia recognize Panama; it remained offended with the United States, however, for in giving the money to Colombia, our government abstained from an outright apology and admission of its guilt.

At any rate, the United States *can* be proud of its technical accomplishments in Panama. Between 1907 and 1910 a commission under Colonel G. W. Goethals ingeniously eradicated yellow fever from the area, and after seven additional years and a cost of $336,650,000, the brilliantly-engineered Canal was opened in 1914.

The current scene: The Canal has come to play a role in Panama not unlike that of the Nile in Egypt; Panama is the Canal and the Canal is Panama, except, of course, for the Canal Zone, a strip five miles wide on either side of the waterway, which is a United States government reservation, administered by an appointed governor, currently Major General William A. Carter, who also is president of the Panama Canal Company.

The country itself has developed relatively little. Much of its land remains unexploited. Attempts have been made at industrialization, but they have been relatively minimal. Some progress is being made in agriculture, in order to cut down on imports of foodstuffs. Exports of bananas, cacao, and abacá, mostly grown and shipped by the United Fruit Company, are increasing. There are still clusters of Indians who have not been integrated into the general society. Although there is no racial color bar, the Negro community—descendants of workers imported many years ago from the British West Indies—remains on the bottom rung of the economic ladder, and the great majority of mestizos, or mixed-blood Panamanians, are poor, too.

Wealth, and political power, rests in the hands of a relatively few aristocratic families of Spanish descent, whose members have taken turns in recent years at being elected president.

The incumbent, Roberto F. Chiari, has made considerable advances over his predecessors. He became president in 1960 and within a year his administration had a great deal to show in such areas as low-rent housing, slum clearance, social security, new schools, hospitals, and vigorous enforcement of the minimum-wage law. Still, widespread discontent remains. Farmers complain over the government's lack of progress in much-needed agricultural reform, Canal workers still smart over higher salaries paid to U.S. citizens in the Canal Zone, pro-Castro and pro-Communist sentiment has abated only a little. Despite his intelligence and energy, and even though his point of view is more progressive than that of the majority of the members of the legislature, President Chairi, whose family is the principal sugar producer in the country, is essentially a rich businessman, and a symbol of the oligarchic-type ruling faction which the Panamanian on the street cannot be expected to support indefinitely.

YOUR VISIT TO PANAMA

One would think that Panama, joining North and South America as it does, would run in a north-south direction. But it doesn't, and one finds, after taking a sharp look at a map, that it extends itself, roughly, on an east-west level, Colombia being its eastern

neighbor, and Costa Rica flanking its western frontier. One
travels east to reach the Pacific from the Atlantic, and the Pacific
gate of the Canal is almost thirty miles east of its Atlantic
entry.

The entire country is small, even by the standards of Central
America, of which Panama is often considered a part. (It did not
join the Organization of Central American States until 1961.)
Though not the smallest of the Central American regions, it is
exceeded by all but the tiny colony of British Honduras in population; there are still only about a million Panamanians, two-fifths
of which are clustered about the edges of the Canal. There are
some forty thousand residents of the Canal Zone, about half of
whom are Americans.

Small though it is, Panama cuts a wide topographic swath,
ranging from quite substantial mountain ranges—the highest peak
is more than eleven thousand feet high—through middling hills,
into coastal lowlands.

Because of its topsy-turvy east-west layout, to which are added
the complications of a canal and a foreign territory flanking it,
Panama at first glance can appear confusing. One can simplify
it by bearing in mind these salient facts: Panama City, the
capital, and Balboa, the principal city of the Canal Zone, lie side
by side at the Pacific gate of the Canal. Cristóbal and Colón are
the principal twin towns of the Atlantic side, the former within
the republic, the latter in the Canal Zone, both blending into one
another, much like Panama City and Balboa. The Canal can be
traversed by ship in eight or nine hours; by train, bus, or car in
considerably less than that. Even on a short visit one can easily
visit both the Atlantic and Pacific sides of Panama, as well as
a point or two in the interior, and, perhaps, one of the intriguing
islands off the coasts.

All too often Panama is either the first stop on a Latin American journey, and given short shrift by the traveler anxious to get
on; or it is the last point en route home, and is again skimmed over,
this time by the tired tourist who can't wait to call the milkman
at home to have deliveries resumed. For the visitor who is not

impatient for a look at Lima, or Stateside-bound and ready to collapse from exhaustion, Panama is not without its attractions.

Panama City: Polyglot Panama City is not, at first glance, particularly appealing. And for some visitors, who never get beyond its honky-tonks, or who, on the other hand, hole themselves up at the swimming pool of its most luxurious hotel, it remains without special appeal up to the moment of departure. Still, there are nooks here, and crannies there which merit exploration and which help to dispel the notion that this city is no more than a slapped-together community of a quarter of a million people, without rhyme or reason.

It has, to be sure, handsome residential sections—some less opulent than in other Latin capitals, but along the same lines, and hardly stimulating. It has appalling slums, which are only gradually beginning to disappear, and while perhaps of interest to the sociologist, are without any special distinction, as slums go. It has a not terribly handsome business area, where the merchandise is invariably more attractive (and this includes price) than the setting. It has a populace which has grown so accustomed to tourists that there are those among them not at all averse to being rude, indifferent, or even dishonest. And it can be a little hot and humid during the middle hours of the day.

But on the other side of the coin are the plus factors. The Plaza de Francia, for example, is small, gay with the scarlet of poinciana trees, dignified by the obelisk honoring the abortive French attempt to build the Canal, and surrounded by a substantial group of mellowed Colonial-vintage buildings. Nearby is one of the glories of the Spanish architectural genius, dating from the days when the city was rebuilt in 1672 to replace the earlier capital virtually destroyed by pirates. I refer to that part of the old protective wall known as Las Bóvedas (the dungeons). Steps from it lead to a handsome promenade, Paseo de las Bóvedas, which affords a stirring view of the Bay of Panama and a trio of islands within it, each still the site of venerable battlements. Directly under Las Bóvedas are the dungeons in which prisoners were incarcerated centuries ago—thick-walled, with arched ceilings and windows which afforded their occupants amazingly delightful views of the water.

Old churches? More than you might imagine in a city so superficially new as this. One, Santo Domingo, is considered to be indirectly responsible for Panama having been selected as the Canal site, rather than Nicaragua. Its flat arch has stood for three centuries with no internal support, and engineers are believed to have deduced from it that Panama is earthquake-immune, whereas volcanic Nicaragua would not be. The cathedral, on Plaza Cathedral, embellished with statues of the country's founders, is a graceful double-towered building, its unusual domes encrusted with mother-of-pearl. San José Church, nearby, is notable for its glittery baroque altar—a work of art in gold, and a relic of the original Panama, not filched by the pirates only because a resourceful priest quickly painted it black just before they approached. La Merced's stones were carried, piece by piece, from a church by that name on the site of Old Panama, and its statue of the Virgin dates from the original capital, too.

The National Museum offers the interested traveler a graphic view of the country's history, dating back to Indian times, and there are museum-type displays, too, in the old Colegio La Salle, where Bolívar first proposed a federation of South American republics, in 1826. The presidents of the republic now live in the lovely palace which was the home of the Colonial governors. Now known as La Presidencía, it is graced by an exceptionally handsome tiled patio, alongside whose fountains strut proud egrets. Some of the public rooms within are open to visitors.

The National Theatre, properly elegant in the best Latin American tradition, is one of the city's best old buildings, and the gleaming white El Panama Hilton Hotel, designed in 1951 by American architect Edward Stone, is probably its best modern one, the forerunner of most of today's streamlined resort hotels the world over. Interesting, too, is the new University City, whose buildings house the University of Panama. Students and/or staff members are usually available to show visitors about; most speak English and are glad to chat with visitors from the country which now so much occupies their thoughts—and part of their national territory.

In great contrast to this façade of streamlined Panama are the ruins of Old Panama—or *Panamá Vieja,* as it is called. Just a few miles from town, they make for a pleasant half-day excursion, or better yet, a moonlight drive. To be seen are the remnants of the once-great cathedral, a plaza now disguised with moss-covered pillars, bits and pieces of other buildings including San José Church, whose great altar is now in its namesake in the capital, and dungeons facing the sea where, so the stories go, inmates were executed by neither hangman nor firing squad; the high tides simply drowned them when they flooded their cells.

Balboa: The "capital" of the Canal Zone, Balboa adjoins Panama City—one can cross from one to the other without knowing it. Balboa is not without the antiseptic air of an army post, at least in its more official areas, which house, among other things, a monument to Goethals and the Canal Zone Administration Building, whose murals tell the story of the Canal's construction. Beyond is the residential section of *Ancón* where the most important institution is the Gorgas Hospital, whose specialty is tropical diseases.

Excursions from Panama City or Balboa: *Madden Dam* makes a good half-day (or longer) outing, with the car passing through thick jungle as well as near the Canal and two of its outstanding locks: Miraflores and Pedro Miguel. *Taboga Island* is a delightful resort, with such inducements as swaying palms, wide sandy beaches, boats for deep-sea fishing (a Panama specialty), a good hotel and restaurant, and an ancient church which is one of the oldest in the Americas, the Spaniards having settled the island in 1515. Only twelve miles offshore from Balboa (reached by launch, with two or three departures each way every day), this is a fine spot for a rest, and it is truly quiet, there being no animals, domestic or otherwise, and, believe it or not, no cars allowed. Considerably more distant—and the goal of avid deep-sea fishermen, on occasion—are the *Pearl Islands,* whose only settlement is a tiny fishing village atop one of the mountains which hug the shores. Reasons for going: corvina, sailfish, marlin, red snapper.

Colón and Cristóbal: The twin towns of the Atlantic coast, Colón and Cristóbal, are relatively little-visited by air travelers who arrive in Panama City, on the Pacific side. Ship passengers frequently pass them over, too. This is justifiable in the case of little Cristóbal, but Colón is worth an acquaintanceship. Second only to the capital in size, it is a town of about sixty thousand, quite as lively at night as Panama City, and with an almost Oriental main thoroughfare, known as Front Street. Besides that street, with its crowds and its crowded bazaars, cabarets, and bars, one might also take a look at the attractive cathedral; the impressive statuary (with subjects ranging from Columbus to de Lesseps) on the Paseo Centenario; Beach Drive, the site of the beginnings of the ill-fated French-engineered canal, and for the visitor who will not otherwise see the Canal, a drive to the Gatun Locks. An hour's ride from Colón, the locks are in jungle country, and en route to them, and crossing over them, one can come across such fauna as giant lizards, land crabs, and snakes. The old fort of San Lorenzo—sacked by Henry Morgan—is in the vicinity and can be combined with a Gatun tour, as can a view of the American community called Margarita, within the Canal Zone.

Portobelo: Twenty miles from Colón is Portobelo, where Columbus landed in 1502, and where the Spanish constructed a town which thrived for some two hundred years. Nearby is the site of Nombre de Dios, the terminal of the old Spanish gold route. Still to be seen are a trio of forts which guard Portobelo's once-bustling harbor, and there are, as well, other memorabilia of the conquistadors' days: a building where was stored the gold transported from Peru, venerable cannon, and a remarkable Black Christ statue in the centuries-old cathedral.

The San Blas Islands can be reached conveniently by boat from Colón—or about as quickly by plane from Panama City, and constitute what is possibly the most curious anomoly of modern Panama. There are 365 of them, but only the larger ones are inhabited. Residents are the Cuna Indians, who assure themselves privacy by means of a treaty with the Panamanian government, to the extent that visitors cannot even remain overnight on their islands. Women members of the tribe never leave the islands, wear rings in their noses, and dress in costumes made out of superbly hand-appliquéd cloth known as *mula*—squares of it make wonderful wall hangings.

The Canal: See it by *driving* to one or more of its locks, by *train* (there are several daily connecting Panama City and Colón in an hour and a half), or, of course, by *ship*. (Sorry, no plane hops; against the law.)

Each method is not without advantages. The auto route allows for stops at the Miraflores Locks on the Pacific, or the Gatun Locks on the Atlantic, where one can watch the massive gates open and close to admit ships. Trains alongside on the shore line pull ships through the rough spots. The train trip offers the varied countryside, besides frequent views of the Canal; it is quick and comfortable. And, of course, the journey by ship is the genuine article: forty-two miles from Balboa to Cristóbal, taking about eight hours, give or take an hour, with the highlights the trio of Gatun Locks and the immense, man-made, 163-square-mile Gatun Lake. Facts and figures? There are enough to make one's head spin, and are easily come by on the spot. But for anyone wondering how heavy the traffic is, it might be worth noting that some ten thousand ships pass through on a busy year, and the average toll per vessel is four thousand dollars —although some pay thrice that. More than a quarter of a million ships have gone through the Canal since it opened, carrying a billion tons of cargo.

Other Panama highlights: There are small bathing resorts along the coasts, none terribly close to Panama City. These include *Río Mar, San Carlos, El Valle,* and *Santa Clara*—all accessible within a day from the capital. I would rather head instead for *David,* the republic's third largest city, in the interior. From there one can visit the Montuno people, whose strange agricultural communities, little changed in centuries, are centered around the nearby town of *Ocú* and the *Chiriquí Highlands* (around *Boquete*)—great mountain plantations of sugar and coffee, for fine fishing and hunting, with an excellent resort inn. Not far are *El Baru,* a fifty-eight-hundred-foot inactive volcano with a small hotel on its inactive slopes, and *El Volcán,* at an elevation of eleven thousand feet, on the Pan American Highway near the Costa Rica frontier. David itself, from which all of these places can be excursion points, is amid interesting Indian country, with a colorful market, a still-Colonial façade (with a cathedral and other old churches), a river which meanders through its center, and a good modern hotel.

WHAT TO BUY

This is it: shopper's paradise. Free-port prices on cameras from Japan and Germany, silver from Peru, watches from Switzerland, emeralds from Colombia, perfumes from France, leather goods from Argentina, chinaware from Britain, silks and ivory from India, Irish linens and English woolens, ceramics and crystal from Scandinavian countries, film from the United States; and from Panama, strikingly handsome *mula* cloths, with intricately-layered appliqué-work in vivid colors, marvelous for framing on walls, and made by the Cuna Indians of the San Blas Islands. Other Panamanian items include *panasillas,* coat-shirts for men, of linen or poplin, which often look more attractive in Panama than at home, and *polleras,* the elaborate (and expensive) dress worn by Panamanian women for ceremonial occasions or to dance the *tamborito,* Panama's national dance. Also available: free-port whisky and liqueur, sold in bond and delivered to one's airplane in advance of departure; ideal for travelers en route home. Most reputable shops are experienced in shipping merchandise to the United States. In *Colón*—sometimes cheaper than Panama City—they include: Slim's, French Bazaar, Maduros, Novedades, Atlantico, all on Front Street. In *Panama City:* American Bazaar, Motta's, Quinta Avenida, Fastlich Jewelry, International Jewelry, Salomon's (for Oriental wares), all on or near Central Avenue, the main shopping street. Branches of a number of these stores, with the same prices as downtown, are found in the arcade of El Panama Hilton Hotel.

CREATURE COMFORTS

HOTELS—**Panama City:** El Panama Hilton is one of the handsomest hotels in the hemisphere, with particularly huge and attractive bedrooms, all with bath and terrace, some with air-conditioning (which is not a necessity, thanks to the ingenious ventilation system). Facilities are first-rate, and include a twenty-four-hour coffee shop with good, inexpensive food; a swimming pool (which could stand expanding, at least on weekends); fifteen acres of gardens; several bars (indoor and outdoor); dining room; *boîte* with entertainment and dancing; a government-supervised casino; tennis courts and a variety of shops, and services including airline branch offices and bilingual staff; $10–$12 single April 1 to December 15; $15–$18 single December 16 to March 31. Number Two is the more central and cheaper International— modern, fully air-conditioned rooms, all with shower or bath; roof garden; restaurant; *boîte;* bar; $8 single. Others: Roosevelt, Colombia, Tropicana, Colón, Central, Ambassador. **Colón:** The Washington, until recently a U.S. government operation, is an elderly, rambling hotel with a delightful seaside veranda, swimming pool, and, sad to relate, accommodations, meals, and service which have deteriorated with the change in ownership. Single $4–$8. Number Two is the Plaza. **Taboga Island:** La Restinga—a quiet, attractive resort hotel, with a good dining room and friendly bar. **Santa Clara:** Santa Clara Inn. **David:** Nacional—modern and comfortable; $4–$6 single. **Boquete (Chiriquí Highlands):** Panamonte Inn—restful, cool mountain retreat serving appetizing meals, offering riding, fishing, and hunting facilities; $10 single, American plan. **Bambito** (*El Baru Volcano*): Hemmerling's Lodge, primarily for fishermen—simple but clean.

RESTAURANTS AND NIGHT LIFE: Besides the restaurants and

coffee shops of El Panama Hilton and the International Hotel, try the delightful, unique Panama City beer gardens, which often serve excellent meals (and other beverages besides beer). These include El Rancho, Sky Chef, and Atlas Club. Others: Gran China (Chinese), Tabaris, El Intimo. Colón's best restaurants are the dining room of the Washington Hotel, Bilgray's, Ciro's, and the Tropic Bar. There are a multitude of bars and honky-tonks in both Panama City and Colón; you pays your money, you takes your choice. Better night spots in the capital include, besides the Casino in the Sky and Bella Vista Roof of El Panama Hilton, and the Hotel International's supper room, such spots as O.K. Amigo and the Grill Aloha, both opposite the Hilton, Maxims, No Me Digas, Ritz Cabaret, Happyland, Bahia, and El Intimo. Colón's leading cabarets are the Copacabana and the Club Florida.

PRIVATE CLUBS: Panama City's poshest is the Union. Others: the Panama City Golf Club and the Strangers Club in Colón, open through introductions by members. There are, as well, both Rotary and Lions in the capital, and the clannish Americans in the Canal Zone have all manner of organizations of their own.

Panamanian food specialties: The marvelous jumbo shrimp are a great treat, and everywhere available; other sea foods are good, too, particularly corvina, tuna, and lobster. Then, too, there are such things as the quite special Panamanian tamales, *patecones de plantano yerde* (fried plantains), often served as a cocktail canapé; *sancocho,* a vegetable-chicken stew-soup; the inevitable *arroz con pollo,* again with a Panamanian twist, and *seviche*—marinated fish seasoned with hot peppers, not unlike that of Peru. Steaks are excellent, and American-style dishes, including hamburgers, are popular. Local beer is fine, and—good news—American and European whiskies and liqueurs are cheaper than in the United States. Even milk drinkers may live quite dangerously: the stuff is pasteurized.

PERU

(República del Perú)

Entry requirements: *A tourist card, obtainable through transport company or travel agency; or a visa, obtainable from Peruvian consulates; onward or return transportation required for either.* **Best times for a visit:** *I would not hesitate to visit Peru at* any *time of year, but December–April is the pleasantest period, particularly in Lima. There is little rain in the capital, but from May to November there are often heavy clouds or fog, known as* garua. *The mountain regions, including Cuzco, range from cool to cold. Along the coast it is never extremely hot, even in summer, thanks to the Humboldt Current.* **Currency:** *The sol, (plural: soles), worth about a nickel, and divided into one hundred cents.* **Film availability:** *Plenty in stock, but the prices are considerably steeper than in the United States.* **Language:** *Spanish is the official language, but many of those Peruvians who are Indian—and that means about half the population—speak only Quechua or Aymara. There is a good bit of English spoken in hotels, restaurants, shops, and transport terminals.* **Domestic transport:** *Good air service via Faucett*

Airlines to major and lesser points throughout the country; flights to many fewer points via Tapsa and Tam airlines; about two thousand miles of good roads and the same mileage of railroads. **Tipping:** *Most hotels add 10 per cent service charge and 6.5 per cent tax; additional small tips are nonetheless expected. Fifteen per cent is the average tip where no service charge is added. Taxi drivers are not tipped.* **Business hours:** *Shops and offices take a two-hour lunch break (noon to 2* P.M.) *in winter, and even longer— three to four hours—in summer; closing hour is about 7* P.M. **Further information:** *Panagra, Chrysler Building, New York, and Gran Hotel Bolívar, Lima, Peru; Peruvian Touring and Automobile Club, Lima, Peru; Peruvian Embassy, Washington, D.C.*

INTRODUCING PERU

It was from Peru that the Incas administered their enormous empire, and it was in Peru that the Spaniards established their vast Colonial domain. The cultures of both peoples are at once the glory of Peru and the bane of its existence. These two incredibly diverse ways of life have existed side by side for more than four centuries, but they have not yet been melded. And so, even today's Peru is in reality two Perus—modern republican Peru, with its increasingly streamlined façade and its gracious, aristocratic Spanish *ambiance,* and Indian Peru—largely pastoral, apallingly poor, undeniably exotic and magnetic. Though Ecuador and Bolivia have similar backgrounds, the divergencies between the two cultures in those countries is never as striking as it is in Peru. For it was Peru that the conquistadors and their descendants made the show place of the New World. Ecuador and Bolivia, though hardly without remaining evidences of Spanish grandeur, were backwater territory, in contrast.

The Incas and pre-Incas: No country's history is more literally

and utterly fantastic than Peru's. It had seen a good deal of noteworthy activity long before the Incas made their impact on the
scene. Substantial indigenous cultures thrived for most of the
Christian era: the Chavin civilization, the earliest known, from
the third to seventh centuries; the Nasca-Paracas culture, which
succeeded it for three hundred years; the Mochica civilization,
whose skills in ceramics, weaving, sculpture, and metalwork was
equaled—and possibly improved upon—by the Aymara peoples,
the great architects of the Tiahuanaco area adjacent to Lake
Titicaca in what is now part of Bolivia.

The Incas' star began to rise in the eleventh century in the
vicinity of Cuzco, their capital in the Peruvian highlands. They
were among the greatest organizers—and Organization Men—
of all time. Unabashedly imperialist, their goal—and they went
a long way toward fulfilling it—was an Incaic continent. The
secrets of their success were basically twofold: (1) a brilliant
sense of over-all planning and control, with which they evolved
a smooth-functioning pyramidal-type dictatorship where people
gave up individual liberties in exchange for a full stomach, and
(2) a lack of pride to the extent that they avidly incorporated
the best of the cultures of the peoples they conquered. Their
religion, which was basically worship of the sun, was borrowed
from Tiahuanaco, and so possibly were their ingenious architectural
and engineering skills. Their craft traditions—the glorious textiles
which their descendants still weave, the pottery they still produce
—were no doubt in part a result of what they had acquired by
other imperial victories.

The Inca greatness: These people were great metallurgists, great
statisticians, great political scientists, great agriculturalists, great
builders and engineers, great artisans. They mined silver, gold, and
copper, and they were skilled at smelting it, making alloys such
as bronze, and fashioning objects both practical and aesthetic.
They counted by means of knotted ropes, which allowed them
to compile statistics that even Washington would admire today.
They built—with no knowledge of the arch—stone temples,
houses, public buildings, and great walls, deftly fitting immense

blocks in place without the use of mortar. Through skillful planning they assured their peoples of adequate food supplies, storing harvests in great warehouses for lean years and fully utilizing the near-barren mountain terrain for such crops as potatoes and corn, which, incidentally, were their culinary contributions to the world. (They had no cows, pigs, or horses, but they domesticated the llama, the alpaca, and the dog.)

Their roads ranked among the wonders of the world, and provided fast communications with every corner of their immense empire. (And that empire, by the time they reached their peak of greatness, extended from Ecuador to parts of Chile and Argentina, from the Pacific on the west through Bolivia in the east.) The incredibly well-engineered roads totaled some ten thousand miles and were used principally by trained couriers. Bearing messages, they would run in relays and the journeys they were able to make in a few days were later to take the Spaniards several weeks, on horseback or by carriage.

The basis of Inca society—again inherited from previous cultures—was the ayllu, or clan. Its various families were under the jurisdiction of a kind of village elder, who in turn controlled the land—commonly held—on behalf of the state, to whose officials he was subordinate. The Incas' system was harsh, but so was the environment in which they lived; their way, they believed, was the only one which would assure a viable state, and systematic distribution of limited resources.

Conflict at the summit: The gap between the ayllus and the summit was a great one. At the top of the government structure was the Sapa Inca, considered to be divine and the earthly representative of the sun god. He surrounded himself with an elite in whose various ranks were priests of the church, government administrators, chiefs of conquered nations, and the leading artisans and professional men, both Inca and conquered. The Sapa Inca (the Inca people, incidentally, derive their collective identification from the title of their sovereign) had as his chief advisers the governors of the four regions—north, south, east, west—of the empire. Probably the greatest of the Sapa Incas was Pachacutec (1400–48). It was he who solidified the empire, united it by the bond of a common language—Quechua—and made possible its continued expansion under his successors, one of whom, Huayna Capac, was indirectly responsible for its demise.

By the time Huayna Capac became emperor, Incaland was so big as to be unmanageable from the splendid capital, Cuzco, and so it was divided into two segments, one ruled from the capital, the other from Quito. Just before the Spaniards arrived, the two rulers, Huáscar in Cuzco, and his half-brother Atahualpa in Quito, had taken to quarreling. The moment could not have been a more propitious one for Francisco Pizarro, the illiterate, power-mad, status-hungry ex-swineherd who was out to make a name for himself and carve an empire of his own.

Enter the conquistadors: Pizarro and his henchman, Diego de Almagro, with a force of but two hundred men and a couple of dozen horses, landed on the coast in 1532, and proceeded into the mountains, with Atahualpa's knowledge. The ruler was no doubt anxious to have allies in his struggle against half-brother Huáscar. He encountered the foreigners at the town of Cajamarca, at which point things began to move with lightning-like rapidity. Pizarro's band ambushed the Inca, killed the guards protecting him, and then promised him freedom in exchange for a roomful of gold. Atahualpa, considering the ransom reasonable enough, at once offered it. It was accepted with alacrity and its donor was forthwith murdered with even greater speed.

By the time the Pizarro forces arrived in Cuzco, the followers of Huáscar had learned, with great pleasure, of Atahualpa's death. The conquistadors were welcomed as allies—but not for long. They set about with dispatch to loot the rich capital of its treasures, and before long—within a few years—they had subdued not only the Inca leaders, but the masses as well. Never allowed to think for themselves, never leaders but only followers, never having known personal liberty, the Indians, by and large, stoically accepted one dictator over the other, unaware that the newer boss had not the paternalistic, benevolent attitude toward them that their own emperor had had.

And so Peru was conquered. The Indians were subjugated by various means, and under systems with various names, to till the soil and work the mines, first as slaves, then as peons, now as presumably free citizens. Their resistance to the European has been minimal. And until this century, relatively few of their countrymen—Peruvians of either pure or mixed blood—fought their battles for them, although some abortive attempts were made. More than four centuries have elapsed since Pizarro killed Atahualpa, but to this day the Indians of Peru are still the submerged majority. The irony is that the country cannot get along without them, for their countrymen are still not able to work ceaselessly at high altitudes as they are. And without them, the mineral wealth, and other segments of the Peruvian economy, would become meaningless.

The Spaniards were aware of the contribution to be made by the Indians, from the moment of their arrival. They set about to organize the country on the feudal basis which is still largely extant. Needing a port and major city on the coast, they developed the harbor of Callao, and designed adjacent Lima as the capital and cultural center, from which they made further conquests in other parts of the continent. Power changed hands, often violently and ruthlessly. Ambitious Almagro and his men attacked the forces of his boss, Pizarro. They were defeated, and Almagro executed. But a few years later, in 1541, Almagro's son killed Pizarro (his remains are still on view in a glass case in the Lima cathedral).

It was not until three decades later that chaotic Peru—with Spaniards killing Indians, Indians killing Spaniards, and Spaniards killing Spaniards—calmed down, under the administration of Viceroy Francisco de Toledo. He inaugurated a system which lasted for two centuries. It was little more than a modification of the ancient Inca system: local rule was in the hands of Indian administrators, each with an Indian district in his charge, all under the iron thumb of the viceroyalty in Lima. The Indians became more and more Christian and, at the same time, more and more exploited. They revolted twice, abortively, in 1780 and 1814, by which time the creoles—Peruvian-born descendants of the conquistadors—had themselves become irritated with Spanish rule from Madrid. Colonial officials from the mother country had all the cushy jobs, creoles only the minor ones, and taxation was exorbitant.

San Martín comes from the south: The creoles' savior turned out to be José de San Martín, the truly great Argentine leader who had crossed the Andes to help Chile become free, and then continued north to Peru, with the protection of the British Lord Cochrane. San Martín proclaimed Peruvian independence on July 28, 1821, and Bolívar sent Marshal Sucre to lend a hand in fighting the viceroy's forces. After a never-explained meeting with Bolívar at Guayaquil in 1822, San Martín left Peru for Argentina and, shortly thereafter, self-imposed exile, and death, in France. Bolívar was left to reap the fruits of victory, which were made possible by the battles of Junín and Ayacucho in 1824. The Spanish stubbornly held on to the port of Callao but finally gave it up in 1826, and Peru was free—the last of Spain's New World colonies to gain independence.

Its leaders were an oligarchy of creoles whose members darted in and out of the presidential chair, often as a result of violence. By the time the twentieth century was a decade old, nearly a dozen had been deposed, two had been assassinated, and another had been killed in a civil war. Peru, while all this was happening, had been forced into, and forced itself out of, a confederation with Bolivia; has lost (with Bolivia) the War of the Pacific to Chile; embroiled itself in the interminable Tacna-Arica dispute, which lasted until 1929, when the port of Arica went to Chile, the port of Tacna to Peru; loosed itself a year later (1930), by means of a revolution, from the dictatorial but development-minded government of President Leguía, who had been around, off and on, since 1908; and began to approach the modern world.

APRA is born: Foreign corporations were encouraged to come in to exploit the mines and other industry; international trade was stepped up, and, very significantly, the APRA movement began to gain strength. Founded by Victor Haya de la Torre after World

War I as the Alianza Popular Revolucionario Americana, and often outlawed by the government in power, it has an uncompromising reform program: it wants land reform, so that Indians will once again own their own farms; a universal education system, so that Indians will at long last become literate and thereby be able to vote intelligently, an economic program that will bring Indians into industry and out of their subsistence-agriculture rut, advanced labor legislation to afford additional protection to workers. What the Apristas want is the incorporation of the Indian into Peruvian society.

But they have always had the aristocratic landowning class and the army against them. (Haya de la Torre spent a good many years in exile because of his views and the feared potential of his movement.) In 1948 the Apristas revolted against the so-called moderate party in power after it repudiated the support it had originally accepted in order to achieve victory. The revolt was crushed by the army, under General Manuel Odría, who became the dictator-president until he voluntarily relinquished the job in 1958. The Odría period was a time of relative economic progress and stability, but it was ruthless and repressive politically. The Apristas—and virtually all opposition—were outlawed.

Odría bows out: But in 1955 Odría mellowed and announced that elections would take place the following year and that he, in accordance with the constitution, would not be a candidate to succeed himself. The Apristas backed the opposition candidate, Manuel Prado (who had been president from 1939 to 1945), assuring his victory. Dr. Prado's prime minister had been Pedro Beltran, a noted newspaper publisher and a contender for the presidency, in the 1962 elections. He is a friend of the United States, and a strong advocate of aid from abroad, but he had the reactionary forces of the Peruvian legislature to contend with; they still resist any help from abroad which would in any way challenge the vast power of their landowning supporters. Their resistance illustrates the difficulty American foreign-aid programs can encounter. Sometimes, we are finding, we can't even *give* money away, or provide technical assistance. One hopes that the government, in collaboration with the still popular, non-Communist

APRA, will be able to effectuate the social change which Peru has desperate need of. The Indians are beginning to awaken from their centuries-old lethargy and they, with the mostly-poor mestizos, constitute the great majority of the population. The aristocrats will have to give a little if the entire applecart is not to be upset.

YOUR VISIT TO PERU

A South American journey which excludes Peru is inconceivable. This is one of the great travel-nations of the world. Its history, only briefly capsulized earlier in this chapter, lives and breathes every moment of one's visit today. Four centuries have made remarkably little impact on the outlook of the rich aristocrat of Spanish descent, and even less on the way of life on his Indian compatriot. The traveler—be his interests archaeological, sociological, cultural, political, or simply recreational—may well be confused, saddened, amazed, and at times conflicted about his sympathies. But he will never for a moment be bored. And he will invariably be comfortable.

Neither Peru's lack of democratic tradition nor the appalling contrasts between its rich minority and impoverished mass have stood in the way of its developing tourism as an industry. There is, of course, room for improvement, but nonetheless, there is a chain of well-operated government hotels at points of interest throughout the republic, and within the capital there are accommodations ranging from opulently luxurious to comfortably simple. The cuisine, hardly designed for tourists but greatly relished by them, is the most imaginative on the South American continent. Transportation, particularly when one considers the handicaps of terrain, is surprisingly good. Planes now land after a few hours at places where transport by surface conveyances previously took many days or weeks. The railroad traverses unbelievable mountain passes. And there are many good, all-weather roads.

The government, through its excellent museums, its wise policy of preserving antiquities and encouraging continued archaeological

exploration, is doing its fair share. It could do more, of course. A
national tourist office, with branches in New York and other major
cities abroad, would no doubt bring Peru many more visitors.
Meanwhile, Peru lets others—mainly airlines and shipping companies—blow its horn. Panagra and W. R. Grace and Company,
for example, have been its most vocal boosters, and the tourist
industry which has developed is to a great extent a result of their
skilled handiwork. A doff of the hat to them.

And, at the same time, a prefatory note about Lima, the Great
Touristic Stumbling Block. There is no point in attempting to dis-
trust the hard facts: Lima *is* a lovely city, and it is, as well, the
heart and soul of Peru: political capital, industrial center, cultural
mecca, and, by means of its adjacent port (Callao) and a splendid
airport, international transport terminus. But it is, primarily, a
European city. It is not, unlike the capitals of neighboring heavily-
Indian republics such as Bolivia and Ecuador, a city with a traditional Indian community. Those Indians who have migrated to it
have largely absorbed the ways of the creole. One *must,* therefore,
leave Lima if one is to have even a taste of Indian Peru, and I
should say that a trip to Cuzco and nearby Machu Picchu would
be basic and absolute requisites.

Despite its relatively sparse population—some ten millions—
Peru is a whopping big country—more than twice the size of Spain,
its former occupier. Geographically it is chopped in three—a high,
dry Pacific seaboard, a magnificent Andean center, and forested
eastern plains. Most Peruvians live in the mountains, as their
ancestors have for many centuries. They consitute some 60 per
cent of the population; nearly 30 per cent are along the coast, and
the tiny remainder are residents of the largely underdeveloped
eastern tropics.

IN AND AROUND THE CAPITAL

Lima: Proud Lima, the City of the Kings founded by Pizarro in
1535, is no longer the subdued capital which made it the envy of
many a European city during its eighteenth-century heyday, while

it was the seat of administration for all Spanish America. It has, since World War II, burgeoned into a city of a million people—the fifth largest on the continent. Industry has given it a twentieth-century hum, more restrained than that of São Paulo or Caracas, to be sure, but still a mite discordant. One has the feeling that the new skyscrapers—and again they appear in nothing like the profusion of the aforementioned cities—have not been completely accepted by old *Limeñans,* who have not the flexibility or the readiness of the Brazilians and Venezuelans to accept change.

Lima's pace is, then, still essentially slow-moving, and although much of the original Colonial façade has disappeared, enough remains, both original and ersatz, to remind one that this is a city with a great past which it is not yet ready to break with. It is just this facet of its personality which gives it its charm, and which appeals to the visitor who is nostalgic for a touch of Old World ways in the Western Hemisphere.

This sense of antiquity is not without irony. The University of San Marcos, founded in 1551 and the first in the Americas, is today populated by students without the least trace of tradition or sentimentality. They evidence their discontent with the current scene by all manner of politico-emotional demonstrations, which have put the Old Guard in a tizzy. The first printing press in the Americas was set up in Lima shortly after the university opened. But there are still more illiterates than literates, four centuries later. Lima has not in every way fulfilled its expectations, or exploited the advantages of its antiquity as it might have in a more socially stimulating atmosphere.

Still, it has great appeal, most of which comes from those remaining evidences of the bygone elegances to which it still stubbornly clings. There is an air of the haughty at times, but mostly the *Limeñan* is courteous and pleasant; only when he takes the form of a shopkeeper, and then only occasionally, does he take advantage of the tourist in his midst. But shopping will be dealt with on later pages. There is no question but that it is a major occupation with many visitors, but there is the city itself to be seen.

Two great *plazas*—de Armas and San Martín—are the focal

points of central Lima, and they are joined by the Jirón de la Union, whose five blocks constitute the principal shopping area of the town. The Plaza de Armas, though greatly historical, is actually new or near-new. Its oldest authentic building is the cathedral, and even it has been reconstructed a number of times. Still, one does well to look at its older treasures: glittering silver altars, walls whose mosaic designs are the coats of arms of Pizarro and of the city of Lima, the elaborately-carved mid-seventeenth-century choir, and most significant, the bony, rather ghastly remains of Pizarro himself, encased in a glass casket in a tiny chapel near the main entrance. Diagonally across the street is the President's Palace, only a few decades old, but designed and furnished in opulent Spanish Colonial style, on the site, presumably, of Pizarro's palace. Its public rooms—and there are a great many, with the Sala de Pizarro and Salon Dorado particularly sumptuous—are open to visitors, and eminently worth seeing. And its guards—in splendid Colonial-era uniforms—are perfectly amenable to being photographed. Directly opposite the cathedral is the City Hall—even newer than the President's Palace, but again in authentic traditional style, and with an interesting art gallery among its chambers. The Archbishop's Palace, rebuilt in 1924, completes the fastidiously-landscaped plaza's roster.

The other principal square, Plaza San Martín, is without historical significance, but is the site of the Gran Hotel Bolívar, Lima's leading hotel, and of a number of shops, cinemas, restaurants, cafés, and office buildings. Leading streets—most of them modern—lead off from it. It is a favored promenade spot after dark.

The *old churches* are the principal remaining heritage of Colonial Lima, and I should make it a point to visit at least the few most important ones. The list would embrace San Pedro, completed by the Jesuits in 1638, the burial place of a number of viceroys, with a bell which tolled the declaration of independence, an exquisitely-carved gilded choir, and a superb altar; Santo Domingo, which dates from 1549 and contains an urn with the remains of the first Roman Catholic saint of the New World (and the patron saint of Peru), Saint Rose of Lima, and a statue of the saint presented by the Vatican in the seventeenth century; San Francisco, with its Moorish-Baroque décor, features of which are elaborate wood-carving and jeweled embellishments, an adjoining monastery—open only to men—with beautiful tiling and paneled cloister ceilings, an ancient library with thousands of venerable volumes, and a recently-discovered catacomb; La Merced, invariably crowded with white-collar worshipers who work in the neighborhood, and with a handsomer exterior than interior; Saint Rose of Lima Sanctuary, which attracts many pilgrims to see the saint's hermitage, a section of the house where she nursed the sick, and other relics; San Agustín, with early Cuzco paintings and fine, carved choir stalls; Las Nazarenas, built in the mid-seventeenth century and with important venerated images which are borne through the streets by the faithful every October; and eighteenth-century San Carlos in the lovely Parque Universitario, which is the national pantheon, with two of Peruvian leaders in its rotunda.

The best remaining example of Colonial residential architecture is Torre Tagle Palace, which was constructed in the mid-eighteenth century, and is now the headquarters of the Foreign Ministry (foreign ministries in South America invariably are located in the fine old houses). The wood-carved balconies are superb, the patios are lovely, and the ministerial powers-that-be graciously allow visitors to have a look for two hours every afternoon, between one and three. The main hall of the dreaded Court of Inquisition, which functioned in Lima from 1570 until 1820, is now the headquarters of the army's Council of Generals, but is open to visitors, and is interesting principally because of its original function and because of its fantastically intricate hand-carved mahogany ceiling.

The aforementioned University of San Marcos is not at all as attractive as one would hope, considering its four-century history. It is housed in an unprepossessing early-nineteenth-century building which was originally a Jesuit novitiate. The Catholic University of Lima is relatively modern. Both are interesting mainly because of their student bodies and faculties, whom visitors might do well to engage in between-class chats. The Bull Ring, in a now ramshackle neighborhood almost directly behind the President's Palace, is authentically eighteenth-century, and still in use on certain Sundays throughout the year; even more frequently held are cockfights—every Saturday and Sunday at 150 Sandia Street. There are horse races every weekend at the San Felipe Hippodrome.

Lima's *museums,* even though they maddeningly close for lunch in winter and all afternoon in summer, are outstanding, particularly the Museum of Art and Archaeology, with its brilliantly-organized exhibits of pre-Colonial cultures—Inca and pre-Inca—which no visitor is wise to overlook, and which serves as an excellent introduction for trips to Cuzco and Machu Picchu for those headed in that direction, and a worthy substitute for those who are not; the Museum of the Viceroyalty, housed in a lovely seventeenth-century house, and with evocative displays of Colonial furnishings, clothing, *objets d'art,* some purported to have belonged to La Perricholi, mistress of an early viceroy who is portrayed in Wilder's *The Bridge of San Luis Rey;* and the Museum of the Republic, also occupying an old house, in this instance a viceroy's palace where both San Martín and Bolívar lived at different times, and containing portraits, manuscripts, and uniforms of the Colonial and early republican periods.

Fine Arts museums include the Pinacoteca Municipal, with paintings of leading traditional Peruvian painters (including the most noted, Ignacio Merino), the Exposition Palace, where extremely interesting contemporary paintings are on display, and the Museum of Italian Art, whose formal Italian Renaissance building (a gift of the Italian community) is far more interesting than the paintings inside, many of which are reproductions.

Private art collections—Inca and pre-Inca, Colonial and European—include those of Don Pedro de Osma, Don José Antonio Lavalle, Dr. Javier Prado, and Dr. Rafael Lanco Herrera, which deals mainly with the ancient Chimu culture that thrived in the vicinity of Trujillo. Panagra's Tourist Corner and travel agents can arrange for admission.

There are some extraordinarily handsome *parks.* My favorite is the Alamade de los Descalzos, beneath Cerro Cristóbal, the hill which overlooks Lima. *Limeñans* have promenaded among its statue-dotted walks or watched others promenade, while resting on its marble benches, for four centuries. One of the walks was built by La Perricholi's viceregal lover, in her honor. There are, too, the handsome residential sections of suburban Miraflores— much like those in any other Latin American capital and too often, in my view, a destination on travel-agency tours, at the expense of more authentically Peruvian points of interest.

Excursions from Lima: *Callao,* the port adjacent to Lima at which ship-travelers arrive, is an undistinguished harbor town (population about 115,000) with little of interest save a military museum in its ancient barracks, and a pleasant bathing beach at nearby *La Punta* (which also is the site of the Peruvian Naval Academy). Callao is not worth a layover for those arriving at its port, let alone an excursion from the capital. There are, however, other *bathing beaches,* besides La Punta, which are pleasant for day-long outings. Nearby *Ancón* is about the most popular, and near it are a cluster of pre-Inca ruins, which include a town, cemetery, and fortifications. Other beaches include *La Herradura, Punta Hermosa, San Bartolo,* and *Pucusana.*

Considerably more essential would be excursions to *Pachacamac* and *Chosica.* En route to the former, one passes through the much-touted Miraflores residential sections. Pachacamac is pre-Inca, although by the time Pizarro landed, it had been taken over by the Incas and was inhabited by them. Now, astride a hill overlooking the sea, it is a rather pathetic ruin, but one is able to imagine— particularly from the remains of its pre-Inca Temple of the Creator, its Inca Sun-God Temple, and its impressive pyramid— what it was like when Gonzalo Pizarro, brother of Francisco, first came upon it four centuries ago. Chosica, a small but attractive market town some thirty miles east of the city, is gained by a drive through the pretty restaurant-dotted Rimac Valley, and en route one can easily detour to the ruins of the old Inca hill towns of *Puruchoco* and *Cajamarquilla,* whose crumbling walls indicate their onetime strength as strategic Inca and pre-Inca fortress-communities. Interesting, too, are just-discovered pre-Inca ruins in San Isidro. And there is sand-skiing on the coastal mountain slopes at *Pasamayo Grande,* near the resort of *Santa Rosa.*

THE SOUTH

Cuzco and Machu Picchu: Go on an air excursion from Lima, go from La Paz, Bolivia's capital, via Lake Titicaca steamer and train from Puno. But go! There are probably more postcards written home exclaiming over the wonders of Cuzco and Machu Picchu than any other tourist destinations in South America, and with good reason. Cuzco is at once the former capital of the Inca empire and a once-great Spanish Colonial city. Machu Picchu—three breathtakingly beautiful hours distant—was an Inca mountain community which the Indians kept a secret from the conquistadors *and* their descendants, and which was discovered only a few decades ago by a visiting American politician-explorer. In the neighborhood, too, are a number of other interesting spots, including Pisac, whose Sunday fairs are noteworthy; Ollantaytambo, beneath an old Inca fort; and the dramatic terraced farms of the eye-filling Urubamba Valley.

Cuzco was no doubt inhabited long before the Incas reached the peak of their greatness. They chose it for their capital, and by the time Pizarro and his conquistadors arrived in 1532, it was a great walled city. The meticulously planned central area contained the elaborate palaces of the various emperors (each built his own upon ascending the throne), schools for royal children, broad plazas and temples. Only members of the very top of the hierarchy, their families, and the priests lived in this area, but surrounding it were communities of workers imported from throughout the empire to serve as a labor force for the capital. Overlooking the entire complex, which had an estimated population of 100,000 (about twice the current population), was the Fortress of Sacsahuaman, originally military in its function but a religious ceremonial center by the time the empire fell.

The Spaniards, when they came, lost no time in ruthlessly sacking the city of its ornate, skillfully-wrought gold and silver embellishments. They razed a great many of the structures. And they proceeded without delay to build, high in the Peruvian mountains, at an altitude of 11,400 feet, a city as elaborately baroque as those in the Spain of that century. With the aid of Indian artisans and laborers, they superimposed many of their structures on the walls and excavations of the Inca buildings—and so they remain today.

Two disastrous earthquakes, exactly three centuries apart, destroyed much of Colonial Cuzco. The first, in 1650, came during the height of the Colonial period and the rebuilding was in the style of the era. The second, in 1950, was a far greater tragedy, but the Peruvian government, with the help of UNESCO and the Spanish government, has made a great deal of progress in restoration. Interestingly, neither earthquake destroyed any of the Inca foundations which the Spaniards had allowed to remain. The Incas built without mortar, without iron implements, and without knowledge of the curved arch. They fitted together immense stone blocks weighing many tons, after hammering them into size and polishing them with sand and water. And they often had the handicap of steep slopes as building sites.

The Spaniards, so avidly anxious to impose their culture over the Indians, left not a single Inca structure in its entirety. Still, the *Inca work* is evident everywhere in the city. In building after building it serves as the base for a Colonial structure built atop it. A good example is the brilliant curved wall of the Temple of the Sun, a dominant monument of Incaic Cuzco, which has been incorporated on an edifice of another religion, Santo Domingo Church. Still other walls, on Loreto Street, serve as bases of the churches of La Compañía and Santa Catalina. Elsewhere, simple adobe houses are built upon Inca foundations. There is not a street in the old city without some trace of the original Cuzco, and although destruction of the major portions of all of these buildings is hardly to be condoned, one can at least be thankful that they were not razed completely.

Cuzco's contemporary center, the Plaza de Armas, was also its focal point in Indian days. The Spaniards built arcades around it and a quartet of *religious edifices,* the most imposing of which is the Renaissance cathedral. Here the highlights are a glittering pulpit, a bejeweled monstrance fashioned of fifty pounds of gold and more than a thousand precious and semiprecious stones, a painstakingly-carved choir, eleven side chapels, and many paintings, including what is believed to be a Van Dyck of Christ. With an even more magnificent interior is twin-towered La Compañía Church, built by the Jesuits, whose plan was to outdo the cathedral in size as well as splendor. The authorities precluded the priests from making as big a church, but they could not prevent the interior being even more marvelous than the cathedral's. Its exterior features twin towers and an elegant tiled dome. Within are more treasures than one can comprehend on a single visit: ungilded carved-stone walls which are striking in their simplicity; main altar and side altars of gold-splashed wood, enhanced by a number of exquisite paintings; an appropriately ornate pulpit, and, throughout, paintings, sculpture, carving, all of which taken together produce an exceptionally harmonious whole.

La Merced is the oldest church in Cuzco, first built in 1534 and rebuilt a century later, with the tombs of Gonzalo Pizarro and the Almagros, a dazzling jewel-encrusted monstrance, and an adjoining monastery with a true gem of a cloister. Others include Belén de los Reyes, a seventeenth-century Indian-built church with a lovely gold-and-silver altar; the aforementioned Santo Domingo, ingeniously incorporating the curved wall of the Inca Temple of the Sun; El Triunfo and Jesús y Maria, both small churches which flank the cathedral, with the former the more interesting; Santa Catalina, with a cloistered convent and a jewel-like interior; San Francisco, with what is probably the best carved choir in the city, a pleasant cloister with stalls lined with paintings illustrating the life of Saint Francis, and a fascinating old library.

The old University of Cuzco, originally a Jesuit college, adjoins La Compañía Church. Its cloisters are still handsome and there are still several thousand original volumes in the library. (The new university is on the outskirts of the city.)

Other colonial buildings, nonreligious in nature, and badly damaged in the 1950 earthquake (their Inca foundations excepted) include Almirante Palace, the San Borja House (where Bolívar stayed), Concha Palace, and Valverde House.

The Sacsahuaman Fortress, atop a hill overlooking the city, is a sight-seer's requisite, with its parade ground, the massive throne occupied by the emperor while reviewing his soldiers, a bath thought to have been the emperor's, and a curious rock slide, believed to have been used by children. Within Cuzco there are many small curio shops and a vivid market place ablaze with the brilliantly-clad Indians of the city and surrounding region. Because of the altitude, one does well to take things easily the first twenty-four hours or so: walking slowly, climbing inclines or stairways even more slowly, eating lightly and then mainly liquids, and skipping alcoholic drinks.

Machu Picchu is reached in three hours by means of modern, one-car electric *auto-carril,* or by regular train—which takes much longer and is a good deal less comfortable, if cheaper. The distance is seventy-five miles. One can return the same day on the *auto-carril,* allowing for an hour-and-a-half stop—enough to see Machu Picchu, but not enough to really savor it, or to see it when the sun sets over it in the evening and rises above it in the morning. An overnight visit is preferable, with accommodation at the state-operated hotel, adjacent to the site, and a return to Cuzco on the next day's *auto-carril.*

The trip is almost as enchanting as the lost city. It takes one, after ascending to the heights north of Cuzco, through the floor of a broad basin, beneath two overpowering canyons, and then into the green Urubamba Valley with its terraced farms chiseled out of the sides of broad green mountains, neat adobe farmhouses, and the Indians themselves: handsome-featured; wearing clothing they themselves have woven, in wonderfully vivid yellows, greens, blues, reds, and fuchsias; rarely smiling; resignedly chewing on the coca leaves which dull their sensations; pitifully unkempt more often than not. There are no better-looking Indians in South America, none more skilled in the art of weaving or with a more brilliant sense of color and design, and at the same time, none dirtier or more pathetic. One wants to dip them in a tub and scrub them, do likewise with their clothes, often so soiled that the colors are difficult to discern, move them into decent homes, give them decent jobs and wages, send them to school so that they can learn to read and write, and see them evolve as modern Peruvians.

It is at times hard to believe that it was the descendants of these people who built the fantastic mountain town of Machu Picchu, deftly tucked away on the slope of a high mountain, with terraced lands trailing thousands of feet to the Urubamba River below. What was Machu Picchu's function? Some believe that it was one of a chain of agricultural communities which the Incas had begun to build in the near-jungle region below Cuzco, as part of an expansion plan. Others believe, because the skeletons found on the site were all female and the trinkets with them all feminine, that it was used by the ruling caste only in times of disaster, that the women of the Imperial family had been sent to it after the sacking of Cuzco, and that it was for that reason kept secret from the Spaniards.

At any rate, it was never discovered by them, or even by their descendants, though tales of its existence were passed from generation to generation. Hiram Bingham, who was later to become a United States senator from Connecticut, came across it on a 1911 expedition, and it was thereafter explored by a Yale archaeological group, and by other scholars. (A plaque, commemorating the fiftieth anniversary of Bingham's discovery, was affixed to a wall of the ruins during the semicentennial celebrations in 1961.) Its ruins are in good enough shape to allow the visitor to comprehend what it must have been like when inhabited: walls to defend it from attack; marvelously-designed farming terraces; two-story gabled houses (now roofless), a group for each village unit or ayllu; a horseshoe-shaped watchtower whose windows overlook the valley; additional residential areas—one believed to be for the royal princesses, another for the men of the ruling caste, and still another, the highlight of which is a remarkable temple, for the priests.

But a sketchy description of Machu Picchu's ruins can not do it justice. What makes a visit to it so tremendously exciting is the way in which the architecture blends with the setting, the opportunity to observe the genius with which the Inca architects and engineers took nature into account when building. Machu Picchu is anything but a transplanted carbon copy of Incaic Cuzco. In designing it the Incas, after obviously taking great care to choose an aesthetically pleasing site, considered terrain along with function. They achieved what town planners in succeeding centuries have often not accomplished, a city based on a partnership of the works of man and of nature.

Two more Cuzco excursions: It is not always easy to plan, on a complicated trip, to be at a certain place on a certain day of the week. But if at all possible, one should make sure that a Sunday is among the days spent in the Cuzco area, to permit an excursion to *Pisac,* for its exceptional Sunday market. Indians, on that day, trek in from the surrounding countryside to sell their wares and their agricultural produce, to mix and mingle with each other in the market place, and to attend mass at the Roman Catholic church, after marching to it in an elaborate procession, to the accompaniment of music played on traditional instruments. Save that at Huancayo, there is no other market in Peru which is more worth attending, or, for that matter, with a finer selection of hand-crafted textiles, pottery, and silver.

Another destination, out of Cuzco, might well be *Ollantaytambo* (on the route to Machu Picchu), a small town built, like Cuzco, on the foundations of an earlier Inca community, with a quite incredible protecting fort (where individual stones weigh as much as fifty tons!) on adjacent heights, and a charming, pink granite bath (now in the garden of a private home) believed to have been reserved for use by young ladies of princess rank.

Arequipa: Peru's second city, proud, stubborn, and beautiful, is slowly recovering from a recent round of devastating earthquakes which partially destroyed a number of its precious colonial antiquities. Slowly and painstakingly, Italian-imported craftsmen are reconstructing the damaged masterpieces, stone by stone, carving by carving, with the aid of the Peruvian government. The hope now is that Mother Nature has spent herself on this lovely old city. The visitor, until the rehabilitation program is completed, will have to forego much of the pleasure which Arequipa ordinarily conveys.

It is still relatively small—the population is only a little over 100,000. But it has had a past out of proportion to its size. A conquistador colleague of Pizarro, by the name of Manuel de Garcia Carbajal, founded the town in 1540, just a few years after the Spaniards arrived in Peru. He chose an ancient Inca community as the site, and in short order, much as in Cuzco, the Spaniards went about constructing a handsome baroque-style city, inter-mingling uninhibitedly with the Indians—so much so that this town's inhabitants now constitute the most completely mestizo population of any Peruvian city.

Competition between Arequipa, which dominates the south, and Lima, which came to dominate the entire country, has been intense ever since early colonial days. Arequipa held out until the last possible moment before going along with the republicans in the battle for independence. But the rivalry now is of relatively little consequence. *Limeñans* invariably urge visitors from abroad to have a look at the southern metropolis, and their advice is sound.

The city's setting could not be improved upon, even by Holly-wood. And not even the earthquakes can change it: Arequipa straddles a 7500-foot valley, under the shadow of a perfectly-shaped conical volcano known as El Misti, 19,110 feet high, with slopes perpetually frosted by white snows. El Misti itself is flanked by a pair of less aesthetically rounded but nonetheless substantial peaks—Pichú-Pichú (18,600 feet) and Chachani (20,000 feet). They are most visible between April and September; clouds may partially obstruct them during the remaining months, but the city itself, mountain view or no, is pleasant to visit at any time of the year, with cool evenings and days whose temperatures average in the seventies.

Life in Arequipa revolves around the Plaza de Armas. Even now, during the reconstruction period, one can appreciate its beauty. Gracefully arched stones shade three of its sides, and on the fourth stands the immense twin-towered cathedral, built in 1612 and reconstructed in the nineteenth century, with a sparse interior which is in startling contrast to the opulent interior of the Number Two church, La Compañía, built toward the end of the seventeenth century by the Jesuits, and with its outside façade carved of white volcanic rock quite as impressive as the ornate sanctuary.

Other major religious monuments include the lovely church adjoining Santa Catalina Convent, and the churches of San Agustín, Santo Domingo, and La Merced. And I would consider the Central Market a requisite, too, with all manner of stalls, where Indian merchants vend fruits, vegetables, meats, cheap five-and-ten-cent-store-type merchandise, and, most important, handsome hand-woven ponchos, blankets, and shawls.

The Lucioni Gardens, backed by ivy-encrusted walls, are lovely, and the suburban University of Arequipa, with its Rockefeller Foundation-financed School of Medicine, makes for a stimulating morning or afternoon. Beyond the city are a trio of thermal spas in the mountains (of the three—*Jesús, Socosani,* and *Yura*—the latter has the best hotel), and a host of pleasant villages, including *Tingo,* with its popular swimming pools, and *Cayma,* dominated by the steeple of its eighteenth-century church and with pretty picnic grounds.

Arequipa is easily accessible by air from Lima; the flight takes about three hours. It is also a key stopover point for cruise passengers whose ships land at nearby *Mollendo,* on the coast, and who are en route from there to Cuzco by train. The train ride, all the way to Cuzco, is one of the most satisfying in South America. The train circles El Misti and the neighboring peaks, wends its way past wheat and alfalfa fields in the broad valleys, passes through the aforementioned thermal resorts of 'Yura and Socosani and the town of *Pama de Arrieros,* where Indians vend oranges to passengers, and proceeds into even higher country where llamas, alpacas, possibly even vicuñas, graze quietly, glancing up from their occupation on occasion, with an expression which seems to say: "What are *you* doing way up here?" At *Juliaca,* a small market town with a twelve-thousand-foot elevation, Cuzco-bound passengers may stay overnight (there is no good hotel), or continue on a short distance to the comfortable hotel at Puno for a layover preceding the final stretch of the route to Cuzco.

Puno is the chief Peruvian port on *Lake Titicaca,* and the first Peruvian city encountered by travelers arriving in the country by way of the lake, from Bolivia. A cool city (the altitude is 12,641 feet), it is authentically Spanish Colonial, with a history dating back to 1668. The cathedral and the house of the founding viceroy, Count de Lemos, are the principal monuments, although there are Inca ruins nearby at *Sillustani,* lovely old churches at *Pomata* and *Juli,* and the immense lake itself surrounded by neat farms and tiny villages and dotted with ancient-design balsa boats (see Bolivia).

Huancayo: The Indian market at this important little market town ranks with Pisac as one of the finest in the country. Like Pisac's, it is exclusively a Sunday operation, and visitors in Lima are wise to avail themselves of the conveniently-arranged train schedule and hie themselves to 10,958-foot-high Huancayo on Saturday (after purchasing their ticket in advance), stay over that night and Sunday in the pleasant State Tourist Hotel, and return to the capital Monday. The train ride alone makes the excursion worth far more than the seven dollars it costs for the round-trip ticket. The route is roller-coaster in style with the train traveling over the world's highest standard-gauge railroad. (There is oxygen aboard, should breathing become difficult.) Buying and selling at the fair is conducted quite as silently as in the market at Otavalo, in Ecuador. Sellers, who are usually artisans as well, stand behind their merchandise, which is looked over by buyers or prospective buyers. The only speaking considered necessary is the price, given by the merchant only if he is asked it; there is no quibbling or bargaining: take it or leave it. And there's a great deal one might want to take: beautifully woven, strikingly colored blankets, ponchos, alpaca rugs, and ceramics.

Ayacucho: Rarely visited by travelers from abroad, Ayacucho greets the tourist warmly, and with pride: just beyond it, the battle which proved decisive in the Peruvian fight for independence was fought in 1824. The battlefield at La Quinua may be visited, although I have never yet found a battlefield interesting enough to warrant a special trip. Of more interest is cobblestoned Ayacucho itself: the cathedral, Government Palace, and City Hall facing Sucre Park, the main plaza; the lovely old mansions, particularly the still splendid Cristobal de Castillay Zamorra House; such churches as San Agustín, Santa Clara, and San Sebastian, opulent with gilded, elaborately carved altars and impressive façades; and the small but excellent Historical Museum.

Pisco and Paracas: The town which gave its name to the distinctive grape brandy which has made Peru famous among imbibers throughout the world (particularly those who have tasted a pisco sour) is a fairly substantial southern port, with two sections: old Pisco Pueblo, and new, industrial Pisco Puerto. The former is the more interesting for the general visitor, and near its fine old Plaza de Armas is a private club—the Club Social Pisco—which had for a time been General San Martín's headquarters, shortly after his arrival from Chile. A few miles from the harbor is Paracas Bay, where San Martín landed. It is now a pleasant beach resort; there is a good hotel, sea and pool bathing, fishing, golf, and for nonathletic diversion, the nearby ruins of the little-known Paracas civilization, which flourished along the coast more than fifteen hundred years ago.

The North

Iquitos: This remote Amazon river port—more than a thousand miles from Lima and well over two thousand miles from Belém, the Brazilian port at the Amazon's mouth—is the metropolis of Forest Peru, the least-developed, sparsest-populated region of the country. It is worlds away from the Colonial-Inca mountains and the coast. The indigenous people here are Indians whose cultures are vastly different from those of the mountain people, and it is only in recent years that Iquitos—now a town of some fifty thousand—has spruced itself up to a standard where it is glad to welcome visitors.

It boasts now a fully air-conditioned hotel (a link of the State
Hotel chain), a sprinkling of modern buildings, and a public bus
system which entertains its music-loving passengers by putting
musicians aboard to play for them. Among its other attractions
are an aquarium with tanks bulging with exotic river fish; a
museum which tells in part the story of this backwater region of
South America; a humming market, with the wares far more
tropical than those of towns in the mountains and on the coast;
a neighborhood known as Belén, largely inhabited by urbanized
Indians of the district, and most important: facilities for excursions upriver and into outlying villages.

One such, which lasts a full day, takes passengers by speedboat
to Yanamono Island, for a look at a sugar cane mill, and for
introductions to the Yagua Indians, who dress in scanty fiber-cloth
attire, demonstrate their skill at blowing poison darts through
blowguns, and serve as hosts at a meal whose main courses are
smoked monkey, river fish, and *camu-camu,* a potent grape juice
which the Welch people have yet to acquaint us with. Other
trips take one to villages built on rafts, other villages built on
stilts, and to the homes of tribal groups like the Chapras,
Huambizas, and Secoyas—friendly, attractive people all, but
like the Indians of the west, barely integrated into the modern
fabric of the republic.

On the banks of the Nanay, a tributary of the Amazon, there
are beaches for sunning and bathing (the water is considered
swimmable) and a small but intriguing zoo. But it is the Indian
life of Iquitos, and its pervasive tropical atmosphere, that make
it one of the most exciting Peruvian destinations, moisture (it
rains two hundred days of the year) and heat notwithstanding.
One can fly from Lima in a few hours, or come the slower, more
romantic way, by boat all the way from Belém, on the Atlantic,
or from interior Manaus, the Brazilian counterpart of Iquitos;
there are planes from those Brazilian cities, too.

Tingo María and Pucallpa are towns still in the frontier-pioneer
stage, the latter even more so than the former. Tingo María—
and is there a town anywhere with a more wonderful name?—is

at the jungle's edge, and its residents (who have come from four continents, attracted by high salaries) are engaged at raising bananas, sugar cane, tea, rubber, and other tropical produce. Aside from the rugged Wild West nature of the town itself, the chief attraction is a rather bizarre cave, known as Las Lechuzas. *Pucallpa* has been converted from tiny hamlet to bustling town of twenty-five thousand in just two decades, thanks to the colonization activities of Le Tourneau del Peru, Inc., an American-originated firm which is attempting, and with success, to develop a backwater area. Still, Pucallpa has a good way to go: its streets are still unpaved, its hotels inadequate, and its water and sewage systems virtually nonexistent. There are sawmills and rosewood-oil extracting factories, and there is an interesting American Protestant mission whose linguistics programs with the resident Indians are worthy of observation—as are the Indians themselves.

Cerro de Pasco, connected with the coast by plane and by another of Peru's unbelievable and ingenious mountain railroads, is up in the clouds at an elevation of 14,208 feet. It is one of the continent's oldest silver-mining centers; silver was discovered there in 1630. At the turn of this century—by which time Peru had lost out in silver production to other countries where the precious stuff was somewhat more accessible to ports and harbors —mining activity revived with the establishment of the Cerro de Pasco Mining Corporation. The most important ore now is coal, extracted from the world's highest such mine, but there are still yields of gold, copper, zinc, lead, bismuth, and of course, silver. Miners are almost exclusively Indian; others are unable to work at such high altitudes. Quite as interesting as the mines themselves is the model town, operated by the corporation for employees.

Trujillo (and it must be stated forthwith that this city—its name is a proud old Spanish one—was in existence long before the late Dominican Republic dictator named his capital city for himself) is a quiet but charming city, founded by Diego de Almagro in 1534. The *ambiance* is still what it was in viceregal days, despite unobtrusive modern trappings. The Universidad de la Libertad is only a few years newer than San Marcos in Lima, and there are a dozen-odd churches and convents of distinguished vintage, plus a properly impressive cathedral. General Iturregui's House—in which the town's independence from Spain was proclaimed in 1820—is now a private club (the Central) but one does well to somehow or other gain admittance. The Plaza de Armas is still, after more than four centuries, the city center. But it is beyond the city where the attractions are distinctive. Most important are the ruins of *Chan-Chan,* metropolis of a culture known as the Chimu, which the Incas incorporated not long before the arrival of the Spaniards—who in true conquistador fashion looted all of the elaborate gold and silver decorations, many of which adorned the graves of the hierarchy. Today, crumbling walls surround an eleven-mile-square area filled with the remains of temples, artisans' shops, palaces, and gardens. There is still evidence of the skilled decorative work of the Chimus in the exterior embellishments of the walls. The Chiclín Sugar Plantation, a city in itself, and the Hacienda Cartavio, which employs four thousand sugar workers, both welcome visitors.

Huarás, Carás, Chimbote, and the northern mountains: There is no denying the grandeur of the mountains in the region of Arequipa, Cuzco, and Machu Picchu, nor indeed of those traversed to reach Huancayo. Still, the peaks and valleys a few hours north of Lima are spectacular beyond compare, but not, by any means, so close to the clouds that they are devoid of human settlement. Land is tilled on slopes as high as thirteen thousand feet. Indian farmers and villagers follow the ways of life of their ancestors, with nary a thought about rarified atmosphere or acrophobia. Today, plane, train, and car have access to the area and there are even a number of pleasant hotels and resorts scattered about at surprisingly convenient points. With as little as three (but preferably a minimum of five) free days, and a reasonably robust constitution, one can have a look at a region of the continent which is known to very few foreigners.

A relatively quick trip, which of necessity omits one of the high spots of the region but does not neglect the others, is as follows: by air from Lima to *Chimbote,* a small, unprepossessing port less than 250 miles to the north, and the terminus of a crazy-quilt railroad which, by means of sixteen tunnels, crosses the beautiful Santa Valley, arriving some seven hours later at *Huallanca,* a small town at the entrance of the fantastic *Del Pato Canyon.* Cars can be rented at the canyon's pleasant government-operated hotel for a ride through the impressive gorge, and one can spend the night at a comfortable nearby hotel before departing the following day by air for Lima from the nearby town of *Carás.*

With about the same amount of time, one can fly directly from Lima to Carás, drive through the Del Pato Canyon, and return within twenty-four hours to the capital.

With three days—and this should be five, if one is not to rush—one can drive (by rented group-tour car or public bus) from Lima to *Huarás,* via the coastal town of *Pativilca* and the Fortaleza Valley, through rugged rock-hewn countryside—arid, cactus-dotted, and dramatic—gradually ascending into the mountains, crossing the Continental Divide at an eleven thousand-foot altitude, and descending into *Callejón de Huaylas,* the lovely valley whose chief town is Huarás. Small but not without a colorful Indian air about it—most engaging in the busy market place—Huarás is also the site of a unique Archaeological Museum, whose displays include sculpture of ancient Indian civilizations of the region. All about, in the countryside, are tiny villages around which are neat farms straddling the hills, planted with corn, potatoes, alfalfa, and even sugar. The best hotel is not in the town but at the nearby thermal resort of *Monterrey.*

From Monterrey, one proceeds north through the Maracara Valley (where a stopover might be made at another thermal-resort hotel, at *Chancos*) and then covers one of the most breathtaking regions of South America—the route through the valley which divides the Cordillera Blanca (White Range) and the Cordillera Negra (Black Range), passing through the village of *Mancos* at the very foot of the glacial 22,205-foot *Mount Huascarán,* the queen of the White Range; continuing through

Yungay (a base for mountaineers) and the lovely Llanganuco Lagoon to *Carás.* From there one may fly back to Lima, or drive on to Huallanca, and after a night's rest in the hotel there, take the roller-coaster-type train to Chimbote, rest there at a hotel, and fly back to Lima the following morning. The aforementioned schedules are based on the assumption that for most American travelers, time is at a premium. There is nothing to prevent anyone from staying on longer at one of the mountain hotels on the route.

Talara, though a town of but twenty thousand population, has become the nation's Number Two port and a frequent stopover point for northbound international planes, thanks to its location in the heart of Peru's oil territory. Aside from its commercial importance, it is unique in that the International Petroleum Company (which runs an immense oil refinery) has virtually rebuilt it into a hygienic community, with modern homes, schools accommodating some five thousand pupils, varied recreation facilities, and good restaurants. Some thirty miles up the coast is *Cabo Blanco,* justly renowned as a deep-sea fisherman's paradise (swordfish, rooster fish, marlin are among the species caught), and with the members-only Fishing Club, occasionally open to avid anglers who are not members, through arrangements which can be made through Panagra, in Lima or New York.

WHAT TO BUY

Given its two principal cultures, Indian and Spanish, one can easily imagine the wealth of shopping possibilities in Peru. I am not about to give an extensive listing, but I would emphasize two principal categories: *silver*—bracelets, necklaces, rings, cigarette boxes, tea services, flatware, key chains; and *textiles*—blankets, ponchos, shawls, scarves, hand-woven in the brilliant color combinations at which the Peruvian Indians are ingenious. Also significant are *ceramics,* particularly the marvelous beige-and-brown vessel-like bulls of various sizes, made in the neighborhood of

Cuzco, plus pitchers, ash trays, candlesticks, figurines, and other objects. Then, too, bushy alpaca bedroom slippers (which do not have a particularly long lifetime in northern climates but are fun while they last), rugs of pure-white alpaca and the cheaper brown-and-white type (often made up in quite ugly designs, but obtainable in simple solids, as well), dolls in Indian costume, life-size Indian costumes without the dolls, multicolored "stocking" caps and black-and-white wool ski masks, bottles of pisco grape brandy without which one cannot create pisco sours at home, and occasionally, antique pieces dating from the Colonial period.

Now, the big question: where to buy. For the traveler who will tour outside of Lima, I suggest that before buying in the capital he shop the markets and stores of whatever provincial towns are on his itinerary, particularly *Cuzco, Pisac, Arequipa, Huancayo,* and *Trujillo.* Prices in these places are invariably cheaper than in the capital. And even though Cuzco is tourist-ridden, it is a weaving and pottery center, with its ware made, so to speak, right in the neighborhood. Bargaining is the general rule. In *Lima* the Central Market is fun to inspect, but too often has very few crafts on sale. There are a great many tourist-souvenir shops in and about Jirón de la Union, the main shopping street, and although I found the most comprehensive selection and good service at the Casa del Indio, in my considered opinion one shop is very little different from the other. I suggest browsing about before buying. Milly Cook, of Panagra's Tourist Corner in the Gran Hotel Bolívar, keeps up to date on current favorites, but even these can turn out to be disappointing. One does well to get her advice, nonetheless, on shopping—and on just about *anything* Peruvian; she's a charmer and a whiz. One place I *do* recommend, if only for looking, is the suburban studio-shop of Truman Bailey, an American who has devoted many years to perfecting design and workmanship of traditional Peruvian crafts, particularly silver. His prices are high but his things are excellent. Note: (1) Lima is an excellent point for shipping home parcels and overweight, via air freight or parcel post; the aforementioned Milly Cook, at Panagra, can provide the details. (2) For the traveler visiting Bolivia as well as Peru, it is worth noting that silver in La Paz is cheaper than in Lima. Bolivia also has great buys in gold; its Indian textiles can be cheaper than Peru's but are not always as attractive.

CREATURE COMFORTS

HOTELS—**Lima:** The Gran Hotel Bolívar embraces all of the elegance and graciousness of aristocratic Lima: quietly handsome lobbies, restaurant, bars, *boîte,* and bedrooms (all 350 of them), flawless service, both Peruvian and international cuisine, perfect location, overlooking Plaza San Martín; airline offices in the building. This is not only Lima's best; it is one of the finest in the Western Hemisphere. From $7 single. Others: The Crillon is Number Two, recently enlarged and refurbished, with a restaurant noted for its Peruvian specialties; from $6 single with bath. Maury, reputedly the birthplace of the famed pisco sour, recently modernized; from $5 single. Savoy, new and streamlined, from $5 single; Alcazar, another new one; from $5 single. Claridge, Continental, and, in suburban San Isidro, the luxurious Lima Country Club, with three swimming pools, tennis courts, excellent restaurant, bars, and *boîte,* and open to the public; from $8 single. There are also a number of good pensions, starting at about $30 per week, with meals; among the best are the Noetzli and Astoria, both in San Isidro. **Cuzco:** The attractive government-operated Tourist Hotel Cuzco, Spanish Colonial style, pleasant service; single from $4; Savoy-Cuzco—newer and about the same price; Continental—Number Three—and less expensive. **Machu Picchu:** Hotel Machu Picchu—clean, government-operated, and overlooking the ruins of the city; wonderful for an overnight stay to take in both sunset and sunrise; from $3.25 single. **Arequipa:** Choose between the government-operated Tourist Hotel Arequipa (just out of town) or the more central, and noted, Quinta Bates. Others: Sucre, Maccera, Wagner. **Puno:** State Tourist Hotel—clean and comfortable. **Huancayo:** State Tourist Hotel

—very good. **Ayacucho:** Sucre. **Pisco:** Pisco, Humberto, Gran.
Paracas: Paracas—pleasant, with tennis courts, pool, golf course,
ocean view. **Iquitos:** State Tourist Hotel—modern, air-conditioned, comfortable; Malecon. **Tingo María:** State Tourist Hotel—
quite good. **Pucallpa:** Mercedes, Triunfo—neither is recommended.
Cerro de Pasco: America, Venezia. **Trujillo:** Tourist Hotel Trujillo—very pleasant; Jacobs. **Huarás:** Termas de Monterrey (outside of town at a delightful thermal resort; in town, 28 de Julio,
Huarás—neither recommended). **Chancos:** Chancos—thermal
baths. **Huallanca:** Huallanca—comfortable, government-operated.
Chimbote: Chimu, Pacifico. **Talara:** Royal, and at nearby **Cabo
Blanco:** Cabo Blanco Fishing Club, $25 double, American plan;
fishing boats $100 per day, plus $15 for tackle and bait; book
through Panagra.

RESTAURANTS AND NIGHT LIFE—**Lima:** The Gran Hotel Bolívar's dining room is elegant and excellent; dinner plus dancing
and entertainment in its Grill Bolívar, snacks and drinks in the
new main bar and men's bar. At the Hotel Crillon dining room
Peruvian specialties are delicious, and the Skyroom *boîte*-bar-
dining room is pleasant. The most beautiful restaurant in the
city—and one of the loveliest on the continent—is Las Trece
Monedas, in an exquisitely furnished eighteenth-century mansion;
be sure and have a look at every room, and order either Peruvian
or French dishes. Club 91 is atop an office building and affords
a splendid view; steaks and Italian specialties at rather steep
prices. Karamanduka is uninhibitedly Peruvian—and a barrel of
fun, with good beer and wine, wonderful national dishes, moderate
prices, and a delightful pair of sisters who are hostess-proprietors;
a don't-miss place. Cortizo is central and moderately priced, with
fine Peruvian specialties and beef dishes. Chez Victor is posh
and international. Others: Donatello's (Italian and reasonable),
Domino (ditto), Kuo Wa (Chinese), Chalet Suisse (more Peruvian than the name implies, and good), Lucho's and Pavillon
(both French). In the suburbs, try La Toscana, in Magdalena;
Chez André in Miraflores; Marseillaise and S.O.S., La Herradura;
and a marvelous all-you-can-eat chicken-only place called Granja

Azul, on the road to Chosica. For snacks and Yankee-style short-orders (including pasteurized milk shakes and sodas), the Crem Rica chain, throughout town, is very cheap and very good. Leading night spots include the aforementioned Grill Bolívar in the Gran Hotel Bolívar, the also aforementioned effervescent Kara-manduka, where everybody joins the singers and guitarists, and has a ball, the Skyroom of the Crillon, the Aquarium at the Lima Country Club, and La Tradición, with Peruvian music. Interesting bar-cafés include Ed's in Lima, Percy's Candlelight in San Isidro, and Sauco in Barranco. Elsewhere, the leading hotels' dining rooms are generally the best bets, although towns like Arequipa and Trujillo have interesting bars and cafés which are worth exploring.

PRIVATE CLUBS: The beautiful Lima Country Club doubles as a hotel-resort and its pool and tennis courts are open to paying guests, as well as members; cards for the pool are available also, at no charge, to guests of the Gran Hotel Bolívar. Others: Phoenix, Lima Golf, Los Incas, Lawn Tennis (with swimming pool), Rotary, Lions, and at Cabo Blanco, the earlier-mentioned Fishing Club (see Hotels).

Peruvian food specialties: The wonderful spices used by the Indians for centuries have been utilized by the creoles to create the most interesting and imaginative cuisine on the continent, with a number of superb dishes. Among them: *ceviche*—un-cooked fish (usually corvina) marinated in a dressing of lemon juice, hot peppers, onions; corn and sweet potatoes; *anticuchos* —beef hearts (and sometimes merely beef bits, cubes of fish, or chicken livers) skewered and broiled, dipped in a piquant sauce, and served with drinks; all kinds of sea foods uniquely prepared, including excellent shrimp, or *camarones,* and mussels, or *choros;* broiled chicken seasoned with *ají,* a popular local hot chili, is delicious, and so is corn (*cholo*), the Peruvian Indians' contribution to international gastronomy, prepared in many ways. Soup specialties include *sopa criolla* (noodles, spices, chopped beef) and *caldillo de huevo,* an egg dish. *Escabeche* is an unusual fish appetizer; and potatoes, or *papas,* as genuinely Peruvian as corn, are found in many varieties and prepared in many ways; one method, with cheese sauce, is delicious. Fruits are plentiful (particularly avocados). Rice is combined with mixed sea foods and chilies, emerging as *arroz con maniscos*. Milk is pasteurized in Lima, but possibly of more interest is the aforementioned pisco, a unique grape brandy out of which is made the delicious pisco sour. Peruvian wines are plentiful and good; so are the beers. Hardly Peruvian, but worthy of mention, are the Chinese restaurants, some of them excellent.

Index

ABC Shipping Guide, 58
Act of Chapultepec, 9
Aerolineas Argentinas, 53–54, 66, 76, 82
Africa, 6, 147
Agua Dulce River, 282
Air France, 54
Airlines, 21, 50–53. See also under individual countries
Alcoa Line, 58, 159
Alejijadinho (The Little Cripple), 127
Alessandri, Jorge Rodrigues, 239
Alianza Popular Revolucionario Americana, 331–33
Alitalia Airlines, 54
Alliance for Progress, 9, 11–14, 150, 167, 198, 240, 266
Almagro, Diego de, 237, 288, 329–30, 342, 351
Alta Gracia, Argentina, 92
Altiplano, Bolivia, 217, 219, 221
Alto da Serra, Brazil, 122
Alto Paraná River, Argentina, 88
Aluminium Company of Canada, 153
Alvarado, Pedro de, 288
Amigas Northeamericanos del Paraguay, Las, 167
Amapa, Brazil, 137
Ambato, Ecuador, 297–98, 302–3
American Automobile Association, 59
American Council of Learned Societies, 26
American Express Company, 21, 41, 46, 57
American Force for Cultural Popular Action, 23
American International Association for Economic and Social Development, 23
American Museum of Natural History, 27
American Society of Travel Agents, 21, 46
Amerindians, 156
Amazonas Territory, Venezuela, 205
Amazon Basin, Colombia, 269
Amazon River, 3, 4, 112, 135–37, 206, 288, 349–50
Anchieta, Rev. José de, 120
Ancón, Panama, 319
Ancón, Peru, 339
Ancud, Chile, 253
Andes Copper Mining Co., 255
Andes Mountains, XII-XIII, 1–4, 63, 68, 74, 90, 195, 202, 213, 221, 238, 278
Angel Falls, Venezuela, 202, 206
Anglo-Argentines, 70–71, 204
Anglo-Chileans, 244
Angostura, Venezuela, 195

Anthropological Museum, 27
Antillanca, Chile, 247
Antofagasta, Chile, 254
APA Airlines, 53
Apoquindo, Chile, 243
APRA movement, Peru, 331–33
Apure River, 205
Aramburu, Pedro Eugenio, 72
Arani, Bolivia, 230
Araucanian Indians, 214, 237
Arawak Indians, 195
Arcaya, Ignacio Luis, 17
Arequipa, Peru, 34–48
ARGENTINA, 3, 20, 65–100, 126, 163, 166, 219, 239
Argentine Airlines, 53–54, 66
Argentine-American Chamber of Commerce, 25
Argentine State Line, 56
Argentine Tourism Agency, 66
Arica, Chile, 219, 254
Arosemena Monroy, Carlos, 290
Artigas, José Gervasio, 178
Art Institute of Chicago, 27
Art of Brazilian Cookery, The, 143
Art of South American Cookery, The, 38
Asians in South America, 148
Asochinga, Argentina, 92
Association for International Development, 24
Association for Latin American Studies, 26
Asunción, Paraguay, 6, 67–68, 72, 89, 126, 164, 168–70
Atacama Desert, 3, 255
Atahualpa, Inca, 288, 329
Atesa Air Taxi, 286
Atlantic Ocean, 3
Atlantic Railroad, Colombia, 274–75
Atlántida, Uruguay, 186
Audiencia of Charcas, 218
Audiencia of Santa Fe, 264
Avensa Airlines, 54, 193
Avenue of the Americas, New York, 38
Avianca Airlines, 54, 261
Ayacucho, Peru, 348–49
Aymara Indians, 214, 217, 221, 327

Babahoyo, Ecuador, 294
Bahia, Brazil. See under Salvador, Brazil
Bahía Blanca, Argentina, 82
Balboa, Canal Zone, 216, 319
Balboa, Vasco de, 6, 312

Balcarce, Argentina, 82
Balsa boats, XII, 226
Banda Oriental, 58, 106, 178
Bandeirantes, 6, 106
Banditos, Colombia, 266–67
Banōs, Ecuador, 298, 302–3
Bariloche, Argentina, 82–85, 249
Barquisimeto, Venezuela, 195
Barranquilla, Colombia, 268–70
Bartica, British Guiana, 153
Bastias, Rodrigo de, 263, 312
Batista, Fulgencio, 10
Batlle y Ordóñfiez, José, 179
Battle of: Ayacucho, 218, 331; Boyaca,
    195; Ituzaingó, 178; Junín, 331;
    Pichincha, 289; Rancagua, 238
Bay of Panama, 317
Belalcázar, Sebastián de, 264, 280, 288
Belém, Brazil, 112, 134–35
Belém Novo, Brazil, 128
Belgrano, Argentina, 80
Belo Horizonte, Brazil, 64, 112, 127–28
Beltran, Pedro, 32
Berle, Adolph A., 11
Bernhard Dorp, Surinam, 158
Berta, Ruben M., 52
Betancourt, Romulo, 196–97
Bigiston, Surinam, 158
Binational chambers of commerce, 25
Bingham, Hiram, 344
Bío Bío River, 237, 250
Blanco party, Uruguay, 178–79
Bogotá, Colombia, 8, 11, 195, 263–64, 268,
    272, 275, 275–78
Bogotá River Falls, Colombia, 276
Boguete, Panama, 321
Bolívar, Simón, 1, 2, 7–8, 39, 195–96, 201,
    203–4, 218, 231, 264, 271, 274, 276–
    77, 289, 292, 331, 338
BOLIVIA, 6, 8, 15, 38, 68, 73, 86, 163,
    166, 213–14, 215–34, 239
Booth Steamship Company, 58
Botafogo, Dolores, 143
Bowles, Chester, 15
Braniff Airlines, 54
Brasilia, Brazil, 52, 63, 104, 109, 111,
    122–25
BRAZIL, 3, 6–8, 10, 15, 20, 38, 63, 69,
    73, 88, 101–43, 163, 166, 171, 188
Brazil, Northern, 64, 105
Brazilian American Chamber of Com-
    merce, 25
Brazilian Coffee Institute, 25
Brazilian Government Trade Bureau, 102
Brazilian Northeast Development Agency,
    109–10
Bridge of San Luis Rey, The, 338
British Commonwealth, 209
BRITISH GUIANA, 144–61
British Guiana Consolidated Goldfields,
    153
British Guiana Airways, 145
British Guiana Tourist Committee, 145
British Honduras, 316
British Information Services, 145
British in South America, 6, 7, 17, 68–
    70, 85, 93, 178, 195

British Overseas Airways Corp., 54
Brooklyn Museum, 27
Brown, John Mason, 45
Brynner, Yul, XI
Buenaventura, Colombia, 267, 281–82
Buenos Aires, Argentina, XIII, 6, 19, 39,
    63, 66, 68–69, 76–81, 87–88, 90, 114,
    164, 171, 178, 185, 247, 255
Bulnes, Manuel, 238
Bunau-Varilla, Philippe, 313
Burke, Arleigh B., 294
Burnham, Forbes, 150
"Bush" Negroes, 147

Caacupé, Paraguay, 172
Cabot, Sebastian, 67–68
Cabrioles River, 191, 203
Cacheuta, Argentina, 90
Cajamanca, Peru, 329
Cajamarquilla, Peru, 339
Calama, Chile, 254
Caldas, Colombia, 278
Cali, Colombia, 264, 279–80, 282
Callao, Peru, 6, 330–31, 339
Callejón de Huaylas, Peru, 353
Calvo, Samuel, 300
Canada, 109
Canadian Pacific Airways, 54
Canaima, Venezuela, 206
Canal Zone, 311, 314–15, 315–16
Cape Horn, 3, 240, 312
Capiatá, Paraguay, 172
Carabelleda, Venezuela, 202
Caracas, Venezuela, XIII, 63, 195, 199–
    202, 274
Carás, Peru, 352–54
Carahue, Chile, 250
CARE, 24
Caribbean Sea, 3, 146, 195, 267–68, 273
Caribbean Tourist Association, 145, 194,
    262
Carib Indians, 194–95
Cariocas, 113
Carlos Paz, Argentina, 92
Carnival: Rio de Janeiro, 114, 118;
    Montevideo, 183
Carrera, José Miguel, 238
Cartagena, Chile, 243
Cartagena, Colombia, 27–73, 263–64
Carter, William A., 314
Casa Pangue, Chile, 85, 249
Cascaja Island, Colombia, 281
Castro, Chile, 253
Castro, Fidel, 11–12, 15–16, 109–10, 150,
    198, 315
Catatumbo River, 204
Catholic Relief Services, 24
Cauca Valley, Colombia, 279
Causa Airlines, 54, 176
Caxias, Brazil, 128
Cayenne, French Guiana, 147, 155
Cayma, Peru, 347
CEA Airlines, 54
Ceara, Brazil, 134
Central America, 4
Central Magdelena Valley, Colombia, 269

Cerro de Pasco, Peru, 351
Cerro de Pasco Mining Corp., 351
Cervantes, Saavedra de, Miguel, XI
Chacaltaya, Bolivia, 228
Chachani volcano, 346
Chaco, 3, 64, 74, 86, 166, 170–71, 219
Chamber of Commerce of Latin America
   in the United States, 25
Chañaral, Chile, 255
Chan Chan, Peru, 352
Chanchán River, 297
Chancos, Peru, 353
Charles II, King, 88, 313
Charley's Aunt, 1
Charrua Indians, 177
Chase Manhattan Bank, 26
Chavin civilization, 327
Chiari, Roberto F., 315
Chibcha Indians, 4, 6, 214, 263, 276
Chicago Museum of Natural History, 27
CHILE, 3, 15, 20, 50, 71, 73, 83, 85, 90,
   213–14, 219, 235–60, 331
Chilean-American Chamber of Commerce,
   25
Chilean Exploration Co., 255
Chilean Naval Academy, 244
Chillan, Chile, 247, 249
Chillos Valley of Ecuador, 305
Chiloé Island, Chile, 253
Chimbote, Peru, 352–54
Chimu culture, 338–52
Chiriquí Highlands, Panama, 321
Choshuenco, Chile, 247
Chosica, Peur, 339
Christ of the Andes statue, 71, 239, 246
Christian Science Monitor, 57
Chuquicamata, Chile, 255
Church World Service, 24
Chuy, Uruguay, 187
Cincinnati, Colombia, 274
City Service Travel Agency, 77
Ciudad Bolívar, Venezuela, 195, 204–5
Climate, 31. See also under individual
   countries
Clubs, private, 43–44. See also under in-
   dividual countries
Cochabama, Bolivia, 220, 226, 229–30
Cochrane, Lord, 244, 331
Coffee-growing, Brazil, 106
COLOMBIA, 3, 4, 8, 10, 15, 20, 195,
   202, 213–14, 261–85
Colombian National Tourist Board, 262
Colombian Safaris, Ltd., 269
Columbus, Christopher, 5–6, 146, 195,
   312, 320
Columbia University, 45
Colón, Archipiélago de, 306
Colón, Canal Zone, 316, 319–20
Colonia, Uruguay, 177, 187
Colonia Suiza, Uruguay, 187
Colorado parties: Paraguay, 167; Uruguay,
   178
Colorado River, 74
Color bar, 14
Commercial Bureau, 8
Commewijne District, Surinam, 157
Commewijne River, 157

Communist countries, 11, 14–16, 315
Comodoro Rivadavia, Argentina, 86
Compañía Ecuatoriana de Turismo, 306
Concepción, Chile, 249–50
Concepción, Paraguay, 171–72
Concon, Chile, 245
Condado Caribbean Hotel Corp., 160
Congress of Panama, 8
Congress of the United Provinces of the
   Rio de la Plata, 90
Conquest of Peru, The, 213
Conquistadors, Spanish, 6
Conservative parties: Chile, 238; Colom-
   bia, 264, Ecuador, 289
Constitución, Chile, 249
Continental Divide, 353
Cook, Milly, 355
Copa, Airlines, 310
Copacabana, Bolivia, 227–28
Copiapó, Chile, 255
Cordillera Blanca, Peru, 353
Cordillera Negra, Peru, 353
Córdoba, Argentina, 6, 64, 91–92
Coro, Venezuela, 195
Coroico, Bolivia, 229
Coronel, Chile, 250
Corrientes, Argentina, 89
Costa, Lucio, 123
Costs, 47–50, 54–57. See also under indi-
   vidual countries
Cotopaxi volcano, 303
Cottica River, 158
Crafts, 39–40. See also under individual
   countries
Credit cards, 41
Creoles: Guianas, 148; other countries, 6,
   69, 331
Creole Week, Uruguay, 183
Cristóbal, Panama, 316, 319–20
Cruzeiro do Sul Airlines, 54
Cuba, 10–11, 198
Cuenca, Ecuador, 214, 295
Cuisines, 38. See also under individual
   countries
Cultural exchanges, 15
Cumaná, Venezuela, 195
Cuna Indians, Panama, 320–21
Curitiba, Brazil, 64–125
Currencies, 41. See also under individual
   countries
Customs, 36–37
Cuyuni River, 153
Cuzco, Peru, 31, 214, 272, 287, 329, 340–
   45

D'Aguiar, Peter, 150
Damas River, 251
Darwin, Charles, 293, 306
Daule, Ecuador, 294
David, Panama, 321
Declaration of Punta del Este, 13
Defoe, Daniel, 210
De Garay, Juan, 68
De Lesseps, Ferdinand, 313, 320
Del Pato Canyon, Peru, 353
Delta Line, 56–57

Demerara River, 153
De Solis, Juan Diaz, 67
Devil's Island, French Guiana, 155
Devil's Nose, Ecuador, 297
Dichato, Chile, 250
Dirección Nacional de Turismo: Argentina, 66; Bolivia, 216; Ecuador, 287; Venezuela, 194
Dockstader, Frederic, 27
Domburg, Surinam, 158
Dominican order, 88
Dominican Republic, 10, 72, 197–98
Don Quixote, XI
Douglas, William O., 14
Drake, Sir Francis, 271, 273, 312
Drinking water, 30
Driving, automobile, 59
Dutch Guiana ex-, 144–61
Dutch in South America, 6, 146
Dutra, Eurico Gaspar, 108
Duty-free purchases, 37–37

Eboué, Félix, 148
Eastern South America, introduction to, 61–64
ECUADOR, XIII, 213–14, 264, 286–309
Ecuadorian-American Chamber of Commerce, 25
Ecuadorian Naval Academy, 294
Ecuadorian-Peruvian border dispute, 290–91
Eisenhower, Dwight D., 11–12, 220
Ekeko, god of, 233
El Baru, Panama, 321
El Bolsón, Argentina, 84
El Dorado, 63, 262, 264
El Misti volcano, 364
El Salvador, Chile, 255
"El Supremo," 165
El Valle, Panama, 321
El Volcán, Chile, 243
El Volcán, Panama, 321
Eloy Alfaro, Flavio, 298
Emanuels, S. D., 149
Embassies and consulates, American, 40–41
Empresa Colombiana de Turismo, 262, 268
Encantado Valley, Argentina, 84
Encarnación, Paraguay, 88, 172
Ensenada, Chile, 252
Entre Rios, Argentina, 89
Esmeraldas, Ecuador, 288, 294
Esmeraldas River, 294
Espejo Peak, Venezuela, 203
Essequibo River, 153
Estancias, 74, 80, 184
Europeans in South America, 6, 213–14

Falcón, Juan, 196
Falkland Islands, 93
Fares: air, 48–50; ship, 55–57
Farrelones, Chile, 247
Fascists, Chile, 239
Faucett Airlines, 53, 325–26
Febrerista party, Paraguay, 167

Federation of the West Indies, 209
Federmann, Nikolaus, 195, 264
Feldman, Susana Redondo de, 45
Ferdinand VI, King, 271
Fiat factories, Argentina, 92
Filho, João Café, 109
Film availability, 35. See also under individual countries
First Bank of Boston, 26
Fishing, Uruguay, 188
Flores, Juan, 298
Fonda del Sol Restaurant, 38
Food and Agricultural Organization, 22
Food specialties, 38. See also under individual countries
Ford Foundation, 24
Foreign Policy Association-World Affairs Center, 27–28
Fortaleza, Brazil, 133–34
Fort Santa Teresa, Uruguay, 186
Forty-niners, 313
Foz do Iguassú, Brazil, 126, 187
Francia, Jose Gaspar Rodrigues, 88, 165
Franciscan order, 177, 279, 300–1
Franco, Francisco, 72
Freighter travel, 58
French Government Tourist Office, 145
FRENCH GUIANA, 144–61
French in South America, 6, 146
Friedlander, Paul J. C., 37
Frondizi, Arturo, 72–73
Fusagasugá, Colombia, 276

Galápagos Islands, 293, 306
Gallegos, Romulo, 196
García Carbajal, Manuel de, 346
García, Diego, 67
Garcia, Lou, 45
Garua, 325
Gatun Locks, Panama, 321
Gauchos, XI, 2, 66, 69, 178, 184
Georgetown, British Guiana, 151–52
Girard, Alexander, 38
Goethals, G. W., 314
Goiaz, Brazil, 122
Gómez, Juan Vicente, 202–3
Gomez, Laureano, 265
Gonzales, Godofredo, 199
Good Neighbor Policy, 10
Goodwin, Richard, 11
Gordon, Lincoln, 11, 110
Goulart, João, 110
Grace, J. Peter, 26
Grace, W. R., and Co., 25, 55, 334
Grace Line, 20, 25, 55–56
Grace Log, 25
Graf von Spee, battleship, 186
Gran Chaco, 168
Gran Colombia, Republic of, 6, 195, 204, 264–65, 289
Guaíba River, 128
Guamba Indians, Colombia, 281
Guaqui, Bolivia, 226
Guarani Indians, Paraguay, 88, 163–65, 172
Guarani language, 164

Guarujá, Brazil, 122
Guayaquil, Ecuador, 50, 291–94, 331
Guayaquil, Gulf of, 293
Guayaquil-Quito Railway, 295–98
Guayas River, 291, 294
Guevara, "Che," 110
Guiana region, Venezuela, 199
GUIANAS, THE, 3, 7, 63–64, 144–61
Guide to All Cruises, 57
Gulistān, 19

Handa, Colombia, 276
Harlem, Surinam, 157
Harman, Archer, 296
Harman, John, 296
Harrison, Faustiono, 180
Hawkins, Sir John, 270–71
Haya de la Torre, Victor, 331–32
Hay-Pauncefote Treaty, 313
"Hear How to Converse in Spanish," 45
Hemispherica, 24
Heredia, Pedro de, 270
Hilton Hotels International, 21, 209–10,
    257, 311, 318, 321, 323
Hilton, Ronald, 27
Hispanic American Report, 27
Holy Week celebrations, Popayán, Co-
    lombia, 281
Hotel Corporation of America, 21, 308
Hualanca, Peru, 353
Huancayo, Peru, 345, 348
Huaráa, Peru, 352–54
Huáscar, Inca, 288, 329
Huatajata, Bolivia, 226, 228
Huayna Capac, Inca, 329
Huigra, Ecuador, 297
Hull, Cordell, 10
Humboldt Current, 294, 325
Hurlingham, Argentina, 80
Hutterites, 171

Ibañez, José, 239
Iguassú Falls, 64, 74, 86–87, 112, 125–27,
    170–71
Iguassú River, 86–87
Iles du Salut, French Guiana, 154–55
Inca Indians, 4, 6, 90, 214, 217, 236, 287,
    303, 326–30, 338–39, 341
Indian markets, Ecuador, 303
Indians, South American, 6, 7, 213
Inoculations, 30
Inquilinos, Chile, 237–38
Institute of Hispanic-American and Luso-
    Brazilian Studies, 26
Insurance, Travel, 41
Inter-American Association for Democracy
    and Freedom, 24
Inter-American Children's Institute, 9
Inter-American Commission on Women, 9
Inter-American Conferences, 8, 11, 13,
    110, 176, 185
Inter-American Development Bank, 23, 220
Inter-American Driving Permit, 59
Inter-American Highway, 310
Inter-American Indian Institute, 9

Inter-American Institute of Agricultural
    Sciences, 9
Inter-American Press Association, 24
Inter-American Schools Service, 26
Inter-American Statistical Institute, 9
Inter-American Treaty of Reciprocal As-
    sistance, 9
Intercom, 28
Intercontinental Hotels Corp., 21, 189, 207,
    283
International Bank for Reconstruction and
    Development. *See under* World Bank
International Confederation of Free Trade
    Unions, 25
International Driver's License, 58
International Petroleum Co., 354
International Union of American Re-
    publics, 8
Iparanga River, 107
Iquique, Chile, 254
Iquitos, Peru, 137, 349–50
Isabel, Princess, 108
Islands of Sun and Moon, Bolivia, 228
Islas Malvinas, 93
Isle of Marguerita, Venezuela, 202
Itatiaia National Park, Brazil, 119
Itineraries, 47–48
It's Not Too Late in Latin America, 26

Jagan, Cheddi, 149–50
James, Preston, E., 63
Jesuit order, 5, 86, 88, 120, 164–65, 172,
    177, 272, 337–38, 342
Jesús, Paraguay, 172
Jesús, Peru, 347
Jesús Maria, Argentina, 92
Jewish settlement, Surinam, 158
Jivaro Indians, Ecuador, 305–6
Joden Savannah, Surinam, 158
John VI, King, 107
Johnson, H. L., 26
Joint Committee on Latin American
    Studies, 26
Journal of Inter-American Studies, 27
Jujuy, Argentina, 91
Juli, Peru, 348
Juliaca, Peru, 347
Juliana, Queen, 149
Junín de los Andes, Argentina, 251

Kaieteur Falls, British Guiana, 153–54
Kaiser factories, Argentina, 92
Kellogg Foundation, 24
Kennedy, John F., 10–12, 14–15, 36, 109,
    150, 167, 198, 220, 266, 290
Kennedy, Mrs. John F., 198, 266
Kipling, Rudyard, XI
KLM Royal Dutch Airlines, 54
Knight, Frances G., 29
Kubitschek, Juscelino, 109, 123

La Asunción, Venezuela
La Coronilla, Uruguay, 187–88
La Cumbre, Argentina, 92
La Dorada, Colombia, 276

La Falda, Argentina, 92
La Guaira, Venezuela, 200, 202
La Herradura, Peru, 339
La Paloma, Uruguay, 187
La Parva, Chile, 247
La Paz, Bolivia, XII, 31, 39, 218, 220, 222–26, 254
La Paz River, 217
La Plata, Argentina, 81
La Punta, Peru, 339
La Quinua, Peru, 349
La Serena, Chile, 214, 255
Las Rabonas, Argentina, 92
Las Salinas, Chile, 245
Las Toscas, Uruguay, 186
LAB Airlines, 54, 216
Labor party, Bolivia, 220
Lagoa dos Patos, Brazil, 128
Laguna Beach, Venezuela, 202
Lagunillas, Chile, 247
Lake: Buenos Aires, 86; Caburgua, 25; Calafguén, 25; Colico, 251; Epuyén, 84; Frias, 85; Guillelmo, 84; Gutiérrez, 84; Lacar, 84; Llanquihue, 251–52; Maracaibo, 3, 194, 199; Mascarai, 84; Mirim, 187; Moreno, 84; Nahuel Huapí, 83–84; Panguipulli, 251; Pirehueico, 251; Puelo, 84; Puyehue, 252; Quilleihue, 251; San Roque, 92; Titicaca, 217, 221, 226–28, 327, 348; Todos los Santos, 251–52; Traful, 84; Valencia, 203; Villarica, 251; Ypacaraí, 170
Lake Districts: Argentina, 74, 82–85; Chile, 240, 247–52
Land of Lace and Legend, 167
Language, 44–45. See also under individual countries
Lanín National Park, Argentina, 84
Laraquete, Chile, 250
Larrazabal, Wolfgang, 197
Latacunga, Ecuador, 298–99
Latin America, 63
Latin American Business Highlights, 26
Latin American Institute, Columbia University, 27
Latour Travel Agency, 237, 257
Laundry service, 32
LAV Airlines, 193
Lavalleja, Juan Antonio, 178, 187–88
League of Women Voters, 24
Leguía, Augusto B., 351
Lezo, Blas de, 271
Liberal parties: Colombia, 265; Ecuador, 289; Paraguay, 167
Lima, Peru, 6, 39, 50, 68, 90, 330, 334–39
Limay River, 84
Lindbergh, Charles A., 51
Lippmann, Walter, 111–12
Llaima, Chile, 247
Llanos, Venezuela, 3, 199
Llao-Llao, Argentina, 84
Lleras Camargo, Alberto, 266–67
Llolleo, Chile, 243
López, Carlos Antonio, 165
López, Francisco Solano, 69, 107, 165–66, 169, 173
Los Caracas, Venezuela, 202
Lota, Chile, 250
Luján, Argentina, 81
Lynch, Eliza, 165, 173

Maca Indians, Paraguay, 170
Macapá, Brazil, 137
Machachi, Ecuador, 298–99
Machu Picchu, Peru, 340–45
Mackenzie, British Guiana, 153
Macuto, Venezuela, 202
Madden Dam, Canal Zone, 319
Magdalena River, 3, 263, 267, 269, 275
Magellan, Ferdinand, 6, 67, 85, 180
Magellan, Strait of, 3
Mahdia, British Guiana, 153
Mail, 44
Maipo, Chile, 243
Maldonado, Uruguay, 186
Mallasilla Valley, Bolivia, 229
Mamelucos, Brazil, 103
Mamiña, Chile, 254
Manaus, Brazil, 112, 135–37, 350
Mancos, Peru, 353
Manizales, Colombia, 278
Mannerville, Gaston, 148
Mansfield, Mike, 17
Manta, Ecuador, 295
Maracaibo, Venezuela, 203–4
Maracara Valley, Peru, 353
Maracay, Venezuela, 202
Maranhão, Brazil, 134
Mar Chiquita, Argentina, 82
Mar del Plata, Argentina, 81–82
Margarita Island, Venezuela, 205–6
Martin Tours, 46
Marowijne District, Surinam, 158
Marowijne River, 158
Maryknoll Missioners, 25
Mato Grosso tablelands, 3
Mayan civilizations, 4
Mazaruni River, 153
Meals for Millions, 25
Medillín, Colombia, 267, 278–79
Melocotón, Chile
Mendoza, Argentina, XII, 90, 243
Mendoza, Pedro de, 68
Menetue, Chile, 251
Mennonites, Paraguay, 171
Mera, Ecuador, 298
Mercedes, Uruguay, 187
Mérida, Venezuela, 203
Mesopotamia, Argentina, 86
Mestizos, 7, 214
Metropolitan Touring, 287
Mexico City, 9
Mina Clavero, Argentina, 92
Minas Gerais, Brazil, 106, 127
Minas, Uruguay, 187
Miramar, Argentina, 82
Miranda, Carmen, XI
Miranda, Francisco, 195
Misiones, Argentina, 86
Misiones settlements, 88, 172
Mistral, Gabriela, 255

Mitre, Bartolomé, 69, 79
Mochica civilization, 327
Moengo, Surinam, 158–59
Mollendo, Peru, 347
Monte Alegre, Brazil, 135
Montecristi, Ecuador, 295
Monterrey, Peru, 353
Montevideo, Uruguay, XII, 9, 63, 177, 180–84
Montt, Manuel, 238
Montuno people, Panama, 321
Moore, Lloyd R., 51
Moore-McCormack Line, 57
Moors, 5, 7
Mora, José A., 9
Morgan, Henry, 312, 320
Morrison, deLesseps, 14
Motilone Indians, Venezuela, 204
Mount: Aconcagua, 3, 74, 248; Avila, 200; Cotopaxi, 298; Huascaran, 353; Illimani, 223; Pichincha, 301
Movimiento Nacionalisto Revolucionario, Bolivia, 219
Mulattoes, 7
Muñoz-Marín, Luis, 16
Museum of the American Indian, 27
Museum of the Hispanic Society of America, 27

Nación, La, 72
Nanay River, 350
Napoleon, 107, 264
Napo River, 288
Nasca-Paracas civilization, 327
Natal, Brazil, 105, 133–34
National Catholic Welfare Conference, 24
National Council of Churches, 24
National Federation of Coffee Growers of Colombia, 25
National Front coalition, Colombia, 266
Nazis, German, 166, 186, 219
Negro Creek, Surinam, 158
Negroes in South America, 6–7, 38, 103–5, 147, 272, 289
Neocohea, Argentina, 82
Nevado del Ruiz, Colombia, 278
Neves, Tancredo, 111
New Amsterdam, British Guiana, 153
New Amsterdam colony, 146–47
New Granada, 195, 264, 312
New Orleans, Louisiana, 14
New York City, 146
New York Herald Tribune, 57
New York Times, 17, 37, 57, 150
New York University Junior Year in Brazil, 27
Niagara Falls, 87, 154, 206
Nicaragua, 10, 167, 275, 313
Niemeyer, Oscar, 38, 123, 127
Nieuw Amsterdam, Surinam, 137
Nieuw Nickerie, Surinam, 158–59
Niterói, Brazil, 115
Nixon, Richard, 12, 198
Nono, Argentina, 92
North America, 6
North Americans, designation of, 18
Nova Friburgo, Brazil, 119

Nova Lima, Brazil, 128
Novo Hamburgo, Brazil, 128
Nueva Helvecia, Uruguay, 187

Obrajes, Bolivia, 224
Ocú, Panama, 321
Odría, Manuel, 10, 332
Official Steamship Guide, 58
Oficina Nacional de Turismo del Uruguay, 176
O'Higgins, Bernardo, 238, 249–50
Ojeda, Alonso de, 146, 195
Ojeda, Ponzo de, 263
Old Panama City, Panama, 318
Oligarchial governments, 7
Olinda, Brazil, 105, 133
Olivos, Argentina, 80
Ollantaytambo, Peru, 345
Operation Bootstrap, 15
Orcellana, Francisco de, 288
Organization of American States, 8, 9, 14, 16, 22, 23, 59, 198, 266
Organization of Central American States, 315
Orinoco River, 3, 5, 146, 202, 205–6
Oruro, Bolivia, 232
Osorno, Chile, 247, 251–52
Osorno volcano, Chile, 251
Otavalo, Ecuador, 303–5, 348
Ouro Preto, Brazil, 112, 127–28

Package tours, 47–48
Pachacamac, Peru, 339
Pachacutec, Inca, 238
Packing, 32
Paez, José Antonio, 196
Pama de Arrieros, Peru, 347
Pampa, 3, 64, 70, 74, 90, 92
Pampatar, Venezuela, 206
Pampulha, Brazil, 127
Panagra Airlines, 20, 25, 43, 45, 50–52, 66, 176, 216, 236, 246, 262, 280, 287, 311, 326, 334, 338, 354, 355
Panair do Brasil Airlines, 54
PANAMA, 6, 32, 50, 68, 213–14, 264–65, 310–24
Panama Canal, 10, 214, 311, 315, 321
Panama City, Panama, 316–19
Panama, Isthmus of, 3, 312
Panama National Tourist Commission, 311
Panamá Vieja, 318
Pan American Airways, 54
Pan American Coffee Bureau, 25
Pan American Health Organization, 9, 10, 23
Pan American Highway, 9, 21, 59, 202, 204
Pan American Institute of Geography and History, 9
Pan Americanism, 7
Pan American Sanitary Bureau, 23
Pan American Society of the United States, 25
Pan American Union, 8, 22
Paracas, Peru, 349
Paraguana Peninsula, Venezuela, 204

Paraguarí, Paraguay, 172
PARAGUAY, 8, 10, 13, 64, 69, 72–73, 86, 88, 126, 151, 162–74, 176, 178, 219
Paraguay River, 67, 166, 168, 170–71
Paramaribo, Surinam, 156–57
Paraná, Argentina, 67, 89–90
Paranam, Surinam, 159
Paraná River, 3, 67, 89
Parnaíba, Brazil, 133–34
Pasamayo Grande, Peru, 340
Passports, 29
Pasto, Colombia, 264
Patagonia, 3, 4, 64, 66, 74, 85–86
Patiño family, 216, 230
Pativilca, Peru, 353
Paulistas, 114, 122
Paz Estenssoro, Victor, 219, 220
Peabody Museum, 27
Pearl Islands, Panama, 319
Peasants' Leagues, Brazil, 109
Pedro I, Emperor, 107, 118, 121
Pedro II, Emperor, 108
Penalolen, Chile, 243
People's National Congress, British Guiana, 150
People's Progressive Party, British Guiana, 149
Pereira, Colombia, 278
Pérez Jiménez, Marcos, 10, 196–97, 199, 200–1, 203
PERU, XII, 2, 3, 6, 10, 21, 68, 213–14, 217, 226, 264, 287, 312, 325, 359
Peruvian-American Chamber of Commerce, 25
Peruvian-Ecuadorian border dispute, 290–91
Peruvian Naval Academy, 339
Peruvian Touring and Automobile Club, 326
Peru, Viceroyalty of, 312
Perón, Eva, 71–72
Perón, Juan D., 11, 66, 71–72, 75, 110, 167
Petrohué, Chile, 252
Petropólis, Brazil, 108, 118
Peulla, Chile, 85, 252
Philip IV, King, 271
Photography, 34–36
Pica, Chile, 254
Pichú-Pichú volcano, 346
Pilar, Paraguay, 172
Piriápolis, Uruguay, 186
Piribebuy, Paraguay, 172
Pisac, Peru, 340, 345, 348
Pisco, Peru, 349
Pizarro brothers, 388
Pizarro, Gonzalo, 239, 342, 388
Pizarro, Francisco, 2, 6, 213, 237, 264, 280, 288, 312, 329–30, 336, 346
Pizón, Vicente Yáñez, 104
Playas, Ecuador, 294
Pluna Airlines, 54
Pomata, Peru, 348
Ponce Enriquez, Camilio, 290
Popayán, Colombia, 264, 267, 280–81
Porlomar, Venezuela, 206
Portales, Diego, 238

Porteños, 76
Portillo, Chile, 246
Pôrto Alegre, Brazil, 52, 64, 112, 128
Portobelo, Panama, 312, 320
Port of Spain, Trinidad, 209
Portuguese in South America, 5–7, 17, 68, 105, 146, 178
Porvenir, Chile, 253
Posadas, Argentina, 88–89, 172
Potosí, Bolivia, 214, 218, 230–31
Potrerillos, Argentina, 90
Prado, Manuel, 332
Pradomar, Colombia, 269
Pre-Inca civilizations, 326–27, 338–39
Prensa, La, 72
Prescott, William H., 213
Press of the Americas, 24
Primavera, Paraguay, 171–72
Providencia Island, Colombia, 275
Pucallpa, Peru, 350–51
Pucón, Chile, 251
Pucusana, Peru, 339
Puerto Alegre, Argentina, 85
Puerto Ayacucho, Venezuela, 205
Puerto Blest, Argentina, 85
Puerto Cabello, Venezuela, 196, 204
Puerto Colombia, Colombia, 269
Puerto Deseado, Argentina, 86
Puerto Frias, Argentina, 85
Puerto Iguazú, Argentina, 87, 126
Puerto Madryn, Argentina, 85
Puerto Montt, Chile, 85, 240, 249, 252
Puerto Rico, 15–16
Puerto Varas, Chile, 252
Punata Valley, Bolivia, 230
Puno, Peru, 226, 348
Punta Arenas, Chile, 253
Punta del Este, Uruguay, 14, 184–86, 188
Punta Hermosa, Peru, 339
Puracé, Colombia, 281
Puruchoco, Peru, 339

Quadros, Jânio, 109–11, 120
Quechua language, 329
Quesada, Gonzalo Jimenerez de, 263
Quetrupillan Volcano, Chile, 251
Quillacollo, Bolivia, 230
Quintero, Chile, 245
Quito, Ecuador, 6, 31, 39, 214, 272, 299–302, 329
Quito-Guayaquil Railway, 295–98
Quito, Kingdom of, 288

Radical party, Chile, 240
Radicals of the People party, Argentina, 73
Rahue River, Chile, 251
Railroads, 21
Raleigh, Sir Walter, 147
Rancagua, Chile, 249
Ransa Airlines, 193
RAS Airlines, 54
Real Airlines, 53
Recife, Brazil, 64, 105, 132–33
Renison, Sir Patrick, 150

Reyes, Argentina, 91
Reynolds Metal Co., 153
Rincón del Bonete, Uruguay, 188
Riobamba, Ecuador, 297
Rio de Janeiro, Brazil, XII, 2, 9, 63, 102, 105–6, 110–12, 113–19
Rio de Janeiro, state of, 119
Rio de Janeiro Tourist Office, 102
Río de la Plata, 3, 6, 67, 74, 80, 177
Río Gallegos, Argentina, 86
Rio Grande de Norte, Brazil, 133
Rio Grande do Sul, Brazil, 52
Río Mar, Panama, 321
Rio Negro, Brazil, 135–36
Río Negro, Uruguay, 188
Río Primero, Argentina, 92
Rio Treaty, 9
Rivera, Uruguay, 188
Rocafuerte, Vicente, 289
Rocha, Uruguay, 186
Rockefeller Foundation, 24, 347
Robinson Crusoe, 210
Rojas Pinella, Gustavo, 10, 265
Roosevelt, Franklin D., 10, 166, 311
Roosevelt, Mrs. Franklin D., 12
Roosevelt, Theodore, 311, 313
Rosario, Argentina, 89
Rosario, Paraguay, 171
Rosas, Juan Manuel de, 69, 107
Rosas, Juan Martínez de, 238
Royale Island, French Guiana, 155
Rule, Colter, 30
Rusk, Dean, 12, 17

Saadi, 19
Saavedra, Hernando Arias de, 68
Sabará, Brazil, 128
Sacsahuaman Fortress, Peru, 340
Safaris, Colombia, 269
Saint Laurent, French Guiana, 155–56, 158
Saint Rose of Lima, 336–37
Salinas, Ecuador, 294
Salta, Argentina, 64, 91, 255
Salto Chico rapids, Uruguay, 187
Salto Grande, Uruguay, 187–88
Salto, Uruguay, 187
Salvador (Bahia), Brazil, 38, 64, 112, 129–32
San Andrés Island, Colombia, 275
San Bartolo, Peru, 339
San Bernardino, Paraguay, 170
San Blas Islands, Panama, 320–21
San Carlos, Panama, 321
San Fernando de Apure, Venezuela, 205
San Ignacio Miní, Argentina, 88
San Isidro, Argentina, 81
San José de Maipó, Chile, 243
San José, Uruguay, 188
San Martín de los Andes, Argentina, 84
San Martín, José de, 7, 39, 75, 78, 90, 218, 238, 292, 331, 338, 349
San Pedro Claver, 272–73
Santa Clara, Panama, 321
Santa Cruz, Argentina, 86
Santa Cruz, Bolivia, 232

Santa Fe, Argentina, 89–90
Santa Marta, Colombia, 263, 273–75
Santarém, Brazil, 135
Santa Rosa, Peru, 340
Santiago, Chile, 6, 83, 85, 241–43
Santo Amano Island, Brazil, 122
Santo Domingo, Chile, 243
Santo Domingo de los Colorados, Ecuador, 303, 305
Santos, Brazil, 105, 112, 119–22
São Jerônimo, Brazil, 128
São Luiz, Brazil, 133–34
São Paulo, Brazil, 38, 102, 109, 112, 119–22, 171
São Vicente, Brazil, 105, 120, 122
Sapa Inca, the, 328
Saquisilí, Ecuador, 303
Saramacca River, 157
SATGA Airways, 145
Saturin Travel Agency, 114
Scandinavian Airlines System, 54
Schlesinger, Arthur A., Jr., 11
School of Inter-American Studies, University of Florida, 27
Sears Roebuck, 26
Segregation, racial, 14
Selvatours Travel Agency, 136
Serra dos Orgãos National Park, Brazil, 119
Sertão, Brazil, 64, 104, 122
Servicio Nacional de Turismo de Chile, 236
Sheraton Corporation of America, 21, 207
Shipboard life, 57–58
Shipping companies, 54–58
Shopping, 39–40. *See also* under individual countries
Sierra de Aconquija, Argentina, 90
Sierra de Cordoba, Argentina, 92
Sierra Nevada de Santa Marta, Colombia, 274
Sierra Nevada, Venezuela, 203
Sight-seeing and guides, 42–43
Siles, Herman, 220
Sillustani, Peru, 348
Silva, Colombia, 281
Skiing: Bolivia, 229; Chile, 245–47; Colombia, 278
Smithsonian Institution, 254
Society of Brothers, 171–73
Socosani, Peru, 347
Solgar, Colombia, 274
Solís, Juan Diaz de, 177
Solís, Uruguay, 186
Somoza family, Nicaragua, 10, 167
South Africa, 71
South America: Alphabetically, XVI; area, 2; population, 2; geography, 2–4; climate, 4, 31; history, 4–17; tourism, promotion of, 19–22; organizations dealing with, 22–28; costs of travel, 47–50; tourist cards and visas, 28; inoculations and health, 30; customs, 36; food specialties, 38; shopping, 39–40; currencies, 41; tipping,

41; sightseeing, 42–43; private clubs, 43–44; language, 44–45. *See also* under individual countries
Soviet Union, 10, 109
Spaniards in South America, 5–7, 17, 64, 68, 72, 146, 195, 213–14, 312–13, 329–31
Stado Novo, 108
Stanley, Falkland Islands, 93
Steamships, 21
Stevenson, Adlai E., 12, 13, 198
Stoelmans Islands, Surinam, 158
Stone, Edward, 318
Strait of Magellan, 73, 93, 253
Stroessner, Alfredo, 10, 13, 72, 166–67, 173
Sucre, Antonio José de, 218, 231, 289, 300–1, 331
Sucre, Bolivia, 218, 231–32
Sucúa, Ecuador, 305
Sugar estates, British Guiana, 152–53
SURINAM, 20, 144–61
Surinam Airways, 145
Surinam District, Surinam, 158
Surinam Tourist Bureau, 145
Surinam Tourist Development Board, 145, 147
Suriname River, 157
Swissair, 54

Tabarangué, Paraguay, 172
Taboga Island, Panama, 319
Tacna-Arica dispute, 331
Tacna, Peru, 254
Taganga, Colombia, 274
Talara, Peru, 50, 353
Talca, Chile, 249
Talcahuano, Chile, 250
Talsa Airlines, 310
TAM Airlines, 326
Tapsa Airlines, 326
Temuco, Chile, 250
Tequendama Falls, Colombia, 276
Teresópolis, Brazil, 119
Termas de Puyehue, Chile, 252
Tiahuanaco culture, 217, 232, 327
Tiahunaco, Bolivia, 228
Tierra del Fuego, 3, 22, 74, 86, 253
Tingo, Peru, 347
Tingo María, Peru, 22, 350–51
Tipping, 41–42. *See also* under individual countries
Tiquina, Bolivia, 227
Tirsteza, Brazil, 128
Tobago island, 10, 209
Tobatí, Paraguay, 172
Toledo, Francisco de, 330
Tomé, Chile, 250
Topo, Ecuador, 298
Touring Club de Colombia, 270
Travel agents, selecting, 46
Travel magazine, 30, 57
Treinta y Tres Orientales, 178
Treinta y Tres, Uruguay, 188
Trelew, Argentina, 85–86
TRINIDAD, 158, 204, 209–10

Trinidad and Tobago Tourist Board, 210
Trinidad, Paraguay, 170
Triple Alliance War, 69, 166, 178
Trujillo, Peru, 338, 351–52
Trujillo, Rafael, 10, 72, 197–98
Tucumán, Argentina, 69, 90–91
Tumuc-Humac Mountains, 154
Turbaco, Colombia, 273
Turbol Travel Ageny, 216
Turja, Colombia, 263

UCLA Museum, 27
Ultima Esperanza, Chile, 253
United Force Party, British Guiana, 150
United Fruit Co., 274, 314
United Nations, 9–10, 12, 22–23 71, 123, 219, 341
United Provinces of la Plata, 69
United States Government: Customs, 36–37; House Foreign Affairs Committee, 23; Information Service, 23, 40; libraries in South America, 40; National Museum, 27; Passport Offices, 29; Peace Corps, 262; Senate Foreign Relations Committee, 23; Travel Service, 28; Treasury Department, 36
United States of New Granada, 265
United States-South American relations, XIV, 9–18, 73, 109–11, 163, 166–67, 176, 197, 217, 220, 239, 294, 311, 313–14, 332
Universities: Andes, 203; Arequipa, 347; Atlantic, 269; Austral, 251; Bahia, 131; Bogotá, 277; Buenos Aires, 79–80; Caracas, 200; Cartagena, 272; Catholic (Chile), 242; Catholic (Peru), 337; Chile, 242; Catholic Guayaquil, 293; La Plata, 81; Liberdad, 351–52; Panama, 318; Paraná, 125; Popoyán, 280; Rosario, 89; San Andrés, 225; San Carlos, 91; San Francisco Xavier, 218, 231; San Marcos, 335–37, 352; São Paulo, 27, 121
University of Pennsylvania Museum, 27
Upsallate Pass, 51
Urubamba River, 344
Urubamba Valley, Peru, 343
URUGUAY, 3, 8, 13, 16, 20–21, 64, 68–69, 73, 93, 106, 110, 112, 166, 175–92
Uruguay River, 3, 187–88

Valdivia, Chile, 247, 251
Valdivia, Pedro de, 237, 251
Valencia, Venezuela, 195, 202
Valparaiso, Chile, 243–45
Vargas, Getúlio, 108–9
Varig Airlines, 20, 50–54, 66, 102, 176
VASP Airlines, 54
Vatican, the, 6
Velasco Ibarra, José Maria, 290
VENEZUELA, 3, 5, 10, 17, 20–21, 39, 63–64, 193–210
Venezuelan-American Chamber of Commerce, 25

Venice, Italy, 194
Vernon, Sir Edward, 271
Vespucci, Amerigo, 67, 146, 194–95, 204
Viasa Airlines, 54
Viceroyalty of Peru, 218
Victoria Falls, 126, 154, 206
Vicuña, Chile, 255
Villa Concho, Colombia, 274
Villarrica, Chile, 251
Villavicencio, Argentina, 90
Villeta, Paraguay, 170
Viña del Mar, Chile, 245
Vinces, Ecuador, 294
Vinto, Bolivia, 230
Visas and tourist cards, 28
Vision Latin American Letter, 26
Vision Magazine, 26
Volta Reaonda, Brazil, 119
Von Hagen, Victor W., 213

Waldo, Myra, 38
War of the Pacific, 219, 239, 331
Washington, George, 271
Welles, Sumner, 10

Western South America, introduction to,
    211–14
Wilder, Thornton, 338
Woodward, Robert F., 15
World Bank, 23, 73, 274
World Health Organization, 10, 23
World War I, 108
World War II, 10, 15, 71, 146, 166, 171,
    219, 239

Yacanto, Argentina, 92
Yagua Indians, Peru, 350
Yaguarón, Paraguay, 172
Yale University, 344
Yanamono Island, Peru, 350
Yungas valleys, Bolivia, 229
Yupanqui, Tito, 227
Yura, Peru, 347
YWCA, 25

Zabala, Bruno Marico de, 177
Zipaquirá, Colombia, 276